The Audubon
Society
Field Guide
to the
Natural Places
of the
Mid-Atlantic States:
Inland

Other titles in this series include:

**The Audubon Society
Field Guide
to the Natural Places
of the Mid-Atlantic States:
Coastal**

**The Audubon Society
Field Guide
to the Natural Places
of the Northeast:
Coastal**

**The Audubon Society
Field Guide
to the Natural Places
of the Northeast:
Inland**

The Audubon Society Field Guide to the Natural Places of the Mid-Atlantic States: Inland

Susannah Lawrence and
Barbara Gross

A Hilltown Book
Pantheon Books, New York

Staff for this volume

Editor:	Caroline Sutton
Reporters:	Susannah Lawrence
	Barbara Gross
Cartography:	Rebecca Lazear Okrent
	Gene Gort
Essays:	Jake Page
	Edward Ricciuti
	Gene Wilhelm
	H. R. DeSelm
	Jack L. Ferrell
Consultant:	Richard Plunkett

Library of Congress Cataloging in Publication Data

Lawrence, Susannah.
    The Audubon Society field guide to the natural places of the Mid-Atlantic States.

    Bibliography: p.
    Includes index.
    Contents: Coastal—Inland.
    1. Natural areas—Atlantic States—Guide-books.
I. Gross, Barbara. II. National Audubon Society.
III. Title.
QH76.5.A87L39   1984   917.4'0443   83–21417
ISBN 0–394–72279–5 (v. 1)
ISBN 0–394–72280–9 (v. 2)

Text design: Clint Anglin

Manufactured in the United States of America
First Edition

To E.K.G.

The National Audubon Society

For more than three-quarters of a century, the National Audubon Society has provided leadership in scientific research, conservation education, and citizen-action programs to save birds and other wildlife and the habitat necessary for their survival.

To accomplish these goals, the society has formally adopted the Audubon Cause: TO CARRY OUT RESEARCH, EDUCATION, AND ACTION TO CONSERVE WILD BIRDS AND OTHER ANIMALS, TREES AND OTHER PLANTS, SOIL, AIR, AND WATER, AND ALSO TO PROMOTE A BETTER UNDERSTANDING OF THE INTERDEPENDENCE OF THESE NATURAL RESOURCES. To carry out the Audubon Cause, the society's programs are structured around five specific missions that encompass the tremendous scope of the organization:

—Conserve native plants and animals and their habitats
—Further the wise use of land and water
—Promote rational strategies for energy development and use
—Protect life from pollution, radiation, and toxic substances
—Seek solutions for global problems involving the interaction of population, resources, the environment, and sustainable development.

Our underlying belief is that all forms of life are interdependent and that the diversity of nature is essential to both our economic and our environmental well-being.

Audubon, through its nationwide system of sanctuaries, protects more than 250,000 acres of essential habitat and unique natural areas for birds and other wild animals and rare plant life. The sanctuaries range in size from 9 acres around Theodore Roosevelt's grave in New York State to 26,000 acres of coastal marsh in Louisiana. Most of the sanctuaries are staffed by resident wardens who also patrol adjacent natural areas not owned by Audubon.

Audubon's 500,000 members provide the underpinning for all the society's programs and activities. Two-thirds of our members also belong to local Audubon chapters, now numbering more than 480, which serve in their communities as focal points for conservation, nature education, and citizen action on environmental issues.

We also maintain ten regional offices, each staffed by two or more full-time professional conservationists who advance Audubon programs throughout the fifty states.

Our staff conducts wildlife research to aid such endangered species as the bald eagle, whooping crane, eastern timber wolf, and bog turtle and to provide knowledge of the ecologically sound management of our sanctuaries. The society also publishes the award-winning *Audubon* magazine and *American Birds* magazine.

For further information about the society, write or call:

> National Audubon Society
> 950 Third Avenue
> New York, N.Y. 10022
> (212) 832-3200

Contents

x   **Contents**

Caverns of the Great Valley   262

Mountain Lake Wilderness Study Area   307

The Appalachian Plateau: A Furrowed Upland   313

Acknowledgments

This was an enormous project, requiring the contributions of great numbers of people. I would first like to thank all those who bravely tried out the directions and the maps.

Without the sponsorship of the National Audubon Society this project would never have been undertaken, and thanks to Richard Plunkett's careful review of the manuscript many mistakes have been corrected.

Special thanks to John Serrao for his work on Piermont Marsh and the Palisades, to Don Miller for his work on Devil's Hole, and John Kunsman for his description of Carbaugh Run.

The staffs of the national wildlife refuges and national, state, and local parks described in this book have been universally helpful and supportive. Both the national office and the local branches of the Nature Conservancy have provided assistance and encouragement in covering certain Conservancy preserves. I would also like to thank the Virginia Society of Ornithologists and the Maryland Ornithological Society for their help in compiling information.

The following people provided invaluable aid in reviewing material and answering innumerable questions, and in some cases even acting as guides. Dr. Peter Patton, Wesleyan University; Dr. Earl Core, West Virginia University; Dr. Harlan P. Banks, Cornell University; Earl Hodnett, Northern Virginia Regional Park Authority; David Coffman, Westvaco Corp.; Paul Engman, Riverbend Park; Walter McMann, National Park Service; Keith Van Ness,

Maryland Wildlife Administration; Dr. Charles Baer, West Virginia University; Dr. Robert Behling, West Virginia University; Ray Blum, Monongahela National Forest; Martin Borko, Orange County Community College; Michael Brown, National Park Service; Dennis Carter, National Park Service; Tom Colefield, Maryland Wildlife Administration; Bob Ford, National Park Service; Dr. Richard Jaynes, Connecticut Agricultural Experiment Station; Lee Kramer, United States Forest Service; Dr. Michael Kudish, Paul Smith College; Elizabeth Murray, Ivy Creek Foundation; John Orth; Tolly Peuleche, Maryland Department of Natural Resources, Land Planning Services; David Tice, Mid-Atlantic Forestry Services, Inc.; Steve Croy and Tom Weiboldt, Virginia Polytechnic Institute; Dr. L. K. Thomas, National Park Service; Doug Welker, West Virginia Geological Survey; Hal Wierenga; Claudia Wilds; Dr. Charles R. Worth, University of Virginia; Lytton Wood, Red Oak Forestry Services; Dr. Elmer and Jean Worthley; Dr. Thomas Berg, Pennsylvania Geological Survey; Don Miller, Meesing Nature Center; John Serrao, Greenbrook Sanctuary; Robert Schutsky; Russell Titus, Paterson Museum; Jerry Schierloh, New Jersey School of Conservation; Annie Bohlin; Richard Kane; James Yolton, Upsala College; Dr. Edward Buckley, Boyce-Thompson Institute; Frank Buser; Ben Lefever, Pennsylvania Power and Light; Paul Weigman, Western Pennsylvania Conservancy; Dave Hubbard, Virginia Division of Mineral Resources; Karl Beard, Mohonk Preserve; Sioux Baldwin, Andorra Natural Area; Dr. Stan Shetler, Smithsonian Institution; Wade Wander; Dr. Gerald Johnson, Department of Geology, College of William and Mary; Dr. Thomas Pickett, Delaware Geological Survey; Lorraine Fleming, Delaware Nature Education Society; Dr. Richard Forman, Department of Botany, Rutgers University.

Thanks also to Dan Okrent for giving us the opportunity to learn and be paid for it.

We particularly wish to thank David Frederickson and our editors at Pantheon for their meticulous work and for their encouragement, and Caroline Sutton, who has been editor, friend, and supporter.

Finally, to all you friends and relations who humored, housed, and accompanied us, Barbara and I offer eternal gratitude.

How to Use
This Book

The aim of the Audubon Society Field Guides is to enable the reader to explore and enjoy the natural history and ecology of selected natural areas in the United States. Unlike any other guide to the outdoors, this series describes the interaction of plants, animals, topography, and climate so that the hiker, birder, or amateur naturalist will be able to understand and more fully appreciate what he or she sees. Today, almost all the sites presented in these guides, whether in public or private ownership, are maintained for public education and enrichment. All offer geological, botanical, or biological points of interest, as well as the beauty, excitement, and tremendous variety of the outdoors.

This guide is one of an initial set also including a Mid-Atlantic coastal volume, a Northeast coastal volume, and a Northeast inland volume. The areas covered in each guide have been determined, as often as possible, according to geological rather than governmental boundaries. The separation of coastal and inland volumes in the Mid-Atlantic series, for example, is clearly indicated by the *fall line*. This roughly north–south demarcation running from New York City into Georgia occurs where the flat Coastal Plain rises to meet the rolling hills of the Piedmont.

Each guide contains descriptions of over a hundred natural areas, and each site description pinpoints what is most significant, intriguing, or unusual about that area. More important, it explains *how* the site came to look as it does, and *why* certain species of vegetation and wildlife can be found there. Thus, while one narrative unravels the geological history of a region as it is revealed in the rock outcrops along a trail, another centers on a rare and ancient stand of Atlantic white cedar, and still another highlights the waterfowl that gather in an area, explaining their feeding, breeding, and migratory habits. Indeed, if the diverse entries about a particular area such as the Catskill Mountains are read as a group, the visitor can reach a fuller understanding of both the existing biotic climate and the workings of human and natural history. Furthermore, the sites have been organized by geological and ecological regions, each prefaced by an introductory essay providing a general look at the geology, vegetation, and wildlife in that region and the human influence on it.

This volume is divided into five regions or provinces; these follow physiographic boundaries established in the 1930s by N. M. Fenneman for the U.S. Geological Survey and still widely used today. (Physiography is the study of the earth's physical geography.) In the eastern United States, these provinces are laid out on an axis running generally northeast to southwest. Where necessary, rivers have been used to provide other boundaries. The regions are organized from east to west, and, within each region, the site descriptions move from north to south.

The gently rolling topography of the Piedmont Province is bounded on the east by the fall line. A small nub of the province reaches north along the Palisades into New York. From there it broadens and runs southward into Alabama. The southern boundary for this volume is the Roanoke River in southern Virginia. On the western edge of the Piedmont, the land rises, often imperceptibly, into the Blue Ridge.

The New York–New Jersey Highlands Province forms the northwestern border of the Piedmont. It is part of a long peninsula of ancient rock and an extension of formations found in New England. Also called the Reading Prong, it extends southwestward from the Hudson River across north-central New Jersey and dips into Pennsylvania, where it ends at Reading.

South of the Reading Prong, the Blue Ridge Province begins. This narrow mountain ridge, made up of ancient, deeply eroded rock, is the western boundary of the Piedmont. For the purposes of this volume, its southern boundary is also the Roanoke River, which divides the Blue Ridge into a northern and southern section.

The Ridge and Valley Province, commonly called the Appalachians, is a long, sinuous series of mountains running the length of the eastern United States. The Catskill River in upper New York and the New River in southwestern Virginia are the northern and southern boundaries of the area as it appears in this book. The western edge is bounded by the Allegheny Front, which is often indistinct along the southern Appalachians but becomes an impressive escarpment in some areas of Virginia. In central Pennsylvania, the Ridge and Valley Province swings almost due east.

To the north and west of the Ridge and Valley is a vast area known as the Appalachian Plateau Province. Of this region, this guide includes the Catskill Mountains in New York, the Poconos in northeastern Pennsylvania, and other sites on the plateau as far west as the Pine Creek Gorge in north-central Pennsylvania.

All sites in this guide are numbered, and a system of cross-referencing throughout enables the reader to locate the most thorough discussion of a particular species or geological formation. For example, ospreys may be mentioned briefly in one description, but there will also be a reference to a fuller discussion elsewhere in the book. Each site opens with precise directions to the area and ends with a section called *Remarks*. Here is included such practical information as the length and difficulty of a recommended walk; what equipment to bring; possible activities such as swimming, fishing, and skiing; the availability of boat rentals; nearby places to camp; and best times of the year to visit.

Most site descriptions include a map, keyed by letter to the narrative, which leads the visitor along a suggested walk or boat trip. A sample map follows, along with a key to the various symbols that appear throughout the book.

Each guide includes a brief glossary, a bibliography of works on related subjects, and an extensive index. The Index is cross-referenced to enable the reader to find a particular site of interest, whether because of a species or geological formation or because of certain sports and other activities.

It may be useful to read about a site before visiting, to learn the length of the trip and what equipment to bring. While principal species of vegetation or wildlife are identified in the entries, others are mentioned in passing, and the amateur birder or botanist may therefore wish to bring along a field guide to birds, trees, or wildflowers. Recommended supplementary guides are listed in the Bibliography.

Finally, it is important to remember that natural sites are never unchanging places, rather always in flux. Wind and wave action alter the profile of the coast; bogs fill in with vegetation; some animals learn to adapt to the influx of civilization while others vanish. Many natural areas reflect the human impact of the past two centuries, be it the draining of marshes or the reseeding of forests. No such change is an isolated event. As an old field returns to forest, for example, pioneer seedlings give way to mature forest, and the birds of prey that once hunted the open field are replaced by their forest counterparts. Similarly, our knowledge about such phenomena is

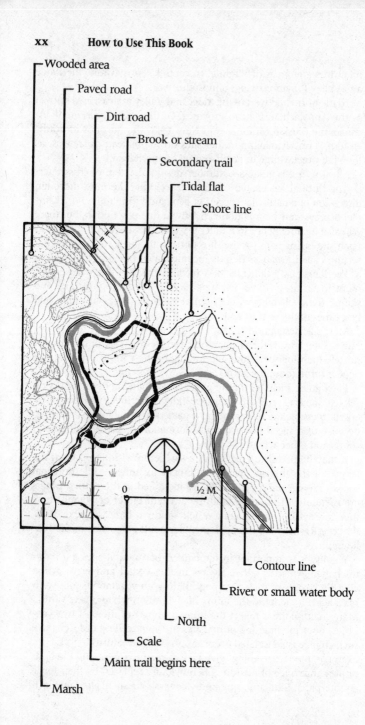

Wooded area

Paved road

Dirt road

Brook or stream

Secondary trail

Tidal flat

Shore line

Contour line

River or small water body

North

Scale

Main trail begins here

Marsh

0   ½ M.

interdisciplinary, and forever changing as further observations are made and past theories uprooted. In these volumes, we have attempted to present the most widely accepted geological and ecological theories. We do not presume to be comprehensive, nor to judge the validity of other recent theories and conclusions. Our aim is to introduce some of the processes botanists, biologists, and geologists believe to be at work in the natural world, thereby offering the reader a deeper appreciation and understanding of the complexity, beauty, and vulnerability of our natural areas.

The Piedmont:
The Foot of the
Mountains

A sinuous boundary starts in the north at the Hudson River's Palisades and winds in a southerly direction through the capitals of five states and that of the nation, ending in Montgomery, Ala. Early settlers called it the *fall line,* the place at which Atlantic-bound rivers became unnavigable, often because of rapids or falls. Between the fall line and the formidable barrier of the Appalachian Mountains lay hilly wooded land. Here colonists found single, isolated hills (called *monadnocks*) and saw a resemblance to the landscape of southern Europe, the Italian *piemonte.* Thus did this region—between the fall line and the Appalachians—come to be known as the Piedmont, literally the foot of the mountains.

The key to understanding the 85,000 square miles of the Piedmont is twofold: soil moisture and the hand of man. At one time or another, 95 percent of the region has fallen under cultivation and about half of it remains so. Except for a few pockets of wildness here and there, the Piedmont is a study in ongoing plant succession.

Four hundred years ago, the entire Piedmont region was uniformly forested with huge old trees—chiefly chestnuts and oaks—virtually none of which remain. Settlers cut down the mature forest and began to till the land. It was an ancient landscape the farmers exposed, one shaped by violent upheavals.

The geology of the Piedmont Province is obscure. The rock has been so changed by heat and pressure that geologists have yet to completely unravel its age and origins. The province is made up primarily of thick wedges

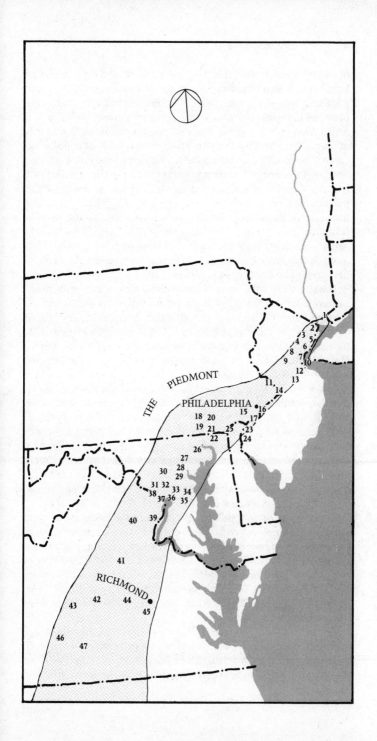

THE PIEDMONT

PHILADELPHIA

RICHMOND

of metamorphic rocks, principally gneiss, schist, and quartzite. These have been shoved westward, one on top of another, and slope gently eastward toward the sea. About 500 million years ago, continental plates of the earth's crust, carrying western Europe, America, and Africa, were thrust together in a vast, grinding collision. Over a span of several hundred million years, two more periods of collision occurred, eventually closing a wide sea known as the Proto-Atlantic. Although the line of impact was far to the east of the present North American coastline, the force of that impact was so immense that millions of tons of rock were thrust westward as easily as a boat thrusts aside the skim of ice on a November pond. To the west the collisions created a high mountain range which would become the Appalachians. As each new layer of rock was thrust onto the Piedmont, it was heated, made malleable, and compressed. As it cooled, new crystalline structures took shape.

The stresses of collision also fractured the rock, and in some places molten magma from beneath the earth's crust was forced upward through these fractures to cool and harden into granite. This granite determines the fall line along much of the southern Piedmont. In New Jersey, much later volcanic intrusions associated with the opening of the Atlantic Ocean 200 million years ago resulted in the Palisades and the Watchung Mountains.

As the winds and rains inexorably wore down the land, sediments ran off toward the sea, creating the Coastal Plain with its sandy soils. Weathered by chemical reactions with air and water, the crystalline rocks decayed yet further into the Piedmont's characteristically clayey soils. The Piedmont has eroded into a place of gentle, rolling hills. Crisscrossed with the fences of farms and dotted with woodlots, these hills give the region its own particular geometry: unlike the Midwest, it is an area where humans have been hard put to it to create a seemingly straight line on the land.

Beginning perhaps 2 million years ago, ice sheets came and went at least four times, covering much of North America as far south as northern New Jersey. The ice sheets left behind huge glacial remnants that melted and became lakes in what is now the Piedmont of New Jersey. These lakes eventually filled in, becoming ponds, marshes, and finally woods. There are no natural lakes now in the Piedmont—the only standing water has been impounded by dams, built by bulldozers or beavers.

Yet there is plenty of water. Rivers and countless streams plunge toward the ocean. The entire region enjoys between 40 and 50 inches of precipitation a year. There are few areas in the Piedmont that are either extremely wet or extremely dry. The growing season is nowhere less than 180 days, usually with 60 percent of those days being sunny. It is a generous land.

In spite of the similarity in the amount and timing of precipitation throughout the region, there are considerable variations in the amount of moisture found in the soil. Ecologists refer to such conditions as *xeric* (meaning dry), *mesic* (well drained), and *hydric* (wet). Much of this has to do with topography: as one would expect, water, given its determination to head downward, leaves the steep slopes of hills dry, or xeric, whereas bottomlands are wetter, or hydric. Thus, from the edge of the Appalachians to the Coastal Plain, there is an overall tendency of the soil to become damper. Most of the land in the Piedmont is in between—mesic. But there are many anomalies, more often than not the result of different kinds of bedrock underlying the soil (and which in turn become soil). Some soils are coarser, so water can drain out of them more readily. Others are finer, retaining water. In some cases the bedrock itself is less porous, causing more water to accumulate in the soil above. The Piedmont is a mosaic of subtle differences in soil moisture. And in each piece of the mosaic is a differing collection of plants and therefore animals.

For example, the forests of Maryland are nowhere older than 150 years, most of them being less than 100. One can walk through Maryland's woodlands, mostly deciduous, and find the dominant trees to be chestnut oaks and bear oaks. Abruptly one will pass into an area of post, blackjack, and chestnut oaks, or into an area of willows and loblolly pines. Each area has its characteristic association of tree types. Yet in a beginning forest, one will find the saplings of all or most of Maryland's trees represented because there is little or no canopy to block the sunlight. Saplings of all sorts—borne as seeds by wind or bird—take hold in the soil. But then at some critical time the roots of certain species and the specific soil-moisture level become incompatible, and those trees suffer and die, leaving only the association of tree types that thrives best on that particular amount of moisture.

By the mid-1800s, most of the Piedmont's forests had given way to the farmer's axe, and much of the farming was hard on the soil, depleting it of minerals and nutrients. Thus, farms were abandoned by the thousands, (and at an increasing rate in this century). After the Civil War, many of the old cotton plantations were planted with pines, mostly loblolly, and became one of the world's richest sources of wood pulp for papermills. Farmland in Alabama dropped from 75 percent in 1900 to 10 percent today. So the key to nature and landscape in the Piedmont is what happens in abandoned fields.

In a well-drained (mesic) field that is abandoned and left to itself, a relatively rigorous and predictable process takes place over the years. In the first year crabgrass becomes the dominant plant, followed by horseweed, then aster, then broom sedge and goldenrod. In the fifth year, saplings begin to emerge above the goldenrod. In the southern Piedmont, these pioneers are generally redcedar or various pines. In the northern Piedmont, the early arrivals will be deciduous trees like maples and beech, to be supplanted by a climax forest of oaks and hickory. In a large area, from South Carolina to the Potomac River, both conifers and hardwoods do the work of colonization, with the conifers eventually giving way to the deciduous hardwoods. Eventually, after some 50 to 90 years, the oaks take over, spreading their great canopy of leaves high above the ground, and the forest can be said to be mature. Beneath this canopy is an understory of trees like flowering dogwood and redbud, under which are a large variety of shrubs and herbs. In the spring, the forest floor is blessed with ephemeral wildflowers—trout lilies, spring beauties, Dutchman's breeches—delicate splotches of color that grow, flower, and set seed in the 30-day interval between the warming of spring and the appearance of the forest's leaves, which cut off the sun.

As a mesic field changes into a forest, the animal population changes with it. Among insects, for example, at first grasshoppers and ground beetles enjoy the crabgrass environment. When asters and daisies become dominant, so do bees, moths, and butterflies—pollinators. When the trees take over, grasshoppers and bees are reduced and the site becomes a breeding ground for moth and butterfly larva, as opposed to adults. In the mature forest, during the time of the ephemeral wildflowers, certain solitary bees and various flies are on hand as pollinators, timing their activities, as do the ephemerals, to the tyranny of the trees.

In drier (xeric) areas, the soil is usually coarser and thinner, the result of greater erosion on steep slopes or the depletion caused by farming. In such areas, a less predictable collection of grasses emerges first, followed by a variety of herbs, to be succeeded more often than not by pines, especially noted for their tolerance of dryness and poor soil. As the pines mature—and the process takes longer in drier sites—they are joined by various oaks of the kind that tolerate aridity. As each generation of leaves falls to the forest floor, the soils gradually build up, making the site suitable for yet more oaks. Ridgetop forests, dominated by chestnut oaks, are usually gnarled and not as tall as mesic forests, rarely exceeding 60 feet in height. Life is less diverse in these dry, ridgetop forests, but here one finds populations of that great and uncommon soaring bird, the raven.

The richest, wildest, most diverse and magical lands of the Piedmont are the wet (hydric) bottomlands, where alluvial soils, sediments deposited by streams and rivers, exist near flowing water. Often relatively inaccessible, they have not been as widely farmed and often retain a primeval quality. Here plant succession is speeded up. Soils are rich combinations of sand and silt, and a profusion of herbs takes hold immediately after such a place is abandoned. Swamp milkweed, sedges, and rushes soon abound; before long, shrubs like buttonbush emerge, followed by alders, willows, and maples, beaver fodder. Alongside streams and rivers, the trees, seeking sunlight, lean out over the open water, often to have their roots flooded and, as the banks expand or change course, often to topple into the water. In such areas, particularly north of the James River, silver maples predominate as a kind of premature climax forest, maintained in adolescence by regular floods.

Such bottomland forests host a profusion of spring ephemerals and are often lush with ferns. In some cases they sport horsetails—primitive holdovers from the Carboniferous Period, some 300 million years ago. In the rivers and streams that course through such places, the American eel matures, later heading out into the ocean south of Bermuda where, in the Sargasso Sea, it lays its eggs and dies. In one of the miracles of animal navigation, the tiny hatchlings find their way back to the Piedmont's watercourses.

It is to such places—busy woodlands in one stage or another, streams, rivers—that most naturalists go, seeking birds, wildflowers, fish, or simply peace. But a large part of the Piedmont's acreage is of quite a different sort, a more tailored beauty. Some 50 percent of the Piedmont is farmland, more often than not given over to cropland and pastureland in equal amounts, and more often than not bordered by wild-growing hedgerows. It is from the hedgerows that a great variety of birds issue forth to patrol the fields, a major form of insect control, while overhead, turkey vultures wheel on the thermals, joined by an occasional watchful hawk, pursuing its useful affairs. Carefully maintained, the farms of the Piedmont—fences and hedgerows snaking across emerald fields—are as much a part of the region's natural beauty and charm as its woodlands and plunging rivers.

Pasturelands and hayfields provide a traveler not only lovely vistas of hills and valleys but excellent places to observe some extraordinary associations of nature not available in forest or swamp. The grasshopper sparrow, for example, is not as spectacular as a scarlet tanager, but it is rarer. Killdeers, dapper birds, make their precarious nests in pebbly spots in pastures, their keening calls echoing oceanic matters. Where a bovine hoof scars the pasture, a thistle will soon colonize, and from the surrounding hedgerows, goldfinches will visit the thistle in their undulating flight. Under cover of the hedgerow's tangle, the gray fox lurks, patrolling for "varmints," such as insects and mice. The gray fox will climb up into the hedgerow to feast on wild raspberries and pokeberries. Hedgerows are more than barriers; they are the headquarters for much of the Piedmont's wildlife.

The Piedmont is an ancient region, a welcoming landscape shaped and reshaped by the hand of man, sculpted essentially by even more powerful forces, diverse and always changing, always seeking some momentary ecological equilibrium for the present short moment of geological time.

—Jake Page

1.

Piermont Marsh

Directions: Rockland County, N.Y. From New York City take the Palisades Interstate Parkway 10.6 miles to Exit 4. Turn north on U.S. 9W and go 2.2 miles to the entrance of Tallman Mountain State Park. Turn east (right) onto the entrance road and bear right into the park. Park in the lot; continue along the road toward the river to the traffic circle. Go left toward the North Picnic Ground and turn right immediately on the blue-blazed Long Path. Parking is also available in the picnic area.

Ownership: Palisades Interstate Park Commission; New York State Department of Environmental Conservation; Town of Piermont.

From spring, when the marsh is just starting to turn green, until winter, when the dried, yellow grasses rustle in the wind, an extraordinary array of birds make use of Piermont Marsh and the river at its edge. This is one of the most diversified and interesting birdwatching sites in the Hudson valley. The northernmost brackish marsh on the river, Piermont Marsh harbors both freshwater and salt-marsh species.

Walk a few hundred yards along the Long Path into a picnic area (**A**). From here, on top of the 150-foot Palisades cliffs, you can look down on the entire 940-acre Piermont Marsh. The top of Tallman Mountain is a broad, wooded plateau with fine examples of old mixed-oak forests including red, white, black, and chestnut oaks as well as some large American beeches, shagbark hickories, and flowering dogwood in the understory. This forest is typical of the Palisades (see **#2**).

The Long Path runs left out of the picnic ground, down a short, steep hill, to the edge of the river. Turn left along the paved bike path. To your left, where the steep escarpment of the cliffs ends, are tall specimens of sugar maple, chestnut oak, black birch, hemlock, basswood, black locust, and pignut hickory. These trees are considerably larger than the trees at the top of the Palisades, even though they may well be the same age. Being at the bottom of the slope, they grow taller as they compete with each other for sunlight. Soils also tend to be deeper, richer, and more fertile at the base of cliffs, for sediments are washed off the uplands with each rainstorm.

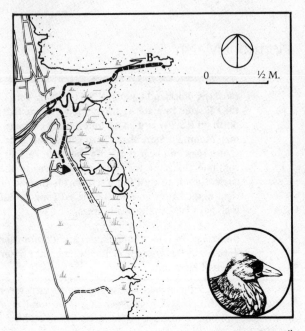

Inset: *Sora rail*

Continuing north about a quarter-mile, the path crosses Sparkill Creek, which flows out of a magnificent gorge or *gap* in the Palisades. Many geologists hold that this gap marks the former course of the Hudson River, cut millions of years ago. At that time, it flowed around the back of the Palisades. Others maintain that the gap was carved by torrential meltwaters from the ice sheets that covered the region intermittently during the last 1 to 2 million years (see **Piedmont**). After crossing the creek, turn right on Paradise Ave. and walk about a quarter-mile to the entrance of the Paper Board Co. Turn right and walk out along the mile-long Erie Pier, which forms the northern border of the marsh.

The pier was built in 1841 as the eastern terminus of the Erie Railroad. Here passengers and freight were transferred from trains to boats bound for New York City. The pier was also the site of a thriving ferry landing for steamboats crossing the river or heading north to West Point and Albany.

From the pier, you have a wide view of the brackish marsh. Salt-marsh cordgrass, salt-meadow cordgrass or salt hay, big cordgrass, and freshwater cordgrass grow here. They are all members of the same genus, the Spartinas. Each species has its own niche. Salt-marsh cordgrass grows along the wet edges of the marsh and salt-meadow cordgrass grows on slightly higher ground inland. These two species are among a handful of plants that can survive in salt water. By a combination of chemical pumps in their root systems and salt glands that excrete excess salt, these plants are able to maintain the correct water balance within their cells and to draw in nutrients. Plants without these adaptions quickly lose their cell water when immersed in salt water. Salt-meadow cordgrass and salt-marsh cordgrass reach their northern limit in New York State at Piermont.

Big cordgrass is a brackish-to-freshwater species of wet marsh soils. Look for it along the borders of Sparkill Creek. Freshwater cordgrass grows on the dry upper edges of the salt marsh. It is a prairie species, which grows in vast, pure stands on the moist bottomland soils along the Missouri River. Along with other prairie species, this grass probably moved eastward in the warm period following the retreat of the last glacier about 10,000 years ago. At that time, the climate was considerably hotter than it is today.

Other marsh plants visible from the pier include marsh elder, a shrub that grows on higher ground in salt marshes, cylindrical bulrush, narrow-leaved cattail, swamp rose mallow, purple loosestrife, and phragmites. The last two species have become problem plants. Purple loosestrife is an alien plant that is aggressively replacing many freshwater marsh species in the northeast (see **#49**). Phragmites is a native grass that grows well where marshland has been disturbed by diking, construction, drainage, or some other activity. Once phragmites is established, it too spreads vigorously, excluding other species. While phragmites does stabilize marsh soils and resist erosion, it replaces plants that are far more important sources of food for wildlife.

The salinity of the river here may be as high as 12 parts per thousand. (The salinity of seawater averages about 35 parts per thousand.) This explains the presence of fiddler crabs and the occasional diamondback terrapin, both of which are salt-marsh species. This section of the Hudson is also one of the river's most productive fishery areas. The shallows of the Tappan Zee and the Haverstraw Bay, just to the north, represent a major spawning and nursery habitat for striped bass, shad, and other marine species. An estuary such as this offers better protection to vulnerable young fish than the ocean, because there are fewer predators. Salt levels can vary widely depending on the cycle of the tides and the flow of the river. Relatively few species have adapted to this changeable habitat.

From the pier, scan the marsh for bird life. In spring and summer, four species of the secretive rail family—the king, the Virginia, the clapper, and the sora—nest among the grasses. Both the American bittern and the least bittern also breed here. The best time for seeing or at least hearing these inconspicuous birds is very early in the morning, at or just before dawn. The rails are very narrow in front, enabling them to move through small passageways in the thick grasses, well out of sight of predators. The American bittern is quite a large bird but is almost as difficult to spot because of its amazing protective coloring. On the front of its long neck is a series of muted brown and tan vertical stripes. When hiding, the bird stands with its bill pointing straight up in the air, the striping on its throat blending perfectly with the marsh grasses. The bittern's eyes are placed so that even in this pose it can look straight ahead at the intruder.

More easily seen are nesting common gallinules, marsh wrens, and seaside and sharp-tailed sparrows. In August hundreds of swallows, which are early migrants, pass through on their way south, stopping to feed on insects in the air above the marsh.

Beyond the marsh, the pier extends out into the river. Low tide bares wide mudflats, which attract over twenty species of shorebirds during the peak migration times in May and again from August through September. They stop to feed on the flats, which are full of small worms, crustaceans, and mollusks.

At the end of the pier on the north side, open fields attract water pipits and horned larks in winter (**B**). Winter is also the time to look for the great rafts of diving ducks that gather in the river shallows, including canvasback, common goldeneye, scaup, and the occasional loon (see **#18**).

In autumn the pier is a good place to watch the flights of ospreys, northern harriers, and broad-winged, sharp-shinned, red-tailed, and other hawks migrating south from New England and then west across the Hudson before turning south again (see **#2** and **#5**). Along the disturbed ground of the pier itself, there are a variety of shrubs and trees typical of the early stages of succession (see **Piedmont**). White mulberry, silky dogwood, ailanthus, blackberry, staghorn sumac, and the vines of Japanese honeysuckle form thickets where numbers of warblers, vireos, flycatchers, and thrushes can be found during spring and fall migrations. From the pier, retrace your steps to your car.

Remarks: *In warm weather be prepared for mosquitoes. The walk to the end of the pier is about 2 miles. You can also drive to the Paper Board Co. factory and leave your car there. From the park entrance continue driving north on U.S. 9W into Piermont and turn east (right) on Piermont Ave. and then right onto Paradise Ave., which leads to the factory. Activities in the area include fishing from the pier (no license required), hiking along the Long Path and the Bike Path, and swimming at the state park. The best way to explore the marsh is by canoe.*

2.

The Palisades of the Hudson

Directions: **Bergen County, N.J. From New York City, cross the George Washington Bridge and follow signs to the Palisades Interstate Parkway. Go about 7 miles north to Exit 2 (Alpine Approach Rd.). From the exit ramp turn north (right) onto Route 9W. Continue north for about 1.7 miles and park at the pedestrian overpass that crosses the Palisades Parkway. Cross the overpass and pick up the blue-blazed Long Path. Walk a few hundred yards to the Women's Federation Tower on the edge of the cliffs (A).**

Ownership: **Palisades Interstate Park Commission.**

Within sight of the cluttered skyline of New York City, this 5-mile trek takes you into wild rocky ravines shaded by towering trees. Here red foxes raise their pups and white-tailed deer browse. From the ramparts each fall you can watch hawks—the broad-winged, the red-tailed, the Cooper's, and the sharp-shinned—as they cross the Hudson on their southern journey. The cliffs themselves are unique, a wall of solidified lava lining the Hudson for 45 miles.

Standing at the cliff's edge (A), you are on the highest point of the escarpment. After emerging from the ground as a low ridge in Staten Island, the Palisades cross the narrow straits called the Kill van Kull river into New Jersey, gradually increasing in height past Jersey City, Weehawken, Fort Lee, and Englewood; at Alpine they loom 530 feet above the Hudson. Along this section there are sheer vertical drops exceeding 300 feet. The cliffs continue northward into New York State as Tallman Mountain, Clausland Mountain, Hook Mountain, High Tor, and finally Mount Ivy. Then the ridge once again descends beneath the ground.

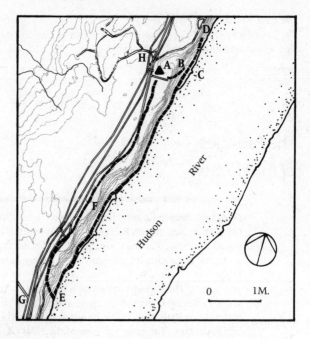

The stone tower commemorates the efforts of the New Jersey Federation of Women's Clubs, which led the battle to preserve the Palisades. After much lobbying, the Palisades Park Commission was formed in 1900. Its primary purpose was to save the cliffs from destruction by the quarrying industry. During the last few decades of the nineteenth century, countless tons of hard, durable diabase rock were blasted away from the cliffs for ship's ballast, sea walls, cobblestones, railroad beds, and crushed gravel. Today virtually all of the Palisades from Fort Lee to High Tor have been preserved as one long, 75,000-acre public park, and designated a National Natural Landmark.

Here at the very brink of the escarpment, vegetation must endure harsh conditions. The soils are thin and dry; winds are strong. The forest of large oaks that covers most of the ramparts is replaced here by stunted hackberry, redcedar, shadbush, pignut hickory, and black cherry growing from the crevices in the rock. Columbines, wild pinks, and pussytoes bloom at the cliff's edge in May. In spring and summer, look for the five-lined skink, the only species of lizard in New Jersey, warming itself on the sunny rocks. Indigo buntings, birds of open sunny places, sing from the exposed treetops. This is an excellent place to watch the autumn hawk migrations. A dozen different species may be seen, including an occasional bald eagle and peregrine falcon, both endangered species. The hawks make their way south through New England, fly west over the Hudson, and turn south again. They can be seen at close range as they rise over the cliffs on updrafts of warm air (see **#5** and **#78**). Five to ten thousand broad-winged hawks have been seen on a single September day.

From the tower the Long Path bears northward (left) and descends into a shaded ravine past chestnut oaks, pignut hickories, black birches, flowering dogwoods, blackhaws, mountain laurel, and maple-leaved viburnum. Herbs include partridgeberry, pink lady's slipper, and three parasitic flowers: the smooth false foxglove, wood betony, and squawroot. The false foxglove and the squawroot draw some of their nutrients from the roots of oak trees. In the ravine, the trail forks.

Turn right off the Long Trail down into the ravine and descend toward the Hudson River. The forest changes from the typical mixed-oak forest of the Palisades ridge to a denser, more mature woodland of sugar maple, American beech, eastern hemlock, black birch, white ash, and tuliptree. The first four species are unusual in this area, being more characteristic of the northern hardwood forests of upstate New York and New England (see **Catskill Mountains**). They grow well in the shaded, cool, and moist conditions of the ravine.

Stone steps have been built into the trail to make the steep, winding 30-minute descent easier. The trees gradually increase in size toward the bottom of the ravine. Many of the tuliptrees exceed 120 feet in height and 9 feet in circumference (see **#23**). Some of the larger red oaks, hemlocks, and sugar maples in the canopy are certainly over two centuries old. As in a great many other sections of the Palisades, the forests here seem almost untouched. Although the forests of the Palisades are second growth, none have been cut for at least 80 years. Stands in ravines such as this are older, protected by the steep terrain.

The trail is bordered by a great profusion of wildflowers in spring. Some of the species found include early saxifrage, Dutchman's breeches, herb robert, and sweet cicely which grow in rocky woodlands. In the moister soils you will find jack-in-the-pulpit and trout lily (see **#12**). Look for Christmas, polypody, and evergreen wood ferns on the shaded slopes in summer. Along the rockier sections of the trail where light strikes the boulders, vines such as poison ivy, Virginia creeper, and Canada moonseed grow vigorously. Where trees have fallen over, they are being broken down by fungi, bacteria, and a wide variety of insects. You may spot huge millipedes as thick as a child's finger. Millepedes were probably living on the earth 400 million years ago. They are one of the more primitive creatures, resembling segmented worms, from which they may have evolved.

The rich insect life of the woodlands and the seclusion of the ravine bring many nesting songbirds. Carolina wrens, worm-eating and black-and-white warblers, veeries, ovenbirds, scarlet tanagers, red-eyed vireos, wood thrushes, and pileated woodpeckers can all be found here in the spring and summer breeding season. The worm-eating warbler is found only in undisturbed woodlands, and therefore is uncommon in this vicinity. Even the rare and beautiful cerulean warbler is occasionally seen here in spring and summer.

Near the bottom of the slope, some very large sugar maples, black birches, hemlocks, and white pines grow among the huge blocks of diabase that have tumbled down from the cliffs. Beneath these are tall clumps of witch-hazel and some big sassafras trees. Now the ravine trail meets the white-blazed Shore Path (**B**). Turn north (left) and walk a few steps to explore Forest View (**C**). Here, overgrown fields attract birds that nest in shrubby thickets—blue-winged and yellow warblers, yellowthroats, and white-eyed vireos. Just beyond this open expanse is a stone dock on the river from which, at low tide, the hiker can view the steep cliffs in a unique panorama.

Less than a quarter-mile farther north along the Shore Path is a rugged area (**D**) covered with immense blocks of diabase that crashed down the escarpment during a landslide. Here, in the caves and cavities at the base of the rocks, is one of only two eastern wood-rat colonies in the entire state of New Jersey. A southern species, the wood rat was once found in much of New Jersey but has nearly disappeared. Two species of snake, the poisonous northern copperhead and the large but harmless black rat snake, also inhabit this rocky expanse, sunning themselves on the ledges in late spring (see **#72**). The copperhead is not aggressive but rather lazy; nonetheless, be careful where you step.

If you poke around in the mud of the riverbank at low tide, you will find clamshells and maybe a blue-clawed crab. The Hudson River is actually an estuary here, mixing fresh water with salt. The ocean tides reach all the way up to Troy, N.Y., 135 miles to the north, and the river is still slightly salty 66 miles upstream at Hyde Park. The mixing of fresh and salt water accounts for the extraordinary diversity of fish in the Hudson. Depending on the time of year, saltwater species such as striped bass, shad, bluefish, and herring can be found side by side with freshwater species like largemouth bass and sunfish.

Retrace your steps to the junction of the Shore Path and the ravine trail (**B**). Just to the south of the intersection is a grove of slender white paper birches, a species more commonly found in New England and Canada; this cool, sheltered site is its only natural location in the entire Palisades.

Continuing south, you will pass through some of the most magnificent scenery of the Palisades. The Shore Path becomes a broad level trail skirting the bottom of the steep 500-foot cliffs. These cliffs prominently display the vertical rock columns that are responsible for the modern name Palisades (a wall of upright posts, as used in old forts) and the older Indian name Weeh-awk-en, "rocks that look like rows of trees." The entire Palisades ridge originated 190 million years ago during a series of underground volcanic eruptions. These upheavals were connected with the separation of the continents of North America and Africa (see **#3**). Molten magma was forced upward through fractures in the earth but never reached the surface. Instead, it was injected as a long *sill* between layers of the sedimentary sandstones and shales that covered this region (for shales and sandstones see **#111**). Like the 1000-foot-thick filling in a layer cake, the molten magma slowly cooled and hardened underground into the igneous rock called diabase or dolerite. This rock, comprised mainly of the minerals pyroxene and feldspar, is very similar to the basalt of the nearby Watchung Mountains, but since it cooled more slowly underground, the crystals in the diabase are larger and coarser than those in basalt and are more easily seen with the naked eye.

As the diabase solidified, it shrank and fractured into a series of vertical columns, roughly polygonal in cross section. After millions of years of erosion, the softer sandstone layers covering the diabase sill were removed, and its eastern edge, the Palisades cliffs, was exposed by the Hudson River. The fractures in the rock have been further eroded by the action of water freezing and expanding in the cracks over millions of years. In some places, large pillars of rock have separated from the cliff; elsewhere, great sections of the cliff face have tumbled down, forming extensive talus piles below (see **#66**).

One of the dominant trees of the lower slopes is royal paulownia or princess-tree, a beautiful oriental species with huge leaves and fragrant lavender flowers that bloom in May. Originally planted as an ornamental tree in the large clifftop estates in the late nineteenth century, this tree has now spread to the wild.

If time permits, continue south along the Shore Path about 2 miles to the Alpine Boat Basin (**E**). Otherwise, retrace your steps to the ravine trail, which will lead you back up to the Women's Federation Tower (**A**). In winter, the river is a resting place for thousands of canvasback ducks, some common goldeneyes, and other diving ducks (see #18). Along the shore can be seen the unaltered reddish sandstones underlying the Palisades—the bottom layer of the diabase "sandwich." This was the rock used in building many of the brownstone houses of New York and New Jersey. Just south of the Alpine Boat Basin, the Henry Hudson Drive has cut through the diabase and the sandstones, revealing the contact zone between the two formations. Wherever the hot molten magma contacted the sedimentary rocks, its intense heat baked them into new metamorphic rocks.

On the north side of the boat basin is a white colonial house supposedly used by Lord Cornwallis the night before his assault on the Palisades on the morning of November 20, 1776. Just north of the house turn west and walk a half mile up a ravine trail, which will lead you back to the blue-blazed Long Path. Turn north (right) and go past the Palisades Interstate Park Headquarters. From here it is about 2 miles back to your car.

This section of the Long Path passes the remains of several former estates and gardens that existed before the park took over the land early in this century. There are several stands of mature mixed oak and sweetgum forest, the sweetgum being at the northern limit of its range. One fascinating feature, about three-quarters of a mile from the headquarters, is the Gray Crag, a huge rock pillar, 300 feet long and 10 to 20 feet wide (**F**). To reach it you must cross a bridge over a deep, narrow canyon. Just beyond the crag is another detour to the right, leading to an overlook and a 300-foot waterfall. In summer it's dry, but in winter it becomes a cascade of ice and snow, and the hemlocks beside it are shrouded in ice. The Long Path does an abrupt turn to the left at Ruckman Point, one of the "pitching points" where trees cut from the Palisades forests were tossed down to boats and shipped to the city for winter firewood. From the point it is half a mile back to the parking area.

Remarks: *The entire round-trip hike described here is 5 miles of energetic walking. Wear hiking boots and take binoculars. You can return to your car by bus from Closter Dock Rd., half a mile south of the park headquarters on U.S. 9W (**G**). You can avoid the use of a car completely by taking a bus across the George Washington Bridge and up 9W to the starting point of this hike (**H**).*

3.
Great Falls
of Paterson

Directions: Paterson, N.J. From New York City go west on
I-80 about 15 miles to Paterson. Take the Main St. exit and
turn left onto Main St. After 2 blocks turn left onto Grand
St., proceed 5 blocks, and turn right onto Spruce St. Fol-
low Spruce St. 3 blocks and bear right onto McBride Ave.
Then turn left into Overlook Park.

Ownership: City of Paterson.

This dramatic geological site, a National Natural Landmark, stands
in the middle of the old industrial city of Paterson, N.J. The Great
Falls of the Passaic tumble 77 feet from a gap in the First Watchung
Mountain, enlarged by the river during the glacial ages. Tall cliffs of
columnar volcanic rock lie along the riverbanks. The power and
beauty of the falls remain in marked contrast with the surrounding
site, now marred by trash and neglected nineteenth-century industrial buildings. Although the area is part of the Great Falls Historic
District, little has been done to restore it. A recent fire has destroyed
a number of the old buildings.

The formation of the Watchung Mountains is linked to the opening of the Atlantic Ocean, which began about 200 million years ago.
The continents of America and Africa sit on large plates of the earth's
crust. Once these plates and the continents they support were joined
together in a huge land mass known as Pangaea. The plates began
to pull apart, moved by forces that we still do not understand. This
occurred far to the east of the present North American coast.

Throughout much of what is now the Piedmont Province, the
stress of the separation caused the land to sink, creating basins. These
basins then filled with sediments eroded off the surrounding highlands; slowly the sediments hardened into red shales and sandstones.

The separation of the plates also caused the underlying rock layers
to break and crack. As a result, there were several periods of volcanic
activity 180 to 190 million years ago, and blankets of lava were
spewed over the sedimentary layers. (Lava is molten rock or magma
from deep within the earth that is forced to the surface.) The lava
cooled to form a dark fine-grained rock called basalt. Later, more

sedimentary material covered the basalt, encasing it like the filling in a sandwich. Over millions of years, the upper layers of sedimentary rock have been eroded away, revealing the underlying basalt.

The record of these events is clearly visible at Great Falls. Standing at the overlook, you can see the basalt—the grayish material—in the cliff opposite. The meeting point or contact of the basalt and reddish brown sandstone is down at the water line. Downstream on the right, outcroppings of rock show a contact that is much higher, about 75 feet above the river. At one time these sedimentary strata were on an equal level, but the rock formation split apart, and the two parts shifted positions so that the two bands of sandstone now sit on different sides of a fault.

For a closer look at the falls, walk back to the road, McBride Ave., turn right and then right again onto Wayne Ave. Cross the river, go one block, and turn right into the other section of the park. Walk to the overlook. Huge blocks of basalt lie at the foot of the falls, broken off by the relentless force of water pushing through cracks in the rock. On the cliff face, ferns, mosses, and even a few small trees have taken hold in the crevices. The roots of these plants slowly work their way into the solid rock, thus contributing to the gradual destruction of the cliffs. In some places on the cliff, *slickensides* are visible, smooth planes of rock where the faces of a fault have rubbed against each other (see **#63**).

Cross the bridge and walk down the far side to the Valley of the Rocks. Here the cliff face rises 130 feet, and the layers of sedimentary rock and various forms of basalt are particularly beautiful. The red sedimentary material is on the bottom, usually formed in layers roughly parallel to each other. In some places the layers appear to run into each other; this phenomenon, called *cross-bedding*, occurs when the sediments are deposited in water currents that change direction and speed. The basalt, which is at the top of the cliff, appears in three distinct bands, formed by differences in the rate at which the molten lava cooled. The uppermost layer cooled quickly and fractured into fluted structures. Below them lie large, cruder columns, which cooled more gradually, and below those, a solid, unfractured layer.

Remarks: *Allow an hour for the site.*

4.

Troy Meadows

Directions: **Morris County, N.J. From New York City, take I-80 west about 20 miles and take the exit for Route 23 south. Turn west (right) immediately on U.S. 46. Go about 6 miles and turn south (left) on New Rd. Cross over I-280 and take Edwards Rd. (the service road) on the right. Park immediately on the right opposite a dirt road going in to the left with a chain across it. Walk down the road heading due west. Go straight across an open meadow to the woods on the far side. Pick up the path again and in a few moments you will reach the edge of the marsh. A rough walkway of two planks leads out to the boardwalk that stretches several miles beside the power line. The southern end of the boardwalk is more beautiful than the north.**

Ownership: **Wildlife Preserve, Inc. No entry permit required. Closed during hunting season.**

This National Natural Landmark is the largest remaining cattail marsh in New Jersey. An island of unspoiled land in the midst of a densely populated area and several major highways, it is beautiful at any time of year: a golden prairie ringed with flaming maples and sour gum in the autumn, green and full of birds and animals in the spring, haunted by screech, barred, or great horned owls on cold February nights. Many of the species that live in the marsh are specifically adapted to freshwater wetlands that are rapidly disappearing. As a result, these creatures are becoming rare, and in some cases their survival is threatened.

Bog turtles have probably never been abundant because of their unusual requirement of swampy or boggy land combined with a slow-moving stream passing through. Troy Meadows is one of the few places in New Jersey where these turtles can be found. The meadows are an unusual site for the blue-spotted salamander, whose normal range is from the Gulf of the St. Lawrence to upper New York state. The salamander requires a marshland environment for breeding, and in New Jersey it is found only in the Passaic watershed. These animals are difficult to see; one would be very lucky to spot them on a casual visit to the meadows. In March, though, you might well see muskrats weaving their lodges from cattails and mud, and snapping and spotted turtles often appear around the boardwalk.

Birdlife is incredibly rich in Troy Meadows. Swamp sparrows and long-billed marsh wrens nest in the marsh, weaving intricate structures from the cattails. Northern harriers, a species of hawk which is threatened in New Jersey, swing in low arcs over the meadows, looking for rodents. At dawn, during the breeding season from April into June, you may hear the queer, croaking cries of rails and the oddly mechanical calls of bitterns. If you are lucky, you may even see them. Both the least and American bitterns nest here, as does the sora rail. The bitterns are usually found in freshwater marshes, adapted to a diet of toads and frogs. The best time of year for Troy Meadows' birdlife is in April and May. The cattails are not so obtrusively high, and the birds are more active. In April, snipe migrate through in large numbers, performing mating flights above the marsh, soaring high into the air and thrumming as they plummet to earth.

Troy Meadows is a remnant of the last glacier. A huge mass of ice broke off the glacier and rested here, enclosed in a thick layer of

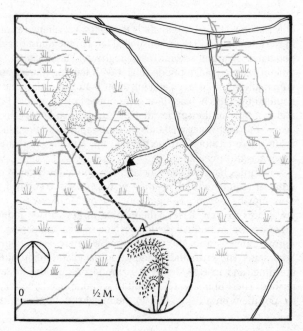

Inset: Phragmites

glacial debris. As the ice melted and settled, a depression formed, lined with the sediments deposited by the glacier. At one time the meadows were part of a vast lake of glacial meltwater that drained through the Great Falls of Paterson (see **#3**). Gradually, the water level dropped and marsh plants invaded the area.

From the boardwalk, one can see a range of successional stages, from open water to hardwood forest (see **Piedmont**). In patches of open water there are the tiny, bright-green leaves of duckweed. Such floating plants are the first intruders onto open water following algae. They have threadlike "roots" that hang below the small leaves and act as stabilizers. The cattails and the sedges, on slightly higher ground, follow the floating plants. These plants gradually help build up the soil: silt from the water collects around the leaves and stems, and when they die and fall over, they add to the soil below. Eventually, islands are formed, covered with buttonbush, willows, and alders. After them come red and silver maples, pin oaks, green ash, and sweetgum. Look out to the west from the boardwalk: colonies of this last succesional stage line the horizon. The swamp woodlands are also a favorite habitat for wood ducks (see **#7**).

At the southern end of the boardwalk (**A**), a small river wanders through the marsh. Sediment washed down by the river has collected along the shores in low levees, slightly higher than the level of the marsh. Here alders, willows, and buttonbush have sprouted.

Looking out over the marsh, you will see patches of feathery reeds, phragmites. These plants are more tolerant of pollution than cattails and have taken over large portions of New Jersey wetlands. They provide little food for birds and other animals, and sometimes pose a threat to wildlife habitats.

Wetlands are considered by ecologists to be the most productive ecosystems. They produce more tons of vegetation per acre than the richest grainfields. The saturated soils contain little oxygen, drastically slowing the decay of dead plants. They become part of a thick, stringy layer of peat, which forms the soil of the marsh and gives it its special character (see **#120**). The peat acts like a sponge to absorb and hold excess water, a natural form of flood and drought control. Many amphibians and insects require wetlands to carry out their breeding cycles. A rich variety of bird and animal life results from the abundance of food.

The continued existence of these areas is greatly threatened by development. Raising or lowering of the water level of a marsh will totally disrupt its wildlife and vegetation. Pollution of local streams can also irrevocably change or destroy a marsh. Although Troy Meadows itself is protected, the heavy use of the surrounding area may endanger its survival.

Remarks: *In spring the walkway out to the boardwalk is often covered with water. Biting insects may be unpleasant in summer. From the walkway to the river to the south is about three-quarters of a mile. The marsh is best seen alone or with one other person—a large group will scare the wildlife and crowd the narrow boardwalk.*

5.

Montclair
Hawk Lookout

Directions: **Essex County, N.J. From New York City, take I-80 west about 8 miles to the Garden State Parkway. Go 6 miles to Exit 151 at Bloomfield. Go west 2.1 miles on Watchung Ave. to Upper Mountain Ave. Turn north and go 0.7 mile to Bradford Ave. Turn west and go 0.1 mile to Edgecliffe Rd. Turn north (right); go 0.3 mile and park on the left (north) side of the street. Do not park on the south side; you may be ticketed. Cross Edgecliffe Rd. and walk up the short, easy path to the lookout.**

Ownership: **New Jersey Audubon Society.**

It is a warm sunny day in mid-September. You are standing on an outcrop of the First Watchung Mountain. The skyline of New York City, from the towers of the George Washington Bridge to the Verrazano, is clear and sharp on the horizon to the east. A steady wind is blowing out of the northwest. During the next few hours, two thousand broad-winged hawks will wheel and turn into view in the sky overhead. Spiraling higher and higher, each hawk will suddenly set its wings and, like a fighter plane peeling off formation, dive off to the southwest.

This spectacle doesn't happen every day during the fall migrations, but in mid-September, at the Montclair Hawk Lookout, it is not uncommon. Every year from September through November, anywhere from ten to seventeen thousand broad-winged hawks, thousands of sharp-shinned hawks, hundreds of American kestrels, ospreys, and red-tailed hawks, along with dozens of less common migrants, pass over this ridge, which has been designated as a National Natural Landmark.

It is the ridge that brings them here. From their breeding grounds in New England or Canada, the hawks follow the mountains south. Along the ridges, the hawks find the updrafts which are essential to the larger birds in the long flight to the wintering grounds; the updrafts enable them to soar, to gain altitude, to fly with a minimum of effort. The updrafts are created in two ways. As the sun strikes the earth, the air over an open field or a rocky outcrop heats more rapidly than air over a forest, and it rises. The other source is winds out of the northwest that strike the ridges at right angles forcing currents of air skyward.

The large soaring hawks have broad wings, shaped to provide them with maximum lift. Each wing ends in five fingers of feathers, with each feather also shaped to provide additional lift. The hawks can thus soar for hours over marshes, fields, and woodlands as they hunt for small animals. Smaller hawks such as kestrels and merlins hunt birds—and even insects—on the wing. Their faster, more maneuverable flight enables these hawks to catch their flying prey. They flap their wings and pass rapidly over the ridge, relying less heavily on the rising air currents.

Broad-winged hawks breed in most of the eastern United States. Those from New England fly south to the coast of Connecticut, swinging west over the Hudson and the Palisades until they strike the Watchung Mountains. Those from areas farther west fly south over different mountain ridges (see **#78**). Many broad-winged hawks migrate all the way to South America. Their flight is the most spectacular both because of their large numbers and because their migration is concentrated into a few short weeks. They are the first hawks to move south because they have the farthest distance to travel. Other species winter in the southern United States and Central America.

The Watchung Mountains are two ridges of igneous rock, the result of hot lava that was forced up through fissures in the earth's surface and embedded between layers of sedimentary rocks about 180 to 190 million years ago (see **#3**). In that same geological period, the surface buckled and heaved upward, propelled by tremendous pressures from within the earth. The beds of sandstone, shale, and igneous rock were tilted up toward the southwest. Gradually, over millions of years, the softer sedimentary rock eroded while the harder igneous rock remained, exposed as the escarpments of the First and Second Watchung—like two long fish hooks, side by side, running northeast and southwest.

The vegetation on top of the ridge is typical of hilltops in the Piedmont. Red, white, and chestnut oaks predominate with sweet birch, gray birch, and sassafras. Species that fruit in the fall—maple-leaved viburnum, dogwood, and wild grape—attract migrating songbirds, so that the hawk watch is a good place for observing finches and warblers, too.

Remarks: *Bring binoculars, a chair, and some dark glasses if the sky is very bright.*

6.

Kearny Marsh

Directions: **Essex County, N.J. From New York City take the New Jersey Turnpike south to Exit 15W, the first exit after the Lincoln Tunnel. Take Route 508 towards Kearny. After 1 mile turn north (right), onto Schuyler Ave. (Route 507) and go 1.2 miles to the Gunnell Oval on the right. Park at the northeast corner of the playing fields and walk out to the railroad tracks. Walk north (left) along the tracks a few yards and up onto the railway embankment, running east-west. Turn east (right) and walk along the embankment, stopping frequently to scan the marsh. You can walk about a mile and a half to a wildlife area, which appears on the left. Caution—the tracks are still in use despite their dilapidated appearance. The best time to visit the area is on Sunday when almost no trains are running.**

Ownership: **Town of Kearny.**

In the midst of the most depressing section of the New Jersey Turnpike, surrounded by landfill strewn with tires, plastic, and glass, and under the smoke plumes of industrial plants, lies a vibrant island of life: Kearny Marsh. The marsh is a flooded area in the midst of broad wetlands called the Hackensack Meadows. During the 1970s an extension of the New Jersey Turnpike was built here, blocking the drainage of the area. The marsh hosts the largest breeding populations of American coots and pied-billed grebes in the state of New Jersey and is one of the few nesting sites in the state for the ruddy duck, a bird that generally nests in the prairies of Canada and the north-central United States. Other nesting species include many dabbling ducks (see **#18**)—mallard, blue-winged and green-winged teal, gadwall and wood duck—common gallinules, least and American bitterns, as well as black- and yellow-crowned night herons. Six other species of heron and egret feed in the marsh, eating the small killifish, which in turn feed on mosquito larvae. Look also for muskrats and snapping and eastern painted turtles during the warm months.

Throughout the year, American kestrels and northern harriers hover over the marsh, and during fall migration, ospreys, merlins, and sharp-shinned hawks are regular visitors. Peregrine falcons are also occasionally seen. Winter is the time to see short-eared owls patrolling the landfills, along with the thousands of herring and great black-backed gulls. Intermingled with these may be the uncommon glaucous and Iceland gulls, which have white rather than dark wing tips. Rough-legged hawks, birds of the northern tundra, often winter in the marshes, along with many species of waterfowl, including canvasback, northern shoveler, bufflehead, and pintail. Another resident is the seven-spotted ladybug, which is present in such quantities that many are captured here and sent to gardeners all over the country for aphid control. This ladybug is a European species, which apparently established itself here on its own. The insects may have found their way here from Newark Airport.

The 22,000 acres of the Hackensack Meadows, which include Kearny Marsh, were once covered by the waters of the ancient Glacial Lake Passaic (see **#9** and **#7**). Because the meadows lie over impermeable layers of clay that accumulated at the bottom of the lake, and because the area catches water from the high ground to the west, drainage is poor, and the soil is always soggy. It is this factor which has saved some of the wetlands from full-scale development, in the midst of one of the most industrialized strips of land in America, providing a haven for so much birdlife. In spite of all the abuse—in the form of solid waste and chemical pollution—suffered by the meadows in the past, life now flourishes at Kearny Marsh. These wetlands are a testament to the self-cleansing action of marshes and swamps. The deep layer of peat and the rapid growth of abundant vegetation absorb some of the water-borne pollutants, significantly raising the water quality of the streams filtering through the marsh. The raised railroad beds that border the marsh also protect it, blocking the seepage of pollutants into the area from nearby towns and chemical dumps. The water quality of the marsh has been steadily improving over the last several years. Although the marsh has been leased to two companies for development, 40 percent of the area is to be preserved as open space.

Remarks: *To see shorebirds, continue north on Schuyler Ave. about a mile to a dirt road leading east (right) marked North Arlington–Lyndhurst*

Joint Meeting. Follow the road across the railroad tracks to the environmental center and park. Walk around the pool ahead of you. Some of the unusual species that come here every year are golden plover, ruff, Baird's and buff-breasted sandpipers, marbled and Hudsonian godwits, and Wilson's and northern phalaropes. For further information contact the New Jersey Audubon Society, P.O. Box 693, Bernardsville, N.J. 07924, (201)766-5787, or the Hackensack Meadowlands Development Commission, 1 Dekorte Park Plaza, Lyndhurst, N.J. 07071.

7.

Great Swamp
National Wildlife Refuge

Directions: **Morris County, N.J. From New York City take I-80 west, about 30 miles. Go south on I-287 about 12 miles to the Basking Ridge exit. Go east (left) on North Maple Ave. and drive 0.8 mile to Madisonville Rd. Turn east (left) and drive 0.5 mile to Pleasant Plains Rd. Turn east (right) and go 2.7 miles to the refuge headquarters, where you can obtain information and maps of the refuge. To reach the observation center (A), continue on past the headquarters to the next crossroads and turn left on White Bridge Rd. Go 1.1 miles to New Vernon Rd. Turn left and go 1.2 miles to the entrance to the observation area on the left. For a view of one of the impoundments, drive beyond the tower entrance to the first bridge (B). The pool is off to the left. To explore the wilderness area, park at the designated area on New Vernon Rd., a quarter-mile north of the bridge at C, or return to White Bridge Rd., turn east (left), and drive about a half-mile to the end of the old Meyersville Rd. (D). Other parking areas are at E and F.**

Ownership: **U.S. Fish and Wildlife Service.**

Surrounded by the New Jersey suburbs and about 45 minutes from New York City, the Great Swamp Refuge is an island of wildness. This National Natural Landmark contains more than 5000 acres of swamp woodland, dense thickets, marshy pools, and pockets of up-

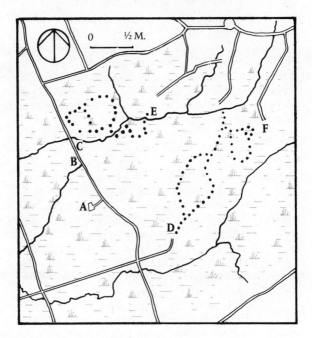

land woods. Thousands of wood ducks breed here each spring, and there are more bluebirds nesting on the refuge than anywhere else in the state. Miles of trails wander through a designated wilderness area big enough to get lost in.

As you approach the swamp by car, you will notice that it lies in a shallow depression surrounded by higher ground. Like Troy Meadows to the north, Great Swamp is a remnant of Glacial Lake Passaic (see **#4** and **#9**). The Wisconsin ice sheet stopped just to the north of where the swamp now lies. Route 24 runs on top of the glacier's terminal morraine, the dike of gravel, boulders, and other debris left behind as the glacier melted northward. The meltwaters of the glacier were caught between the Watchung Ridge to the south and east, the massive ice sheet to the north, and the high ground to the west. The resulting lake lasted about 4000 years, laying down a thick layer of impermeable clays 60 to 80 feet deep. Gradually the lake filled in with the remains of plants and animals, being gradually colonized by sedges and other wetland plants, and finally becoming a wooded swamp. Begin your trip to the swamp with a stop at the wildlife observation area (**A**). There are two blinds, each by a small pond.

Waterfowl and other birds gather here, and you can watch them from close range.

During the last two centuries, the swamp has been logged, burned, drained, farmed, and then abandoned. Only a few pockets of large mature trees remain scattered through the area. Local citizens organized in 1960 and purchased the swamp to prevent it from becoming a jet airport. They then turned the land over to the Department of Interior to be preserved as a refuge.

The thick bed of clays is what maintains the moisture levels in the swamp. The water-bearing strata or aquifers of the region actually lie below the clays. Water levels in the swamp depend solely on precipitation and the flow of two streams, Great Brook and Black Brook. Throughout much of the swamp, the clays are covered by sands, in turn covered by a layer of mucky peat. The peat, partially decayed vegetation, is stringy, spongy, and loosely woven. It can store large amounts of water, which helps the swamp stay moist during droughts. As in a bog, peat in a swamp develops because there is little oxygen in the still waters. Bacteria that break down organic matter need oxygen to survive. Some decay does go on in oxygenless or *anaerobic* conditions, but it is very slow.

Swamps help control flooding. Swollen streams spread out across the flat land and lose much of their momentum. Excess water is absorbed by the peat and by the living vegetation. As the swamp succession proceeds and less moisture-tolerant species take over, the land loses some of its ability to absorb water. Paradoxically, the drier the habitat becomes, the less moisture it is able to hold. Unfortunately, Great Swamp is still vulnerable to farming and development activities in the vicinity, which drain water from the swamp.

From the bridge (**B**), you can look out over one of three pools created to maintain water levels in the swamp and to keep succession from progressing too quickly. These pools are dotted with nesting platforms and dead trees where thousands of young wood ducks are hatched each spring. Logging and draining of mature woodlands has destroyed many potential nesting sites over much of the eastern United States. The birds prefer to nest deep in wooded swamps but will also nest as much as a mile from the water. Great Swamp has become a major refuge for them.

The male wood duck is startlingly beautiful—an iridescent green head with white facial markings, a soft brown breast speckled with white, and a dark iridescent back tinged with purple.

The female wood ducks arrive as early as February and have often already mated on the wintering ground. The males will arrive later. Only if there is an ample supply of food will the females lay eggs.

The females must find a nesting site. The birds will nest about 30 to 50 feet above the ground in a hole in a tree or in one of the artificial nesting platforms scattered through the marsh. Often there are not enough sites to go around. The homeless females will then dump their eggs into nests already inhabited by other wood ducks. Sometimes forty or fifty eggs are found in one nest. When the eggs hatch, the resident female will probably abandon them, for she will be unable to feed them all.

At the break of dawn from mid-April to mid-May, the young hatch. The mother calls to them with a unique cry. The babies have very long toenails enabling them to climb out of the nest cavity. They fall to the ground and start off after the female, who makes straight for the water. The babies instinctively know how to swim and begin to feed on minute crustaceans and other bits of animal life. Mature wood ducks, however, are vegetarians. They are dabbling ducks (see **#18**), living on shallow-water vegetation such as the seeds of arrow arum, smartweeds, pickerelweed, duckweed, and a variety of grasses: They also forage in the woods, eating acorns and berries.

The marsh stage in Great Swamp is maintained partly by muskrats. They pull up aquatic vegetation by the roots, using it for food and building material. This keeps the water open. In the past, beavers may also have played a part, constructing dams that kept water levels high. Beavers have been restored to the area and are thriving. Though rarely seen, minks live in and around the pools and streams. They are skilled at fishing, and they swim well (see **#44**). Their tracks can sometimes be seen in the soft mud at the water's edge.

The ponds and the slow-moving streams of the swamp are inhabited by a variety of turtles and fish. Snapping turtles are ferocious and are particularly fond of baby ducks. Other turtles are the eastern mud, spotted, wood, and eastern painted, and the musk turtle or stinkpot. The musk turtle gets its name from the odoriferous secretion it exudes when caught. The bog turtle, a rare species, has also been reported (see **#23**).

A number of snakes favor the wetlands. The northern water snake can often be seen basking on branches above the water. It is common on waterways throughout the Mid-Atlantic region. The eastern garter snake and the eastern ribbon snake are also commonly seen. The ribbon snake swims on the surface of the water; it feeds on salamanders, frogs, and fish.

The refuge pool at (**B**) has stands of cattails and buttonbush and hummocks of sedges and bur reed, where other marsh birds nest. For another look at the marsh vegetation, go to the observation center (**A**) and walk out along the boardwalk trail there. Mallards, black ducks, green-winged and blue-winged teals, Canada geese, green herons, least and American bitterns, secretive king and Virginia rails, soras, and common gallinules can all be found here.

The arrow arum, pickerelweed, cattail, and other wetland species have had to find solutions to a variety of problems. The muck of the swamp is virtually devoid of oxygen, yet the roots of these aquatic plants need oxygen. Most of them have air tubes that run from the emergent leaves and stem down to the roots. Terrestrial species have small openings, or *stomata,* on the lower surface of their leaves, through which they take in carbon dioxide for photosynthesis and release oxygen. These openings are on the underside of the leaf, to prevent the loss of too much moisture. But on aquatic plants like the water lilies, which have floating leaves, the stomata are on the upper surface of the leaf. These plants are important to the many tiny animals that lay their eggs on the stems and undersides of the leaves.

Duckweeds—tiny green leaves floating on the surface of the pond—are another important group of aquatic plants. As their name implies, they are a favorite food for waterfowl. A small rootlike filament dangles down from beneath the plant. This filament stabilizes the duckweed and keeps it from turning over. It also draws in nutrients from the surrounding water. To survive the winter, duckweeds develop a dense bud during the summer. This bud sinks and sprouts in the bottom of the pond. Then when the warm spring arrives, the bud develops leaves with air spaces inside. The leaves then float to the surface.

Most aquatic vegetation reproduces by sprouting from roots or other parts of the plant. Fertilization of flowers is difficult because pollen—the dust of tiny male reproductive cells—is not particularly waterproof. Some species, such as the water celery, send up a flowering stalk so that the flower blooms above the water. Once the flower is fertilized, the flower stalk is retracted so that the seeds develop underwater. Some seeds—for example, those of the water plantain—are equipped with small floats, helping to disseminate the species.

Aquatic vegetation is an important source of oxygen for fish, crustaceans, and other forms of aquatic life. During daylight hours, the plants manufacture excess oxygen as a by-product of photosynthesis. At night, both plants and animals draw on this reserve as they transform food into metabolic energy.

To explore the wilderness area, walk in from any of the parking areas at **C**, **D**, **E**, or **F**. (If you have two cars, you can leave one at each end of the trail and avoid retracing your steps.) From **C** to **E** is about 1.5 miles. From **D** to **F** is also about 1.5 miles. Other trails loop away from these paths and back again. The trails will take you along flat but wet terrain, through lowlands, where red maple, American elm, and willow are common, and islands of slightly higher ground, where you will find American beech, white oak, shagbark hickory, and gray birch. On these higher patches, rhododendron and mountain laurel are abundant in the shrub layer. Pink lady's slipper blooms each spring on these islands of drier ground.

The woods are rich with birdlife. On late winter evenings, barred owls, screech owls, and great horned owls call. These birds mate in winter, and their calling is part of the breeding ritual. Barred owls prefer a wetland environment, nesting near streams or swamps. Great horned owls and screech owls nest in a variety of woodland habitats. Owls are legendary hunters. They are equipped with powerful night vision and highly sensitive hearing, which enable them to stalk the small rodents and other mammals that are active at night. The two ears of an owl are of unequal size; this apparently hones their ability to fix the location of prey.

Throughout the area, spring migrations of warblers, thrushes, and vireos are wonderful. About twenty-seven species of warblers are likely to be seen or heard during migration.

Remarks: *Spring and fall are the best times here. Early morning and late evening are best for seeing wildlife. The refuge is open year round from dawn to dusk. In addition to the many miles of hiking trails through the wilderness area, the Morris County Outdoor Education Center ([201] 766-2489) also maintains trails and offers a number of nature programs. To reach the center drive south on Long Hill Rd. to Meyersville. Turn east on Meyersville Rd. to Fairmount Ave. Turn left on Fairmount Ave. to Southern Blvd. Turn left on Southern Blvd. and drive to the center. West of Pleasant Plains Rd. along White Bridge Rd. is the Somerset County Lord Stirling Park. Canoeing on the Passaic is allowed by permit at this park. Camping is available by permit at a nearby county park, Mahlon Dickinson. Contact the Morris County Park Commission, P.O. Box 1295 R, Morristown, N.J. 07960, (201) 285-6166. To explore the wilderness area, be prepared for wet hiking. Rubber boots are a good idea in colder weather. With the warm weather come mosquitoes and ticks.*

8.

Scherman-Hoffman
Wildlife Sanctuaries

Directions: **Somerset County, N.J. From New York City take I-80 to Exit 43. Take I-287 south, toward Morristown, for 11.8 miles to Exit 26B for Bernardsville. Travel north on Childs Rd. 0.5 mile; bear right on Hardscrabble Rd. Sanctuary parking is 1 mile on right.**

Ownership: **New Jersey Audubon Society.**

The lush floodplain of the headwaters of the Passaic River, stately second-growth forests, and open meadows make this small sanctuary of 250 acres a haven for diverse plants and wildlife. It is bounded by Morristown National Historical Park, and trails lead from the sanctuary to the site of George Washington's encampment during the bitter winter of 1779. Across Hardscrabble Rd. from the parking lot is the floodplain of Indian Grave Brook (**A**), which features a short guided nature trail about half a mile long.

Floodplains exist along streams that have carved out broad, gently sloping valleys. Soil is brought downstream by runoff and high water and deposited along the banks. Then, as the stream cuts farther into its channel, the banks become fertile, well-watered terraces. During floods the excess water flows along a channel on the floodplain, sweeping away much of the vegetation in its path. The flooding breaks the sequence of succession that began when the farms on the floodplain were abandoned. These conditions favor light-loving species, and luxuriant thickets of vines, shrubs, and ferns cover the moist, rich soil. Numerous species produce fruits, which attract many birds during migration and throughout the winter.

From the parking area follow the red-blazed Dogwood Trail as it rises over rocky terrain through a late-succession forest of mixed oaks and hickory. Except for the absence of chestnut trees, the composition of this forest is virtually the same today as in George Washington's time. (The chestnuts were wiped out by a blight brought from Europe at the turn of the century [see **#30**].) Oaks and hickories are only moderately tolerant of shade. They reproduce most readily in clearings where a fallen tree or some other disturbance has created an opening in the canopy. This forest has been disturbed frequently since the eighteenth century and never allowed to reach

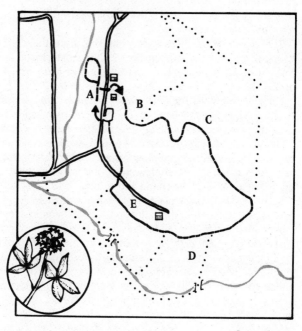

Inset: Ginseng

a climax stage. Only over the past few years have the woods been left to themselves, and beeches and sugar maples—species of the northern climax forest—are becoming increasingly common here.

On the southern slopes of the trail (**B**) are many fine, tall tulip-trees, a fast-growing, sun-loving species that will decline but not totally disappear as the beeches and sugar maples take over. Their soft wood breaks easily at the top in high winds; this creates an opening in the canopy and a sunny place where young tuliptrees can sprout.

The shrub layer here, where the forest is closing in, is much less luxurious than that down on the floodplain. Dogwood dominates the understory and fills the woods with white blossoms in May.

As the trail approaches the ridgetop (**C**), one encounters boulders of granite bedrock strewn over the ground. The igneous rock is probably one billion years old and forms the backbone of the New Jersey Highlands, part of a spur of mountains—the Reading Prong—that runs from Vermont down to Pennsylvania (see **New York–New Jersey Highlands**). These are the oldest exposed rocks in the eastern United States. The huge, rounded boulders sitting on the very top of the hill are debris left by the Wisconsin Glacier, which retreated about 10,000 years ago.

The vegetation up here is very different from the slope forest. Chestnut oak and lowbush blueberry, which can thrive on these dry, rocky soils, predominate. Look for ruffed grouse and pileated woodpeckers here.

Now the Dogwood Trail moves downhill toward the Passaic River. Bear left where the trail bends to the right and spend a few minutes exploring the river's floodplain. Here a climax forest of yellow birch and beech has developed (**D**; see **#41**). This area is at a much later stage of succession than the floodplain of Indian Grave Brook, because it was not cut over as recently. The banks of the river host many wildflowers in the spring and summer, including dwarf ginseng, downy rattlesnake plantain, and showy orchis.

Retrace your steps to the Dogwood Trail and continue on it as it moves out into the open. Hoffman's Fields (**E**) are mowed every few years and represent early succession on an open field. Tall grasses and a great assortment of flowering plants are typical of this stage. Occasional pioneer oaks are scattered in the grass. The abundance of flowers—violets, bergamot, asters, butterfly weed, goldenrod, and more—make this an ideal habitat for many species of butterflies in the summer months. The rare wood turtle, which is actually quite common in the sanctuary, can be seen in May, when it comes into the meadows to lay eggs.

Remarks: *Wear sturdy shoes and be prepared to climb. Allow two hours to see the sanctuary. The trails are open every day until 5 p.m. A trailside museum is open Tuesday through Saturday, 9:00 a.m. to 5:00 p.m. and Sunday 12:00 to 5:00 p.m. The sanctuary is closed the last two weeks of December and the last two weeks of June. Nearest camping is at Round Valley Recreation Area, Lebanon, N.J. For further information contact Scherman-Hoffman Sanctuaries, P.O. Box 693, Bernardsville, N.J. 07924, (201) 766-5787.*

9.
Moggy Hollow

Directions: **Somerset County, N.J. From New York City take I-80 west about 30 miles to Exit 43. Follow I-287 south 19.2 miles to Exit 18. Go north on U.S. 202 and 206 toward**

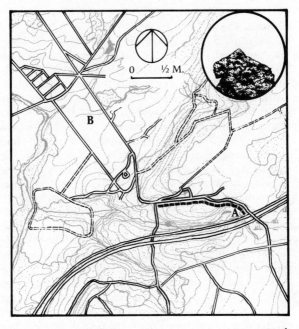

Inset: Basalt

Bedminster, about 1 mile, bearing right on U.S. 202 into Far Hills. Go 1.2 miles and turn south on Route 512, Far Hills Rd. After 1.3 miles pull into the dirt road on the right and park. Walk from the dirt road south along Far Hills Rd. until you reach the chain fence along I-287. Follow it downhill to the right. Here the slope is less precipitous, and you can work your way down into the ravine more easily.

Ownership: **Upper Raritan Watershed Association.**

Moggy Hollow, a National Natural Landmark, is a narrow, steep-sided ravine walled off at one end by a ledge of basaltic rock. On wintry afternoons it is a fascinating and forlorn spot, oddly out of place with the rich, rolling countryside of Somerset County and the incessant hum of I-287 just to the east.

After a short scramble of a few yards, you will find yourself on a ledge of basalt rock (**A**). As the Wisconsin Glacier began its retreat about 15,000 years ago, the meltwaters filled a basin formed by the New Jersey highlands to the west and the ridge of the Second Watchung Mountain to the south and east (see **Piedmont**). This body of water, Glacial Lake Passaic, stretched for many miles and rose until it reached the height of the ledge at Moggy Hollow, 331 feet above sea level. From this first outlet, the water drained southwestward. Later, two lower outlets at Little Falls and Great Falls were uncovered as the ice sheet continued to retreat northward (see **#37**).

The ledge across the notch is basalt, a dark igneous rock deposited about 180 to 190 million years ago (see **#3**). Because of the fine-grained crystalline structure of basalt, scientists know that it was formed as molten material was forced up through fissures in the earth's surface by volcanic eruption and was spread over the ground in a sheet. Exposed to the air, the material cooled rapidly, so that the crystals remained small. Molten rock that cools more slowly within the earth's rocky surface layer—granite, for example—develops larger crystals. There were three major periods of lava flow, each resulting in a new layer of basalt over layers—hundreds of feet thick—of sandstone and shale (see **#111**). Subsequent disturbances within the earth tilted these layers upward to the east and south. As erosion ate away the softer sandstones and shales, the basalt was exposed, forming the ridges of the First and Second Watchung Mountains and a series of outcroppings from the third period of volcanic activity. Looking down from the ledge to the west (I-287 is behind you), you will see a steep-walled ravine dropping to a marshy flat about 40 feet below. For thousands of years this ledge was the spillway of Glacial Lake Passaic, which lay to the east and north (see **#7**).

At the intersection of Far Hills Rd. and Route 202, stop and look at the fields stretching away to the southwest (**B**). The rolling green hummocks are really terraces of glacial debris brought here by the meltwater and deposited as the flow of water slowed.

Remarks: *The route down to the ledge is a short, very steep and rocky scramble. Wear sneakers and be careful.*

10.
Hutcheson Memorial
Forest

Directions: Somerset County, N.J. From New York City take the New Jersey Turnpike south to Exit 10 (about 25 miles) and go northwest on I-287 about 14 miles to Route 527

(Easton Ave.) toward New Brunswick. Go 0.3 mile and turn right onto Cedar Grove Lane. Go about 3 miles to the end. Turn right onto Amwell Rd. (Route 514). The entrance to the forest is 1.3 miles up the road on the left. Look for the huge arch. The woods are open only by appointment and during regularly scheduled tours. Write to the Director, Hutcheson Memorial Forest, Rutgers University, Department of Botany, New Brunswick, N.J. 08903. The preserve is protected by a caretaker.

Ownership: **Rutgers University.**

A small, quiet woodland with a number of tall, impressive white oaks and the open understory of a mature forest, this is one of the oldest undisturbed stands of oak-hickory forest remaining in the United States. Some of the trees are 300 years old. The wood, a National Natural Landmark, is a living museum of what much of the eastern United States was like 200 years ago and a laboratory in which the natural cycles of succession, of cause and effect, are studied.

Although this is an old stand, it is not virgin timber, nor is it at climax (see **Piedmont**). Before colonists settled in the area, forest fires were fairly common. Once started, a fire could burn miles of unbroken forest before being extinguished by a rainstorm or being halted by the edge of a wetland. Fire opened up the canopy and allowed light, which is essential to the regeneration of oaks and hickories, to reach the forest floor. The predominance of oaks and hickories in the canopy today (roughly 70 percent) is probably due to the frequency of fires prior to the eighteenth century. But when the colonists cleared patches of land for farming, breaking up the forests, fires could no longer rage across thousands of acres at a time; since the fires were stopped in 1711, few young oaks and hickories have taken root here. Without further disturbance, the forest may develop into a mix of sugar maple, red maple, beech, and ash.

Over time, another factor has favored the oaks and hickories. The soils here are quite shallow—only about 30 inches thick above the bedrock—and since the area is well-drained, these soils dry out during the occasional periods of drought. Oaks and hickories are better suited to these dry conditions than are beeches and maples.

Events over the last few years are again changing the complexion of the forest. The understory is dominated by flowering dogwood, which has recently been hard hit by disease. Even more than the canopy, the understory determines how much light will reach the forest floor, and the defoliation of many dogwoods has been followed by a great increase in tree seedlings. In 1981, the first serious attack of gypsy moths took place, opening up the woods still further. Only after many years will the effects of these changes on the forest be clear. The university is allowing these natural disturbances to run their course and will monitor their effect.

Remarks: *Easy walking over flat terrain. Guided walks through the forest take about an hour and are designed to show you various successional stages as well as the mature forest.*

11.

Bull's Island

Directions: **Hunterdon County, N.J. From New York City take the New Jersey Turnpike south about 25 miles to I-287. Turn north on I-287 and go about 18 miles. Take U.S. 202 southwest 26.5 miles to Route 29 on the east bank of the Delaware. Turn north and drive 5.5 miles to Bull's Island on the left. Parking is by the headquarters. From the parking area walk east to the canal and follow the trail, which runs north and south the length of the island.**

Ownership: **New Jersey Division of Parks and Forestry.**

Early on a June morning, sunlight filters down through the tall sycamore trees and glitters on the Delaware River. Warblers sing from the trees and cliff swallows dart over the river, catching insects to feed their young. Bull's Island is a part of the Delaware River floodplain, separated from the mainland by the Delaware River and Raritan Canal. A trail follows the edge of canal from one end of the island to the other, a distance of a little over a mile. Head south first into the wilder section of the island. The vegetation is like that of the river islands to the north (see **#68**). In addition to sycamore, other species such as tuliptree, silver maple, and black walnut cover the island with mature forest. On the forest floor, a rich tangle of ostrich fern, pale jewelweed, and nettles crowds the path.

A distinct race of yellow-throated warblers inhabits the tops of the sycamores along the canal. In the southeastern states, where the birds are quite common, they prefer to nest in the clusters of Spanish moss draping the live oaks. Prothonotary warblers, another southern

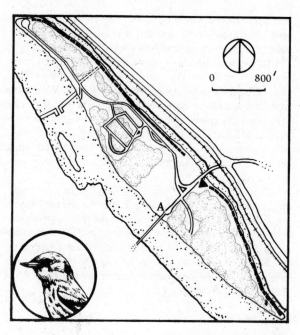

Inset: Cerulean warbler

species, are also regularly seen here in the breeding season. Look for them low down in shrubs by the water's edge. Other species that nest at Bull's Island, perhaps easier to find here than elsewhere in New Jersey, include the warbling and yellow-throated vireos, seen at the southern end of the island, and the cerulean warbler (also a southern species), which frequents the treetops at the northern end. Northern parula warblers, which also like the treetops, nest on the island as well.

After exploring the trail, return to the parking area and continue westward to the bridge over the Delaware River (**A**). Around the entrance to the bridge are black-locust and red-mulberry trees, species commonly found in disturbed areas. The red mulberry produces delicious fruits which are eaten by squirrels, songbirds, and people. Black locust has beautiful drooping white flowers in spring and distinctive compound leaves made up of seven to nineteen leaflets. It can grow on barren soils and is an important tree in the process of succession. Certain bacteria that grow on its roots can absorb inorganic nitrogen. The bacteria pass some of this nitrogen to the tree and some to the surrounding soil, enriching it and making it suitable for other species. The bridge itself has been built with a number of limestone blocks. Growing in the tiny crevices are two interesting small ferns, purple-stemmed cliff brake (smooth form), a fern of calcium-rich outcrops, and blunt-lobed woodsia.

Cliff swallows nest underneath the bridge. They do not commonly breed in New Jersey. Once true to their name, they built their colonies of mud nests on rocky walls and ledges. With the advent of buildings and other man-made structures, especially in agricultural areas or near rivers, the cliff swallows began a partnership with people, building nests under the eaves of barns, on the walls of dams, and underneath bridges like the one at Bull's Island. Look for their distinctive light-colored foreheads and rumps as they swoop under your feet.

Remarks: *The best time to come is late spring and early summer. Camping facilities are located at the northern end of the island. Other activities include fishing (with a license) in the canal and the river, swimming, and boating. There are rental operations scattered along Route 29. Watch out for stinging nettles on the path. Bring bug repellent. For further information contact Bull's Island State Recreation Area, R.D. 1, Box 4—Canal, Belle Mead, N.J. 08502, (201) 873-3050.*

12.

Herrontown Woods

Directions: **Mercer County, N.J. From New York City, take the New Jersey Turnpike south about 30 miles to Exit 9. Follow signs for New Brunswick. Drive 0.7 mile on Route 18 west to the overpass for U.S. 1 and follow signs for U.S. 1 south. Drive 16 miles. Go northwest (right) on Route 571 (Alexander St.) for 1.7 miles. Turn northeast (right) on Route 27 (Nassau St.) and go 1.0 mile to Snowden Lane. Turn northwest (left) and go 1.4 miles to the entrance to the woods; turn left and go to the end of the road.**

Ownership: **Mercer County Park Commission.**

Herrontown Woods is a small, richly varied forest with wet woods, a stream, moist and well-drained slopes, and old fields reverting to forest—a range of habitats which illustrate the process of succession. This diversity brings warblers in great numbers in the spring. The

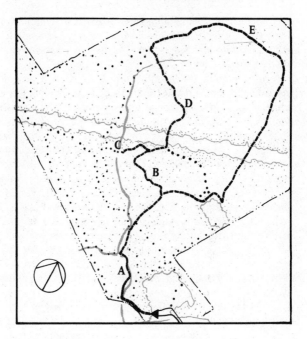

deep, moist soils support a wealth of flowers in the spring and fall, as well as an outstanding assortment of ferns.

From the parking lot walk west on the Red Trail and then east on the Green Trail. This area (**A**) is a "late old field," an early stage in the transition from abandoned farm land to mature hardwood forest. The first trees to encroach on the open field were redcedars, trees which need abundant sunlight. Scattered through the woods here, a few cedars still remain, but they are dying off in the shade created by the growing forest. Gray birches, which followed the redcedars onto the open land, also thrive in sunny areas, and they, too, are disappearing as other trees crowd in.

Now a young stand of pin oak, a tree associated with swampy conditions, is the dominant species, but it is also a step in the succession. The saplings and younger trees are largely red oaks, red maples, and sweetgum, and eventually they will probably become the dominant trees. Flowering dogwood is the main understory species. Its presence, along with red oaks, indicates that the soil here is drier than that usually associated with pin oaks; one possible explanation is that conditions have changed and that the site has become drier over time. There are abundant vines here that are typical of an early-forest stage of succession, in which a considerable amount of sunlight can still strike the forest floor. As the trees grow, the vines climb upward, seeking light.

Turning left onto the second Yellow Trail, you will pass along the east side of the stream and climb through a mixed oak forest (**B**) of white, black, and red oak with some sweetgum. These are trees one would expect to find on the deep, moist soil of this well-drained slope. Judging from the young trees, the forest here may eventually be dominated by red maple, sweetgum, and white ash, with a few white and black oaks present. One theory holds that the mixed oak forest that today covers much of northern New Jersey is the direct result of human disruption—logging, farming, quarrying, fire, and the like. As clearings reverted to forest, the oaks were able to flourish in the open woodlands of the earlier successional stages; later, in the shade of other trees, they will do less well. This theory is in dispute, for the abundance of other trees among the saplings and seedlings may be deceptive. We do not know what effect the heavy defoliation of the oaks by gypsy moths will have on the evolution of the forest. By opening up the canopy, the infestations may encourage young oaks. On the other hand, the moths may kill the young trees, too. Only time will tell.

In the deep and moist soils of the slope, spring flowers are abundant. Spring beauty, mayapple, skunk cabbage, jewelweed, jack-in-the-pulpit, and Solomon's seal are common. Typically, deciduous forests are full of flowers in the early spring, when leaves are sparse and ample sun strikes the ground. In full summer, the trees provide too much shade for flowering plants to flourish. In more open ecosystems, such as the open grassy strip along the gas pipeline that cuts across the woods, flowering continues through the summer.

Follow a spur of the Yellow Trail to **C**, where a stream descends from the high ground to flow hidden from view beneath boulders of the weathered bedrock. These huge stones are chunks of diabase, formed from molten rock forced up through the earth's surface and sandwiched between layers of sedimentary rock 180 to 190 million years ago (see **#2**). Erosion exposed the diabase. Then, in the bitter climate accompanying the advance and retreat of the last glacier, the rocks were broken apart by countless cycles of freezing and thawing (see **#118**).

Across the pipeline of the Red Trail is a grove of American beech trees (**D**). Beeches are able to reproduce both by seed and by sprouting from the roots of larger trees. The young trees you see here are probably all sprouts of a parent tree. Since the beeches are reproducing themselves, this grove will look much the same in 100 years. For the moment the process of succession has finished, and the stand is at climax. Beeches will continue to grow here until some disturbance—fire, clearcutting, disease, etc.—begins a new cycle of succession. In a climax woods, one would not expect to see many plants in the shrub and herb layers, for the shade is intense. In beech stands the understory and shrub layer is especially sparse because the root systems of beeches are very shallow and take from the soil the water and nutrients that other species require in order to grow. Maple-leaved viburnum is the common shrub, an indication that the soil is moist but never saturated for long periods; this viburnum does not like very wet conditions.

To return to your car, either retrace your steps or continue along the Red Trail to the Blue Trail (**E**). Turn right and follow the trail back to the Red Trail.

These are merely the most notable of the succession communities in Herrontown Woods. A more complete description is available from the Stony Brook–Millstone Watersheds Association, Inc., R.D. 1, Box 263A, Pennington, N.J. 08534, (609) 737-3757.

Remarks: *The walk around the perimeter of the woods takes about an hour and a half. Wear good shoes and be prepared to scramble over logs. Beware of poison ivy. Nearby camping by permit; write or call the Mercer County Park Commission for reservations: P.O. Box 1777, Trenton, N.J. 08607, (609) 989-6530.*

13.

Princeton Institute Woods

Directions: **Mercer County, N.J. From New York City, take the New Jersey Turnpike south about 30 miles to Exit 9. Follow directions for Herrontown Woods (#12) to Nassau St. Turn west (left) on Route 27 0.3 mile and turn south (left) on Mercer St.; go 0.8 mile to Olden Lane. Turn left again; drive 0.6 miles to the end of the road. Parking is on the left.**

Ownership: **Princeton University Institute for Advanced Studies.**

These 500 acres of upland forest, streambanks, and marshland are a primary way station for migrating spring warblers; on a given day during the first three weeks of May a seasoned birder may see and hear over thirty species. The males are brilliant in their breeding plumage: the sharp orange and black of the Blackburnian, the fiery color of the prothonotary, the delicate blue of the cerulean. Each sings a distinctive song; even those that will nest farther north are practicing their declarations of territory and courtship (see **#17**).

From the parking area, walk to the right along a broad dirt track. This is one of the best vantage points, for the trail is bordered by the woods on one side and the open fields of the institute on the other. Search the shrubs out in the field for the yellow warbler, the yellow-breasted chat, and the chestnut-sided warbler. Several trails lead southward (left) off this path, winding through the woods toward the marsh on the far side. Large oaks and hickories dominate the canopy; flowering dogwood is abundant in the understory. The damp forest floor is covered with large stands of skunk cabbage (see **#51**) and lush cinnamon fern. The Kentucky warbler, a southern bird of wet woods, nests here along with four species of vireos: the white-eyed, the yellow-throated, the red-eyed, and the warbling.

The warblers that migrate through these woods fly north from Central and South America and the Caribbean. They expend tremendous amounts of energy, which they must replenish daily by eating. They habitually migrate at night, when they will be safer from hawks, and rest and feed in the daytime. These woods are an oasis where hatching inchworms and other insects provide ample food. An excellent time to see many warblers is during a cold spell just after heavy rains, when the birds gather, waiting for better weather.

Other landbirds such as thrushes and flycatchers also move through in large numbers each spring. During the fall migrations, the greatest concentrations of songbirds move south along the coast. At that time coastal woods are rich with berries and seeds (see Mid-Atlantic coastal volume).

Remarks: *Adjoining the Institute Woods is the Carl Rogers Sanctuary. Drive one block north on Olden Lane to Hardin Rd. Turn east (right) and go one block to Springdale Rd. Turn south (right) and drive to the end. Turn west (right) on West Drive and park by the observation tower. Purple martins nest in white boxes by the marsh. Prothonotary warblers nest along the marsh edge. In winter the pine plantings around the woods are often a roost for great horned, barred, long-eared, and saw-whet owls. Look for their droppings at the base of the tree; then search the branches, especially near the trunk. When roosting, the birds will allow you to approach quite close. Camping at Bull's Island State Park (see **#11**).*

14.

Bowman's Hill
State Wildflower Preserve

Directions: Bucks County, Pa. If going south from points along the Delaware, follow either Route 32 on the west bank or Route 29 on the east bank south. From U.S. 202 go south on Route 32 for 5.3 miles; turn right at the sign for Washington's Crossing State Historic Site and Bowman's Hill State Wildflower Preserve. Bear right at the fork just inside the entrance and drive to the end. From Trenton go 9 miles north on Route 29 to Washington's Crossing, and turn west (left). Go over the bridge and turn north (right) on Route 32. Go 5 miles to the park entrance on the left.

Ownership: Pennsylvania Bureau of State Parks.

Bowman's Hill is a living museum of the native plants of Pennsylvania and their habitats. Hardwood forest, a sphagnum bog, limestone outcrops, serpentine barrens, (see #15, #28), and extensive plantings of ferns are all found along the trails. Unusual species as well as those typical of the area have been planted. A great many of the plants here are found throughout much of the region covered by this book, so the preserve is well worth a visit. Printed guides to the preserve are provided; nothing is tagged, however, so you must make your own identifications.

During spring migrations (the first three weeks of May), songbirds are plentiful here. Bowman's Hill (directions available at the preserve) is a good vantage point for observing treetop migrants, such as the Tennessee and cerulean warblers.

15.

Tyler Arboretum

Directions: Delaware County, Pa. From Philadelphia take U.S. 1 southwest about 13 miles beyond I-76. Go north on

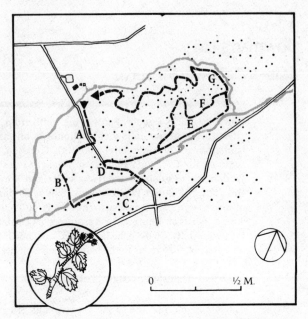

Inset: New Jersey tea

Route 452 for 0.5 mile; continue straight on Barren Rd. for 1.1 miles. Turn left on Painter Rd. and go 1 mile to the arboretum, on the right.

Ownership: Tyler Arboretum.

Tyler Arboretum combines plantings of native and introduced species, cool, wooded slopes of mature forest, stream-valley vegetation, a variety of successional stages, and the one remaining serpentine barren in Delaware County. Spring and fall songbird migrations are outstanding both here and in the neighboring Ridley Creek State Park.

Starting out from the education center, the Painter Brothers Trail (red blazes) and the Pinetum Trail (green blazes) run together through open meadows planted with a variety of conifers, including a giant sequoia (**A**). Eastern bluebirds nest in this area, in the boxes put up for that purpose (see **#7**). In winter, this habitat and the evergreens around the Arboretum buildings provide food and shelter for a number of birds. Kinglets, purple finches, brown creepers, and white-breasted nuthatches are joined in some years by such northern species as pine siskins, red-breasted nuthatches, evening grosbeaks, and white-winged and red crossbills. These birds appear over much of the eastern United States when their normal wintering grounds far to the north are overpopulated or when the crops of seeds there are inadequate. Evening grosbeaks have gradually become more regular winter visitors.

Just beyond the giant sequoia, the Pink Hill Trail (pink blazes) leads off toward the serpentine barren. Along the trail are a number of black walnut trees. Highly valued for their wood, which is used for veneers, walnuts are becoming increasingly rare. Their presence indicates that the soil here is moist and well-drained. At **B** there is an old abandoned farm. What is left of the buildings has been concealed beneath a thick tangle of vines, honeysuckle, bittersweet, wild grape, and multiflora rose. The vines, along with mosses and lichens, are colonizing a habitat unsuitable for other plants—the stones of the old farmstead. Around the buildings is a young forest dominated by Kentucky coffeetree, an escaped ornamental.

Continuing on the Pink Hill Trail, you will eventually emerge into what appears to be open field reverting to forest (**C**). There are beard grasses or broom sedges, redcedars and asters (in the fall), all typical of the early stages of secondary succession in the Piedmont (see **#41**). This area was never farmed, however, because the soil is too poor, and while the timber may have been cut or burned off, the clearing will never have exactly the character of the woods around it. Lying below the grasses is serpentinite, a metamorphic rock containing the mineral serpentine, heavy metals such as nickel and chromium, and a variety of other minerals. The soils that form from serpentinite are arid and infertile, and the vegetation that grows on the barren is therefore dramatically different from that which grows in the woodland (see **#28**). Each serpentine barren supports a different mix of plants depending on varying qualities of the rock—that is, the degree to which it has been changed and shaped by heat and pressure under the earth's surface, plus the mix of various mineral components. The character of the serpentinite and the amount of water available will affect the character of the soil and the rate at which it is formed. This, in turn, determines the mix of vegetation that will grow.

Some of the plants seen here are typical of the serpentine barrens, but they are found in other dry, sandy soils as well; these include blackjack oak, New Jersey tea, slender mountain mint *(Pycanthemum tenuifolius)* and whorled milkweek *(Asclepias verticillata)*. Other plants like the three species of barren chickweed (spring flower) and the barren aster (autumn flower) are associated only with serpentine barrens. The outstanding feature of this barren is the display of moss pink, a small creeping plant that flowers in late April and early May. This plant is not confined to the serpentine barrens but grows on dry, sandy soils throughout the Mid-Atlantic region. All of the plants that grow here benefit from the lack of competition from other species. Young red maple and sassafras trees, typical of many barren communities, are growing on some parts of the barren (see **#28** and **#25**).

Here and there one can see outcrops of the serpentinite rock. Known locally as honeycomb rock, the exposed surface has developed pockmarks as the more soluble minerals eroded away, leaving behind the more resistant rock.

When you reach Painter Rd., turn left and walk about a quarter-mile back to where the Dismal Run Trail and the Wilderness Trail go off to the right (**D**). This is a good place to see winter wrens and hermit thrushes, northern breeding species which spend the cold months here. Farther along the trail listen and look for the Louisiana waterthrush, the hooded warbler, and the Kentucky warbler during the breeding season from April into summer. Warblers, vireos, and flycatchers are abundant in the upland woods along Rocky Run during the spring and fall migrations.

Down in the valley of the Dismal Run (**E**) is a rich woodland growing in the alluvial soils bordering the stream. Alluvial soils are formed from sediments carried downstream by rivers and brooks. They are fertile soils because of the abundant moisture and the high content of organic material and nutrients, washed down from the slopes above. The streambanks have an abundant and varied array of plant life. Beeches, oaks, and hickories, with scattered black birches and black cherries, form the canopy. Flowering dogwood and iron-wood are principal understory trees, with witch-hazel and spicebush as the main shrubs. Notice as you walk up out of the valley that spicebush gives way to maple-leaved viburnum, a sign that the soils are drier on the hillsides. In spring, the stream valley is full of wild-flowers, including Jacob's ladder, spring beauty, wood anemone, and bloodroot (see **#12** for discussion of woodland flowers).

On the slopes above Dismal Run (**F**), and along Rocky Run (**G**), are many tall tuliptrees as well as mature black, scarlet, and white oaks, beeches, and young red maples. This part of the forest is at a later stage of succession than the woods at **B**. It has reached the climax stage, which in this region is considered to be oak-hickory. Tuliptrees were once considered successional species here; now, however, they seem to be part of the climax forest, taking the place of the vanished American chestnut. The well-drained soils and temperate climate of the region create an ideal habitat for them. (See **#41** for discussion of climax; also **#30**.)

Remarks: *The Pink Hill Trail takes about 45 minutes and includes some hills. The Dismal Run Trail takes about 2 hours; most of it follows the stream valley. There are over 20 miles of trails in all. Ridley Creek State Park which lies directly north of the arboretum, offers excellent spring birding along the creek, particularly during the first three weeks of May. Where Sycamore Mills Road borders the creek it is often possible during migration to sight as many as twenty-five species of warblers, six of vireos, and six of thrushes. To reach Sycamore Mills Rd. walk north along Painter Rd. to Forge Rd., which is closed to cars. Turn right and walk about 1 mile to the end, at Sycamore Mills Rd., which is also closed to traffic. Nearest state park camping is at French Creek State Park, about 30 miles northwest, off I-76. Fishing for trout in Ridley Creek; a license is required. For further information contact the Tyler Arboretum Education Center, P.O. Box 216, Lima, Pa. 19060, (215) 566-9133.*

Wissahickon Valley

The Wissahickon Valley, a National Natural Landmark, is just minutes from downtown Philadelphia, yet its steep slopes are covered with tall oaks, tuliptrees, and maples where warblers, thrushes, vireos, and other migrants gather in the thousands. The waters of the creek are fresh enough to support a sizable population of stocked trout, while numerous outcrops and old quarry sites display the ancient and tortuous geological history of the region.

Up until the middle of the nineteenth century the Wissahickon Valley was the site of many mills. Then when coal replaced steam as a source of power, the mills were abandoned and the valley became a touring spot, dotted with inns. In 1868 the area was included in Fairmount Park; the inns were demolished and the forest was allowed to grow back. One of the earliest environmental organizations in the country was the Friends of the Wissahickon. The group helped to restore the vegetation of the valley by planting native trees, shrubs, and flowering plants. Still active today, the organization continues to watch over and tend the valley.

Along the upper slopes of the valley the tall trees of the canopy are white and northern red oaks, American beech, and tuliptree. Other species include sugar maple, mulberry, and white ash. The typical shrubs are witch-hazel, spicebush, and maple-leaved viburnam. (See **#14** for discussion of Piedmont forest.) In the shadiest ravines, such as Cresheim Valley (see **#17**), hemlock, rhododendron, and mountain laurel may be found.

Although bears and wolves vanished completely in the

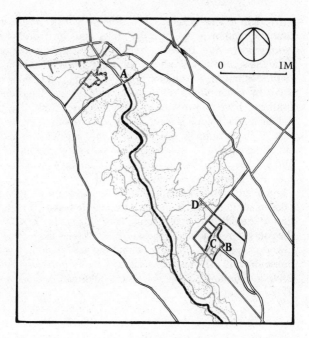

1700s, other mammals have returned to the Wissahickon since the nineteenth century. Deer are common, and there are healthy populations of other animals such as skunk, opossum, raccoon, and red fox. The more than 2000 acres of the park provide ample range for these creatures.

All along the west side of Wissahickon Creek runs an old carriage road, now used by bicyclists, joggers, horseback riders, and walkers. Closed to cars, it is called Forbidden Drive. A number of other trails, winding along the upper slopes of the valley, are much less traveled. Maps of the trails are available from the Friends of the Wissahickon, Box 4068, Philadelphia, Pa. 19118 for $1.50, and from the Andorra Natural Area.

Besides maps, Andorra has information such as lists of birds and plants, as well as a series of trails all its own. The naturalist offers walks throughout the park all week long. For further information write or call the Andorra Natural Area, Northwestern Ave., Philadelphia, Pa. 19118, (215) 242-5610. To reach the Natural Area follow directions to Wissahickon Ave. as given in the Geology Walk (see **#16**) and drive north about 1.5 miles to Allens Lane. The road turns right at Allens Lane. Go 1.2 miles and turn northwest (left) onto Germantown Ave. Go 2.7 miles and turn southwest onto Northwestern Ave. Drive 0.2 mile to the junction of several roads. Take the second road from the left, a gravel road that winds uphill to the Natural Area. Although the valley is in the midst of a big city, there are few incidents of crime. Some purse snatchings and thefts from cars have occurred in the busy, overused Valley Green area. Taking a friend along is a good idea on any expedition. Remember that all plants, animals, and rocks within the park are protected. No collecting is allowed. But the creek is stocked with trout each year, and you may fish if you have a license. Camping is available outside the city at French Creek State Park.

There are no horse rentals nearby. Sleighrides in winter and hay-rides in summer can be arranged through Robert F. Dougherty, 12 East Mermaid Lane, Philadelphia, Pa. 19118, (215) 248-4490; and the Monastery Stable, (215) 843-7433. Bicycles are for rent at the lower end of Fairmount Park behind the Art Museum at #1 Boat-house Row, (215) 236-4359. Sailboats are for rent along East River Drive in Fairmount Park. For further information call (215) 686-2176.

16.
Geology Walk

Directions: **Philadelphia, Pa. From downtown Philadelphia, drive northwest on East River Dr. along the Schuylkill River following signs for Wissahickon Dr. About 1 mile beyond U.S. 1, the Roosevelt Expressway, turn northeast (right) on Wissahickon Dr. After about 1.5 miles turn left on Wissahickon Ave. Follow it about 1.5 miles to where it ends at Allens Lane. You must turn right on Allens Lane. Go 1.2 miles and turn northwest (left) on Germantown Ave. Go 2 miles and turn southwest (left) on Bell's Mills Rd. Go to the bottom of the hill and turn right into the parking area just before the small stone bridge. Walk across the bridge and turn north (right) on Forbidden Dr. (A: see map, p. 53).**

If you are coming from north of the city, take Exit 25 off the Pennsylvania Turnpike and drive southeast on U.S. 422, which becomes Germantown Ave. If coming from the

south on I-95, get onto I-76, the Schuylkill Expressway, going northwest. Follow it about 11 miles to the exit for Wissahickon Dr. and U.S. 1 going south. Go north (right) across the Schuylkill and onto Wissahickon Dr.

Ownership: Fairmount Park, City of Philadelphia.

All along the Wissahickon Creek, many outcroppings of rock reveal clues to the complex geological history of the region. Throughout the area are found various forms of igneous and metamorphic rock. (The third type of rock, sedimentary rock, is not found here; see **#111**). Igneous rock began as molten material deep within the earth; it cooled and hardened as it was forced up close to the surface or erupted out into the open (see **#2** Falls and **#3**). Metamorphic rock is the result when other rock—either igneous, sedimentary, or other metamorphic—has been changed and remade by intense pressure or heat or both. Both of these types of rock are associated with disturbances within the earth that occur as mountain ranges are thrust upward. Their presence here is due to the building of the Appalachian Mountains (see **Ridge and Valley**).

Go north along Forbidden Dr. from Bell's Mill Rd. about 100 feet. To the left of the path you will see some dark green metamorphic rocks. The coloring is best seen on protected faces where the chemical interaction of air, water, and rock has not darkened the stone. The rock here is made up mostly of the mineral chlorite, which accounts for its dark green color. Touch the stone; it feels slippery. This is due to the presence of another mineral, talc.

All rocks are made up of minerals which are various combinations of elements such as silica, potassium, magnesium, oxygen, and hydrogen. These elements can combine into different crystalline structures to form minerals. Familiar minerals are table salt (which is the mineral halite, made up of sodium chloride), ice, and corundum, an extremely hard mineral that in some of its forms is known as sapphire and ruby. Each mineral has its own crystalline structure that differentiates it from every other mineral and that makes it hard or soft, brittle, or strong. The greasy feel of talc, for example, is due to its particular crystalline structure: it forms in microscopic flat plates, which fit one on top of another and which break apart easily, sliding over each other and producing the slippery sensation. When rocks undergo metamorphosis, entirely new minerals are formed, which are almost always associated with metamorphic rock. Talc is one of these. We generally cannot see the individual structure of a given crystal within a rock because its development has been constricted by that of many other crystals all packed together. The shiny flakes in this rock are chlorite, one of the mica minerals. This family contains large amounts of silicon and tends to form flat, platelike crystals which reflect the light.

The rock here is called schist, a metamorphic rock. This schist formed when shale or mudstone (sedimentary rocks made up of mud) was subjected to intense pressure and heat below the surface of the earth. It has several distinct characteristics. The mica minerals it contains are large enough to see with the naked eye. As the rock was compressed by the pressures within the earth, the minerals within it were pushed into an orderly alignment. Think of the game pick-up-sticks. When you spill the sticks on the table, they lie every which way. Take your hands and push the sticks together, and they will line up in a bunch parallel to each other. In this schist it is the crystals of talc and chlorite which are aligned in parallel rows. One of the chief characteristics of schist is that it tends to flake apart along the parallel planes of the crystals. This kind of cleavage is referred to as schistosity. All the schist in this area is part of the Wissahickon Formation, the principal formation in the area.

About 150 feet farther up the road is a small hollow which has been cut out of the hillside. It is probably the site of an old quarrying operation; there are still some blocks of stone sitting on the ground. Find a portion of the rock protected from the weather and examine it. On the surface are dark blotches surrounded by greenish-gray stone that glistens. The lighter material is made up of chlorite and talc. The dark areas consist of serpentine similar to the outcrops which underlie the serpentine barrens at Tyler Arboretum (**#15**) and Soldiers Delight (**#28**). Serpentine was used as a building material in Philadelphia until it was discovered that it is easily corroded by pollutants in urban air.

Continue for about 500 feet and look to the left. More examples of schist are exposed. These rocks are dark gray or brown with no green, which means that they do not contain chlorite. The exposed surfaces are shiny, for other types of mica are abundant in this rock. As shale or mudstone is compressed, the first mineral to crystallize is mica. Most of us are familiar with its thin, papery crystals. It comes in a variety of colors; some of it is so transparent that it was once used instead of glass for lanterns and windows.

The cleavage in this rock is nearly vertical and very straight. Further on you will see schist which has been folded and bent so that the line of cleavage is rippled and contorted.

To your right a line of schist rock extends across the creek. Because of cleavage, schist erodes into angular shapes. Water seeps in along the parallel planes of cleavage in the rock and works both chemically and mechanically to break it apart.

You can also see rounded boulders in the stream bed. This is granite, an igneous rock that is much, much harder than the schist and that does not have its planar structure. In granite the minerals are welded together, the crystals interlocked. As a result, erosion produces rounded shapes. These boulders have come from an outcrop of granite a little to the north, which you can see if you walk another 150 feet. To the left is a tall cliff of rock, also the site of a quarry. In the middle of the cliff is a band of granite. It is light to dark gray and is shaped into large, massive blocks which seem almost artificial. When subjected to massive pressure, or as the molten rock cools and shrinks, granite breaks naturally into these blocky shapes. This makes it a good stone for quarrying. The fractures that shape the blocks are called joints. On either side of the granite are bands of schist. Looking closely at the schist you will see that the cleavage runs vertically. You can also see that there are bands of color within the schist. These bands are reminders of the sedimentary rock from which the schist was formed (see **#111**). As layer upon layer of mud was deposited under water, conditions changed and the composition of the layers or beds changed. These changes were recorded in the changing bands of color of the beds. The beds of sedimentary rock were laid down horizontally; then at some later point, the rock was thrust on end (see **Piedmont**).

Because the bedding planes in the schist on each side of the granite are parallel, we know that this is a granite sill. When still molten, the granite was pushed in between the beds of rock. If the granite were perpendicular to the bedding planes displayed in the schist, we would know that this is a dike, formed by molten rock forced up through a fracture or a fault across the grain of the rock.

Another line of rocks extends across the stream at this point. Most of them are hunks of granite, rounded and smooth. At the far side, however, is the meeting point or contact between the granite and the schist. The different patterns of erosion in the two rocks are very clear. As in the cliff face, the beds and planes of cleavage in the schist are vertical; water has attacked the weaker layers more vigorously, leaving thin ridges of tougher material behind.

Proceed up the path about 100 feet. Across the stream is a dam of worn and ridged schist. To the left is a small cut into the hillside—another old quarry. On the north side of the schist exposed here, the surface of the rock is gently curving. This rock has been folded by pressures exerted during the building of the Appalachians. If you look closely, you will see that there are also very small ripples or crenulations over the face of the rock. These are tiny folds. The axis of the large fold and the axes of the tiny folds are all in the same direction. It is probable that they also indicate the direction of very large folds which underlie the region. These folds were created when the rocks here were buried deep within the earth. In the high temperatures there, the rocks were softer, more malleable; when pressure was exerted on them, they bent and crinkled instead of breaking (see **#95**).

The last station is 500 feet along the path. Through an opening in the fence make your way down to the stream bank and backtrack to where a series of pinkish rocks juts out into the water. This rock is quite different from those downstream. Unlike schist, it doesn't break into small plates. It is also much harder and lacks the shiny crystals of mica. If you look closely you can see banding of pink and black across the surface of the rock. This is gneiss, part of a formation called the Baltimore gneiss. It is the oldest rock in the region, being probably over one billion years old. The pink bands are made up of one of a group of minerals called feldspar while each of the dark bands is made up of one of several minerals. Gneiss is a metamorphic rock. It has formed under greater pressures and temperatures than the schist to the south. Under these conditions the different minerals contained in the rock recombined into distinct layers that have no connection to the original beds of mud, sand, or silt.

Now return to the parking area and cross the road into the picnic ground. Follow the path which leads south. At the top of the rise are exposed sections of the Wissahickon schist. The surface of the rock is dotted with small round red dots about ⅛ to ¼ inch in diameter. These are crystals of garnet, another mineral mainly associated with metamorphic rock. If you look closely, you can see the facets of the crystals. Each face has four sides. One of the characteristics of metamorphic rock is that as pressure and heat increase, the size of the crystals grows.

Elsewhere in the rock are bands up to 5 inches wide of lighter-colored quartzite. Quartzite does not flake like the portions of the schist which contain mica; it is also much harder. The predecessor of quartzite is sandstone, not shale or mudstone. At several places on the rock face the layers of quartzite have been doubled back on themselves. These are folds in the rock just like those in the exposures on the west side of the creek.

Remarks: *The whole tour is about a mile long. Remember that all the rock in the park is protected; there is absolutely no collecting. Much of the information for this walk was taken from the* Guidebook to the Geology of the Philadelphia Area *(Bulletin G 41), written by Bruce K. Goodwin for the Pennsylvania Geological Survey. It describes three other walks in* *the valley, and although the information is somewhat out of date, it is an excellent resource. Copies are available for $1.50 from the Department of General Services, State Book Store, P.O. Box 1365, Harrisburg, Pa. 17125.*

17.
Carpenter's Woods

Directions: Philadelphia, Pa. Follow directions to Wissahickon Ave. as given in the previous entry (#16). Go north 1.5 miles to Sedgwick St., just before Wissahickon Ave. turns sharp right to become Allens Rd. Turn right and go one block to Wayne Ave. Park on the left (**B**: see map, p. 53).

Ownership: Fairmount Park, City of Philadelphia.

Nestled in a valley covered with mature forest is one of the best known birding spots in the area. White oaks, northern red oaks, tuliptrees, and American beeches share the canopy on the slopes while tall sycamores line the banks of the small stream that runs through the valley. Sugar maple, beech, and sassafras are common in the understory. At the center of the woods is a small clearing surrounded by a tangle of shrubs and vines. This diversity makes an excellent refuge for great numbers of warblers, thrushes, vireos, and other landbirds which migrate through here each spring and fall.

From the small parking area, a wide trail leads northward. To reach the stream side (**C**: see map, p. 53), follow the trail for a few minutes as it slopes gently down into the valley. Other trails crisscross the 40-acre wood.

The height of the migration is during the first three weeks of May and again from the end of August through the middle of September. Spring migration is particularly spectacular. At that time you may expect to see a great variety of warblers, including the black-and-white, northern parula, magnolia, black-throated green, black-throated blue, yellow-rumped, Blackburnian, and bay-breasted warblers, and both the Louisiana and the northern waterthrush. Many warblers also nest here and can be seen or heard during the summer months; among these are the chestnut-sided, yellow, and blue-winged warblers, plus the common yellow-throat, American redstart, and ovenbird. Carpenter's Woods is a good place to look for some of the rarer species of warblers like the cerulean, Tennessee, worm-eating, and Wilson's warblers. These birds tend to migrate up the Mississippi Valley and are infrequently seen along the east coast.

The particular glory of the spring warbler migration is the breeding plumage of the male birds: the striking Blackburnian, his black cheeks setting off the intense orange of his face and chin; the lemon-colored breast and throat of the Canada warbler with his delicate black necklace; the beautiful blue of the cerulean. The females are generally much duller versions of the males, harder to see in the foliage and harder to identify. Before the fall migration, after the breeding season is past, the males molt and grow new feathers, losing their bright colors and becoming more like the females.

The bright colors of these birds are caused by various pigments in the feathers and also in some cases, the construction of the feathers. The darker colors—black, brown, and dull yellows—are made up of a pigment called melanin. The brighter reds, yellows, and oranges are due to carotene. Blue feathers are caused by the physical configuration of the feathers rather than by a pigment. The outer layer of cells of these feathers breaks up white light, in somewhat the same way a prism does, while the inner cells of the feathers contain pigments which provide a dark background that allows the reflected blue color to be seen. If you crush a blue feather, its color disappears.

Feathers have a variety of uses. They insulate birds from the cold, shield their skins from the sun, and help camouflage the birds from predators. Almost all birds are lighter colored on their underparts and darker above. This is called countershading. Because the sun shines from above it tends to lighten the color of their backs and to shadow their underparts. Countershading counteracts this effect, making the outline of the bird less visible to predators.

During the breeding season, camouflage is less important to warblers than is the ability to attract females of the right species. Because these birds generally nest, roost, and feed among the thick foliage of trees and shrubs, they can afford bright colors. Ground-dwelling birds such as grouse and pheasants, and those that nest out in the open like nighthawks and sandpipers must rely on their subtle coloring to protect them.

The change from winter to breeding plumage is directly tied to day-length. As spring approaches, the longer daylight hours stimulate certain hormones in the males, and their bright plumage begins to appear. Their glowing colors in turn stimulate sex hormones in the females so that they, too, are ready to breed.

One of the best ways to identify warblers in the spring is by song. Each species has its own distinct song or songs, and each individual has its own slight variation. Females have distinctive call notes but generally do not sing. All species sing most often during the breeding season. Among warblers, songs help the birds find each other in the thick foliage, identify the male birds, attract females, and establish territory. Although males on migration sing with gusto, they do not really begin to defend their territory until they arrive at their breeding grounds. The males will sing all day at the start of the breeding season; later they will be most vocal in the early morning and again in the evening.

A wide variety of species can share a small woodland like Carpenter's Woods because each species makes use of different combinations of resources. In the forest, different habitats are stacked one on top of the other like stories in a building. Each has its characteristic bird life. The cerulean warbler is a treetop bird, hunting insects on the wing as a flycatcher does; the northern parula hops around in the upper branches eating such things as beetles, wasps, gypsy-moth caterpillars, and spiders. Other species like the blue-winged warbler and the common yellowthroat favor brushy thickets in old fields or at the edges of clearings. The yellowthroat often nests in tussocks of grass or in the lower branches of shrubs close to water where it feeds on mayflies, dragonflies, leaf rollers, ants, and damselflies. The blue-winged also nests close to the ground in blackberry bushes, old tree stumps, and tall grasses. Its diet includes beetles, ants, and caterpillars. The ovenbird, an inconspicuous brown warbler, is a ground-dweller, building a small roofed shelter of dead leaves, moss, and grasses, which protects the nest from rain and the eyes of predators. It hops around on the forest floor, rooting for slugs, snails, earthworms, crickets, and other terrestrial creatures.

Competition between species in this woodland is also reduced by varying schedules of migration. Some warblers, like the black-and-white and the palm, are early migrants. Others, like the Blackburnian, arrive later. The various species of thrushes, vireos, flycatchers, and other landbirds found in Carpenter's Woods follow similar patterns of dispersal and staggered migration.

Remarks: *For further information on birds of the area contact the Andorra Natural Area (see* **Wissahickon Valley***) and the Delaware Valley Ornithological Club, Academy of Natural Sciences of Philadelphia, 19th and Parkway, Philadelphia, Pa. 19103. There are several good recordings of bird songs which will help you learn to identify warblers (see* **Bibliography***).*

Nearby Place
of Interest

In Cresheim Valley the second-growth forest is especially
beautiful, an unexpected pocket of northern woods (D).
At the mouth of Cresheim Creek a waterfall cascades into
Devil's Pool. Like the potholes at the Tubs (#75) and at
Archbald Pothole (#115), this one was formed as water
coming down over the falls swirled stones and gritty particles against the rocks at the bottom. The rock along the
lower portion of the creek is schist containing large
amounts of mica, bands of quartzite, and small, round
crystals of garnet (#16). Like Carpenter's Woods this
streamcourse is an excellent place to observe the spring
landbird migration. To reach Cresheim Valley, continue
along Sedgewick 3 blocks to McCallum St. Turn north (left)
and go 3 blocks to Allens Lane. Turn right and go one
block to Emlen St. Turn left and go to the bottom of the
hill and park. Cross the road and walk into the valley along
Cresheim Rd.

Susquehanna
River Gorge

From the Conejohela Flats to the Conowingo Islands the Susquehanna has carved a deep gorge through the Piedmont rocks. Steep ravines lined with massive hemlocks and other old trees appear almost untouched. Southern species that are rare elsewhere in Pennsylvania are common along lower stretches of the river, and each spring and fall the river becomes a flyway for thousands of whistling swan and other waterfowl. Just above the Maryland line, rocky islands, worn and sculpted by the glacial meltwaters, are covered with a mosaic of upland vegetation and riverine species. Surrounded by development, crisscrossed by dams, its waters impounded for five power plants, the 30-mile gorge is spectacular in spite of it all.

Just below the Conejohela Flats the river leaves the lowlands to cross the Piedmont uplands. The northern section of the gorge is cut through the Wissahickon schist, a metamorphic rock about 500 million years old (see **#16**). This rock is extremely hard and resistant to erosion, and the gorge is narrow and deep here. Below Susquehannock State Park, the river widens out as it flows through softer Peters Creek schist.

Although geologists estimate that the river began to carve its pathway 10 million years ago, the real shaping of the gorge occurred during the Ice Age, which began about 2 million years ago. Four times a huge ice sheet covered much of North America. Each advance was followed by a warming period when the ice sheet retreated northward, releasing vast quantities of water (see **Piedmont**). The meltwaters carried tons of debris, large boulders, and fine sand. Wielding a ferocious cutting power, the river hollowed out the potholes of the Conowingo Islands, and gouged out the mysterious clefts, called *deeps*, that lie below the surface of the river. In some places the riverbottom is 130 feet below the original level of the river, 30 feet below sea level. Formed at the same time as the islands, these deeps occur mainly on the east side of the river.

The glacial meltwaters coursing through the main gorge rapidly eroded a deep channel. The smaller tributaries, draining only the surrounding countryside, carried much less water. By the time the waters dropped and grew quieter, the smaller-stream valleys were left high above the river. Three general patterns of erosion have since developed along these streams, depending on the rate of flow, the formations through which they cut, and the shape of the original beds. Some, like Kelly's Run (see **#20**), have incised a channel into deep rocky gorges. Others, like Counselman Run, Oakland Run, and Rock Run (see **#19**), were apparently smaller streams; their beds became a series of steps and falls. Otter Creek, with its hairpin meanders, represents the third type (see **#18**); the meanders reflect the earlier course of the stream as it wandered over a gentler slope (see **#94**).

North of the Wissahickon schist is the Conestoga limestone. There is an ongoing debate as to the relative ages of these two formations. Apparently at some point during the long sequence of mountain-building, the schist was given a tremendous shove by immense forces originating from deep within the earth and was pushed on top of the limestone. In Grubb Glen, where Shenks Ferry Wildflower Preserve is located, a thumb of the limestone protrudes into the schist. Here, rich soils have developed and created a nursery for a garden of spring wildflowers.

18.

Conejohela Flats

Directions: **York County, Pa. From Lancaster go west on Route 999 about 10 miles to River Rd. (Route 441). At the intersection of these roads there is a parking area. Cross the railroad tracks toward the river. From here scan the river for birds (A). Small boats and canoes can be launched at Long Level on the west bank of the river. Go north on**

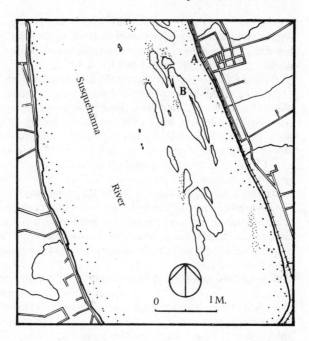

Route 441 about 4 miles to Route 462. Turn west (left)
across the bridge and then go south on Route 624 for 5.9
miles to Long Level.

Ownership: **Safe Harbor Power Co.**

From the banks of the Susquehanna at Washington Boro (**A**), the
river is a broad lake dotted with low islands. The checkered pattern
of mudbanks, riverine woods, marshy thickets, and calm waters is a
focal point for waterbirds of all varieties. The Conejohela Flats are
unique throughout the Piedmont.

In October and November, and again in March and April, concentrations of migrating waterfowl gather here. Twenty-five species of
duck have been recorded, attracting many hunters in the fall. Mallard and black duck fly through in great numbers. Many breed here
as well. Other common dabbling ducks are the blue-winged teal,
which is an early migrant, often passing through in August and
September, American wigeon, and pintail. Diving ducks seen along
the flats include scaup, common goldeneye, canvasback, and bufflehead. Ruddy ducks, common mergansers, common loons, horned

grebes, pied-billed grebes, and double-crested cormorants are also regular visitors. Redheads were once a common sight. This species is becoming increasingly rare largely due to the disappearance of their nesting grounds in the prairies and the Great Plains of the United States and Canada. This has affected the canvasback as well.

Dabbling ducks tend to feed in shallow waters, eating floating plants like duckweed, and tipping down to forage for vegetation and small aquatic mollusks and crustaceans on the bottom. With relatively large wings in proportion to their bodies, dabbling ducks are able to spring straight up from the water. This enables them to make use of small lakes and marsh ponds. They can also slow their flight speed for precision landings. Diving ducks, on the other hand, are better suited for larger bodies of water. They have smaller, pointed wings—well designed for fast flight, but not for quick takeoffs. Divers must run along the water to become airborne. Their high-speed landings also require more room. Diving ducks' feet are set far back on their bodies; this helps them swim underwater but makes them very clumsy on land.

Shorebird migrations peak here in April and May and especially from late July to October. Species seen here include the greater and lesser yellowlegs, least sandpiper, semipalmated sandpiper, dowitcher, and western sandpiper. The killdeer and the spotted sandpiper nest in the area. When the Safe Harbor Dam was constructed in the 1930s, it began to create low sandbars and mudflats which attract the birds. The dam blocks the river's flow. As the current slows, sediments are deposited. New islands have formed and the old ones have changed shape. The slightly higher ones become covered with vegetation.

Close to the eastern shore is a large island, which is an important heron rookery (**B**), known as Rookery, House, or Middle Island. From March through July, this sanctuary is posted to keep the birds safe from disturbance, but from **A** you can watch hundreds of birds flying in to roost on summer evenings. Cattle egrets are the most numerous species, followed by the black-crowned night heron, glossy ibis, and snowy egret. The cattle egret, glossy ibis, and snowy egret have been gradually extending their range northward; the Conejohela Flats are their first known nesting grounds in Pennsylvania. The birds nest in the deciduous trees on the island. The most common tree species are silver maple, boxelder, and river birch. These trees are generally confined to streambanks, where light is abundant and where occasional flooding prevents many other species from growing.

In August, flights of thousands of swallows wheel and flick through the sky. Rough-winged, barn, tree, cliff, and bank swallows and purple martins can all be observed as they fly south to their wintering grounds.

The featured event here is the arrival of the whistling swans in November. Some of them winter on the river, feeding in the nearby grainfields by day, resting on the water by night. Once the birds fed almost exclusively on submerged aquatic vegetation. This vegetation has almost disappeared from Chesapeake Bay, where large numbers of swans spend the winter. (Scientists are not sure why the plants have vanished. Pollutants and sedimentation in the bay waters may be responsible.) As a result the birds have changed their diet, and now depend largely on waste grain left on the fields after harvest. By March thousands of swans have gathered, waiting for the increasing length of the days to signal the time to move north again. Almost overnight they are gone, heading for nesting grounds in the Arctic.

Remarks: *The best time to see the herons, egrets, and glossy ibises is on an evening in June, July, or August, when the birds are flying home to roost and the night herons are leaving to feed in the shallows. The only way to explore the islands is by boat or canoe. Boats can be rented at the Long Level marina on the west shore (see Directions above). It takes about 20 minutes to row out to the islands. Rookery Island is a sanctuary of the Pennsylvania Game Commission. If you have a motorboat, be wary of shoals and stumps. Bring binoculars; a spotting scope is useful for watching birds from shore.*

19.
Otter Creek
Natural Area

Directions: **Lancaster County, Pa. From Lancaster take Route 272 south for 13 miles to Route 372 and turn west (right). Drive 9.2 miles (crossing the Susquehanna) to Route 74. Turn northwest (right) and drive 3.3 miles to Route 425. Turn north (right) and drive 4.2 miles to the Otter Creek parking area. The red-blazed trail begins by the bridge next to the parking area.**

Ownership: **Pennsylvania Power and Light Co.**

This trail follows Otter Creek as it winds its way through a narrow gorge lined with tall trees. Eastern hemlocks dominate the glen. The trees are huge, some of them 30 inches in diameter at breast height. Along more open areas in the stream valley and on southern exposures are a variety of other trees, including tuliptree, sycamore, red maple, and basswood, with umbrella magnolia in the understory. This forest type, called *mixed mesophytic*, develops on soils that are neither very dry nor very wet.

As you walk along the trail, look for a small tree with large leaves, the umbrella magnolia. It is a southern tree rare throughout the rest of Pennsylvania; this is its northern limit. River valleys are often passageways for the spread of both plants and animals. Seeds are borne downstream by water, and carried upstream by wildlife, particularly birds.

In May, the umbrella magnolia produces large cream-colored blossoms. Magnolias were one of the first families of trees to develop flowers. Like other flowering species, they depend on insects for pollination—that is, the fertilization of ova, or egg cells, by male pollen grains. Scent, color, and nectar are adaptations that attract an

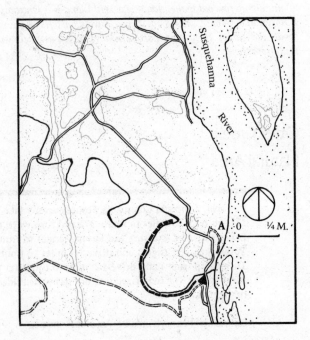

insect into the flower, where it will become dusted with pollen. Then the insect goes to the next flower and deposits some of the pollen there. Magnolias have very simple flowers, not nearly so well designed as more advanced flowers—those of fruit trees for example. The cup of the magnolia blossom is very large and open, which means that an insect could land and fly away without ever having touched one of the sexual parts of the flower. Apple or cherry blossoms, on the other hand, are small and cupped, which directs the insect more precisely to the pollen-covered stamens, the male organ of the flower. The flowers of the magnolia are few and scattered widely over the tree, while fruit trees produce many blossoms bunched together—a much more effective arrangement.

The stand of trees in Otter Creek may well be 200 years old or more. Because of the long history of settlement in the region, it probably is not a virgin stand, but inaccessibility and private ownership have protected this site, and others along the river, from destruction.

In winter, hemlocks are important for a number of species. The small cones are a source of food for birds and small rodents. Animals will not eat the strongly scented needles. Because they are so tolerant of shade, the smaller hemlocks do not lose their lower branches as they grow; when snow weighs down the lower branches, rabbits and other small mammals find shelter beneath the trees. Owls often roost in hemlocks and other conifers, generally crouching by the trunk on the inner branches. Among the wintering owls found here are the long-eared, great horned, and screech. Look for whitewash and pellets on the ground beneath the trees. The pellets are regurgitated wads of fur, bone, and other indigestible bits of the owl's prey. Other wintering species include both the black-capped and the Carolina chickadees; usually, the ranges of these two species do not overlap. The Carolina chickadee is another southern species not found in most parts of Pennsylvania.

As you follow the course of the creek, you will work your way over large boulders of Wissahickon schist and chunks of limestone (see **Susquehanna River Gorge**). Notice that the stream meanders in its deep ravine. This is an example of an *entrenched* meander, which means that the stream was already a winding waterway before it cut into the formation and has kept its original course, simply cutting its way deeper and deeper. Other tributaries such as Kelly's Run (see **#21**) cut through the rock in straight paths.

Remarks: *The nature trail is a loop trail three-quarters of a mile long. Although not steep, the path is rough and rocky. You can continue for another half-mile up the stream before cutting back sharply southeast (right) up the hill. At the top turn right on the blacktop road to return to your car. If you are adventurous, you can continue upstream, using the streambed itself as a trail. This is a good way to explore many of the small ravines leading into the Susquehanna, such as Muddy Run, Counselman Run, and Oakland Run. Be sure to wear rubber-soled shoes. The easiest access to these streams is by boat from the river (see* **Susquehanna River Gorge***). Just north of Otter Creek, Urey Overlook boasts a good view of the river (***A***). Walk north from the parking area along the river on a yellow-blazed trail, a walk of about half a mile to the top of the bluff.*

Camping is available at Otter Creek Campground and Pequea Campground (see **#20***), which are owned by Pennsylvania Power and Light Co. There are many hiking trails in the area. The Conestoga Trail runs 15 miles from Lock 12 near the Holtwood dam north to Martic Forge. For a trail map and for camping information write to George Aukamp, Lake Aldred Superintendent, Pennsylvania Power and Light Co., Holtwood, Pa. 17352. West of the river, the Mason-Dixon Trail goes north to join the Appalachian Trail. For further information on hiking trails throughout Pennsylvania, write to the Keystone Trails Association, P.O. Box 251, Cogan Station, Pa. 17728. Canoeing and boating are very popular, but the river's currents can be surprisingly strong, and storms can come up quickly. Canoe rentals and trips can be arranged through the Wildernest, 1339 Fruitville Pike, Lancaster, Pa. 17601, (717) 291-5881. They also rent camping equipment. Fishing is excellent all along the river—walleye, muskellunge, bass, catfish, crappie, and perch are commonly caught. Otter Creek and many of the other tributaries are stocked with trout. A license is required. Fall, winter, and spring are especially beautiful. Summer can be hot and muggy. In warm weather be prepared for ticks. Poisonous northern copperheads do inhabit the rocky areas, but your chances of running into this shy snake are slim.*

20.
Shenks Ferry
Wildflower Preserve

Directions: **York County, Pa. From Lancaster, go south on Route 324 about 10 miles. Just across Pequea Creek, turn northwest (right) onto River Rd. (Route 441), and go about 2 miles to Shenks Ferry Rd. Turn left, drive to the bot-**

tom, and park by the sign for the preserve. A half-mile walk along a dirt road and an abandoned railway bed will take you through the area.

Ownership: Pennsylvania Power and Light Co.

This wide, gentle valley is strikingly different from the rocky ravines elsewhere along the river. It lies above easily eroded limestones, a peninsula of the Conestoga Valley to the north (see **Susquehanna River Gorge**).

As with all limestone soils, the earth here is rich in nutrients (see **#73**). Every spring, wildflowers bloom in profusion. From early spring when the hepatica, bloodroot, and trillium appear, to May when cranesbill, wild ginger, mayapple, and mertensia blossom, and on into mid-June, there is always something in flower. Some, like the columbine, are particularly associated with lime soils.

About halfway along the path near a small stream, there is a stand of chinkapin oak or Muhlenberg oak on the left side of the trail. This tree is more common to the Ohio valley; it is found on limestone outcrops and is an uncommon species in most of the Piedmont. The leaf resembles that of the chestnut oak, but the bark is generally thinner and more scaly.

Remarks: *The whole preserve covers only about 30 acres. Stay on the trail and do not pick any flowers.*

Nearby Places of Interest

There are interesting outcrops of the Wissahickon schist along the Conestoga Trail just south of Shenks Ferry. Go back to Route 324 and turn west (right). Drive about 2 miles to a covered bridge on the left side of the road. Park by the bridge. Cross the creek and walk north along the orange-blazed trail, which follows an old trolley bed along Pequea Creek. There are huge tumbled boulders and deep pools in the streambed. To reach House Rock and Wind Cave, either walk from the covered bridge, following the orange blazes west and south about 3 miles, or drive west on Route 324 to the river. Turn south (left) at the T junction, go over the bridge, and park at the PP&L public boat launch on the other side. Continue on foot about 1 mile to where the road curves sharply east. An orange-blazed trail leads south (right) along the river. There is a backpack campsite at Reed Run, about 1.5 miles down the trail. To park overnight, drive back to the covered bridge, cross the creek, and turn right to the Pequea Campground. The Wind Cave sits high above the river, made up of huge broken chunks of Wissahickon schist. With 1000 feet of passages, it may be the largest fault cave in the eastern United States. The Allegheny cave rat lives here, its only known habitat in this region. House Rock is another huge outcrop of the schist, with prominent bands of quartz running through it. The hike to House Rock is rugged; allow about an hour to cover the 2-mile round trip. Remember a flashlight with new batteries if you want to explore the cave. Summer can be hot and humid, and there are some poisonous snakes—northern copperheads. Ticks are out from spring to fall.

21.
Kelly's Run and
Pinnacle Overlook

Directions: York County, Pa. From Lancaster, go south on Route 272 about 12.5 miles to Route 372. Turn west (right) and drive about 4.5 miles to Street Rd. Bear right and go another 0.5 mile to a picnic ground on the right. The orange-blazed trail begins at the north corner of the picnic ground.

Ownership: Pennsylvania Power and Light Co.

Kelly's Run falls down to the Susquehanna through a small gorge, 300 to 400 feet deep at the bottom. Cliffs and massive boulders of Wissahickon schist (see **Susquehanna River Gorge**) overhang the stream. Kelly's Run—unlike Otter Creek (see **#19**) a meandering stream—is a typical product of another type of erosion. This stream has worn a straight path to the river.

The upper portion of the trail passes through a young forest of oaks (**A**). Chestnut oak is the principal species, indicating that the soil here is dry. Other oaks include northern red, white, and black. In the understory the thick stands of mountain laurel bloom in late

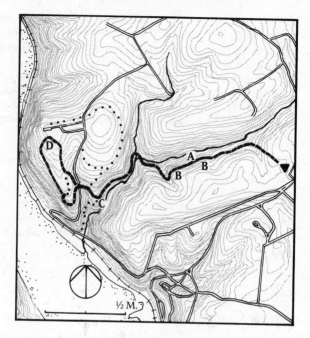

½ M.

May and early June and are another indicator of the dry, acid soils. At **B** there are also the remnants of charcoal pits. In the early nineteenth century before the age of coal, teams of woodcutters cleared much of the forests of the northeastern United States. The wood was partially burned in round pits covered with earth, turning the wood into charcoal. The earth and charcoal of the pit were purged of organic material and nutrients, and it has taken a long time for plants to recapture these sites.

About three-quarters of a mile from the trailhead, the path descends to the streambed of Kelly's Run, passing through dense stands of hemlock and rhododendron; in July, the latter is covered with pinkish flowers. After another quarter-mile the creek turns left around a rockface. Cross the stream on the rocks and continue half a mile downstream. At **C** a spur trail heads steeply uphill to Pinnacle Overlook. After climbing 500 feet the trail meets Pinnacle Trail, which affords several good views of the gorge. The overlook sits on top of an anticline (see **#95**). The Wissahickon schist has buckled upward here, creating a ridge of resistant rock that runs across the river.

The soils are very dry on the ridgetop, and there is a stand of table mountain pine. This species is usually found only on the dry ridgetops of the Appalachians. It is growing here with Virginia pine and chestnut oak. The two pines look similar; the best way to tell them apart is by the spines on the scales of their cones—the table mountain pine has stout, curved spines, while those on the Virginia pine are long and slender.

To return to Kelly's Run, you can take the Fire Line Trail, marked by a large wooden sign at the overlook. It follows the edge of the canyon until it strikes the Conestoga Trail, marked in orange. The Conestoga Trail leads back down to Kelly's Run. Turn upstream and return to the picnic area.

Remarks: *The walk along Kelly's Run can be slippery and treacherous and is quite rugged. Wear sneakers or hiking boots. The trail down to the bottom of Kelly's Run is 3.5 miles roundtrip; allow about 2 hours. Add another hour for climbing the mile up to Pinnacle Overlook and back. You can also drive to the overlook—return to River Rd., drive north about 1.3 miles, and turn left onto Pinnacle Rd., which leads to the overlook.*

22.
Lower Gorge
of the Susquehanna

Directions: **York County, Pa. From Lancaster, go south on Route 272 about 12.5 miles to Route 372. To reach Susquehannock State Park, turn west (right) and go 2.7 miles to Susquehannock Rd. and the sign for the park. Turn south (left). The road turns sharp right at 3 miles. Continue 0.5 mile and turn right into the park. Drive to the end of the road and park. A well-marked path leads to the overlook (A). To reach the launching area for the Conowingo Islands, drive west on Route 372 across the Norman Wood Bridge and make the first left turn onto Slab Holtwood Rd. Drive 1.5 miles and bear left toward the Muddy Run Boat Launch Area. To reach the Ferncliffe Wildlife and Wildflower Preserve, go south from the state park entrance 1.4 miles down into a glen; cross the creek and bear left on Harmony Ridge Rd. After 0.7 mile turn right on Bald Eagle Rd. Continue 0.7 mile to Benton Hollow and park. A dirt road leads down about 1 mile into the preserve.**

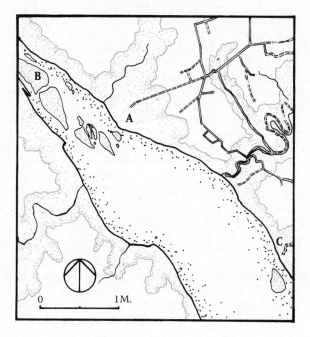

0   1 M.

Ownership: **Pennsylvania Bureau of Parks; Philadelphia Electric Co.**

Go first to the overlook at Susquehannock State Park (**A**). From here you can see how the narrow river gorge opens out as the stream passes from the resistant Wissahickon schist to the softer Peters Creek schist just to the south. On the opposite (western) shore is the Peach Bottom nuclear power plant.

Immediately below the lookout are the Conowingo Islands, an array of rocky islands in the middle of the river. They were shaped by glacial meltwaters that rushed through the gorge about 15,000 years ago (see **Susquehanna River Gorge**). Today, they are covered with varying types of vegetation related to their shape and their height above flood level.

From the boat launch take a boat out to Upper Bear Island (**B**), the largest and one of the most unspoiled of the islands. Beach the boat and explore the island on foot. Growing side by side are stands of eastern hemlock, which do best on moist, shady sites; stands of red, chestnut, and other oaks, characteristic of drier sites; and stands of red maple, tuliptree, black birch, American beech, blackgum, white ash, and other species that grow in moderately moist (mesic) soils. Understory species include flowering dogwood, sassafras, pawpaw, and hornbeam. In summer look for the zebra swallowtail, a southern butterfly that feeds exclusively on the pawpaw. There are also trees and plants characteristic of disturbed habitats, such a black locust, various species of blackberry, and numerous vines. Floodwaters occasionally flow over the island, interrupting succession on the lower parts of the island.

American holly, a Coastal Plain species, and indigobush, a southern species, are both found at their northern limit here. Birds migrating northward may have eaten the fruits farther south and dropped the seeds on the islands. Plant species may also move southward as river waters disperse seeds downstream.

Upper Bear has several pools that fill with rainwater. The pools are fringed with cattail, spatterdock, water plantain, burr reed, and other aquatic species. Bullfrogs, spring peepers, leopard frogs, and green frogs make use of the ponds. Many more species of amphibians and a variety of reptiles probably inhabit the islands. The black rat snake, common watersnake, box turtle, and wood turtle have been recorded. White-tailed deer occasionally swim between the islands and the shore. Other mammals found on the islands include Virginia oppossum, striped skunk, eastern cottontail, eastern mole, beaver, muskrat, raccoon, and woodchuck.

The islands are a very popular roost for turkeys and black vultures. Black vultures are gradually extending their range northward. Dead fish washed up on shore are a prime source of food. Ospreys are also commonly spotted along this section of the river from April to mid-May and from mid-August to mid-October, along with a diverse population of gulls.

A trip to the lower gorge should include the Ferncliffe Preserve. Follow the road along the south bank of Rock Creek (**C**). The stream has cut its way through the Peters Creek Schist down to the Susquehanna. There are a number of small falls and cascades typical of tributaries that carried less water during the glacial retreat (see **Susquehanna River Gorge**).

The forest in the preserve is another good example of old-growth mature forest, with hemlocks 30 inches in diameter and a mixture of mesic hardwoods including American beech trees of great size, tuliptrees, white ash, northern red oak, scarlet oak, sugar maple, chestnut oak, and basswood (see **Catskill Mountains**).

Remarks: *Plan to spend at least half a day exploring the Conowingo Islands. All the islands are open to the public. There is no overnight camping. If you have a motorboat, go very slowly and watch for submerged rocks. Stay away from the Muddy Run Power Plant on the bank. The Wildernest in Harrisburg rents canoes (see #19). There are several hiking trails at Susquehannock State Park.*

23.

Brandywine Creek
State Park

Directions: New Castle County, Del. From downtown Wilmington drive northwest on Route 52, the Kennet Pike, to Route 100. Turn north (right) and go about 2.3 miles to the junction of Adams Dam Rd. and Route 94. Turn right and then left into the park. Drive to the end of the road and park by the nature center.

Ownership: Delaware Division of Parks and Recreation.

The 786 acres of this park are a collection of diverse and intriguing habitats: a rounded hill crowned with fine old tuliptrees, a freshwater marsh, the rich floodplain of the Brandywine River, old fields tangled with blackberries and alive with birds.

From the nature center parking lot, the well-marked Tuliptree Trail winds through huge tuliptrees towering 100 feet high (**A**). These trees have a particularly light, soft wood. Among the Indians and the early colonists, the trunks were prized for canoes. The wood is still valued for making furniture, toys, and musical instruments. Fast-growing, tuliptrees grow best on moist soils—flood plains, for example—though they also pioneer drier, more mesic sites (see **Piedmont**). Tuliptree seedlings do not grow in deep shade, but the seeds remain viable for many years, which allows the species to take advantage of openings in the forest canopy or of more major disturbances such as logging or storm damage. The tuliptree is named for its large pale flower, which appears in spring. Its blossom is reminiscent of its relative, the magnolia.

As you see here, tuliptrees are often the largest trees in a mature stand. In the Piedmont, oak-hickory is considered the climax forest type, yet here the tuliptree holds dominion, an indication that these particular soils retain moisture well. In amongst the tuliptrees are

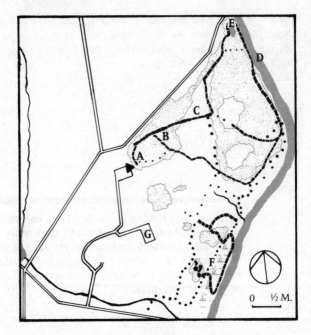

large American beech, white oak, and red oak. This stand is about
170 years old, and aside from the removal of blighted chestnuts in
the early 1900s, it has seen little disturbance since the early 1800s.

Beech and flowering dogwood are the principal understory species. Below them is the shrub layer, where maple-leaved viburnum
is most common, followed by spicebush. The big heart-shaped leaves
of wild ginger carpet much of the forest floor all summer long. Look
for its unusual three-pointed red flower in the notch of the two leaf
stalks, which appears in April. In amongst the ginger are clumps of
dwarf ginseng. Ferns are also abundant. Rattlesnake fern, silvery
spleenwort, New York fern, cut-leaf grape fern, and broad beech fern
are among the species found in these rich woods.

The deep soils that support this ecosystem have formed over millions of years from the ancient metamorphic rocks of the Piedmont,
which lie below. The formations are Precambrian, over 575 million
years old. They are made up of a wide range of minerals that have
weathered into fertile loam, a mixture of sand and clay. Loam soils
hold moisture and retain nutrients well but also allow good drainage, ensuring an adequate supply of oxygen to the roots.

At **B** take the right-hand trail down hill into the open. Beyond the woods these old fields are reverting to forest (**C**). The fields have not been cut in about 15 years. Secondary succession is approaching the middle stage, when young trees begin to shade out the early shrubs. Here an assortment of species such as red maple, black cherry, hackberry, post oak, ailanthus, and persimmon are thrusting up through a dense tangle of Japanese honeysuckle, sumac, and bush blackberry. Take the left-hand path toward Brandywine Creek.

Down by the creek is a floodplain (**D**; see **#44**) where silver maple, tuliptree, sycamore, and a mixture of other species dominate the canopy. Red maple and boxelder fill the understory, while box-elder and spicebush are the common shrubs. Japanese honeysuckle, tall blackberry, greenbriar, and multiflora rose grow thickly along the ground. Back from the stream edge is a small pond (**E**). This is typical of the structure of the floodplain. A levee of higher ground lines the stream, with a zone of lower, wetter ground behind it. The red-spotted newt, the northern two-lined salamander, and the spotted salamander are found in and around this area. The red-spotted newt is the adult stage of the bright orange eft, the salamander commonly seen in the woods, especially after a rain. The larvae of the newt change into the eft stage, which may last for several years. The efts can afford to be bold: due to toxic or irritating skin secretions, few predators will eat them (see **#58**). To return to your car, go south along the creek and take one of two trails back to the tuliptree woods.

To the south of the nature center is a freshwater marsh (**F**). A boardwalk allows you to explore the interior of the marsh. A large population of bog turtles inhabits the marsh, though they are so secretive that they are rarely spotted. This turtle is so shy that its status is uncertain. Much of its habitat has been drained, and scientists fear that it is rapidly disappearing. The bog turtle is highly sensitive to changes in water level and even a minor fluctuation may destroy its habitat. Snapping turtles, eastern box turtles, and stinkpots are more commonly seen. A variety of amphibians use the marsh, including bullfrogs, green frogs, pickerel frogs, and spring peepers.

Cattail, broad-leaved arrowhead, rice cut-grass, sweet flag, giant bulrush, and wild rice are the more prominent emergent plants, which you can see from the raised path crossing the marsh.

Though small, the marsh is used by a surprising array of mammals as well, including mink, long-tailed weasel, star-nosed mole, muskrat—and of course, raccoon, opossum, and white-tailed deer, found in almost every habitat in the Piedmont.

The entire park is a haven for birds. Censuses have recorded 185 species using the area throughout the year. The peak of activity is during spring migration when thrushes, vireos, many species of warblers, and other landbirds are seen. The marsh plants, the shrubs of the understory, the old-field invaders, and a helathy population of insects all provide food in good supply. The open hill south of the nature center (**G**) is a good place for hawk-watching in autumn (see **#5** and **#58**).

Remarks: *A full circuit of the west section of the park is about a half hour walk on gently rolling terrain. There are numerous trails in the new section of the park just across Brandywine Creek. They wind through a spectacular mature forest punctuated by rocky outcrops of Precambrian gneiss (see* **#16**). *The park is beautiful at any time of year. It is open daily from 8 a.m. to sunset. An entry fee is charged in summer. The nature center is open Wednesday to Sunday. Camping is available at Lum's Pond State Park, about 20 miles southwest of the park along the Chesapeake and Delaware Canal. Look for signs on U.S. 13. Other activities include a fitness trail, tubing, fishing (with license), and canoeing on the creek. For rentals contact Coat's Canoe and Kayak in Chadds Ford, Pa., (215) 388-7613; or Wilderness Canoe Trips, at the junction of Route 141 and U.S. 202 outside of Wilmington, (302) 654-2227. For further information write or call Brandywine Creek State Park, P.O. Box 3782, Wilmington, Del. 19807, (302) 571-3534, or the nature center at (302) 655-5740.*

24.
Alapocas Woods

Directions: **New Castle Co., Del. From Wilmington go north on I-95 to Exit 8, U.S. 202 north. Go 1.6 miles to Route 141 and turn south (left). Go 1.2 miles and turn south (left) at the second traffic light on Alapocas Road. Go 0.4 mile and pull off to the right into the parking and picnic area. Drive through it to a slightly larger area just beyond. From here several trails wander through 110 acres of woods.**

Ownership: **City of Wilmington, under the supervision of the New Castle County Parks and Recreation Department. A small portion is privately owned.**

Large oaks, beeches, and tuliptrees stand 100 feet tall in this small wood that overlooks the Brandywine River. Several small clear streams run down the steep slopes to the creek below. On the high ground, the tops of the trees on the floodplain are at eye level, perfect for watching warblers, thrushes, and vireos during the spring and fall migrations (#17).

As you walk along the trails, especially along the stream beds, you will see many boulders tumbled about. The predominant rock in the area is gneiss, a metamorphic rock (see #16). Extreme heat and pressure have caused the minerals in this rock to form bands of different colors. The primary minerals in the gneiss here are hypersthene, quartz, and andesine. Quartz is the only common mineral composed exclusively of silicon and oxygen. Andesine belongs to the group of minerals known as feldspar. Together with quartz, they account for 75 per cent of the continental crust.

The white oaks that once dominated this woodland have been severely affected by recent infestations of gypsy moth. The female gypsy moth lays its eggs on the trunk of the tree in late summer. The eggs look like a furry tan mass on the bark. In spring the eggs hatch out into capterpillars, which eat voraciously, feeding on the oak leaves. The caterpillars then build cocoons and transform themselves into adult moths. After just one year's infestation, an oak tree can recover, but with each defoliation it grows weaker, and with the third, the tree will probably die. This may encourage greater growth of understory species that now include flowering dogwood, red maple, tuliptree, and American beech, and below them such shrubs as maple-leaved viburnum, southern arrowwood, and American hazelnut. There are a number of American chestnut stumps and young saplings scattered through the stand. (see #30).

At **A** the canopy opens up all at once. Only a few tall trees remain, and a thick growth of shrubs almost hidden by a variety of vines such as Japanese honeysuckle, posion ivy, Virginia creeper, fox grape, and common greenbrier are taking advantage of the light now available. This is probably the path of a tornado that passed through, leveling the trees. This area extends down to the banks of the Brandywine, offering enticing cover to landbirds that prefer brushy, dense habitat, including such songbirds as the blue-winged warbler, the common yellowthroat, the yellow-breasted chat, the yellow warbler, and the white-eyed vireo.

Remarks: *This is a particularly lovely place in May, when the dogwood is in bloom and spring warblers are passing through. Nearby camping at Lum's State Park, south of Wilmington along the north bank of the Chesapeake and Delaware Canal. Look for the sign along U.S. 13.*

25.

Nottingham Serpentine Barrens

Directions: Chester and Lancaster Counties, Pa. From Philadelphia, go southwest on U.S. 1 about 50 miles to the Nottingham exit. Turn southeast (left) on Route 272 and drive 0.2 mile to Old Baltimore Turnpike. Turn right and drive 0.8 mile to the entrance of Nottingham Park on the left (**A**).

Ownership: Chester County Parks and Recreation Department.

In the midst of the fertile farmlands of southeastern Pennsylvania are 1000 acres of rolling upland where pitch pines and patches of prairielike grassland interrupt the sweep of cornfields and pastures. This is the last remaining serpentine barren in Pennsylvania, containing a unique and arresting blend of plants. Outcrops of serpentine occur sporadically from Nova Scotia to Georgia. This rock is apparently formed out of material which came from the mantle, the dense layer that lies between the crust and the inner core of the earth. This rock weathers very slowly into a thin, acid, infertile soil inimical to many species of plants (see **#28**).

To get to the serpentine barrens, walk south from the parking area along the yellow-blazed Chrome Trail. After 800 feet it joins the Doe Trail (white blazes). Stay left and continue for about 0.5 mile to the Buck Trail (red blazes). Turn west (right) and look for several unmarked trails leading southward (left) to the most open part of the barrens.

Some of the species found here, although common elsewhere, are rare in this part of Pennsylvania. It is thought that their presence here records the climatological changes that occurred during the advance and retreat of the most recent ice sheet, the Wisconsin (see **Piedmont**). The Aleutian maidenhair fern, for example, is found only in Canada, Alaska, and the Nottingham Barrens. When the Wisconsin ice sheet reached its southern limit, it was still many miles to the north of this area. Even so, the climate here was arctic; only tundra vegetation could survive. This fern, adapted to harsh, mineral-poor environments, established itself in the region. Once the

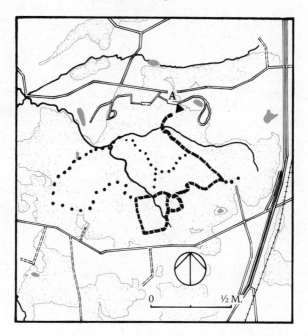

climate warmed again and other species returned, the fern was relegated to the barrens, where there was little competition from other species.

In contrast, Small's ragwort is a plant common in the southeastern United States but not found north of Virginia except on serpentine outcrops. During the warm interglacial period, when the climate was warmer than it is today, this plant extended its range northward. Then, as conditions cooled, other species crowded this southern interloper out of the more favorable soils.

Also found in the grassy areas are little bluestem, grama grass (*Boutelous curtipendula*), and Indian grass. These were originally grasses of the western prairies. When the climate grew warmer, prairie species advanced eastward. Other interesting plants in these openings include moss pink, fameflower (here at the northern edge of its range), lyre-leaved rock cress, whorled milkweed, tiny serpentine aster, and serpentine chickweed. The last two plants are endemics—species found only on the barrens.

The extensive forest of pitch pine is also unusual. It may well be the largest in the state. A northern species, pitch pine is generally confined to the mountains in regions south of northern Pennsylvania.

The barrens, with its range of habitats, is rich in birdlife. Whippoor-wills, otherwise scarce in this part of the state, are numerous here in nesting season. Seventeen nesting species of warblers have been recorded, including finds unusual for the region such as the yellow-throated, worm-eating, pine, and cerulean warblers. White-tailed deer and eastern cottontails are common, but little is known about other mammals.

Remarks: *Walking is easy. Allow an hour or two to explore the area. The two park ponds are stocked with bluegills and bass. Fishing from the shore is allowed, with a license, during the season. Octoraro Creek is stocked with brown trout. The creek also offers some challenging whitewater canoeing. Camping is available at the park. There are poisonous northern copperhead snakes in the area, though it is unlikely that you will ever see one. Spring and fall are especially lovely. Be prepared for ticks in warm weather (see* **Susquehanna River Gorge***). There are 8 miles of hiking trails here. In winter, the trails are open for cross-country skiing and there is ice skating on the ponds. For further information contact Nottingham Park, Nottingham, Pa. 19362, (215) 932-9195.*

26.
Rocks
State Park

Directions: **Harford Co., Md. From Baltimore, take I-95 northeast about 12 miles to Exit 4. Take Route 24 north; about 8 miles north of Bel Air, turn left onto Rocks Chrome Hill Rd., just beyond the nature center. Park in the small lot at the trailhead, 0.1 mile past the corner on the right.**

Ownership: **Maryland Forest and Park Service.**

The rocks of Rocks State Park rise loftily above Deer Creek. Legendary tribal council meetings held by local Indian chiefs at the rocks have given them the name "King and Queen Seats." Reached by a

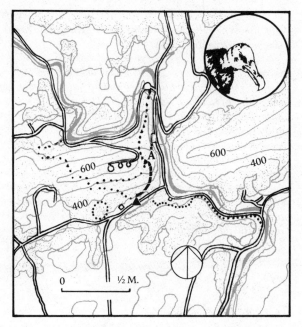

Inset: Turkey vulture

moderately steep, quarter-mile trail (see Remarks), these towering rock outcrops (**A**) delight visitors with their impressive height and broad views of the neighboring countryside. Turkey vultures, red-tailed hawks, and an occasional osprey soar on the currents, often at eye level or even below. The trail passes through a forest dominated by oaks and hickories, with thickets of mountain laurel tangling the understory. In contrast, the moist soils of Deer Creek's floodplains support black walnuts, tuliptrees, and Virginia pines. Because the area that is now the park was recently farmed and logged, most of the trees are less than 50 years old.

The King and Queen Seats crown a nearly sheer 170-foot cliff that drops down to Deer Creek. Another steep wall rises on the creek's other side. Both highlands are part of the same ridge, into which Deer Creek has carved a wide gorge, or water gap (see **#97**). Composed of a hard, metamorphosed conglomerate, originally a sedimentary rock containing a large proportion of pebbles and gravel, this ridge is more resistant to erosion than the surrounding rocks and remains in high relief against the adjacent gently rolling hills.

Take the same trail back to your car. Or, for a somewhat longer walk, follow the Red Trail away from the King and Queen Seats to make a loop totaling 1 mile.

Remarks: *Several other trails also lead to the King and Queen Seats. In summer, you can drive to the ridgetop and walk across a short, level stretch to the rocks. To reach this point, continue 0.6 mile on Route 24 past Rocks Chrome Hill Rd., and turn left before the bridge onto St. Claire Bridge Rd. Drive about 0.7 mile, then turn left onto a park road and follow it up to the picnic area. The rocks are off to the left. Be careful near their precipitous edges. Activities include picnicking, hiking, tubing, swimming, and fishing (with a license and trout stamp). Climbing on the rocks should be attempted only by experienced technical climbers. Pets are prohibited. The park is open year round. In summer, it gets crowded and the dense foliage blocks the view. For information contact Rocks State Park, Route 1, 3318 Rocks Chrome Hill Rd., Jarrettsville, Md. 21084, (301) 557-7994.*

27.
Gunpowder Falls
State Park—
Hereford Area

Directions: **Baltimore County, Md. From Baltimore, take I-83 to Exit 27 nearly 12.5 miles beyond the Beltway (I-695). Turn right onto Mount Carmel Rd., which ends after 0.4 mile at a T intersection. Turn left onto York Rd. and go about 1.7 miles. Two small parking areas straddle York Rd. just before Gunpowder Falls. Walk down to the grassy area on the right (east) side of the road, along the river's south bank, to pick up the trail.**

Ownership: **Maryland Forest and Park Service.**

The Hereford area is the most remote section of Gunpowder Falls State Park, characterized by rugged wooded hills, damp floodplains, narrow creeks, and a meandering river. Its features, from the forest of oaks and hickories that shrouds the slopes, to the mayapples thriving on the floodplains, are typical of the Piedmont (see **Piedmont**). A half-day hike along this 4.2 mile loop trail provides ample opportunity to explore the various aspects of the park.

The first 2 miles of this route, following the blue-blazed Gunpowder South Trail, parallel Gunpowder Falls. Throughout most of the year the water level of the river is quite low. Since the 1930s, the flow of the Gunpowder has been impeded by Prettyboy Dam. Located 4.5 miles upstream, Prettyboy Reservoir holds much of Baltimore's water supply.

The meandering river has cut its way through the hard mica schist, a metamorphic rock common throughout the Piedmont (see **#37**). As it wears its way into the rock, the river is confined by a steep wall on one side (**A**), where the trail climbs high onto the rocky bluffs. Across the river, the land slopes away from the water more gently. Apparently following some weakness in the rock, the river swings back at **B**. Here, a steep wall rises on the far side of the river, where a tributary tumbles over Raven Rock Falls, and the trail crosses a narrow floodplain, formed where sediments and soil have accumu-

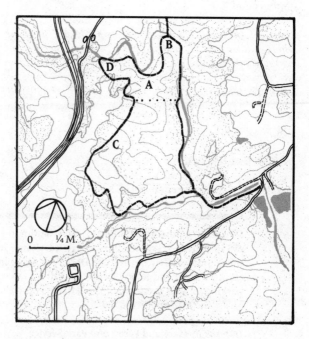

lated along the inside of the meander (see **#94**). Skunk cabbage and other moisture-loving spring wildflowers flourish on the floodplain, where many tree stumps indicate the presence of beavers.

Turn right onto Panther Branch Trail just before crossing Panther Branch. (Look carefully for the pink blazes so as not to bypass this trail. It follows Panther Branch upstream for more than half a mile, then leads back to the uplands.) Like most of the Piedmont region, this area was farmed some 50 years ago. The trail crosses fields presently in use, then leads along a lane shaded by tall white pines (**C**). When land is no longer cultivated, trees are often planted to prevent erosion and retain moisture. White pines are most often used because of their rapid growth, forming forests whose dense shade inhibits the evaporation of water. Evergreens such as white pines require very little maintenance. Pines are frequently planted around reservoirs, as here near Prettyboy Reservoir, because the additional organic material of deciduous leaf litter speeds the eutrophication of the water. In addition, white pines provide food and shelter for a variety of wildlife and have commercial value as lumber. At **D** the trail files between numerous saplings where an unused area is naturally reverting to forest (see **#41**), then returns to the starting point.

Remarks: *Other activities include picnicking, hiking, horseback riding, fishing (with a license), and canoeing. Nearly 20 miles of trail, well-marked with color-coded blazes, crisscross the park or follow the Gunpowder. Contact park headquarters for more information: Gunpowder Falls State Park, 10815 Harford Rd., Glen Arm, Md. 21057, (301) 592-2897.*

28.
Soldiers Delight
Natural Environmental Area

Directions: Baltimore County, Md. From Baltimore, take I-695 to Exit 18. Travel west on Liberty Rd. (Route 26) for 5 miles. Immediately beyond the Deer Park shopping center, turn right and follow Deer Park Rd. 3.4 miles to the parking lot and overlook on the left. Several trails begin across the road and to the right.

Ownership: Maryland Forest and Park Service.

Soldiers Delight Natural Environmental Area is an uncultivated, desolate place where expanses of grasses and stunted trees contrast sharply with the dense oak and hickory forests on the adjacent rolling hills. Only plants tolerant of little soil, desiccation, and nutrient imbalances grow here. Soldiers Delight, which owes its unique appearance to the underlying rocks, is the only virtually undisturbed serpentine barren left in Maryland. Its name dates back to colonial days, but the origin remains unknown. According to one story, the soldiers of King George III gave this place its name because the Indians' surprise attacks were less successful in these barren areas than in the forests. A quainter account holds that the local women made pies and cakes, to the delight of the soldiers.

The Natural Environmental Area includes 1500 acres of serpentine barren and forest, with an additional 1000 acres scheduled for acquisition; the serpentine barren is more extensive. Both the 2-mile orange-blazed trail and the 3-mile yellow-blazed trail (which coincide for some distance) lead across the serpentine barren into the surrounding forest and back again.

The massive rock, commonly termed serpentinite, is primarily composed of the mineral serpentine. A number of other ultrabasic minerals (those containing much iron and magnesium and little silica) are also present in small amounts (see **#16**). Heavy metals such as chromium, nickel, lead, and zinc are also present in the rock. The first chromium discovered in the United States came from a nearby serpentine barren in the early nineteenth century. Chromium was mined at many of the serpentine barrens in the region during the 1800s, until richer deposits were found in other countries. Near the beginning of the orange- and yellow-blazed trails is the abandoned Choate chromium mine. Other less-obvious mineshafts are scattered throughout the area; all are dangerous and should not be entered.

As you walk across the serpentinite, notice that on fresh surfaces, it is blue-black, or greenish when wet, while oxidation has quickly bleached out the exposed rock. The rock decomposes slowly, though, and most of the erosion products are washed away. The remaining shallow soil is acidic, clayey, and infertile. Reaching a maximum depth of 6 to 8 inches, the soil retains little water, creating a semi-desert environment. What nourishment plants can get from the soil depends on the parent rock; soils derived from serpentinites characteristically lack calcium (lime) and potassium (potash), while iron and magnesium abound. Magnesium apparently substitutes for calcium within the plant cells. Although the plants can survive, they are dwarfed. The heavy metals limit the number of species able to grow here as well as the height and size each can attain. The trees, about 50 years old, are equal in age to the larger oaks and hickories not on the serpentinite. On more fertile soil, the plants of the serpentine barrens would flourish but generally cannot compete with the plants typical of better soils.

Only three species of trees live here on the serpentine barren: blackjack oak, post oak, and Virginia pine. A number of unusual plants have found a niche at Soldiers Delight, including Maryland's largest stand of fringed gentian and its only populations of the rare vanilla-scented holy grass and tufted hair grass. Turkeyfoot, beard grasses, indian grass, and many others grow throughout Soldiers Delight. Blazing star and bird-foot violet are among the wildflowers that add color to this somewhat drab spot.

A hike through this unique area on either trail, or simply a gaze outward from the overlook, will reveal the striking demarcation between the oak-and-hickory forest and the scrubby blackjack and post oaks and Virginia pines. This boundary indicates the precise extent to which the serpentinite interrupts the deeper, richer soils formed from the surrounding metamorphic quartzite and schist (see **#37**). The trails then return to the serpentine barren and eventually emerge on Deer Park Rd. Turn left and follow the road a short way back to the parking area.

Outcrops of serpentinite are not common in the eastern United States, although they exist in the Piedmont uplands from New York to Georgia. The rock is altered material derived from the earth's mantle—the interior section between the crust and core. Under the continents, the mantle is some 20 to 30 miles below the surface, while beneath ocean basins, it is only about 6 miles below the surface, as oceanic crust is thinner than continental crust. Serpentine barrens are thought to be fragments of the upper mantle and oceanic crust that were thrust onto the continents as Africa and Europe eventually collided with North America, building the Appalachian Mountains and closing the proto-Atlantic Ocean (see **Piedmont**).

Without the detrimental influence of people, Soldiers Delight serpentine barren would remain relatively unchanged long into the future. Unfortunately, this natural area, like so many others, suffers from pollution. Illegal use of motorcycles and off-road vehicles has trampled the vegetation and speeded erosion, creating areas that are truly barren. The dumping of trash that occurs both in and around Soldiers Delight is adding much organic material to the soils, allowing weedy plants, not indigenous to serpentine barrens, to invade. Atmospheric pollution from Baltimore, acid rain, and automotive emissions cause additional ill effects.

Remarks: *Three other trails lead through the area; a large wooden map is posted by the parking lot. Each trail is well-marked with color-coded blazes, but watch carefully for the markers to avoid getting lost. The trails, muddy in spring and hot and buggy in summer, are open year round for hiking and horseback riding (no rentals available). A picnic area, by an old hunting lodge (Red Dog Lodge), is located on the Green Trail. For more information, contact E. Vernon Tracy, superintendent of Soldiers Delight Natural Environmental Area, at 4830 Deer Park Rd., Owings Mills, Md. 21117, (301) 922-3044.*

29.
Patapsco Valley
State Park—McKeldin Area

Directions: **Carroll County, Md. From Baltimore, take I-70 west about 9 miles from the Beltway to Exit 81. Bear right onto Marriotsville Rd. and head north for 4.2 miles. The park entrance is on the right; parking is at the top of the hill. Walk back along the entrance road to where the Switchback Trail begins (A).**

Ownership: **Maryland Forest and Park Service.**

The wide array of plant and animal life at the McKeldin Area of Patapsco Valley State Park typifies the Piedmont region. The 5-mile, yellow-blazed Switchback Trail begins in the upland forest that covers most of the park. Several species of oak and hickory grow here, along with tuliptree, beech, and Virginia pine. Spindly American chestnut sprouts challenge the imagination to picture the forest of magnificent chestnut trees, sometimes 100 feet tall and 4 feet across, that graced these hills a century ago, before the chestnut blight arrived from Asia and wiped out one of the most valuable species of hardwoods. (see **#30**).

As it descends to the South Branch of the Patapsco River, the trail passes by one of the two types of metamorphic rock that are clearly exposed in the park (**B**). A strip of micaceous quartzite runs northeast across the park, from the South Branch to the North Branch of the river. Notice the tiny flakes of mica, which catch the sun's rays and set them dancing. The rock, a metamorphosed sandstone, was mined for flagstones because it splits easily into flat slabs along its thin, uniform beds. At the bottom of the hill are mechanical remains of the quarrying operation.

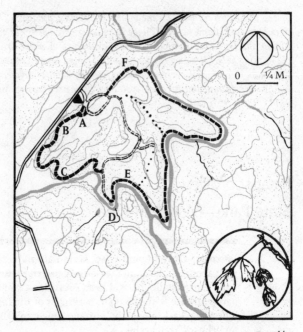

Inset Box elder

Leveling off, the trail follows the South Branch as it meanders through the bottomlands (**C**). These moist floodplains along the branches of the Patapsco are covered with sycamore, willow, river birch, silver maple, white ash, boxelder, and American hornbeam. Dogwood, spicebush, and laurel grow beneath them.

When this area was a plantation, the uplands were cultivated, while the low, moist sections with poor drainage were used for grazing. The dense woodlands have covered most of the evidence of the past. Furthermore, the park management has planted fruit trees and berry hedgerows, for wildlife food, and white pines, to prevent erosion and retain moisture (see **#27**). Beneath the tall trees a variety of wildflowers blooms in spring, before the lush foliage prevents the sunlight from penetrating to the forest floor. Dogtooth violets, spring beauties, mayapple, bloodroot, and lady's slippers are among those one is apt to find (see **#36**). Roaming the forest and waterways are numerous small mammals and reptiles that, like the vegetation, are typical of the region. White-tailed deer, raccoons, squirrels, muskrats, snapping turtles, lizards, salamanders, and snakes are sometimes seen.

The trail meets a road at the picnic area; turn right and go to the end of the road, then scramble down to the waterfall (**D**), where a trail leads alongside the river. Swimming in the large waterhole here is prohibited because of the dangerous undercurrents.

Once again marked by yellow blazes, the trail crosses broad out-crops of gneiss, the second, much older rock type (**E**), where Hurricane Agnes stripped all soil from the bedrock in 1972. Probably over a billion years old, this gneiss is the oldest rock found in the Piedmont uplands. The folded layers of dark and light minerals that decorate it are the result of the high pressures and temperatures that altered this rock and obliterated all clues to its original identity.

The trail roughly parallels the river to the confluence of the Patapsco's two branches, then continues along the narrow floodplain of the North Branch. Zigzagging up the steep slope, the trail climbs back to the uplands. It ends at an overlook of the Liberty Dam (**F**), built in the 1950s to supply Baltimore city and county with water. The enormous white wall containing that great expanse of brilliant blue water explains why so little water and so much vegetation lie between the banks of the North Branch. Continue through the picnic area back to the parking lot.

Remarks: *This area of Patapsco Valley State Park sees the fewest visitors. Open year round. There is an entrance fee of $3 per car on weekends and holidays from April through September. The trails are open for hiking and horseback riding (no rentals available); tubing and fishing (with a license) are permitted in the river. For more information contact the park at: 1100 Hilton Ave., Baltimore, Md. 21228, (301) 747-6602.*

30.
Sugarloaf Mountain

Directions: **Frederick County, Md. From Washington, D.C., take I-270 about 22 miles northwest to the exit for Route 109. Following signs to Sugarloaf Mountain, turn right, pass under the highway and go 2.9 miles southwest on Route 109 to Comus. Turn west (right) onto Route 95. After 2.4 miles you will come to the base of Sugarloaf Mountain. Turn right through the gateway and continue 1.4 miles up the mountain to the end of the road. A steep quarter-mile**

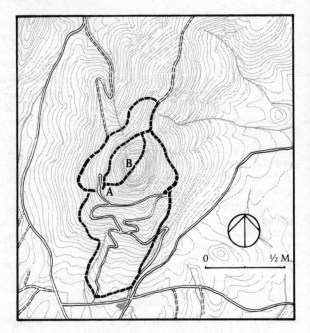

trail, beginning at a set of stone steps, leads from the lower end of the parking area (**A**) to the top of Sugarloaf Mountain (**B**).

Ownership: **Stronghold, Inc.**

Although Sugarloaf Mountain rises only 1282 feet above sea level, it is the most prominent feature for many miles. The mountain was privately owned and maintained for many years by Gordon Strong, a nature lover, who declined to develop it. He established Stronghold, Inc., which now manages the area, and it has been designated a National Natural Landmark. This small island of forest lies close to several urban centers. It is not spectacular, but offers woodland in which to wander and pleasing views of the surrounding farmlands.

The only rock exposed on Sugarloaf Mountain is quartzite, a tough, metamorphosed quartz sandstone. The structure of the mountain is a complex dome or anticline (see **#95**) with smaller secondary folds across it, similar to that of Catoctin and South Mountains to the west. The quartzite here is considered to be the equivalent of the

Weverton quartzite which forms those ridges as well as Elk Ridge (see **#52, #54,** and **#55**). The stratigraphy, or the arrangement of the rock layers (strata), around Sugarloaf Mountain corresponds to the sequence in the vicinity of South and Catoctin Mountains. Fossils found to the west in Washington County lead geologists to believe that Weverton quartzite is about 570 million years old. Because Sugarloaf Mountain lies in the Piedmont near the border of the Blue Ridge Province (see **Piedmont** and **Blue Ridge**), understanding of its geological time-frame may shed light on that of the Piedmont. Geologists can determine when the crystalline rocks of the Piedmont were metamorphosed, but their origins remain a mystery. If the relationship between the highly metamorphosed Piedmont rocks and the relatively unmetamorphosed rocks of known age to the west can be ascertained, the structure of the Piedmont will become better understood.

The thick oak-and-hickory forest that covers Sugarloaf Mountain is typical of Maryland's uplands. Chestnut oaks have replaced the American chestnuts that were once dominant throughout the Appalachians. One way to tell the difference between seedlings of the chestnut oak and sprouts of the American chestnut is to look closely at their leaves. For both species, they are elongated and have toothed edges, but while the American chestnut leaves have sharp teeth, those of the chestnut oak are rounded. Around the turn of the century, a fungus (*Endothia parasitica*) was introduced from Japan or China which killed American chestnuts. It was first discovered around New York City in 1904, and from there it spread rapidly, at a rate of some 20 miles per year. In New England, the chestnuts were destroyed by the 1920s; the blight reached the southern Appalachians by the 1940s. It not only altered the landscape but caused a terrible loss of highly valuable and useful trees.

American chestnuts grew tall and straight. Shaded by the thick canopy above, the lower branches died, or self-pruned. Because of this, these trees yielded good timber. They sometimes grew to be 100 feet tall with 7-foot diameters. Because the wood was extremely resistant to rot, was moderately strong, split easily, and had a nice grain, it was used widely for fences, poles, shingles, and furniture. The nuts were harvested by both humans and many forest animals. The trees also provided tannin, needed to tan leather.

The chestnut blight is a parasite that destroys the thin cambium, the living layer of a tree, located beneath the protective outer bark. It enters through any crack or wound in the bark, forming a canker that girdles the tree and stops the flow of sap, which sustains a tree's life. Eventually, the tree weakens and dies. However, the fungus cannot live underground, and so the roots remained unaffected, allowing chestnuts to sprout from the stumps. By the time the sprouts reach diameters of 1 to 5 inches, though, they usually are infected and, within a year or two, die.

Stronghold, Inc., is helping coordinate research efforts to return healthy chestnut trees to the forests. Since the 1930s, attempts have been made to hybridize the American chestnut with the blight-resistant, but shorter, Japanese and Chinese chestnuts. Researchers are making progress, but they have not yet satisfactorily combined the desired traits of each. Another approach taken has been to speed the natural process of change through mutation, by exposing seeds to ionizing radiation in the hope that advantageous characteristics will develop.

However, the most promising research involves a biological control of the fungus itself. In the 1950s, biologists noted that Italian chestnuts, also susceptible to the blight, were healing themselves. It turned out that the strain of fungus associated with these trees was "hypovirulent," or less capable of causing disease. Because the fungus is less virulent (it actually has a virus), trees can fight back and heal the cankers; thus this strain of the blight can live in the outer bark without killing its host. When a hypovirulent strain comes in contact with a "normal" strain, the former infects the latter, which likewise becomes less harmful. Scientists are trying to find a way to make what occurrred naturally in Italy happen here. They have had some success and, eventually, may get the hypovirulent fungus to spread from tree to tree on its own.

The wildlife at Sugarloaf Mountain is also typical of Maryland's uplands. Deer, red and gray foxes, weasels, and raccoons are joined by a variety of small mammals. The secretive bobcat may still prowl these woods. Wild turkeys, reintroduced to Frederick County in the 1960s, have found a home here. Screech and great horned owls roost in the trees. The lower stretch of the Sugarloaf Mountain Rd. is a good place to look for migrating warblers and thrushes, particularly when the mountaintop is clouded over. Summer tanagers and worm-eating warblers nest along the lower slopes. The mountaintop can be a good place for hawk-watching in both spring and fall (see **#5** and **#78**).

Remarks: *Sugarloaf Mountain is open during daylight hours year round for hiking, horseback riding (no rentals are available), and picnicking. A water fountain is located at the base of the mountain. Stop along the mountain road only at designated viewpoints; certain areas are restricted for educational purposes. Motorcycles are not allowed. Plants should not be picked. Dogs must be kept leashed. For more information contact Stronghold, Inc., P. O. Box 55, Dickerson, Md. 20842.*

Nearby Place
of Interest

Lilypons, where great numbers of goldfish and water lilies are raised, is a very productive birding spot. Varying water levels in the many ponds attract shorebirds, migrating ducks, wading birds, and breeding marsh birds. Landbirds are also found here. From Sugarloaf Mountain, turn south (left) from Route 95 (from where you first approached the mountain) onto Mt. Ephraim Rd. Continue to Dickerson, and go north and west 3.8 miles on Route 28. Turn north (right) onto Route 85, travel 3.8 miles, then turn right onto Lilypons Rd. Hours are 9:00 a.m. to 4:30 p.m. Mondays through Saturdays, noon to 4:30 p.m. Sundays. For more information contact Lilypons, Lilypons, Md. 21717 (301) 874-5133. Many of the back roads in the vicinity of the Monocacy River also provide good birding.

Chesapeake and Ohio Canal

The Chesapeake and Ohio Canal extends 185 miles from Washington, D.C. to Cumberland, Md. Together with a wide towpath, the canal parallels the Potomac River as it passes from the Ridge and Valley Province (see **Ridge and Valley**) through the gap in Catoctin Mountain at Point of Rocks, across the redbeds of the flat Frederick Valley, and between the Piedmont hills of hard crystalline rock below Seneca. The canal bypasses Great Falls and ends in Georgetown—the colonial part of the District of Columbia—where the coastal plain begins. Seven dams cross the river, diverting its water into the canal.

Begun in 1828 to improve trade and transportation with areas to the west, the canal competed with the Baltimore and Ohio Railroad, which was also being built. Problems with construction and property rights resulted in numerous delays, and the entire length was not completed until 1850. Because the costs were far greater than anticipated and the railroad had already reached Cumberland, plans to extend the canal to Pittsburgh were abandoned. Damaged by floods in 1889, the canal was rebuilt and used until 1924, when it was ruined by another flood.

The C&O Canal National Historic Park, which includes the canal and towpath, and a number of adjacent parks, forests, and wildlife management areas provide many recreational opportunities. Bird-watching, especially along the lower reaches of the canal, is a favorite activity throughout the year. It is excellent during spring and fall, when warblers, vireos, thrushes, and hawks, among others, migrate past the canal. Waterfowl winter on the river, and many birds nest in the thick bordering deciduous forest in summer. One can picnic, hike, and bicycle along the towpath. The surface is unpaved and somewhat rough outside of the city. Horses are permitted beyond Seneca, and camping is allowed at designated sites, located about every 5 miles. Canoeing on the canal, between Georgetown (Lock 4) and Violets Lock (Lock 23) near Seneca, requires portage around the locks. Rentals are available at Swains Lock (Lock 21) and Fletchers Boat House (Mile 3). Only experienced boaters should venture into the Potomac River; certain dangerous areas are to be avoided, and a number of dams require portaging. Numerous boat ramps—maintained by the National Park Service, the state, or private owners—provide access to the river for fishing (a license is required) and boating. Two private companies run boat trips on the river by Great Falls (see **#37**) and Harpers Ferry (see **#55**). Barge trips along the lower canal are scheduled from spring through fall by the National Park Service.

For more information, stop at the visitors' center in Georgetown near the beginning of the canal, or contact Great Falls Tavern, 11710 MacArthur Blvd., Potomac, Md. 20854, (301) 229-3613, or C&O Canal National Historic Park, Box 4, Sharpsburg, Md. 21182, (301) 739-4200.

31.

McKee-Beshers
Wildlife Management Area

Directions: **Montgomery County, Md. From Washington, D.C., take I-495 to Exit 39 and head west on River Rd., passing through the town of Potomac. After 11.2 miles, at the intersection with Route 112, River Rd. turns left. Continue about 3 miles, watching for Hunting Quarter Rd. on the left. There are three parking areas at the Wildlife Management Area:**

A.   **Turn left onto Hunting Quarter Rd., and continue 0.6 mile to the parking area on the left.**

B.   **From *A*, go another 0.8 mile to the second parking area, also on the left.**

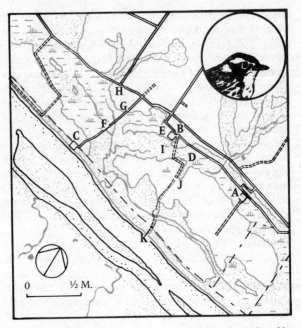

Inset: Yellow-throated warbler

C. Continue 0.1 mile on Hunting Quarter Rd., then turn
    right on Hughes Rd. and go 0.1 mile, back to River
    Rd. Turn left, proceed 0.3 mile to Sycamore Landing
    Rd. Turn left and drive 0.8 mile to Sycamore Landing
    and park at the road's end.

Ownership: Maryland Wildlife Administration.

Within easy reach of metropolitan Washington, McKee-Beshers
Wildlife Management Area—known locally as Hughes Hollow—has
a large number of diverse habitats within a 1500-acre tract, which
attract ducks, herons, hawks, owls, warblers, and a wealth of other
bird species. This area is well known for its excellent bird-watching
opportunities, especially during spring and fall migrations. Woodland wildflowers burst forth in early spring, while those in the fields
flower later in summer. Deer and red fox inhabit the woods, while
beavers enjoy the impoundments (see **#64**). Also at home in the
wet places are a number of amphibians and reptiles, including red-
cheeked, red-bellied, snapping, and mud turtles. Visitors are free

to explore all of the wildlife management area, slog through the swamps, wander across the fields, and prowl the woodlands.

Three impoundments (**D, E, F**) draw ducks to the area. Both dabbling ducks (such as American wigeons, pintails, teal, and wood ducks) and diving ducks (including buffleheads, common golden-eyes, ring-necked ducks), as well as grebes, come here to feed (see **#18**). The ponds provide them with food such as arrow arum and other vegetation plus small aquatic animals such as insects, snails, and mollusks. A number of herons—common egrets, American bitterns, great blue, little blue, green, Louisiana, and yellow-crowned night herons—wade along the water's edge. The mudflats exposed as water levels lower in summer attract both greater and lesser yellowlegs plus other shorebirds as they migrate south in fall. The shallow marshes (**G, H, I**) also attract waterfowl, herons, and shorebirds.

Crop fields and hedgerows of autumn olive, dogwood, and honeysuckle make up most of the area. Fallow fields are managed to provide various types of cover. Warblers frequent the woodlots, and bluebirds utilize the established nesting boxes. At twilight during the first week of March, male woodcocks present their elaborate mating displays. They spiral up into the sky, the wind whistling through the tips of their wings. After climbing sometimes 300 feet high, they suspend for a moment, singing, then swoop back to earth and approach the female. The American kestrel, northern harrier, and other hawks—red-tailed, red-shouldered, rough-legged, marsh, and sharp-shinned—are seen most often in winter as they hunt for rodents in the fields. At (**J**) an old barn site sits on top of a small rise. This elevated viewpoint is a good place to set up a spotting scope.

The rich bottomland forest bordering the Chesapeake and Ohio Canal provides both seed and insect food and dense cover for birds and other wildlife. Wildflowers bloom here in spring before the sycamores, maples, boxelders, and pawpaws spread their leaves and shade the forest floor. Access to the canal is possible at Sycamore Landing (**C**) and Horsepen Branch (**K**), which can be reached by walking about a mile south from parking area **B** through fields and woods. Although there is no cleared path, one can walk through the woods along the north side of the canal from Horsepen Branch to Sycamore Landing. In spring and fall, a great variety of warblers can be heard, if not seen, in the trees (see **#17**). Large numbers of songbirds rest here during the day while following the Potomac River on their journeys north and south at night. Several warbler species, such as the cerulean, the prothonotary, and the American redstart, nest here in summer, as do white-eyed vireos, blue-gray gnatcatchers, and yellow-billed cuckoos. Wild turkeys (see **#98**) and both pileated and red-headed woodpeckers inhabit these woods throughout the year, along with barred, great horned, and screech owls.

Remarks: *Open year round, but be aware that hunting is allowed in season (permits are sometimes needed, and hikers should be careful during deer season—see #88). Summer weather is hot and humid, and the mosquitoes and ticks are ferocious. Contact the Maryland Wildlife Administration, Seneca Work Center, 11960 Clopper Rd., Gaithersburg, Md. 20878, (301) 258-7308.*

*A National Park Service campsite is located at Horsepen Branch (*K*) on the C&O Canal. This is an excellent place for watching waterfowl on the river at dawn. Boats can be carried in and launched at Sycamore Landing (*C*). Maddux Island (*L*), a forested island with many wildflowers, is part of McKee-Beshers Wildlife Management Area.*

Nearby Places of Interest

A walk to Violets Lock (Lock 23), about 1 mile down the towpath, should be worthwhile for birding. Seneca Creek State Park, another good birding area, is located just downstream from McKee-Beshers Wildlife Management Area. For information, contact the park at 11950 Clopper Rd., Gaithersburg, Md. 20878, (301) 924-2127.

32.
Blockhouse Point

Directions: Montgomery County, Md. From Washington, D.C. Take I-495 to Exit 39 and go west on River Rd. After 10.2 miles (6.7 miles from the junction with Falls Rd. in Potomac), there is a small road, Pettit Way, on the right. Park at the intersection of Pettit and River Rd. (A) or just ahead on the left, where the dirt-road trail begins (B).

Ownership: Montgomery County Department of Parks.

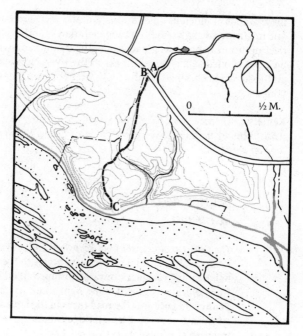

The huge rock outcrops of Blockhouse Point loom nearly 100 feet above the Chesapeake and Ohio Canal and towpath. The dirt-road trail leads about 0.7 mile through heavily wooded, rolling terrain to the top of the bluffs (**C**). The trail branches just before reaching the edge. Take either path. The view from this quiet, lofty spot encompasses a 10-mile stretch of the Potomac River that has not changed greatly over the past decades. On a clear day, Catoctin Mountain (see **#52**) can be seen to the northwest.

The bluffs are composed of mica schist, which underlies much of the Piedmont, extending downstream to Theodore Roosevelt Island (see **#37**). Only Virginia pine and a few other hardy plants are able to cling to the rocky surface, in contrast to the diverse forest that densely covers the hills. Eight different types of oaks, plus hickories, American beeches, tuliptrees, and red maples are among the forty species that have been counted here. Flowering shrubs, such as mountain laurel, pink azalea, and spicebush bloom in spring, as do a multitude of woodland wildflowers (see **#36**).

A typical assortment of small birds—woodpeckers, flycatchers, goldfinches, wood thrushes, and yellow-billed cuckoos—inhabit these woods at different times throughout the year. From the bluffs one might see swallows and common nighthawks as they follow the river upstream during spring migrations. The sharp-eyed visitor might pick out spotted sandpipers on rocks in the river. Northern orioles and eastern phoebes nest on the bluffs. Retrace your steps back to your car.

Remarks: *The view from Blockhouse Point is particularly nice in winter when there are no leaves to obscure it. Be careful along the bluffs, which drop off abruptly.*

Nearby Places of Interest

The C&O Canal towpath from Pennyfield Lock to Violets Lock: Pennyfield Lock Rd. provides easy access to the C&O Canal. Heading east (back toward Washington) on River Rd. from Blockhouse Point, turn right after 1.5 miles onto Pennyfield Lock Rd. The road turns to the left and ends in 0.9 mile. Just beyond, a footbridge crosses the canal to the towpath at Pennyfield Lock (Lock 22).

About 0.5 mile upstream along the towpath, at Milepost 20 of the towpath, is the Dierssen Waterfowl Sanctuary, where dabbling ducks take refuge in winter. Farther upstream, the towpath passes between Blockhouse Point and the river's swift waters tumbling over the Seneca rapids. Ducks, loons, and flocks of gulls may be seen on the river in late fall and early spring as they migrate to and from the coast. Ducks and gulls regularly visit the river in winter, congregating in the slow waters above the diversion dam for Violets Lock (Lock 23) as long as the river is not frozen. This is an excellent place to see other waterfowl, including migrating horned grebes.

33.

Billy Goat
Trail

Directions: **Montgomery County, Md. From Washington, D.C., take I-495 to Exit 39 and drive 3.2 miles west on River Rd. Turn left onto Falls Rd. (Route 189), which ends at MacArthur Blvd. after 2 miles. Turn right and continue 1.2 miles to the Great Falls Tavern (visitors' center). Walk across the bridge over the canal, turn left, and follow the C&O Canal towpath downstream about 0.5 mile to where the blue-blazed Billy Goat Trail begins on the right. There is no sign to indicate the trail, but it is located just above a floodgate.**

Ownership: **National Park Service.**

The aptly named Billy Goat Trail, together with a segment of the Chesapeake and Ohio Canal towpath (see **C&O Canal**), circles the perimeter of Bear Island, the largest island below Great Falls (see **#37**). Although the falls cannot be directly seen from here, the power of the Potomac River is apparent nevertheless. To the steady accompaniment of its thundering roar, one can explore the precipitous brink of Mather Gorge and other rocky features.

Bedrock exposed on the island is metagraywacke and mica schist, the same metamorphic rocks that underlie Great Falls Park. To the right of the trail, as it drops into a wooded valley after about 0.2 mile, is a rock outcrop (**A**) overlooking Mather Gorge. In the wall across the river and just upstream are some vertical breaks in the rock where a foot-wide vertical strip, or dike, of dark igneous rock is exposed. Following the metamorphism was a period of uplift and erosion. As pressure and temperature decreased, the rocks fractured. Molten material intruded into some of these fractures about 360 million years ago. It solidified into lamprophyre, forming dikes, or bands, within the metamorphic rock. This wooded valley sits on the continuation of these dikes. Not easily noticed, the lamprophyre on this side of the river is located to the right of a metagraywacke outcrop nearby, and a second dike lies about 3 feet farther upstream. Fresh surfaces are a shiny dark green, but exposed faces, weathered

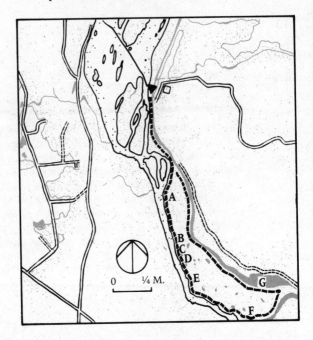

and lichen-covered, are difficult to distinguish from the surrounding rock. Although the lamprophyre dikes extend across the gorge, they do not connect in a straight line. Mather Gorge is carved along a fault (see **#3**); motion along it, which occurred sometime after the lamprophyre was emplaced, cut and offset the dike by some 80 feet.

Before the gorge was carved, the rounded rocks underfoot were washed by the river. Now roughened by weathering, they contrast with smooth rocks currently being polished by the rushing water. Churned by the river, pebbles and boulders enlarged depressions in the mica schist into potholes (**B**), just over 0.3 mile from **A**. Those stones that were too large for the currents to lift out of the potholes remained trapped inside them. Some of those stones, transported as far as 35 miles from their nearest outcrops upstream, are larger than the rocks in the present riverbed that have more recently traveled the same distance, indicating, perhaps, that the Potomac was once more powerful than it is today. The striped appearance of the walls of Mather Gorge, strikingly straight and steep at this point, stems from a variety of gray and yellowish lichen (see **#115**) separated by a strip of dark green moss.

The trail soon enters the woods; after about 100 feet, detours right to the river's edge. This sandy beach (**C**) provides an opportunity to examine the well-rounded rocks, carried by the river, and the nearly vertical beds of metagraywacke, interlayered with the mica schist. A granite dike with sections of pegmatite (see **#37**) cuts across the metamorphic rock.

To survive on this rocky island, on which deep soils are lacking, trees must tolerate dry conditions. Post and red oaks dominate the bedrock terrace community whose other members include white and chestnut oak, pignut hickory, Virginia pine, and eastern red-cedar. While black and southern red oak are common on the richly soiled uplands, they are scarce on Bear Island. A small stream (**D**) flows through a fault associated with the larger one down which Mather Gorge is carved. Trees typical of floodplains—sycamore, green ash, elm, and boxelder—grow here where there is soil to retain the moisture.

A third type of metamorphic rock, amphibolite, is exposed in many places between **E**, about 1 mile along the trail, and **F**, over a quarter of a mile farther. This dark-green or black rock, originally an igneous rock similar to basalt, intruded parallel to the sedimentary layers that were accumulating 550 million years ago. The entire package was metamorphosed: the sediments became metagray-wacke and mica schist, and the thick igneous layer was altered to amphibolite.

There is a large mica schist outcrop, to the left of a flat open area (**F**). The rock has not yet had time, since being abandoned by the river, to break down into soil. The only soil generally available is flood-deposited silt and sand. Rainwater quickly runs off the bare rock into ponds and swamps lying in potholes or other low spots.

When you reach the towpath, turn left and walk a mile and a quarter back to Great Falls Tavern. This section of the C&O Canal, Widewater (**G**), flows down a river channel that was abandoned as the Potomac River cut deeply into Mather Gorge late in the Ice Age (see **Susquehanna River Gorge**). All the canal locks are built of red-brown sandstone quarried eight miles upstream, near Seneca. About 200 million years ago, during the Triassic period, a last epi-sode of uplift caused a series of faults to develop in the Piedmont. Huge keystone-shaped blocks of land dropped down along facing faults, forming basins, which were then filled with the sediments that now compose these rocks. The easily eroded red sandstones and shales are found between Seneca and Point of Rocks in the Frederick and Montgomery Counties, Md. and Loudon County, Va.

Remarks: *The blue-blazed Billy Goat Trail is steep, rough, and rocky; wear proper footgear. It is impassable during high water and very crowded during nice weather. Allow half a day to walk this 5-mile circuit. Below Widewater, a footbridge provides access to MacArthur Blvd. by the Anglers Inn. To get there, turn left from Falls Rd. onto MacArthur Blvd. and drive 1 mile. Park in the small lot on the right or alongside the road. Walk up the towpath toward Great Falls Tavern, and return along the Billy Goat Trail. For more about the geology of Billy Goat Trail and Great Falls, see* The River and the Rocks, *by John C. Reed, Jr., available at the visitors' centers at both locations (see* **Bibliography**). *For more information, contact the National Park Service, 11710 MacArthur Blvd., Potomac, Md. 20854, (301) 299-3613.*

34.
Rock Creek
Park

Directions: **Washington, D.C. From the interchange of Military Rd. and Beach Dr. (where Military Rd. crosses Rock Creek Park), take Beach Dr. north (left) 2 miles. Turn right onto West Beach Dr., go 0.1 mile, crossing the bridge, then make the first left onto Parkside Dr. Park here, walk back to West Beach Dr., and turn right. The bridle trail begins down the small hill by the edge of the creek on your right, just past the corner (A). Follow this trail on the north side of Rock Creek about 1.0 mile to Boundary Bridge (B).**

Ownership: **National Park Service.**

Rock Creek Park lies in the middle of Washington, D.C. and runs nearly the entire length of the city. Many city residents, anxious to escape the urban bustle, flock to the park's deep valleys cut by tumbling streams, hillsides broken by rocky ledges, and open fields. Temperatures here in summer are often 10°F cooler than those on the sweltering streets above.

   The thick woodlands that compose most of Rock Creek Park reflect the human activities that helped shape the natural features present today. Much of the land was once farmed, and during the

Civil War vast areas were completely cleared. Some buildings remain; others are gone without a trace. Exotic species stand alongside the natural forest vegetation, which includes many trees over 100 years old. Some of these exotics, which are not indigenous to the park, such as ailanthus and periwinkle, were intentionally planted by homesteaders. Their locations may be clues to where people dwelled in the past. In other cases, seeds were carried in by birds and other wildlife or were washed downstream from nearby farms and estates.

Over a hundred species of trees and shrubs make up this deciduous forest. Many of these plants grow in the area between West Beach Dr. (**A**) and Boundary Bridge (**B**). The slopes and ridges (which are more prominent farther south in the park) support Virginia pine, redcedar, many species of oaks, several hickories, black and sweet cherry, and sassafras. As throughout the east, the American chestnuts that once spread their branches here have virtually disappeared; only scattered young sprouts remain (see **#30**). River birches, elms, American hornbeams, American beeches, and tuliptrees thrive on the moist, rich soils alongside the streams. A typical array of smaller trees and shrubs comprise the understory: spicebush,

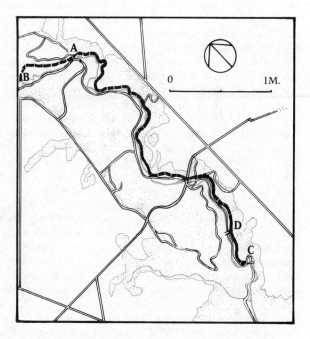

witch-hazel, smooth alder, redbud, dogwood, maple-leaved viburnum, and wild hydrangea. Vines and brambles such as poison ivy, wild grape, greenbrier, blackberry, raspberry, and the introduced Japanese honeysuckle and English ivy are abundant. When a tree falls, creating an opening in the forest, these plants, particularly the troublesome Japanese honeysuckle, often take over. They decrease the amount of light available to the saplings, which would otherwise reclaim the small clearing (see **#41**). Instead, the saplings are stunted and more susceptible to disease. Over twenty species of ferns grace the forest floor with their elegant fronds. Cinnamon and royal ferns grow in low, wet places, while Christmas and rattlesnake ferns are found on drier soil. Rock polypody, northern maidenhair fern, and interrupted fern are uncommon or at the edge of their normal distribution here.

While the surrounding urbanization does not greatly affect the plant community today, it has dramatically influenced the wildlife population. Many mammals no longer live here, and few fish can survive in the polluted streams. Still, a variety of animals do inhabit this relatively undeveloped area. The twenty-five mammals recorded include deer, red and gray foxes, raccoon, and beaver (see **#64**), as well as a good assortment of both large and small rodents. Twelve kinds of snakes (none are poisonous) slither through the park, while eight species of salamanders, seven of frogs, and the American toad join the several types of turtles by the water. Some sixty-one species of butterflies have been seen fluttering across the fields.

The bird population is also varied. Migrating songbirds pause here in spring and fall. Scarlet tanagers, common flickers, and broad-winged hawks breed here in summer, and evening grosbeaks, slate-colored juncos, and white-throated sparrows winter here. The bulk of the bird population is composed of permanent residents—woodpeckers (including pileated), owls, Carolina chickadees, white-breasted nuthatches, titmice, and song and house sparrows. While these birds add a welcome dimension to Rock Creek Park, other places near Washington boast much better birding opportunities (see **C&O Canal** sites and Mid-Atlantic companion coastal volume).

At least forty species of wildflowers bring delicate colors and designs to the forest while sunlight still penetrates through the trees in spring. This area (between **A** and **B**) is one of Rock Creek Park's best wildflower spots. While you may not find a specimen of every wildflower that blooms in the park, many do flower here on the floodplain and in the adjacent woodland. Look for skunk cabbage, Virginia bluebells, bloodroot, hepatica, mayapple, fawn lily, spring beauties, and many others. In May, mountain laurels and azaleas set the hillsides ablaze with their fiery pink blossoms.

This northern edge of Rock Creek Park is less disturbed by usage than its southern portions, which border the Rock Creek and Potomac parkways. Rock Creek itself, however, has not escaped the destructive hand of man. Notice how much silt covers the streambed and stays suspended in the water. Building and road construction have torn up the surrounding land, resulting in increased erosion, the products of which often wind up in Rock Creek. The silt smothers both plants and animals that would normally inhabit the stream.

Many of Rock Creek's smaller tributaries are likewise lacking many of the expected life forms. Silt, other sources of pollution, and the flushing action of floods affect all the park's streams to some degree. Most of the streams begin at the edge of the park as storm-sewer outlets. Because pavement does not allow precipitation to seep into the ground, nearly all the rainwater rushes through the storm sewers into these streams. Floods following heavy rains remove the soil from the stream valleys and wash away many of the water-dwelling fauna. Several species of fish and other forms of aquatic life do manage to survive, though.

Retrace your steps to your car. Return to Beach Dr., turn left, and continue south. Go 1.2 miles past the Military Rd. interchange to the small parking area (Number 4) on the right, just above Boulder Bridge (**C**). From here, walk north (upstream) along Rock Creek. There is no trail next to the creek, but you can easily make your way along the creek next to the road, or walk along the road when it is closed to traffic (see Remarks). A blue-blazed trail, which begins by Boundary Bridge, leads through the valley on the east side of the road.

Here, Rock Creek has cut a steep-sided valley into the hard, metamorphic rock. This stretch, where the water tumbles over boulders and ledges, coincides with the fall line (see **#37**). Although the stream winds along a curved route, its path is controlled by the structure of the rocks. It follows joints, or fractures in the rock, the edges of which have been rounded by years of erosion. (See **#94** for a discussion of stream meanders and structural control.)

The half-mile between Boulder Bridge (**C**) and Rapids Bridge (**D**) provides ample opportunity to examine many of the facets of Rock Creek Park. Walking and bicycling here are particularly enjoyable when the road is closed to automobile traffic (see Remarks). Notice that each bridge is unique in its construction design and materials; a look at the large stones of Boulder Bridge will quickly reveal the origin of its name. Pawpaws, fringetrees, and bladdernuts, plus New York, cinnamon, and beech ferns, can be found by Rapids Bridge.

Remarks: *Activities and facilities include picnicking, hiking, horseback riding (rentals are available), bicycling, a jogging-exercise course, golf course, tennis courts, a nature center, and naturalist activities. Several historical buildings and the National Zoological Park also lie within the Rock Creek valley. It is open for day use only.*

Beach Drive is closed to automobile traffic from Joyce Rd. (just south of Military Rd.) south to Broad Branch Rd. on Saturdays, Sundays, and holidays for pedestrians and bicyclists. In order to reach Boulder Bridge at these times, drive north on Beach Dr. to Broad Branch Rd. Turn left and park at the first area on the left, then walk up the road.

For more information, contact Rock Creek Park, 5000 Glover Rd. NW, Washington, D.C. 20015, (202) 426-6829.

35.

Theodore Roosevelt Island

Directions: **Washington, D.C. The parking area for Theodore Roosevelt Island, located in the Potomac River 0.3 mile north of the Theodore Roosevelt Bridge, is accessible only from the northbound lanes of the George Washington Memorial Parkway. A footbridge leads to the island. From the end of the bridge take the first trail to the right. The Woods Trail leads halfway around the island.**

Ownership: **National Park Service.**

With the incessant rumbling of traffic and the thundering roar of airplanes arriving and departing from National Airport, Theodore Roosevelt Island can hardly be called a wilderness. Yet this 88-acre island in the Potomac River, almost three-quarters of a mile long and just over one quarter of a mile across at its widest, includes more than eight habitats, most of them thick with a great variety of plant species. Forest, two types of swamps, and marsh are the major habitats; wet thickets separate the swamps and marshes; an inconspicuous hemlock grove stands near the center of the island; a small field lies at the island's southern end; and rock, open water, and an intertidal zone circumscribe the island. Human influence is apparent in every aspect of Theodore Roosevelt Island, from the sights and sounds of the city to the plantlife and geological development.

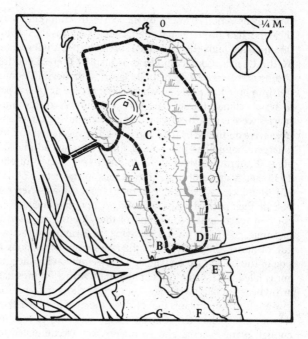

Deciduous forest covers most of the island's higher ground, which reaches a maximum elevation of 44 feet. The Woods Trail passes beneath elms that have survived Dutch elm disease, bitternut hickories, a variety of oaks, and silver maples. Tuliptree, black cherry, and beech are among the many other species of trees that share this dry terrain. A bitternut hickory and a white oak—each stately, over 4 feet across, and about 150 years old—stand beside the trail at **A** and **B**, respectively. Spicebush accounts for more than three-quarters of the shrubs, with wild grape, two kinds of viburnum, and abundant poison ivy adding to the tangled greenery. Mayapple, trout lily, spring beauty, goldenrod, fleabane, and other wildflowers bloom primarily in spring and summer. Intermingled with these native species are a number that were introduced. For example, Kentucky coffeetree grows in certain spots and ailanthus is scattered through the forest, while English ivy and Japanese honeysuckle threaten to take over the island.

This array of vegetation is directly related to the island's history of human activity. From 1632 until it became a monument to Theodore Roosevelt in 1932, the island was used for a number of purposes by its various owners. By the late eighteenth century, much of the land had been cleared for farming and pastures. Fruit trees, ornamentals, and other cultivated species were introduced. In 1935–36 the Civilian Conservation Corps planted over 25,000 trees and shrubs and removed deadwood, Japanese honeysuckle, and other brush in an effort to create what the landscape architects perceived to be a "climax forest" (see **#41**). A number of the introduced species were unable to survive in this environment, and many of the trees were destroyed by the 1936 flood. The vegetation you see today is largely natural, as the existing forest then spread into the open areas. Eastern hemlocks were among those species introduced in 1935–36. A grove of these trees stands in the center of the island (**C**). Hemlocks, which thrive in moist, cool climates (see **#46**), are outside their normal range here and are not reproducing.

Upon reaching the south end of the Woods Trail after nearly a half-mile, go straight ahead, following the Swamp Trail across a tidal gut, or narrow inlet (**D**). Then, the trail swings north along the east side of the island (see Remarks). Nearly empty at low tide, the tidal gut is filled with water by each high tide. Arrow arum, smartweed, arrowhead, cattail, sweet flag, European yellow iris, and rose mallow are freshwater plants that grow in the marsh, which extends up the east side of the island as well. Marsh gives way to swamp where enough plant material and sediments have accumulated to allow trees, such as willows, boxelders, green ashes, and silver maples, to survive. This indistinct border between the two habitats is often marked by wet thickets. These areas are drier than the marshes but still wet enough for marsh plants to flourish beneath the trees and shrubs.

The different habitats here, each with its own distinctive species of plants, are a direct result of differences in topography. The northeast corner of the island is a micaceous schist common throughout the Piedmont. Soft, unconsolidated sediments extend southward. As these sediments accumulated and the water level dropped somewhat, the island developed a relatively high central ridge on which the forest now grows. The land closer to the river is lower and supports the wetlands. The hard metamorphic rock, first encountered here as one travels up the Potomac River, marks the boundary between the Piedmont and the Coastal Plain (see **Piedmont** and Mid-Atlantic coastal volume), although the actual falls have migrated upstream (see **#37**).

Initially, only this hard rock, resistant to erosion, stood above the surface near the middle of the river. Over time, sediments have collected in the lee of the rock wherever the flow of water is slowed. Marshes have developed on these sediments along the edges of the island where it is protected from the river's strong current. Incoming tides hinder the river's journey downstream even more, increasing the rate of deposition. The island has thus grown in length and width, particularly during the past 200 years. Two factors are responsible for this rapid expansion: increased sediment in the river from widespread farming and later development upstream, and the causeway, built in 1810, and in use for about 70 years, that crossed from the island's north end to Virginia.

Before the causeway was built, the main channel of the Potomac shifted between the east side and west side (now Little River) of the island, based on a fine balance of deposition and erosion. Large floods would occasionally clear both channels and add material to the growing island. The causeway changed the river's flow pattern, forcing it into the east channel. With Little River thus dammed, all the sediment from the river was dropped on the east side of the island, causing rapid expansion. Bars formed along the river's edge and, in the protected water behind them, marshes developed. Little River became so narrow and shallow that the inhabitants of the island, fearing disease from the stagnant water behind the causeway, left sometime in the 1830s. Without the cleansing power of the river, the sediments dumped in the channel by occasional floods remained there. In addition, marsh plants were reclaiming the water from both sides. Artificial fill also contributed to the situation.

Deposition exceeded erosion; even large floods did not remove this buildup of material. During this time, the island nearly doubled in length. Then, by the mid-1880s, the natural channel that now separates Little Island (**E**) from the rest of Theodore Roosevelt Island developed. It is located approximately at the point where the bedrock ends and the Coastal Plain begins. The channel (**F**) of Little River to the south of both Theodore Roosevelt Island and Little Island is man-made. Columbia Island (**G**) was also part of Theodore Roosevelt Island. About 1928, the channel was dredged, cutting off Columbia Island and creating Little Island, and Columbia Island was built up with hydraulic fill, in order to support Memorial Bridge and its web of highways. The channel between Theodore Roosevelt Island and Little Island was also dredged, probably at this time.

The Swamp Trail runs into the Woods Trail at the north end of the island. Continue straight through the upland forest, then follow the Woods Trail south, back to the footbridge. \

Remarks: *The route around the island is level and less than 2 miles long. The Swamp Trail becomes impassable after rain, and may be wet at other times. Wear appropriate footgear. To avoid the Swamp Trail, turn left onto the Upland Trail before crossing the tidal gut (**D**). This trail leads across* *the center of the island. The island is open from dawn to dusk year round. Naturalist walks are offered on weekends. For more information, contact Theodore Roosevelt Island, Turkey Run Area, George Washington Memorial Parkway, McLean, Va. 22101, (202) 426-6922 or (703) 285-2600.*

36.
Dranesville District Park

Directions: Fairfax County, Va. From Washington, D.C., take I-495 to Exit 13. Take Route 193 (Georgetown Pike) west 0.2 mile to a small parking lot on the right. Follow the dirt road uphill away from the parking lot.

Ownership: Fairfax County Park Authority.

When the lengthening days of spring prod the wildflowers into bloom, the woodlands and fields of Dranesville District Park comes into blossom. Between mid-March and mid-June, 175 species flower here before the trees, also awakened from winter dormancy, intercept the sun's rays with their expanding foliage. Bursting forth from bulbs or tubers, the earliest bloomers, such as skunk cabbage and harbinger-of-spring, often protrude through whatever snow remains. Heat is generated by last fall's decaying layer of litter, which adds to the heat of the sun's feeble rays. The woodland wildflowers are at their peak from mid-April to mid-June; summer and fall wildflowers emerge later in more open woods and meadows.

The surprising diversity of wildflower species and their abundance at Dranesville is due to the variations in topography and aspect (direction of exposure relative to the sun), which create a variety of microhabitats. Both northern and southern species find tolerable conditions within these 385 acres. Many can flourish within a wide range of sunlight, moisture, soil acidity, and the like, and so are found in numerous habitats. Others that require very specific conditions are not as common. Within the park, which is dominated by a fairly mature oak and hickory forest, there are five basic habitats. The area was last cleared during the Civil War, so most of the trees are over 100 years old. The forest is stable and relatively unchanging. The undergrowth consists largely of wildflowers and other herbaceous ground cover. Among these are bloodroot, one of the first to bloom; Dutchman's breeches and its near look-alike, squirrel corn; several interesting orchids; many types of violets; and profusions of mayapples.

Follow the dirt road to the trail junction (**A**), then turn right and walk to the overlook (**B**). From here, one looks down the palisades that rise from the banks of the Potomac River. Ferns abound around the overlook—there are twenty different species throughout the park. Columbine, yellow corydalis, wild stonecrop, and balsam ragwort are among the flowers that find their niches on these steep rocky outcrops. The river has a large influence on the park's ecosystem. Besides moderately affecting the climate, it carries seeds and pollen from its upper reaches and deposits them here.

Retrace your steps to **A** and continue along the main dirt road to your right. The road passes through an old field (**C**) that was once a homesite but is now growing over with grasses and goldenrod, black locust, and sumac. Black-eyed susan, buttercup, evening primrose (which blooms, as its name suggests, in the evening) and its day-blooming relative, sundrops, all require abundant sunlight and other field conditions.

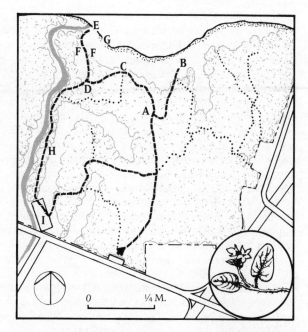

Inset: Trailing arbutus

At **D**, turn right onto a dirt road which leads down to the Potomac River. En route to the river and along Scott Run near the small but pretty waterfalls (**E**) on this narrow creek are hemlock groves (**F**) that thrive on steep slopes facing north or northwest away from the sun and into the cool, moist winds off the river. Only a few plants can adapt to the shaded, acid soils beneath the hemlocks. These include partridgeberry, spotted wintergreen, whorled pogonia, and trailing arbutus. Virginia bluebells, harbingers-of-spring, trout lilies, and wild leeks grow in great profusion beneath the sycamores, maples, and boxelders established on the rich moist soil of the narrow floodplain (**G**). Exploring these steep, dangerous areas is not recommended.

The trail leads back along Scott Run and (noticeably) a sewage line to the lower parking lot. Trailing arbutus clings to the rocky soil exposed in this area (**H**). Cross the parking lot (**I**) and follow the trail up the bluff to the left and back through the oak-hickory forest. Bearing left at the next fork in the trail, continue straight through the following intersection to the next junction. Turn right here onto the main dirt road leading back to the original parking lot. Although many flowers can be seen along the trail, many more, including some uncommon ones, will be encountered on detours off the main trail.

The pleasing shapes of flowers and their bold or subtle colors are designed not to delight us but to insure the species' survival. In order for seeds to develop and subsequently be dispersed, the flower must be fertilized so that the seed-containing fruit can develop. Although most flowers contain both male (stamen) and female (pistil) parts, many must be cross-pollinated (i.e., the pollen from one flower must fertilize another). The pollen is often transported by insects, butterflies, or hummingbirds, which unwittingly collect it during their quests for food or nectar. Flowers entice their pollinators with colors and odors, and are shaped to meet these creatures' needs. For example, bees are attracted by bright colors and sweet smells. They land before searching for food and so pollinate irregularly shaped flowers like violets. Virginia bluebells offer tunnels into which other insects will crawl. Ground insects wander into the low, dark flowers of wild ginger, where they are temporarily trapped by hairs so that sufficient pollen falls onto their backs during their struggles to escape. Jack-in-the-pulpit offers a sophisticated example of this. Flies are attracted to the bottom of the spathe by the carrion odor. Once they discover that there is no food, the purple hood that blocks the entrance hinders escape attempts. Attracted by light filtering through the green striped walls, the flies brush past the male and female flower parts and inadvertently gather or deposit pollen before finding their way up the spike, or spadix, to freedom.

Remarks: *This route of about 3 miles covers varied terrain. Plan to spend a few hours here, allowing time to find and identify the many wildflowers. Please don't pick the flowers; leave them so others can enjoy them too. Most attempts at transplanting wildflowers are unsuccessful. Lists of wildflowers and information about wildflower walks are available from the Fairfax County Park Authority, 4030 Hummer Rd., Annandale, Va. 22003, (703) 941-5008. The lower parking lot (I) is located off Route 193 on the right just beyond the main one. However, entering and leaving this lot are considerably more difficult.*

37.
Great Falls
Park

Directions: **Fairfax County, Va. From Washington, D.C., take I-495 to Exit 13. Drive 4 miles west on the Georgetown Pike (Route 193). Turn right at the light onto Old Dominion Rd. (Route 738). Continue 4.3 miles to the visitors' center parking lot.**

Ownership: **National Park Service.**

Water crashes spectacularly over massive rocks, then surges through a long, deep gorge at Great Falls Park. Elsewhere a placid waterway, the Potomac River here becomes uncharacteristically wild and turbulent as it drops 76 feet within a quarter of a mile. In addition to the breathtaking views of the falls, the park contains other notable, although more subtle, features. The various habitats—woodland, rocky terraces, floodplains, and a swamp—are the result of the area's geological history. Interlaced with the natural history is a record of past human activity.

As you reach the visitors' center, turn right (south). Cross the bridge over the old canal to a wide, level path that parallels the canal. Several short detours to your left will provide terrific views of Great Falls. Each of the four overlooks (**A**) provides a slightly different perspective of Great Falls. The fall line, a zone of large rapids and falls, connects the lowest set of falls on major rivers from Georgia to New York. Large commercial centers developed along the fall line, which marks the upper limit of navigation on these rivers. Here,

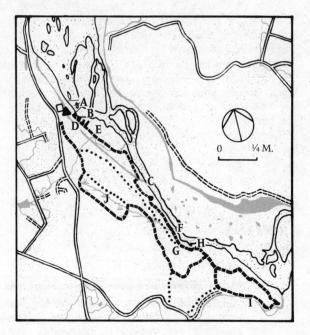

land routes met ocean-going vessels, and water power was available for milling and manufacturing. The fall line indicates the transition from the Piedmont to the Coastal Plain (see **Piedmont** and Mid-Atlantic coastal volume). As they flow from the uplands to the ocean, the rivers slowly wear away the hard, ancient rock over which they flow, then tumble down onto the younger, easily eroded sediments of the Coastal Plain. Ceaseless erosion by the rivers over millions of years has caused the falls to retreat from where the two rock types meet to their present locations upstream (see **#35**).

The course of the Potomac River has not changed drastically since the ice ages began 2 million years ago. At times, sea level was greatly lowered, and the Potomac, moving down a steeper gradient, rapidly deepened its valley (see **Susquehanna River Gorge**). Layers of particularly hard rock occur where the falls are now located. Below this, the somewhat softer rock is weakened by faults and fractures, and is therefore more easily eroded. Over the past 2 million years, narrow rocky channels, studded with tall islands of bedrock, were carved below the falls. The very resistant rock at Great Falls has slowed erosion, leaving the wide, steep-sided river valley above here essentially as it was before the ice ages. Recently, however, it has been modified by a diversion dam for the local water supply, located just above the falls.

The underlying rocks govern the river's path. The rock at the falls is metagraywacke, which is bluish-gray and has a sugary texture where its surface has been weathered. Originally muddy sands deposited on the bottom of a sea some 550 million years ago, the sediments were buried deep beneath subsequent deposits, then folded, fractured, and metamorphosed. The river channels follow these metagraywacke layers. Vertical fractures caused by later uplift have broken up the rock, accelerating the erosion. After careening over the falls, the river encounters a series of closely spaced fractures and makes a right angle turn (**B**) to flow through this zone of weakness. Following another line of weakness, the river again turns sharply to flow through a fault (see **#3**). The shattered rock along this fault has enabled the river to rapidly carve the long, straight channel of Mather Gorge (**C**).

Occasionally, the river will cover these abandoned upper surfaces. A sign at **D**, near the third overlook, marks the water levels reached during the last three major floods (1936, 1942, 1972). The Potomac is normally about 30 feet deep; at the crest of the floods, the water depth had nearly tripled. Torrents rushed everywhere, carrying sand up to these surfaces. Smaller floods, reaching to within 15 feet of the rim, occur about every 2 years.

From the sign at **D**, continue on the path along the Patowmack Canal (**E**). In 1784, George Washington established the Patowmack Company to build a series of canals that would make the river navigable, helping to develop trade with the western regions. The canal, America's first, was begun the next year and took 17 years to complete. Three days were required to pole a flatboat the 185 miles downriver from Cumberland to Georgetown. At the end of the journey, the boats were usually dismantled and sold for lumber; the boatmen then walked home. A small town, Matildaville, existed here until the late 1820s, when use of the canal ceased. The remains of the town, the canal, and its holding ponds are still evident, though largely overgrown.

The path bears left away from the canal, becoming the blue-blazed River Trail. It passes through the woods toward the river, then parallels Mather Gorge (**C**) to the right. Venture carefully off the main trail to the edge of the 65-foot-deep gorge. A silver-gray metamorphic rock, mica schist, is exposed here. Originally mudstone or shale, this material was deposited, folded, and metamorphosed along with the metagraywacke. Weathering has roughened the surfaces of these rocks. At one time they were smooth, polished by the river, which flowed at this level before it cut down into the gorge.

Follow the River Trail south as it crosses the Patowmack Canal and continues along the edge of Mather Gorge. Red and post oaks dominate these dry, rocky terraces. Virginia pines, redcedars, pignut hickories, and several other oaks grow here as well. Blueberry bushes, fringetrees, pawpaws, and blackhaws comprise the understory. St. Johnswort, a flowering plant common in the open rocky areas from here downstream to Chain Bridge, is not found anywhere else locally but occurs to the west in the Appalachian Mountains. A moss that covers the upper walls of the gorge is another mountain species that has found limited footholds in the lowlands.

The period of metamorphism was nearly over by 470 million years ago. At that time, molten granite rock intruded into fractures in the deeply buried metamorphic rock. Veins of granite stripe the mica schist. At **F**, over a mile from the visitors' center, a dike of pegmatite lies near the trail. This coarse-grained pink-and-white igneous rock is very similar in composition to the granite. As magma cools, minerals crystallize from the liquid in a specific order. When the granite has nearly solidified, the most hydrous part of the magma remains. This cools slowly, forming the large interlocking crystals typical of pegmatites. Pegmatites often contain high concentrations of minerals rich in rare elements. When of sufficient size and quality, these minerals are used for gemstones. The dark crystals in this pegmatite are tourmaline.

Pressures from floods have overturned a large number of trees and caused many others to lean downstream. At **G**, however, small trees tilt upstream. When the racing floodwater caused by Hurricane Agnes in 1972 hit the rock wall that lies ahead, some of it was diverted back into an eddy, forcing these trees to lean seemingly in the wrong direction.

As the trail climbs away from the river, the rocks become rougher and more angular. The river-deposited sand is replaced by deep, clayey soil, which results from the chemical weathering of the mica schist. The vegetation also shifts to a community more typical of the Piedmont. A variety of oaks (white, black, southern red, chestnut, and scarlet), mockernut hickory, Virginia and shortleaf pine, and tuliptree grow thickly in the rich soil. Dogwood, mountain laurel, and maple-leaved viburnum commonly flourish beneath the larger trees.

About a mile and a half from the visitors' center, Cowhoof Rock (**H**) rises more than 100 feet above the river, providing excellent views of Mather Gorge and the surrounding terrain. The river at this point is about 60 feet deep, more than twice as deep as elsewhere in the gorge. Perhaps, at some stage of the valley's development, there were falls here that gouged the riverbed. The 1972 floods did not reach this high but did inundate the cliffs across the river.

At the top of the hill, follow the gravel road to the left. This becomes the blue-blazed Ridge Trail. About three-quarters of a mile past Cowhoof Rock, it drops steeply to Difficult Run, where flood-plain vegetation such as sycamore, green ash, silver maple, and boxelder grow beside its lower reaches. Farther upstream, the stream passes through a small gorge (**I**) and breaks over rapids en route to the Potomac. Just as the Potomac River downcut rapidly in response to lowering sea level, so Difficult Run carved more deeply into its valley as it tumbled down to the Potomac. Continue upstream along Difficult Run and watch carefully for the unmarked trail that cuts off to the right and takes you back uphill to the Ridge Trail. Turn left onto the Ridge Trail. Follow this gravel road a third of a mile past the junction with the blue-blazed trail leading to Cowhoof Rock, and turn right onto an old carriage road.

Back on the uplands, away from the Potomac, a swamp (**J**) edges a small stream. After a quarter-mile, turn left off the carriage road onto the swamp trail. The swamp lies in a channel that the river abandoned long ago. The high ground to the northeast was once an island. Peat, composed of dead swamp vegetation (see **#120**), began accumulating on the rocky riverbed 9500 years ago. The plants that grow here, such as red maple, black tupelo, and pin and willow oak, are not found elsewhere in the park. In addition, sweet pepperbush, swamp azalea, poison-sumac, alder, and greenbrier grow in dense tangles in the moist organic-rich soil. Lush stretches of skunk cabbage and lizard's tail mark the wetter areas. The swamp trail re-emerges on the carriage road; turn left and follow it back to the picnic area by the visitors' center.

Remarks: *This route is rough in places; sturdy footwear is recommended. The park is open year round from 9:00 a.m. until dark. It is very crowded in summer. Activities include hiking, horseback riding (no rentals are available), fishing (with a license), picnicking, and naturalist activities. Potomac River Tours offers raft trips through Mather Gorge and canoeing, kayaking, and rock-climbing lessons. For information, contact them at P.O. Box 30061, Bethesda, Md. 20814, (202) 546-7200. Rock-climbing should be attempted only by those with technical experience; climbers should register at the visitors' center. Swimming and wading are forbidden—the strong currents are extremely dangerous. Be careful while walking along the edges of the cliffs. For more information, contact the National Park Service, 9200 Old Dominion Dr., Great Falls Park, Va. 22066, (703) 759-2915.*

38.

Riverbend Park

Directions: **Fairfax County, Va. From Washington, D.C., take I-495 to Exit 13. Go west on the Georgetown Pike (Route 193) for 4.4 miles to Riverbend Rd. (Route 603). Turn right, and after 2.1 miles turn right onto Jeffery Rd. Continue 0.9 mile to the nature center.**

Ownership: **Fairfax County Park Authority.**

Riverbend Park occupies the Potomac River's floodplain and the adjacent hills just upstream from Great Falls (see **#37**). Glorious displays of spring wildflowers decorate the ground (see **#36**), while migrating warblers, flycatchers, and orioles sing from the trees, hidden in the new, bright green foliage. A variety of birds, including wood ducks, cuckoos, and hummingbirds, nest here in summer when butterflies swarm to the fields. Fall paints the leaves with glowing colors but brings fewer birds to Riverbend than does the spring. When the leaves are gone in winter, assorted waterfowl, including ring-necked ducks, buffleheads, goldeneyes and common mergansers, drift on the icy river.

Behind the nature center and to the left, the green-blazed Paw Paw Passage Trail leads through the upland oak-hickory forest to the blue-blazed Potomac Heritage Trail, which parallels the river's edge. The Paw Paw Passage Trail passes a man-made pond, which is spring-fed (**A**). A second man-made pond (**B**), which lies along the Potomac Heritage Trail, is all that remains of an old fish hatchery. Sycamores, silver and red maples, tuliptrees, basswoods, black walnuts, and pawpaws thrive on the rich, moist soil of the floodplain.

Many of the trees along the bank of the Potomac lean out over the water as they reach toward the sun. Contact with the water weakens the roots and intensifies this angle. Three large sycamores, leaning at various angles, are conspicuous in the southern picnic area (**C**). One is merely tilted, but a second lies horizontally on the ground, and what were once branches reaching out from this tree are now vertical shoots that maintain the tree's vitality. The third tree, bent into a peculiar shape, displays a sizable opening in its base. Sycamores are often hollow, and for this reason have sometimes been used to make barrels.

The mottled green, brown, and gray jigsaw-patterned bark of the sycamore is distinctive. The bark is relatively smooth, in contrast to that of other species of trees. On all trees the outer bark is a rough, protective layer of cork. As the tree ages, the trunk grows and expands and the dead cells of the cork layer cannot stretch sufficiently. Furrows and ridges develop as the cork cracks. A new layer of cork grows underneath to maintain the waterproof protection of the tree's inner structures. Each species has a particular pattern and texture. The bark of the sycamore does not expand; instead, it peels off as discrete layers, revealing the new layer beneath.

Return to the nature center by going back along the Potomac Heritage Trail. Just before **B**, turn left onto the Paw Paw Passage Trail and follow it up the hill to complete this approximately 3-mile route.

Remarks: *The park is open year round, but facilities operate on a restricted schedule in winter. Riverbend Park is considerably less crowded than Great Falls National Park. A trail, about 1.5 miles in length, connects the visitors' centers of the two. Activities and facilities include trails for hiking and horseback riding (no rentals are available), picnicking, fishing (with a license), naturalist activities, and a nature center. The visitors' center rents boats and has a launch for boats with engines less than 7.5 horsepower. A fee is sometimes charged for nonresident parking here. For information and hours at the visitors' center call (703) 759-9018. For other park information contact the nature center at 8814 Jeffery Rd., Great Falls, Va. 22066, (703) 759-3211.*

39.
Bull Run
Regional Park

Directions: **Fairfax County, Va. Take I-66 west from Washington, D.C., to the exit for Centerville, about 11 miles beyond the Beltway. Follow signs to the park. Bear right, following Route 28 south 0.6 mile to U.S. 29 South. Turn west (right) and continue 3.2 miles to Bull Run Rd. (Route 621). Turn south (left) and go 2.3 miles to the park entrance. Park in the lot by the swimming pool, 1.5 miles farther. The trail begins across the road at A.**

Ownership: **Northern Virginia Regional Park Authority.**

In early spring, the ground at Bull Run Regional Park is blanketed with a magnificent array of Virginia bluebells. This wildflower display, covering large portions of the park, may well be the best of its kind in the area. The blue expanses are tinged with the pink of the buds and newly opened flowers of the bluebell, as well as an occasional cluster of mature bluebells that never turned blue.

Also adding pink to the fields at Bull Run are masses of spring beauties. These small, delicate flowers are whitish or pink, with dark pink stripes extending from the flower's center along each petal. The stripes help guide pollinating insects to their destination. At night and on cloudy or rainy days, when these insects are not out and about, the flowers close to protect their nectar and pollen from the dew and rain.

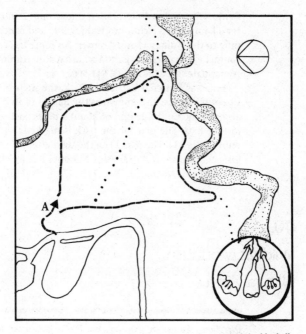

Inset: Virginia bluebells

Mid-April is the best time at Bull Run to see these floral delights which include other spring wildflowers typical for the region (see **#36**). The Bluebell Trail is a 1.5-mile loop.

Remarks: *An annual bluebell walk is held sometime in April; for details contact: Northern Virginia Regional Park Authority, 11001 Popes Head Rd., Fairfax, Va. 22030, (703) 278-8880. Other activities include hiking, swimming, camping, skeet and trap shooting, and indoor archery. The park is closed December 1 to March 15.*

Nearby Places of Interest

Ellanor C. Lawrence Park (Fairfax County Park Authority) offers a mixture of cultural and natural history. From the

Centerville exit on I-66 turn left onto Route 28 north. After 0.2 mile, turn right onto Walney Rd., and continue 0.8 mile to the Walney visitors' center. For more information, contact Fairfax County Park Authority, 4030 Hummer Rd., Annandale, Va. 22003, (703) 941-5000.

Manassas National Battlefield Park, the site of the Battles of Manassas, also known as the Battles of Bull Run, is also nearby. Continue on I-66 about 4 miles past the Centerville exit. The exit for the park is marked. Turn right onto Route 234. The park is on the right after 0.5 mile. For information, contact Manassas National Battlefield Park, P.O. Box 1830, Manassas, Va. 22110, (703) 754-7107

40.
Wildcat Mountain
Natural Area

Directions: Fauquier County, Va. From Washington, D.C., take I-66 west about 35 miles beyond the Beltway. Take the exit for U.S. 17, then immediately turn right onto Route 691 south. Access to Wildcat Mountain Natural Area is about 4.5 miles down this road. (See Remarks.)

Ownership: The Nature Conservancy.

Wildcat Mountain Natural Area lies on the western slope of Wildcat Mountain. These 650 acres of rugged terrain in the foothills of the Blue Ridge Mountains exhibit vegetation typical of the southern Piedmont (see **Piedmont**). Because until 1940 all of Wildcat Mountain was either farmed or logged at various times, different stages of succession are displayed as the forest gradually reclaims the abandoned clearings (see **#41**). Oak and hickory forests of various ages cover the majority of the Natural Area; some portions are more than 150 years old. A good assortment of plants and animals, also representative of the region, lives here, including more than 170 types of wildflowers and at least 94 species of birds.

The trail climbs steeply through the oak-hickory forest with its dense understory, quickly gaining 700 feet in elevation before leveling off. Traces of farming activities remain. Stone walls, now running seemingly without aim through the woods, once bounded pastures. Stately oaks that grew unimpeded in these pastures now dwarf younger trees that have since taken root. More obvious remnants of this history are the buildings at the Smith Place (**A**). Although it has been abandoned for at least 50 years, daffodils that were planted there continue to bloom each spring. The small man-made pond, which usually dries up in summer, is slowly being encroached upon by the surrounding vegetation. It is here, where the clearing is maintained to provide diversified habitats, that the greatest variety of wildlife—including white-tailed deer, raccoons, red and gray foxes, and an occasional bobcat—is apt to be found.

The trail loops to the left, past old stone buildings and alongside several streams. Red maple, sycamore, and white ash grow along the streams, with spicebush, pawpaw, redbud, and dogwood flourishing beneath them. The greenish rock evident throughout the area, out of which the buildings and fences were built, is greenstone, a low-grade metamorphic rock. Low temperatures and pressures altered the original volcanic material, creating this fine-grained, massive rock (see **#56**).

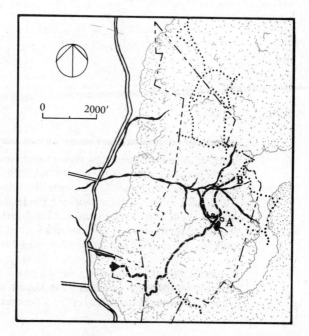

In the vicinity of the Smith Place, where fields were more recently abandoned, patches of Virginia pine and tuliptree, along with black walnut, black locust, and ailanthus, interrupt the oak-hickory forest. At **B**, Virginia pines dominate the old field. The exact successional pattern is largely a function of chance, depending on which sources of seeds are closest at hand and which get established first. However, the seeds of Virginia pine and tuliptree are light and easily scattered over great distances by the wind; they often begin the reforestation of an old field. The larger, heavier seeds of oaks and hickories are dispersed more slowly. After the seeds fall to the ground, they are eaten by animals, transported elsewhere, and deposited in the feces. Once they are established, the oaks and hickories persist, outliving the earlier pioneering trees and preventing their return by shading out the young growth.

Remarks: *For permission to visit Wildcat Mountain Natural Area and specific directions to the area, contact the Virginia field office of the Nature Conservancy at 619 E. High St., Charlottesville, Va. 22901, (804) 295-6106. Species lists are available from the Nature Conservancy. Complete inventories have not been made; additions are welcomed. All wildlife, including plants, is protected and should not be harmed or removed. Camping and picnicking are not permitted.*

41.
Ivy Creek
Natural Area

Directions: **Albemarle County, Va. From Charlottesville, take U.S. 29 north 0.3 mile past the junction with U.S. 250 Bypass. Turn left onto Hydraulic Rd. (Route 743), which bears left after 1.6 miles. Continue another 0.5 mile, then turn left into the Ivy Creek Natural Area. A small, inconspicuous sign marks this road. The parking area is 0.1 mile ahead. Walk past the restored barn to the white-blazed trail.**

Ownership: **City of Charlottesville, and Albemarle County. Managed by the Parks and Recreation Departments, in cooperation with the nonprofit Ivy Creek Foundation.**

The Ivy Creek Natural Area encompasses 215 acres, once a farm, just outside Charlottesville. The fields and woodlands here show what typically happens in the Piedmont when farmlands are abandoned and nature is allowed to take its course (see **Piedmont**). Overgrown roadbeds and old fencelines, barely discernible as they run through the woods, are reminders—less obvious than the fields and restored barn—that this was once a farm. A continuum of plant associations exists here as the fields slowly revert, ultimately, to a forest of oaks and hickories. Grasses give way to shrubs before the pines and redcedars appear. As time progresses, hardwood trees become established and eventually dominate the forest. Since plant succession tends to follow a somewhat predictable pattern, the different plant communities indicate how long ago various sections of the natural area were last disturbed.

Behind the barn, the white-blazed trail enters a forest of oaks, hickories, tuliptrees, and other hardwood species (**A**). Dogwoods, sassafras, pawpaw, red maple, and maple-leaved viburnum grow beneath the taller trees. A number of ferns provide ground cover,

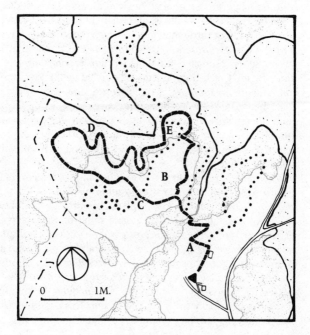

and wildflowers bloom, particularly in spring. Along the White Trail, redcedars, and white, Virginia, and shortleaf pines grow mixed in with the hardwoods. These mixed stands show the transition from earlier stages of succession, when pines dominate, to later stages of mature hardwoods. Prior to this, young pines shade out the grasses and shrubs growing in a field. As they develop, their own seedlings, which require direct sunlight, are unable to grow, and shade-tolerant hardwood saplings spring up in their shade. The transitional stages here find old pine trees joined primarily by younger hardwoods. In the next stage, the pines die out and the hardwoods dominate.

Cross the creek on a small bridge, and follow the trail up the bank on the far side. A field in the early stages of succession stretches off to the right of the trail (**B**). Various grasses, sedges, and other herbaceous plants, like horseweed, broom sedge, and asters, rapidly overrun an abandoned field. Soon, goldenrods, brambles, sumacs, and other shrubs move in. Scattered redcedars, pines, and saplings of such trees as sassafras and black cherry also appear. Summer wildflowers highlight it with color. An older field, more thoroughly invaded by shrubs and trees, lies on the other side of the trail just ahead (**C**). In order to maintain the various stages of succession for educational purposes, some of the fields are mowed periodically.

At the end of the White Trail, bear right onto the Orange Trail, which loops back through woods in which the hardwoods outnumber the pines (**D**). American beech trees abound on this north slope, where the microclimate—the localized climatic conditions—is cooler. Here, the Ivy Creek Natural Area is bounded by the Rivanna Reservoir. The preservation of this undeveloped land helps to protect the watershed. The presence of ground cover impedes the erosion of topsoil. It also impedes runoff, allowing rain water to percolate through the soil and replenish the groundwater. At **E**, turn right onto the Yellow Trail. Go back through the field (**B**) and turn left when you rejoin the White Trail.

When a field reverts to forest, or when any area recovers from a disturbance, the progression of invading plants is called *secondary succession*. (In *primary succession*, plants colonize a place previously devoid of vegetation, such as a sand dune or rocks exposed by glaciers; see **#63**.) The initial changes following a major disturbance are rapid. Pioneering species, tolerant of poor conditions and in need of direct sunlight, appear first. They shade the soil and otherwise alter the immediate environment in such a way as to favor other species. Each successive plant community modifies the environment in some way, usually to its own detriment. This continues until the plant community becomes more or less stable and no longer significantly alters the environment, although some changes are always occurring.

The species which appear in early stages of succession employ very different strategies for survival from the plants which appear later. Those which produce many small seeds (which are easily transported by wind or attached to animals) are the first to become established. These seeds can lie dormant in the soil for a long time, until the environment is suitable for their growth. Once germinated, these sun-loving plants grow rapidly, but remain relatively small even when mature. In contrast, those that dominate the late stages of succession, such as oaks and hickories, produce fewer seeds. These seeds are larger and heavier and are dispersed only by the forces of gravity or by animals that feed on them. The plants grow much more slowly, but they generally attain large proportions. They are also highly tolerant of shade; this increases their competitive abilities. Once established, these late-stage species can live for many years.

When the plant association changes very little and perpetuates itself, a climax community has been reached. As individuals die, they are replaced by species of the same plant association. The term *climax community* has traditionally referred to a specific association of plants that supposedly becomes established in a given climatic region. For instance, the oak-hickory forest has been considered the climax community in the Piedmont. Environmental factors, however, such as topography, exposure, soil nutrients and moisture, temperature, and wildlife activities, are not consistent throughout each region. The composition of the climax communities, then, will vary in accordance with environmental conditions. What were previously thought to be successional stages are now recognized as local climax communities. Pines, for example, may be self-perpetuating on an exposed, rocky ledge even though oaks and hickories comprise the climax forest on adjacent hillsides. A climax community, then, is one that maintains itself under local conditions.

Succession proceeds in one direction, but local factors, such as environmental conditions, the types of plants already present or nearby, and the degree of disturbance, influence the specific sequence of plant succession. This is true even if the climax community for each locality is the same. Disturbances may set back the progression. Clear-cutting can reduce a climax forest to a field, and a severe fire, by burning off almost everything, may create conditions of primary succession. Changes occur even within an established climax community, resulting in a mosaic pattern of vegetation. A tree falls, opening the forest canopy; this allows shade-intolerant species to regain a foothold. The sequence of development may suddenly be altered—a forest fire may destroy all the climax species while leaving a minor, but fire-resistant, species unharmed. Local conditions are then affected by these remaining trees, which dominate the forest until they die. Other climax communities are actually maintained by regular cycles of change. The magnificent sequoia forests of California are a fire-climax community. These giants are resistant to fire, while spruce trees are not. Without fires to remove them from the understory, spruce trees compete with sequoia saplings and prevent their growth.

Debates rage among ecologists over definitions and theories of succession. The ideas discussed here are based largely on the work of Robert E. Ricklets, as presented in *The Economy of Nature* (see **Bibliography**).

Remarks: *The Ivy Creek Natural Area is open for hiking from dawn to dusk. There are 6 miles of trails; maps are available from a bluebird nesting box located near the parking area. Wildlife inventories are not complete, but over one hundred species of birds, most of them typical for the Piedmont, have been recorded to date. Pets are not allowed. For guided walks and information, contact the Ivy Creek Foundation, P.O. Box 956, Charlottesville, Va. 22902, (804) 973-7772.*

42.
Helena's Island
Preserve

Directions: **Nelson County, Va. From Charlottesville, take U.S. 29 southwest about 30 miles. Turn left into Lovington on U.S. 29–Business; after 0.6 mile, turn south (left) onto Route 56. Go southeast 8.9 miles, then turn southwest (right) onto Route 626. See Remarks. For further directions contact the Nature Conservancy.**

Ownership: **The Nature Conservancy.**

Helena's Island Preserve (**A**) beckons curious explorers who enjoy wandering where there are no trails and no guides to the plant and animal life. This 57-acre island in the James River, once farmed, is

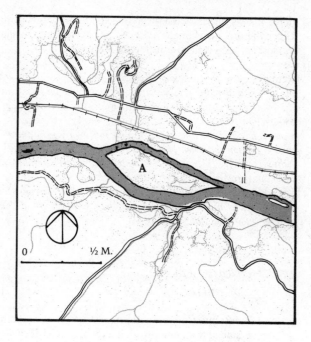

now totally undeveloped. Covered by bottomland vegetation, the tiny island is packed with a variety of plants. A sandy floodplain and small marshy stretches border the perimeter. Sycamores and water willows grow near the ends, while the interior of the island is a junglelike tangle of vines, shrubs, and trees. Spring wildflowers sprinkle the island with color. The island is frequently flooded, which has two major impacts on the vegetation: it keeps the island's forest from maturing (see **#41**), and it also washes in seeds from different environments upstream—hence the diversity of vegetation. One outstanding feature is the grove of 760 black walnut trees that have managed to withstand the floods. This is the only known pure, natural stand of black walnuts greater than five acres in Virginia.

Only a few mammals inhabit the island; a lucky visitor might spot a white-tailed deer or beaver. Amphibians and reptiles, which take to moist habitats, are more plentiful. In spring and fall, warblers pause here on their migratory journeys (see **#17**). Other woodland birds, including red-eyed vireos, Carolina wrens, downy and red-bellied woodpeckers, are present also. Broad-winged and red-shouldered hawks might fly overhead or settle for a moment on a limb. Green herons occasionally pace the sandy beaches, while belted kingfishers keep watch for fish in the water.

Remarks: *The entrance lane is chained off. For permission to visit the preserve and more information on access, contact the Virginia field office of the Nature Conservancy at 619 E. High St., Charlottesville, Va. 22901, (804) 295-6106. The island is accessible only by boat, except when the water is low and you can wade across the narrow river channel. Since you must carry your boat nearly half a mile to the water, use a canoe or other lightweight boat. Once at the James River, put your boat in the water and head downstream, to your left. Helena's Island Preserve is the first island you see. The boat ride takes only a few minutes. There are no boat rentals nearby. The island is labeled "Cunningham Island" on the USGS topographic quadrangle for Shipman, Va.*

Nearby Places of Interest

Just upstream from Helena's Island Preserve, on the south side of the James River, is a calcareous bluff covered with northern white-cedars or arborvitae, hemlocks, and catawba rhododendrons. These and other associated plants, such as bulblet fern and purple-stemmed cliffbrake, are generally found on limestone soils in the Appalachians and are rare in the Piedmont Province. Mixed into this disjunct community are also northern red and chestnut oaks, mountain laurels, and highbush blueberries. The bluffs, which are private property, can be viewed from the river; the best time is in June when the rhododendrons and laurels are in bloom.

Much farther upstream are the Smith Islands, owned by Westvaco Corp. and open to the public for picnicking, fishing, and primitive camping (carry out all trash and do not cut any trees). The closest public boat ramp is at Bent Creek, on the south side of the river, just west of Route 60 on Route 26. Smith Islands are located 0.8 mile above this point. The next public boat ramp is below Helena's Island Preserve, at Wingina on the north shore just west of Route 56. Fishing (with a license) in this 13.6-mile stretch is good for smallmouth bass, redbreast, and channel catfish. For more information about boating and fishing on the James River, contact the Virginia Commission of Game and Inland Fisheries, 4010 W. Broad St., Richmond, Va. 23230, (904) 257-1000.

43.
Sweet Briar
White Oak Woods

Directions: Amherst County, Va. From Charlottesville, Va. travel south on U.S. 29 for about 50 miles. The entrance to Sweet Briar college is on the right. Drive to the public information office, 0.7 mile from the road, and ask for directions. Before starting out, telephone the information office for permission to visit the woods, which are open during the day: (804) 381-6100.

Ownership: Sweet Briar College.

This island of old forest, stretching across the rolling hills of the inner Piedmont (the western edge), is a fine example of mature white-oak woods. In spring and summer the ground is scattered with delicate orchids; thirteen varieties have been identified here. The trees, some of which are over 200 years old, are tall and well spaced. The undergrowth is sparse, as is typical of a mature woodland in this region. A short dirt road winds through the woods.

Before the great chestnut blight that swept America in the early 1900s, this forest was probably a mixed oak-chestnut stand (see #30). Some chestnut sprouts can be found across the road from the sanctuary. Now the white oaks share the canopy with red oaks, tuliptrees, hickories, and blackgums. Beeches and red maples flourish in the cooler, wetter hollows. Throughout the area are several southern species: sourwood, umbrella-tree, and cucumbertree. The abundance of young white oaks indicates that they may continue to be the dominant species in the future. Forecasting forest types from seedlings is tricky; many seedlings will die off or be destroyed by disease or insects. Gypsy moths, which have caused so much damage farther north, fortunately have not infested these woods.

The maximum age for a white oak is generally 350 years. After that, the tree becomes less able to resist disease and the depredations of insects. These trees are considerably younger, no more than 200 years old. Oaks rightly have a reputation for being strong trees. Even a young tree, one that is 30 to 40 years old and growing on rich soils, might have a central taproot that reaches down 5 or 6 feet. Oak trees do not begin to reach maturity until they are 20 to 40 years old, and not until then do they begin to produce acorns. A principal difference between white and red oaks is that the acorns of the white oak family (which includes post oaks, chestnut oaks, and water oaks) are ripe in one year, whereas the acorns of the red oak family take two years to ripen.

One of the striking features of an oak forest is the litter of tough brown leaves that accumulates on the forest floor. Each autumn, deciduous trees must shut down in order to survive the winter. They must reduce the water contained in their cells. If they did not, the cells would burst when the water in them froze. Toward the end of the summer, a corky layer of tissue grows between the branch and the stem of the leaf, cutting it off from the living plant. Now transpiration, the system by which trees pump water from their roots to their leaves and out into the air, can no longer occur. The amount of water within the tissues of the tree is drastically reduced.

The green chlorophyll in the leaves then breaks down quickly, and other pigments become prominent. The brown color of oak leaves is from the pigment in tannin, which is much more resistant to decay than other pigments. When the brightly colored leaves of maples, hickories, and tuliptrees fall to the ground, the yellow and red pigments also fade, revealing the brown of the tannin. As moisture seeps through the dead leaves, it picks up tannin or tannic acid, which contributes to acidity in the soil.

The understory trees, shrubs, and flowering plants are typical of the moist well-drained woods of the Piedmont. Ironwood and dogwood predominate in the understory, while pink azalea, tall deerberry, and American strawberry are the main shrubs. Poison ivy is abundant, especially on the oaks.

It is primarily the absence of human disturbance, not a unique habitat, which makes this preserve an ideal location for orchids. Many of the species found here tolerate soils of varying acidity and moisture content. The majority of them were once quite common in the area.

Red-headed woodpeckers, which have become uncommon in recent years, have begun nesting in the woods, their return coinciding with bumper crops of acorns and beechnuts. The scarcity of these birds throughout the country has been caused by reduction, or elimination, of their habitats, and by the advent of the European starling at the turn of the century—birds that brazenly take over the nesting holes of woodpeckers.

Remarks: *Spring, early summer, and fall are the prime seasons here. No trails have been established in the sanctuary, though there are some old bridle paths. Follow the dirt road that cuts across the woods. Dr. Ernest Edwards, who lives at the sanctuary and knows it well, welcomes visitors. There is camping at Otter Creek in the George Washington National Forest. The campground is on the Blue Ridge Parkway, just north of U.S. 501.*

44.
Willis River
Natural Area

Directions: **Cumberland County, Va. From Richmond go west on U.S. 60, the Midlothian Pike, 46 miles. Turn northeast (right) onto Route 45. Go 5.9 miles to Route 663, a gravel road. Turn north (left) and go 1.9 miles to Route 615. Turn west (left) and go 1.8 miles to Route 608. Turn north (right), go 0.7 mile, and then turn right onto a dirt road. Drive in 0.5 mile to the swinging bridge and park (A).**

Ownership: **Cumberland State Forest, Virginia Division of Forestry.**

On a curve of the Willis River lies a small stand of mature floodplain forest, where willow and pin oaks, tall river birch, black walnut, tuliptree, green ash, sycamore, and other typical floodplain species form the canopy. The lush array of spring flowers includes violets, spring beauties, mertensias, mayapples, trout lilies, and cut-leaved toothworts. To reach the woods, walk southeast from the bridge (upstream) staying close to the banks of the creek, as a guideline, since there is no real trail. The largest trees are found at **B**, many of them over a century old. How this pocket of fine old trees has survived is not clear, for most of the Piedmont has been cut repeatedly.

Floodplains are made up of fine, sandy sediments washed downstream and deposited in terraces along the river bank. This can hap-

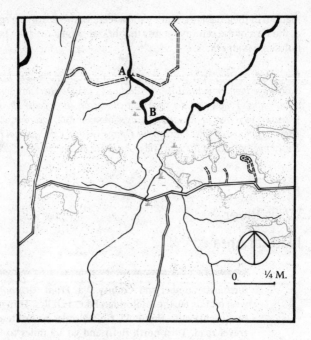

pen during high floods when the rapidly flowing stream runs over the banks. As it does so, the current is slowed by friction as the water spreads out over the land. The water deposits some of its load of sediment, building up the height of the terrace. Terraces may also develop out of a point bar on the inside curve of a meander (see **#94**). Over time, the stream meander becomes more pronounced. As sediments build up on the point bar, the river cuts away further into the outside curve of the meander as well as deeper into its channel. The point bar may eventually become a low-lying terrace, immersed by floodwaters from time to time. Its soils, rich in nutrients and moisture, support a lush growth of trees and other plants.

At the very edge of the stream, life is unstable. There is a tendency for trees to reach out over the water toward the sunlight. This makes them more vulnerable to swift-flowing floodwaters and storm winds. Many trees fall into the river, and succession is often interrupted. River birch dominates the understory and sycamore the canopy at the riverbank. Both these trees are early succession species. Move a few feet back from the stream bank. Here, a climax forest can develop, one made up of species that are shade-tolerant and that reproduce throughout successive generations (see **Piedmont**). The pin and willow oaks, green ash, red maple, hackberry, bitternut hickory, and black walnut you see here are all considered climax species along the floodplains of the Piedmont. Black walnut, a valuable wood for furniture and veneer, has become rarer and rarer as its value increases. Its edible fruits attract birds and mammals. Sweetgum and tuliptree, also found in these woods, are less common in the mature floodplain forest. The understory species include flowering dogwood and hornbeam, while spicebush is the dominant shrub. In the southern Piedmont, spicebush is generally found in the cool, moist bottomlands, while in the north it grows on drier sites. (Compare the floodplain forests at **#8, #11,** and **#68**).

A variety of wildlife is found here and in the adjoining forests: river otter, beaver, bobcat, muskrat, and even a bear from time to time. At dawn and dusk you may spot a mink, a heavy-set animal that is long and sinuous, like a big weasel. The mink is a skillful hunter especially adapted to water. It is a graceful swimmer and its fur is heavy and oily, to keep it from becoming waterlogged. Fierce and quick, it can kill animals larger than itself by biting them on the back of the neck. Minks are solitary creatures—except during the mating season, which begins in early spring. Courtship often involves violent mock battles that last for hours.

Remarks: *At Bear Creek Lake there is camping, fishing, swimming, and boating. To reach the lake go back to U.S. 60 and turn right. Take the third right. No boat rentals are available. In Richmond, Appalachian Outfitters rents canoes (see **#45**). It is possible to canoe Willis Creek, but be prepared for snags. Best seasons are spring and fall.*

45.
James River
Park

Directions: **City of Richmond, Va. The park is a series of scattered parcels of land along the banks of the James from the Huguenot Bridge (Route 147) in the north to Belle Isle under the Lee Bridge (U.S. 301). Most of the park is on the south bank of the river. Coming from the downtown (north) side of the river take I-195, which becomes**

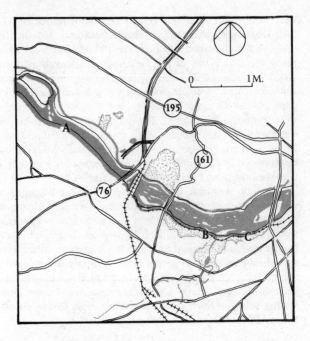

the Powhite Parkway. Cross the James and take the first
exit marked Forest Hill Ave. Turn right. To reach the Pony
Pasture (**A**), proceed 5 blocks to Hathaway and turn right.
After several blocks Hathaway bears left and becomes
Longview. Then bear right on Scottview Dr. Follow it to
the end and bear left where it intersects with Riverside
Dr. Go 0.4 mile to the intersection of Rockfalls Dr. and
Riverside Dr. Turn right and then right again into the Pony
Pasture parking area. To reach the Huguenot Woods An-
nex of the park, continue on Riverside Dr. west for 1.8
miles. Turn right onto Southampton Rd. and park near
the small sign. To reach the nature center (**B**), return to
Forest Hill Rd. and turn east (right). Go to 42nd St. and
turn north (left) to the river. Go to Riverside Dr. and turn
left (west). The entrance is 0.1 mile on the left opposite
Hillcrest. To reach Belle Isle and the Geology Walk (**C**), go
east on Riverside Dr. to 22nd St. and park.

Ownership: **City of Richmond.**

Rumbling over boulders, winding around alluvial islands, the James River wanders through downtown Richmond like a backcountry river, its wooded hills muffling the sound of the city's traffic. Vireos, thrushes, and warblers migrate through the floodplain woods; smallmouth bass of fine size are caught in the river; woodland wildflowers bloom in early spring.

From the Pony Pasture (**A**) you can explore Williams Island and the floodplain of the James. The floodplain is a terrace of soils washed downstream and deposited during very high water. With each new layer of sediment, the plain grows slightly higher, while the river continues to cut down into its bed. The James can rise several feet above normal without running over its banks. Common tree species of the floodplain include sycamore, tuliptree, red maple, boxelder, and hackberry (see **#44**). Spring wildflowers grow abundantly in this environment. Interesting species include germander, speedwell, and bellflower, which are southern plants; morning glory, meadow beauty, and apricot vine, which are northern plants; and a species of western origin, the coltsfoot. Rivers are corridors of transportation for plants as well as human beings (see **Susquehanna River Gorge**). Storm drains bring garden species such as daffodil, snapdragon, and rocket larkspur down to the river and deposit the bulbs and seeds in the alluvial soils. There is one botanical mystery in the region: orchids, which once grew along the floodplain, have disappeared. The Pony Pasture offers the best birding in the city. Spring songbird migrations are impressive in numbers and species. From the parking area, several trails lead eastward through this section of the park.

Just upstream from the Pony Pasture is Williams Island, a beautiful alluvial island with an interesting mixture of habitats. To reach it you can put in a canoe at the Huguenot section of the park or wade across at low water by a small dam half a mile west of the Pony Pasture. The eastern end is high and dry enough to support a forest of mixed hardwoods, including a variety of oaks: white, black, southern red or Spanish, and willow. Other species, such as redcedar, black locust, sweetgum, and winged elm, are early successional species, and thus are indicators of the floods that regularly disturb the area (see **Piedmont**). The western section of the island is covered with more mature floodplain forest. The Pony Pasture and Williams Island, with their assortment of habitats, are excellent places to search for spring migrants.

Retrace your steps to **C**, where the James flows over a ledge of hard igneous rock, part of the fall zone that runs from north to south, marking the division between the uplands of the Piedmont and the lowlands of the Coastal Plain (see **Piedmont** and **#37**). The rocky islands exposed here are made up of Petersburg granite. According to widely accepted theory, the theory of Plate Tectonics, a slow massive collision of the continents of Africa and America, culminating 200 million years ago, created a zone of weakness in the metamorphic rocks here (see **Piedmont**). Molten material was then forced up into the metamorphic rock and hardened into granite. There is considerable debate about the origins of the granite. Was it metamorphic rock which had been heated and melted completely, or was it molten material from beneath the earth's crust? Whatever its origins, this molten material was forced between layers of metamorphic schist and gneiss (see **#16**). Dates for the Petersburg granite cover a wide range from 580 to 330 million years ago.

Along the start of the Geology Trail (**C**), (see directions) the path ascends some steps made from old granite curb stones. To the right are large outcroppings of granite broken by many fractures or joints (see **#16**). In some places you can see examples of slickensides, the smooth surfaces of a fault where two rock faces have moved against each other, polishing the granite (see **#62**). In some of the granite, larger crystals are mixed with much finer crystals. This indicates that the granite had partially crystallized below the earth and then came close to the surface and cooled more rapidly (see **#3**).

Fifty feet higher you will see that the upper surface of the rocks is breaking down into a crumbly, sandy material called *grus*. This is the beginning of soil. The grains are bits of feldspar, quartz, and biotite, minerals of which the granite is composed. The principal agent of destruction is slightly acidic rainwater. As rain falls, it picks up carbon dioxide from the atmosphere and forms a weak carbonic acid that works away at the rock.

The path goes up and over a bridge across the railroad and down to the river again. If the water is low, walk out on the exposed granite. In many of the rocks, potholes have formed. These are tiny versions of the vast cauldrons at the Tubs Natural Area (see **#75**). The pebbles which have shaped these potholes may still be lying in the bottom. If you pick them up, put them back where you found them.

Now walk downriver toward the railroad bridge (**D**). Underneath it, the granite contains irregular dark areas. Here is some of the evidence that molten rock was forced into the schist and gneiss. The dark areas are *xenoliths*, chunks of solid rock that were torn off the existing formations when molten material was injected into the rock layers. These fragments of biotite schist and gneiss can now be found within the granite. The axis of flow is shown by the alignment of parallel bands of minerals in the granite and by the breaking apart of the xenoliths.

Remarks: *The park is closed at night. The visitors' center offers a variety of programs. For further information contact James River Park, Department of Parks and Recreation, 900 E. Broad St., Richmond, Va. 23219, (804) 231-7411. Excellent whitewater canoe and raft trips are run from April through November by James River Experiences, 11010 Midlothian Turnpike, Richmond, Va. 23235, (804) 794-3493. The lower portions of the river have Class 5 rapids at certain times of year. Smallmouth-bass fishing is excellent; largemouth bass, pickerel, and catfish are also caught. State licenses required. Tubing and swimming are popular on the upper portions of the river. Put in at the Pony Pasture. A law forbidding the use of glass bottles on the river and in the park is strictly enforced. Camping is available at Pocahontas State Park about 20 miles to the southwest of the city, west of Route 10 on Route 655.*

46.
Buffalo Creek
Nature Area

Directions: **Campbell County, Va. From Lynchburg, take U.S. 29 south about 8 miles to Route 24. Turn west (right) and drive about 8 miles, passing the town of Evington. The parking area (A) is on the south side (left) in a large field opposite the sign marking the boundary between Campbell and Bedford counties. The trail to the hemlocks crosses the field, then leads into the woods.**

Ownership: **Westvaco Corp.**

In the midst of a rich upland oak-hickory forest stand six acres of eastern hemlocks (**B**). Follow the fairly level trail, about three-quarters of a mile each way, through oaks and hickories to the hemlocks, clinging to the shallow soil of the steep, rocky slope that rises abruptly from Buffalo Creek. The dominant hemlocks, about 130 years old, stand 100 feet tall and 20 inches in diameter. Many others of equal age are smaller, because of less favorable growing conditions, such as crowding. An understory is conspicuously lacking; only a few plants, such as mountain laurel, manage to survive in the dense shade and acidic conditions produced by the hemlocks. Unlike many conifers, hemlocks are exceptionally tolerant of low light levels, and

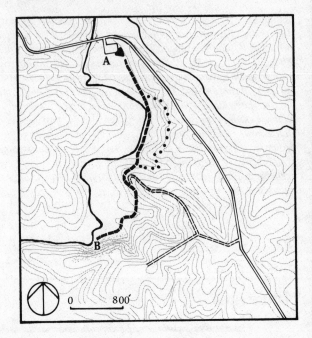

can regenerate in their own shade. Seedlings, in fact, can survive even if they receive only 5 per cent of full sunlight. Hemlocks can germinate on mineral soil, well-decomposed litter, or other poorly developed soil, and this helps ensure their continuance, barring outside disturbances. Fires, for instance, are devastating to hemlocks, for their thin bark offers little protection.

Stands of hemlocks like this are found throughout the upper Piedmont (see **#47**), although they are outside their normal range there. While common in the nearby Blue Ridge Mountains, primarily at elevations higher than 800 feet, here these trees thrive between 550 and 700 feet of elevation. Outside the mountains, hemlocks are usually found only on north-facing slopes, generally undercut by a stream, where the microclimate is sufficiently cool and moist. These stands are relics from the Ice Age, a time when the climate, influenced by the glaciers to the north, was much colder and hemlocks and other northern species prevailed.

The history of this particular stand is not clear. Shortleaf pines, 120 years old, are scattered about. These early pioneering trees indicate that the area was once cleared, possibly by ice or wind storms or other natural catastrophes. However, no evidence of fire has been found in the stand of hemlocks. A number of oaks more than 200 years old rise above the younger hemlocks. Other species of trees, such as beech, blackgum, hickory, tuliptree, and dogwood, are mixed in with the hemlocks. These hardwoods are younger than both the hemlocks and the surrounding forest, which is 80 to 100 years old. The hemlocks are spreading into adjacent hollows and onto the ridge, where the seedlings thrive in the shade of the hardwoods. Evidence indicates that logging activities ceased by the mid-1800s and that at least one fire swept through the adjacent oak and hickory forest in the past. Exactly what sequence of events enabled the hemlocks to become established is still somewhat of a mystery.

Remarks: *Brochures with a map are available at the trailhead. An annual wildflower walk and woodland tour is held in the last week of April. Hunting is allowed by permit only (be careful during hunting season—see **#47**). For more information, contact Westvaco Corp., Timberlands Division, P.O. Box WV, Appomattox, Va. 24522, (804) 352-7132.*

47.
Bannister River
Hemlock Slope

Directions: **Pittsylvania County, Va. From Richmond take U.S. 360 about 105 miles southwest. Before South Boston, turn west (right), staying on U.S. 360 going to Halifax. Drive 6.4 miles and turn north (right) on U.S. 501. Drive 7.1 miles and turn west (left) on Route 642. Drive 2.8 miles and go right on Route 832. Drive 13.5 miles and turn north (right) on Route 640. Drive 2.1 miles and turn right on Route 649. Drive 1.2 miles to the trailhead on the left.**

Ownership: **White Oak Mountain Wildlife Area, Virginia Commission of Game and Inland Fisheries.**

Along north-facing slopes in the Virginia Piedmont are isolated stands of hemlock, far south of the extensive hemlock forests of Pennsylvania and New York and separate from those of the western moun-

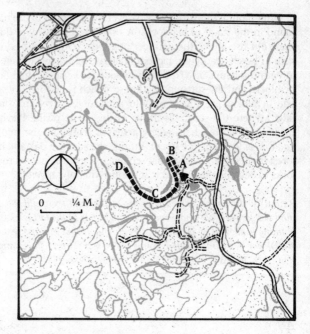

tains of Virginia. One such stand clings to a precipitous hillside on a sinuous curve of the Bannister River.

From the gate, walk about 5 minutes along the rough road past a small man-made pond. The track bears around to the left, and a white-blazed trail turns off to the right. Follow this trail as it passes along the top of the cliff and down to the water's edge. The woods at the top of the cliff are largely mixed oak, with chestnut oak the dominant species. Chestnut oak is common in the dry mountain ridges to the west, an environment similar to this one. It is rarely found in the moister soils of the Piedmont. At **A** a small rocky outcrop overlooks the Bannister Ridge, covered with Virginia and shortleaf pine, the common pines in this part of the Piedmont, in dry, open sites with poor soil. Now the trail heads down to the riverside terrace of deeper, moister soils. Here willow oaks, sweet-gums, hickories, and some beeches come into the forest, and the chestnut oaks disappear. This mixture of species is common on well-watered sites in the Piedmont that have been cut many times. Along the flats (**B**), look for Lewis's heartleaf on or under the leaf litter, in April and May when the small, bell-shaped flower is in bloom beneath the glossy heart-shaped leaves. The blossom is an unusual color, brown on the outside and purple on the inside, with long hairs in the throat. The Lewis's heartleaf is found only in bottomland woods with acid soil in the middle Piedmont, from south-central Virginia to North Carolina.

Now turn south and follow the riverbank around the curve of the meander. At the deepest point of the curve, look up at the slope to your left (**C**). The deciduous forest has given way to hemlocks, a small stand of trees of good size and considerable age. The north-facing slopes, protected from the sun, provide a cool, moist microclimate favorable to hemlock. These hemlock slopes are relics of large evergreen forests that covered much of the Piedmont when the southern United States lay in the shadow of the ice sheet that stopped hundreds of miles to the north during the last glacial advance (see **Piedmont**). Below the hemlock, mountain laurel is abundant—another northern plant that, this far south, is generally found only in the mountains.

The escarpment on the southern side of the river stands in sharp contrast to the gentler countryside on the northern bank. The cliff is part of a belt of sedimentary sandstones and shales from the Triassic period that run through this part of Virginia (see **Piedmont**). The Bannister River has carved out the cliff exposed here.

On the far side of the hemlock slope, the land drops again into another terrace along the river (**D**). Here one finds a second endemic Piedmont plant, *Nestronia umbellula,* known locally as bog asphodel (not to be confused with a different plant called asphodel in the Pine Barrens of New Jersey). This is a low, parasitic shrub that lives on the roots of oaks and pines from Virginia to Georgia. Its small, greenish flowers bloom in May or June. Only one species of this genus lives in North America; the other members are found in Asia.

Remarks: *This is a wildlife management area open for hunting at specific times throughout the year. Deer hunting in Virginia generally runs from mid-November to early January. A number of small ponds on the tract are stocked with largemouth bass and bluegills. There is some fishing in the Bannister River. Many informal trails and dirt roads pass through the area. Camping at Staunton River State Park east of South Boston on Route 344. For further information contact the Commission of Game and Inland Fisheries, P.O. Box 11104, Richmond, Va. 23230.*

The New York–
New Jersey
Highlands:
An Ancient Fastness

When the summer sun broils New York City, many of its residents trek up the Hudson Valley to the cool woodlands of Bear Mountain State Park. There, less than 50 miles from the sizzling pavements of Manhattan, they share a sylvan environment with white-tailed deer, red fox, and other creatures of the countryside that have managed to adapt to life on the city's fringes. In winter, visitors are fewer, mostly skiers and hikers willing to brave the cold. Then in the still woods one hears only the wind rattling the skeletal branches of denuded oaks, hickories, and maples. At this time of year, the Bear Mountain woodlands seem a true wilderness, despite proximity to some of the nation's most thickly-settled areas.

The sense of wilderness at Bear Mountain typifies the upland region to which it belongs, called the Hudson Highlands in New York and the New Jersey Highlands in the Garden State. The division between the two is a political boundary; geologically, they are one.

Although these uplands are not particularly high—the highest are slightly over 1000 feet in altitude—they are rugged, carved into myriad valleys and peaked with rocky crests. The face they present today results from geologic activity that is relatively recent, but their roots are ancient. The rock upon which the Highlands are founded dates back a billion years.

The Highlands stand upon a finger of primal bedrock that extends northeast from Reading, Pennsylvania, to Bear Mountain, then across the Hudson River to Peekskill, New York. From Bear Mountain, the Highlands run

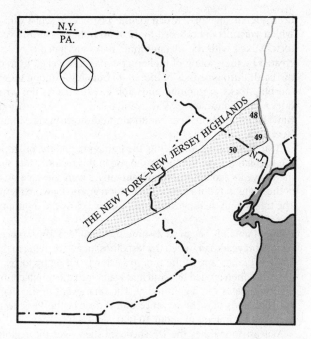

along the border of Rockland and Orange counties in New York and encompass the entire north-central part of New Jersey, centering in both western Passaic and Morris counties and eastern Sussex and Warren counties.

Known as the Reading Prong, the bedrock on which the Highlands are based is an extension of a much vaster complex of similar rock, which underlies mountains from the Blue Ridge of North Carolina and Virginia to the Green Mountains of Vermont. The portion of the Highlands in the Peekskill area is an outpost, separated by the great gorge of the Hudson from the bulk of these uplands, and because of its location it is seemingly linked to the Berkshires of northwestern Connecticut and the Green Mountains. From Bear Mountain to the Pennsylvania border, however, the Highlands constitute an entity, with distinct bounds—the great basin of the New Jersey Lowland on the east and the Ridge and Valley Province of the Appalachians of the west.

Generations of geologists have been fascinated by the age and complexity of the Highlands. Eons of geologic upheavals have jumbled and obscured the story of the Reading Prong, but some of it has been pieced together. Much of the bedrock is schist and gneiss, which was metamorphosed by heat and pressure from even older rock. Mixed with the metamorphic rocks are igneous rocks, those created by the cooling of molten material that welled from deep in the earth during periods of mountain building. Among these metamorphic rocks are granite and diorite, like that in the weathered ridges that stand above Wawayanda Park near Greenwood Lake, New Jersey, and on Bear Mountain and Storm King Mountain in New York.

Bear Mountain, Storm King, the Ramapos, and the other peaks of the Highlands were not the first to rise in this region. More than 500 million years ago, several mountain ranges were elevated on the site of the Highlands but vanished as erosion gradually wore them away. The traces of these ranges are buried deep below the mountains one sees today.

The Highlands began to assume their modern appearance about 70 million years ago, when the last dinosaurs were dying in the dust. The level landscape of the time was slowly raised by forces within the earth, then eroded by wind and water into the rough countryside that dominates the region today. The final event in the shaping of the Highlands was the advance and retreat of the Pleistocene glaciers, from 2 million to about 10,000 years ago.

At least four times the ice sheets pushed over the region, their farthest advance halting in the vicinity of Raritan Bay, New Jersey. As the ice moved over the landscape, it dropped errant boulders about the countryside and scraped and scratched the earth to bedrock. Even the bedrock was gouged in many places, so that valleys and depressions were formed.

The ice also left behind a rubbly mix of sediments, including sands, clays, and gravels of assorted sizes. Some of this material, called *till*, piled up and blocked streams of meltwater flowing from the shrinking ice. The water, thus diverted, flowed into some of the depressions scooped out of the bedrock. Wawayanda Lake grew from such a process. Other depressions became the site of swamps, which in modern times have been cleared and dammed, forming lakes such as Tiorati near Bear Mountain.

Looming above the Hudson River, the Highlands of the Bear Mountain area are dramatically scenic. From a distance, their wooded heights seem as primeval as they must have looked to the European explorers who surveyed them in the seventeenth century. The impression, however, is superficial because the forests of the Highlands have been cut many times since they were first settled by colonists. Even so, the Highlands have forested tracts of surprising extent. And in some areas, such as Black Rock Forest in New York, the mixture of trees is much the same as when Europeans first arrived.

Oaks and hickories dominate the Highlands forests, as they do in nearby areas of southern New England. American beeches, tuliptree, ash, and yellow birch are also abundant. Sweetgum, a southern tree, approaches the northern extreme of its range in the Highlands. Conversely, black spruce, scattered here and there in the Highlands, is rarely found farther south. Striped maple and white-cedar are other predominantly northern trees also growing in the Highlands.

Most of the trees that extend into the Highlands from more northerly areas thrive best at higher elevations, such as along the tops of ridges and the upper slopes of mountain peaks. The difference of hundreds of feet between the highest elevations of the Highlands and the valley floors below makes for a considerable climatic variation between the two. Snow cover often lasts longer in the spring on the ridges, for instance, than on the lower slopes.

In the trees and brush of the upper elevations can be found several birds more typical of northern New York State, such as the Blackburnian warbler and brown creeper. Lower on the slopes are birds that have extended their range northward—the cardinal and tufted titmouse, for instance. Together with birds characteristic of this part of the northeast, such as towhee and ruffed grouse, the mix of northern and southern species makes the Highlands a delight for the birder.

In places like Bear Mountain small herds of white-tailed deer are sometimes seen browsing by the side of roads. In some areas they are so numerous that the forest understory is oddly bare, the result of overbrowsing. The deer are among the prey of a predator new to the area, the eastern coyote, which arrived in the past few decades. The larger forests also support small populations of bobcat and black bear. Flying squirrels, red squirrels, and gray squirrels skitter through the trees, while cottontail rabbits and a variety of small rodents scurry about the woodland floor.

The wildlife of the Highlands is today more varied and abundant than a century or so ago, when most of the forest had been cleared for agriculture. White-tailed deer, for example, were rare in the Highlands during the 1870s. When the European settlers first ventured into the area, however, the area teemed with wild animals; indeed, today's fauna is only a shadow of that of the past. Black bears, now rare, and cougars, which have vanished, once thrived in the Highlands. Myriad passenger pigeons—extinct today as a species—roosted in deep forest groves and filled the air with their flights.

When the settlers arrived, the Highlands were the hunting grounds of a varied group of Indian tribes, including the Esopus, Minisinks, and Haverstraws, who were part of a larger assemblage collectively known as Delawares, although they were never a single tribe. Under the pressure of the Dutch and later the English, the Indians retreated from the Highlands. Long before the Revolution they had relocated westward in such places as the Susquehanna Valley of Pennsylvania. The croplands and pastures of the colonists replaced the woodlands in which the Indians had hunted.

Parts of the Highlands forest were also leveled for lumber and for charcoal. At Bear Mountain charcoal-burning as an industry flourished from colonial times to the mid-nineteenth century. Another industry that developed in portions of the Highlands was mining. Iron was mined at Bear Mountain during the 1800s and in Sussex County near Franklin and Ogdensburg, also a center for zinc mining for many decades.

Lying close to New York City, the Highlands today contain a number of bedroom communities, particularly on their eastern edge, and scattered throughout are sizable towns and small cities. Yet the Highlands are remarkably wild, with their outcrops of ancient rock, lush valleys laced with streams, and miles of woodland hiking trails. From the region's western border, one can see the ridges of the Kittatinny Mountains, the gateway to the more rugged mountains of the interior Appalachians.

—Edward Ricciuti

48.

Bear Mountain and Harriman State Parks

Directions: **Orange and Rockland counties, N.Y. From New York City, take the Palisades Interstate Parkway about 30 miles north to Exit 14A. Follow Tiorati Brook Rd. 4 miles to Lake Tiorati Circle. Go two thirds of the way around the circle and park in the picnic area. Walk about 0.3 mile along that road (Arden Valley Road) to the white-blazed Appalachian Trail and turn left on it into the woods.**

Ownership: **Palisades Interstate Park Commission and N.Y. State Office of Parks and Recreation.**

Bear Mountain and Harriman State Parks encompass 80 square miles about 40 miles from New York City. During the summer, hordes of people throng to the lakes and cool woods of the parks, but during the rest of the year, one can explore the varied habitats in restful solitude. Miles of trails crisscross the wooded hills, passing lakes, streams, and swamps far from the sounds of automobiles. Deer, rabbit, or any one of a variety of birds may be encountered. The parks harbor a great number of different animal species. Records list 39 mammals, 246 birds (94 of which nest here), 24 reptiles, 20 amphibians, and 31 fish. Several unusual species are included, such as otter, mink, weasel, beaver, and bobcat. Birding is good year round. Turkey vultures, broad-winged hawks, and pileated woodpeckers nest here, as do many warblers—worm-eating, black-throated green, black-throated blue, Blackburnian, hooded, and Canada warblers.

Bear Mountain and Harriman State Parks lie in the Hudson Highlands, which is part of the Reading Prong. This upland of ancient rocks extends from Reading, Pa., through New Jersey and southeastern New York, and into Connecticut. It then becomes the Berkshire and the Green Mountains in Massachusetts and Vermont (see **New York–New Jersey Highlands** regional essay). These rocks were subjected to several episodes of mountain-building which folded, faulted, and metamorphosed them. Predominantly banded gneisses, these metamorphic rocks, known as the Highland Complex, are the oldest rocks in the vicinity, the initial major metamorphic event

157

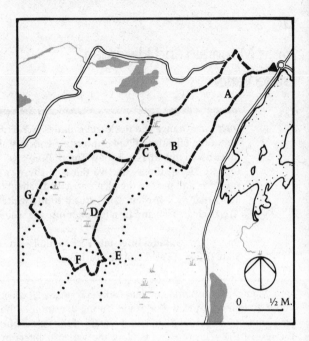

having occurred over a billion years ago. At intervals over the subsequent millions of years, molten rock, or magma, was forced upward into these rocks. The last major intrusion, 600 to 700 million
years ago, yielded the pinkish-gray Storm King granite. Because it is
the most resistant rock in the Hudson Highlands, this granite forms
the crests of the highest ridges, including Bear Mountain.

After millions of years, these rocks were finally exposed at the
surface. During the Pleistocene ice ages that ended some 10,000
years ago, glaciers scraped and scoured the rocks, leaving them polished, scratched, and grooved. They were barren of soil, and littered
with glacial debris, called till (see **#68**) and large blocks, or erratics,
transported from the north. Thousands of years of weathering have
lessened the prominence of the glacial striations. Swamps now lie in
many of the glacier-carved depressions. Of the numerous lakes scattered throughout the park, only Hessian and Brooks lakes are natural. The rest were originally swamps, dammed and cleared by the
Civilian Conservation Corps and other work crews.

The vegetation is influenced by climate and by past human activities. The parks lie in a transition zone between the oak-hickory
forest common to the south and the hemlocks and northern hard-

woods that grow to the north (see **Catskill Mountains**). The Hudson River warms the climate, enabling the oaks and hickories to invade farther north. Differences in habitat, from ridgetops to valley bottoms and from dry rocks to wet swamps, also affect the vegetation. As a result, the forest is quite varied. Red and chestnut oaks, pignut hickories, black birches, white ashes, red maples, and tuliptrees mix with hemlocks, white pines, yellow birches, sugar maples, and American beeches. Wildflowers, ferns, mosses, and lichens flourish throughout the parks.

Many plant species were introduced by early settlers. They are but one aspect of past human influence. The forest has been ravaged again and again. From colonial days until the beginning of this century, people cut trees for firewood, timber, and charcoal-making; and used tannin from the bark of hemlocks to tan leather. Most of the area was cleared during the Revolutionary War. Iron mining flourished in the early and mid-1800s. Scattered farms were active until the turn of the century. Ground fires, often started by careless visitors, have frequently swept across the ridges. Although nature has slowly healed itself and hidden many of the scars, telltale signs linger.

The open woods (**A**) encountered at the beginning of this hike are typical of many ridges in the park, where widely spaced trees rise above stretches of grasses, sedges, or low shrubs. Bluebirds, rare in Rockland County, often nest in these areas. The shallow soil supports rather stunted trees, and much bedrock is exposed. Hot ground fires have killed all the small trees, shrubs, and ground cover. They have recurred often enough to prevent much regrowth, thus creating and maintaining the open, parklike setting.

As the Appalachian Trail (blazed white) drops over the ridge at **B**, the vegetation shifts from mixed hardwoods to predominately hemlocks. These northern trees thrive in the cool ravines and on north-facing slopes. Mountain laurels are abundant. Before crossing Surebridge Brook (**C**), turn left onto Lost Rd., an old, obvious but unmarked road lined with hemlocks and large rhododendrons. On the left, water-filled pits (which are dangerous) mark the location of an iron mine. The dark black rock taken from the mine lies in nearby piles.

Surebridge Swamp (**D**) is located about a half-mile farther down the road. This extensive wetland is filled with sphagnum moss, high-bush blueberries, swamp azaleas, cranberries, and other swamp plants. You may also find buttonbush, spicebush, alders, poison-sumac, swamp honeysuckle, and sweet pepperbush. Many mosses, ferns, skunk cabbage, and blue flag cover the ground, while blackgums, red maples, and tuliptrees stand tall.

Beyond the swamp, at a large rock labeled "Times Square" (**E**), turn right onto the Ramapo-Dunderburg Trail (blazed with a red dot in a white circle). The trail climbs to the ice-smoothed ledges of Ship Rock (**F**) that support some pitch pines and offer good views of the surrounding countryside. Then follow the Lichen Trail (blazed with a blue L in a white square) to the right, across rocks textured and colored by gray, brown, and green lichens (see **#115**). At the end of the Lichen Trail, turn left onto the Arden-Surebridge Trail (blazed red). It joins the Appalachian Trail and weaves through an unusual rock formation called the Lemon Squeezer (**G**). The freezing and thawing of water (see **#118**), and other types of weathering, apparently forced gigantic blocks of rock to separate along joints and to fall askew, creating unusual and narrow passageways.

Follow the Appalachian Trail about 0.3 mile back to Surebridge Brook, turn left and walk along Lost Road to the Long Path Trail (blazed blue), then turn right onto it. The trail passes a small wetland; its fringe of phragmites is another sign of human activity. Phragmites generally grows on land that has been disturbed, such as fill. This trail leads back to the road. The starting point is less than a half-mile to the right.

Remarks: *Allow all day for this hike, which is about 8 miles long. Activities at the parks include fishing (with a license), boating (rentals are available at some lakes; private boats by permit only), hiking (there are over 200 miles of trails), picnicking, and camping. Ski-touring trails are maintained in winter. The Bear Mountain Trailside Museums and nature trails are located off U.S. 6 and U.S. 202, just before the Bear Mountain Bridge. Trail maps are available at the museums and information stations scattered in the park (there is an information station near Lake Tiorati). The park is extremely crowded in summer. Parking is allowed only in designated areas; there may be a fee. Buses and tour boats go to Bear Mountain from New York City. For International Bus Lines schedules, call Port Authority information at (212) 564-8484. Contact the Hudson River Day Line for boat schedules in summer at (212) 279-5151. For more information contact Palisades Interstate Park Commission, Administration Headquarters, Bear Mountain, N.Y. 10911, (914) 786-2701.*

Nearby Places of Interest

The summit of Bear Mountain offers extensive views and good hawk-watching in the fall. Seven Lakes Dr. can be productive for bird-watching. Waterfowl rest on Lake Tiorati in late fall.

West Point Military Academy grounds also offer good birding opportunities. From U.S. 9W by Fort Montgomery, just north of Bear Mountain Circle, follow Mine Rd. west to Route 293. The road is open to the public unless otherwise posted.

Two other nearby places to explore are Black Rock Forest and Schunemunk Mountain. The *New York Walk Book*, revised by the New York-New Jersey Trail Conference and the American Geographical Society, provides trail and other information (see **Bibliography**).

49.

Iona Marsh

Directions: **Rockland County, N.Y. From New York City go north on the Palisades Parkway about 40 miles toward Bear Mountain Bridge. Turn south (left) at the traffic circle on 9W. Iona Marsh is 1 mile south of the Bear Mountain Bridge. Park on the east (left) side of the highway and turn east (left) onto the causeway across the marsh to the railroad tracks and park.**

Ownership: **Palisades Interstate Park Commission.**

Iona Marsh, a National Natural Landmark, lies along the Hudson River, pressed against the hills of the Hudson Highlands. On a sunny autumn evening, it is a golden pocket of cattails seamed with blue canals. In the middle of the marsh is a rocky knoll covered with a deep mantle of mosses.

This is a brackish—slightly salty—river marsh. Fifty miles from the ocean, the Hudson is still tidal here. The salinity of the marsh varies significantly, depending on the rainfall upstream. In the 1970s, when there was abundant rainfall, the Hudson ran full and strong, pushing the seawater downstream, so that the river at Iona was only mildly brackish. Wild rice, a plant with a very low tolerance for salt, was common. The last several years have been much drier, the power of the river weaker. As the sea encroached northward, Iona became saltier, and the wild rice has all but vanished; big cordgrass, which is a brackish-water relative of the salt-marsh cordgrasses, has taken its place.

The rhythmic flow of water through a tidal marsh makes it among the most fertile and productive of all wetland ecosystems, producing more vegetation per acre than even agricultural lands. The river continually carries sediment and soluble nutrients downstream; these feed the marsh plants. Surface roots, stems, and fallen leaves of the marsh plants trap the nutrients and sediments brought by the incoming tide, while partially decomposed plant parts, with their associated microorganisms, are washed out of the marsh with the outgoing tide, feeding organisms in the river throughout the year. Water moving through the marsh brings a good oxygen supply, as does drainage of the marsh at low tide. This is different from the still waters of many swamps and marshes, where lack of oxygen poses major problems for plants, inhibiting both growth and diversity.

The rise and fall of the daily tides adds another dimension to the river marsh. Without it, the marshes would be much smaller, or perhaps nonexistent, for the high tide spreads out over a greater area than does the normal downstream flow of the river. The ebb tide is particularly vigorous, combining the currents of the tide with those of the river. Cutting across the path of the outgoing tide is the causeway. Because it inhibits the free flow of nutrient-rich waters over the southern portion of the marsh, the plantlife is less vigorous in here than to the north. Higher levels of salt undoubtedly play a part as well. The rising tide with its cargo of salt from the ocean filters in, whereas the ebb tide, now less salty because it has mixed with fresh river water upstream, is hindered by the causeway. One sign of changing conditions in the southern marsh is the rapid advance of purple loosestrife, which takes hold and thrives in disturbed areas. This beautiful Eurasian plant, which has little food value for wildlife, appears to be replacing cattail, a very important source of food and nesting material for animals and birds of the estuary.

The causeway is a good vantage point from which to look out over the marsh. The abundance of plant species here is a striking contrast to the uniformity of a coastal salt marsh (see Mid-Atlantic coastal volume). The difference is, not surprisingly, due to the much lower concentrations of salt combined with the flow of the river. Birdlife in the marsh is similar to that in the coastal marshes. During the spring and summer, look for long-billed marsh wrens, swamp sparrows, ospreys, gallinules, least bitterns, and herons. In winter, red-tailed hawks and an occasional bald eagle swing in the sky.

After about a quarter-mile, you will come to the rocky ridge that forms the spine of Iona island. South of the road, the ridge becomes a promontory, where a young mixed-hardwood forest of oaks, birches, and striped maples provides deep shade that, in turn, preserves moisture needed by the mosses on the forest floor. There is no path, but it is only a short scramble to the top of the hummock. At the top, conditions become very dry. Chestnut oaks and blueberry bushes predominate. In an opening in the cover lies a thick mat of eastern prickly-pear cactus, which sports a mass of purple blooms in July. The cactus is uncommon partly because it requires an exceptional amount of sunlight; it is thus an early succession plant and will probably be shaded out here as the forest thickens. The mosses and the cacti are extremely vulnerable, and one should be careful not to walk on them. From the hummock, you can look out over the marsh in several directions. In early morning or evening, this is an excellent place to look for deer grazing or passing through the marsh below you.

Return to the causeway and continue east about a quarter-mile. On your left is a small freshwater swamp, a thicket of crack willow and red maple. The swamp sits in a pocket of the rocky island, protected from the brackish water of the river. In spring you may find Stewardson's jack-in-the-pulpit, a plant of Canada and the Appalachians. Somewhat later greenwoodland orchid and Loesel's twayblade, another orchid, flower on the mossy hummocks of the swamp.

Remarks: *You will need sneakers to climb up the rocky hummock. Avoid entering the marsh, which is full of poison oak; you can canoe along its streams and edges. There are no canoe rentals nearby. Many people come to fish here; a license is required. During high tide the causeway may be flooded. Camping at Bear Mountain State Park, which also has many miles of hiking trails (see **#48**). For further information contact the Palisades Interstate Park Commission, Administration Building, Bear Mountain, N.Y. 10911, (914) 786-2701.*

50.

Wawayanda

State Park

Directions: Sussex County, N.J. From New York City, take I-80 west about 10 miles to Route 23. Turn north (right) and go about 18 miles. Turn northeast (right) on Union Valley Rd. (Route 513) and go 7 miles. Bear left and go 2 miles. Bear left again onto White Rd. and go 1.0 mile. Bear left on Warwick Pike. Go 4.5 miles and turn left into the park. Follow the road 3 miles to Wawayanda Lake. Park in the second lot by the boathouse. Walk east about a half mile from the parking area along the dirt road to the old barn. The Double Pond Trail begins here by a wooden signpost.

Ownership: New Jersey Division of Parks and Forestry.

The Wawayanda Plateau, perched on the New Jersey Highlands, is part of the Reading Prong, a finger of very ancient mountains formed long before the Appalachians (see **New York–New Jersey Highlands**). Wawayanda is one of the few places along the highlands where the granite bedrock is visible. This rock is about 1 billion years old, the oldest rock you will see in the Mid-Atlantic region. The Double Pond Trail, marked with blue blazes, starts at the picnic ground and climbs a small ridge (**A**), where weathered hunks of granite lie. They were exposed by the ice sheets (see **New York–New Jersey Highlands**) and broken up by water freezing in minute cracks within the rock (see **#118**).

Granite is igneous rock, formed by the melting and cooling of a variety of minerals. It is dense and impermeable. Thus, especially on such a flat plateau as this, water collects in small depressions and forms swamps, making the whole area generally moister than land to the east or west. The trees on the ridge are hemlocks, beeches, oaks, and red maples, indicating that even such elevated spots are moderately moist.

After about a mile go south (right) on Cedar Swamp Trail (**B**). In the pockets of the swamp, both the northern and the Atlantic white-cedar are found. The northern white-cedar is at the extreme southern limit of its habitat and is seldom found elsewhere in New Jersey.

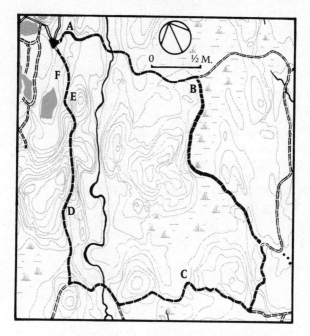

Rhododendron also grows profusely in this acidic, wet environment; it blooms from late June to early July.

Continue to bear right for a mile and a half. The trail ends at Cherry Ridge Rd.; turn west (right). At **C**, groves of beeches dominate. These fast-growing, shade-tolerant trees form part of the climax forest, for their sprouts can flourish in the shade of the larger trees, while the birches, black cherry, and aspens disappear as the forest grows up (see **#41**). Farther along are the remains of old farms (**D**). Creeping red fescue, a lush and delicate grass, grows in the shade, probably planted by the residents of this old homestead. So is the barberry, a thorny shrub that also grows here. A little farther, on the right, is a "wolf tree," an old shade tree that grew in an open spot—a field or yard. With no competition for light, it grew into a spreading, bushy specimen. Now, the forest is taking over and will eventually overshadow it.

Follow Laurel Pond Trail to the northeast (right); it is marked by yellow blazes. The trail passes through an impressive field of granite cliffs and boulders (**E**). A small, pure stand of eastern hemlock lies to the left of the trail at **F**. Borings of soil taken to the depth of the bedrock contain only plant remains from hemlocks, indicating that no hardwoods have grown here since the last ice sheet retreated northward about 15,000 years ago.

Remarks: *Wawayanda is open all year. This walk takes about 2 hours of moderate hiking. Parts of the trail are very wet in the spring; wear rubber boots. Group camping is available in the park. For further information contact Wawayanda State Park, Box 198, Highland Lakes, N.J. 07422, (201) 853-4462. There are extensive hiking trails east of the park on Bearfort Mountain and at Abram S. Hewitt State Forest, and northeast of the park in Sterling Forest in New York. These areas are all on the highlands. For further hiking information see the Hiker Region Map series published by Walking News, Inc., P.O. Box 352, New York, N.Y. 10013.*

The Blue Ridge:
Eastern Rampart
of the Appalachians

Across the western horizon of the Piedmont runs a long, smoky blue line of low mountains, harbingers of the higher peaks to the west. The ancient, gentle hills of the Blue Ridge Mountains form the eastern rampart of the Appalachians from Pennsylvania to Georgia, a distance of some 550 air miles. The Roanoke River, the southernmost stream to flow eastward through the range, divides the Blue Ridge Province into two distinctly different parts and determines the southern boundary of the region covered by this volume. North of the Roanoke River, *ridge* is an appropriately descriptive term, for generally there is a central "backbone" with subordinate ridges grouped about it. At the extreme north, in Pennsylvania, the province actually narrows to a single low crest. Then between the fertile Frederick and Hagerstown valleys of Maryland the range rises abruptly as the Catoctin–South Mountain complex. The drainage descent is precipitous on both sides of the main ridge, resulting in the formation of short canyons and numerous cascades, rapids, and waterfalls such as South River Falls in Shenandoah National Park. In fact, topography is rugged throughout the region, with less than 10 percent of the surface area having a slope of less than 10 percent. The two highest summits in Shenandoah National Park—Hawksbill Mountain, 4050 feet, and Stony Man Mountain, 4010 feet—are in this northern portion of the range. Shenandoah National Park, with its steep wooded hills and abundant wildlife, is the heartland of the Blue Ridge. The Skyline Drive, a 105-mile roadway through the park, extends from Front Royal to

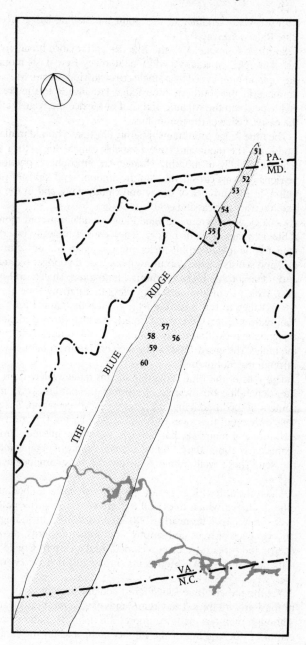

Rockfish Gap, Virginia. At this point the Skyline Drive meets the Blue Ridge Parkway.

South of Roanoke, Va., the Blue Ridge Province broadens; near Asheville, N.C., it attains a width of 80 miles. Here it is a mountainous upland not pierced by a single cross-flowing stream. Most of the drainage of the southern Blue Ridge Province is to the west, the divide between the Atlantic and Gulf of Mexico drainage lying near the eastern edge of the mountains.

The Blue Ridge Mountains superbly illustrate a humid midlatitude landscape. The mountains have a variable climate due to their length, relief, and daily-to-monthly changes in atmospheric phenomena. Seasons contrast considerably in the amounts and kinds of precipitation, in the number of sunny and cloudy days, and in the extent and intensity of heat and cold.

Geologically, the rounded Blue Ridge Mountains record more than a billion years of earth history. They consist basically of very old igneous and metamorphic rocks (pre-Cambrian granites, granodiorites, and schists), which occur as uplands, and younger sedimentary and metamorphic rocks (Cambrian limestones, shales, and quartzites), which form low hills and valleys in a narrow zone along the Great Valley to the west. Catoctin greenstone, named for Catoctin Mountain in Maryland, was formerly massive flows of metabasalt, an igneous rock, that today cap most of the summits and ridges of the range. The greenstone can be seen on a number of highway cuts through the mountains.

The soils of the Blue Ridge Mountains range widely from site to site, depending on the rate of erosion, the hardness and mineral content of the underlying soils, and the local vegetation. The richest soils develop in the coves or hollows. Like basins, the coves collect moisture and materials that have eroded off the hillsides. Trees and plants grow abundantly, adding a steady supply of organic matter to the soil. These well-drained soils are the most productive in the region.

Since the Blue Ridge is not high enough for a timberline—the altitude above which trees will not grow—plants grow practically everywhere. To date nearly 1500 kinds of plants, including about 160 varieties of trees and shrubs, and numerous ferns, mosses, lichens, and fungi have been recorded. In the eastern United States, only the Great Smoky Mountains surpass this rich variety of plant life.

Yet the present Blue Ridge forest contains mostly small, second- or third-growth trees. The virgin stands of yesteryear have vanished. Although man has made an impression upon the natural scene for centuries, the coming of the lumber companies in the nineteenth century greatly accelerated the rate of destruction. Acres upon acres of forest trees were cut for wood products and fuel by the big companies, then needlessly burned before being abandoned. This ruthless method of cut, clear, burn, and move on quickly decimated the Blue Ridge forests.

Fortunately, in a few localities of difficult access, old stands have remained intact. Limberlost, at the head of Whiteoak Canyon in the central district of Shenandoah National Park, is one outstanding example. Sturdy rows of eastern hemlock, approaching 300 years in age and 3 feet in diameter, tower above the surrounding forest canopy. A greenish hue and an almost eternal silence pervade the cathedrallike atmosphere.

The vast clearings made by the lumber companies during the nineteenth and early twentieth centuries are rapidly reverting to forest. Today, 95 percent of the Blue Ridge Province is woodland. On the ridges and dry slopes, oak, hickory, black locust, maple, and scattered ash and pine prevail. In valleys and hollows, tuliptree, sycamore, and basswood grow near watercourses. Eastern hemlock is a common tree along streams, in cool coves, and on north slopes up to an altitude of 4000 feet. Associated with the hemlock are maples, American beech, birches, and tuliptree. At highest elevations (usually above 3800 feet), spruce and fir stand as relics of the Canadian forest type that covered this province during the Pleistocene epoch, or last Ice Age.

Before white men appeared in the Blue Ridge, luxuriant forests provided sufficient food and cover for wildlife. Streams and rivers ran clear—unsilted and unpolluted—while in their depths fish and other water-loving creatures thrived. Bison grazed in the lowlands and majestic elk roamed freely throughout the region. The mountain lion, timber wolf, otter, fisher, and beaver abounded. Most of these mammals are now absent from the Blue Ridge.

With the coming of the white man, conditions changed. Wildlife had to reckon with the rifle, axe, and plow. Consequently, the "land of plenty" began to disappear, and with it, important kinds of wildlife. The wild turkey and ruffed grouse, highly praised game birds, were severely depleted. Of the mammals, the bison was last recorded in 1798. The cougar and timber wolf held out until the dawn of the twentieth century. Evidence of these wild creatures is still apparent in places like Wolf Run, Peaks of Otter, and Elk Creek. Probably the changes in habitat due to human activities had a more profound effect on most wildlife than did man himself.

The Indians also made a deep impression upon parts of the montane landscape. Although the eastern woodland Indians used the mountains primarily as a ground for hunting, fishing, gathering, and chipping, they cleared the forestland at the base of the mountains for agriculture. In the upland forest, they intentionally burned smooth-surfaced areas to form open glades and meadows, both to improve grazing for deer and elk, and to drive game. Fires spread easily over a smooth surface, but normally will not descend a steep valley unless driven by a very favorable wind. The smooth lands were gradually cleared of their trees by oft-repeated burning. Perhaps the most visited clearing lies at Big Meadows in the central district of Shenandoah National Park. This fragrant meadow was once heavily burned and grazed, preventing trees from growing. Today the National Park Service is using controlled burning to maintain Big Meadows as an opening. Otherwise, the meadow would slowly revert to the infringing forest surrounding it.

Burning helped clear grass, brush, and trees from land for farming. Large trees were not felled but were simply girdled by pounding with a stone axe. The combination of burning and "deadening" the forest resulted in extensive open fields, called "Indian Old Fields" by the initial pioneer occupants. These fields were soon settled by German and Scotch-Irish families and became nuclei for future settlement and expansion.

By the time the white settlers arrived in the Blue Ridge in the 1740s, they had acquired vital knowledge from the Indians, especially about agricultural techniques. Besides taking over crops, methods, and cultivated fields, the settlers used Indian guides, transportation routes and methods, and valuable native plants and animals for food, clothing, and medicine. Most of the montane settlers became farmers, growing corn, cabbage, potatoes, beans, squash, and pumpkins. Many lived in "hollows"—long, narrow valleys nestled between mountain ridges. The mouth of a hollow contained the most fertile soil as well as the flattest land available in the valley; thus, settlement occurrred early there. As more land was needed, succeeding generations progressed up the hollow to the headwaters of the stream.

The Civil War, the building of the nearby railroads, the coming of the large lumber companies, and even the substitution of the portable steam sawmill for the old water-driven mill affected the mountain way of life. Many mills and tanyards that served small montane communities through the skill of one family became quiet, then decayed into the landscape. Mountaineers had little cash income left except from moonshining and chestnuts. By 1915 the chestnut blight had destroyed most of the chestnut trees. As the years passed, the mountain population dwindled. However, nearly twenty-five hundred people still lived on the lands acquired by the Commonwealth of Virginia for Shenandoah National Park. More than four hundred families moved to new homes in the adjoining lowlands before the park was dedicated in 1936.

Since the establishment of Shenandoah National Park and Blue Ridge Parkway in the 1930s, the forest has crept back, fire scars have healed, plants and animals now live unmolested by man. Strict park management prohibits hunting, trapping, and lumbering on parklands and protects all wildlife—predators and prey alike. Under these conditions the natural landscape is returning. Once again deer, bear, bobcat, and wild turkey are seen along the Skyline Drive and Blue Ridge Parkway. Today over sixty species of mammals, two hundred kinds of birds, over thirty species of reptiles and amphibians, and numerous species of insects live in the Blue Ridge heartland. Furthermore, these wild and natural areas provide modern man with an escape from the stresses and cares of overpopulated urban existence. Such intangibles are impossible to measure in terms of material wealth, but they are nevertheless real.

—Gene Wilhelm

51.

Carbaugh Hollow
Natural Area

Directions: **Franklin County, Pa. From Harrisburg, go southwest on I-81 about 50 miles to Chambersburg. Turn east on U.S. 30 and go 11.7 miles to Newman Rd. Turn south (right) just before the intersection of U.S. 30 and Route 234. The road sign is about 50 feet off U.S. 30. After 0.2 mile the pavement ends as the road crosses the state forest boundary. Approximately 2.2 miles beyond this point, Newman Rd. intersects the District Rd. Turn right and go about 2.2 miles to a sign and small parking lot for the natural area on the south (left) side of the road. Cross the road and begin walking along the green-blazed trail.**

Ownership: **Michaux State Forest, Pennsylvania Bureau of Forests.**

Carbaugh Hollow Natural Area's 870 acres nestle in the wooded gap between Mount Newman and Snaggy Ridge. The site is drained by Carbaugh Run. The hollow has been logged several times for the manufacture of charcoal, but signs of disturbance are now relatively few.

Although the access trail (blazed with green keystones) is not within the natural area, it does provide an interesting prelude to the hollow itself. This trail descends gradually through a well-drained upland forest consisting primarily of various oaks but including other hardwoods such as blackgum, sassafras, red maple, and flowering dogwood. The shrubby vegetation is typical for a woodland on acid soil, featuring witch-hazel, chestnut, mountain laurel, blueberries, and huckleberries. Prior to the 1920s, chestnut was a major constituent of the forest, but then the chestnut blight left the species nothing more than a mere root sprout; it sometimes reaches sapling size before succumbing to the disease (see **#30**). A visit to the area in late May provides an impressive display of the wild pink azalea (commonly but erroneously called "honeysuckle"). At the same time of the year, the pink lady's slipper or moccasin-flower orchid is scattered throughout the woods.

When the boundary of the natural area is reached, the trail continues along the same abandoned road but is no longer blazed. As the trail descends the ravine toward Carbaugh Run, one finds additional species of plants. Hemlock and black birch become more frequent, and along the stream itself, white pine and rhododendron are conspicuous. Just before the stream, bear left along the old woods road. After an easy 25-minute hike, you will reach the hollow. The cool and shady floor of the hollow and its surrounding ravines provide excellent habitats for mosses and ferns. Dozens of species of flowering herbaceous plants occur—at least twelve species of violets, for example.

Skunk cabbage is an interesting plant conspicuous in the seepy woods along the stream. This member of the arum family receives its name from the fetid odor evident when parts of the plant are bruised. The skunk cabbage is probably spring's earliest "wildflower," in late winter or early spring producing its fleshy, rounded spike of flowers surrounded by a purple-and-green spotted and striped spathe. The plant produces its own heat as it begins its spring activity, which helps it survive early-spring cold snaps. In late spring and summer, the large veiny leaves become quite noticeable. Skunk cabbage contains crystals of calcium oxalate, which cause severe burning sensations if the plant is eaten raw. Thorough drying destroys the crystals, however, and certain parts of the plant were used by the Indians for food.

The hollow is also prime habitat for reptiles and amphibians, particularly salamanders, and the area has been designated as a protected site for these two groups (see **#58**). Native brook trout live in the cold, clear water of Carbaugh Run (see **#53**). Deer inhabit the hollow, and a variety of birds can be found within the area.

Of special interest are the deposits of rhyolite found in the hollow. Rhyolite is a granite-like rock derived from molten material or magma that cooled at or near the surface of the earth. Because such molten rock tends to cool rapidly, rhyolite consists of rather small crystals (see **#3**). The rock is rich in quartz and feldspar and is typically light-colored.

The presence of rhyolite here is notable for two reasons. First, the rock has a very limited distribution in Pennsylvania, being found only within the South Mountain area. Secondly, research has shown that rhyolite was highly prized by the Indians, for making arrowheads and other tools. The fine texture of rhyolite made it especially suitable for chipping. Carbaugh Hollow was reputed to be a very important quarrying site for the Indians.

To return to your car, retrace your steps.

Remarks: *The hike takes two hours. The woods road is generally open and easy, but parts of the trail may be muddy. Camping, swimming, fishing, hiking, and golf are available at Caledonia State Park 15 miles west of Gettysburg on U.S. 30. The Appalachian Trail passes through the Michaux State Forest. For further information write Mr. James C. Nelson, Assistant Director of Forestry, Room 100, Evan Press Building, Harrisburg, Pa. 17120.*

52.
Catoctin Mountain Park

Directions: **Frederick County, Md. From Washington, D.C., take I-270 north about 45 miles to the end, then continue north on U.S. 15 for 17 miles. Go west on Route 77 for 2.7 miles to the National Park Service visitors' center. Turn right onto Park Central Road and go 0.5 mile. Park on the right where the trail to Wolf and Chimney Rocks begins.**

Ownership: **National Park Service.**

Catoctin Mountain, the eastern boundary of the Blue Ridge Province in Maryland (see **Blue Ridge**) is a narrow ridge that extends north-south across Frederick County. It rises abruptly from the lowlands of the Frederick valley to the east. In several places along the ridgetop, bare rock ledges break through the thick forest cover. Two such ledges are Wolf Rock (**a**) and Chimney Rock (**b**). Climb up the short but steep slope to the ridgetop, then follow the level trail to the right. Wolf Rock, nearly a mile from the parking area, lies off the trail to the left. The trail continues another half-mile to Chimney Rock.

Geologically, the mountain lies on the eastern limb of a large, complexly folded anticline, or arch, (see **#95**) which also encompasses South Mountain to the west (see **#54**). Layers of metamorphosed quartz sandstones, the Weverton quartzite, once extended across the entire fold as a thick sheet. This rock is nearly 570 million years old, dating back to the early Cambrian period. Although it is very resistant to erosion, much of the quartzite in the southern part of Frederick County has now been worn away, leaving only the narrow ridges of Catoctin Mountain on the east and South Mountain on the west limb of the fold. The older rocks that occur beneath the quartzite are more easily eroded and have also been worn away,

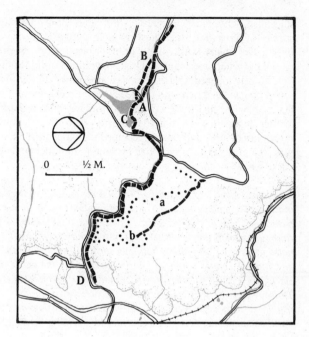

leaving the lowland of the Middletown valley between the two ridges. In the northern part of Frederick County, more of the quartzite has been preserved. Catoctin Mountain occurs as a broad, flat-topped ridge into which streams have carved deep, rocky gorges.

The layers of the quartzite across the large arching structure are tightly folded on a smaller scale. The isolated outcrops at Wolf Rock and Chimney Rock represent the ends of two of these minor folds which have preserved remnants of a massive, 50-foot thick layer of white quartzite. Large fractures cut through the rock. In places, weathering and erosion have formed high, narrow passageways. Walk out to the middle of Wolf Rock, where the largest of these *fissure caves* is located. This 5-foot-wide gap is 35 feet deep and extends for 80 feet. Continue to Chimney Rock, which is as blocky as Wolf Rock but smaller. It offers an excellent view of the adjacent mountains and the lowlands to the east. From here, retrace your steps.

The forest here is dominated by chestnut oaks. Hickories, sugar maples, black birches, and other trees grow here as well. Elsewhere, the moister areas of the park support red and white oaks, tuliptrees, beeches, yellow birches, and hemlocks. The understory is thick with spicebush, serviceberry, greenbrier, and other shrubs. Twenty-seven species of ferns grace the forest floor. In autumn, hawks soar by, over leaves ablaze with color. Spring brings a good assortment of woodland wildflowers and songbirds migrating north. Although it is now mostly forested, this area was cleared in the 1700s and 1800s when people lived here and farmed. They also cut trees for lumber, for charcoal to fuel the Catoctin iron furnace, and for bark to tan leather. It was in 1936 that 10,000 acres were set aside for a demonstration of how land can be reclaimed for parks. In 1954, the park was split in two, with almost half becoming Cunningham Falls State Park (see **#53**); the two parks are managed cooperatively.

Remarks: *Allow 2 to 3 hours for this 2.6-mile round trip. Over activities include a self-guiding auto tour and trails; guided walks; and camping, picnicking, hiking, fishing (with a license and trout stamp), horseback riding (no rentals are available), and cross-country skiing. Park in designated areas only. The park is busiest in spring and fall; summers are hot and humid. Located within the park, but closed to the public, is Camp David, the presidential retreat. An annual Colorfest Weekend is held in Thurmont in the second weekend in October, when the fall colors are usually at their peak. For more information contact Catoctin Mountain Park, National Park Service, Thurmont, Md. 21788, (301) 824-2574.*

53.
Cunningham Falls
State Park

―――――――――――――――――――――

Directions: **Frederick County, Md. Follow directions for Catoctin Mountain Park (#52). Big Hunting Creek parallels Route 77 west of U.S. 15. From the National Park Service visitor's center, continue 0.1 mile west on Route 77, then turn left onto Catoctin Hollow Rd. After 1.2 miles, turn right and go 0.5 mile to the parking area by the beach. Cunningham Falls is about 0.7 mile upstream. A clear trail begins by the outlet of Big Hunting Creek into the lake (A), or take the trail along the wooded ridge. There is also parking by the falls, 0.9 mile past the visitors' center on Route 77.**

Ownership: **Maryland Forest and Park Service.**

Big Hunting Creek, originating in springs on Catoctin Mountain, is a clear, sparkling mountain stream that provides some of the best trout fishing in Maryland. At Cunningham Falls (**B**), near the eastern edge of Catoctin Mountain, the water pours down a narrow chute, dropping 75 feet within a distance of 220 feet. Black-throated green and Blackburnian warblers nest in the hemlocks that shade the falls. Downstream, the man-made Hunting Creek Lake (**C**) interrupts the flow, but below the lake, the creek regains its mountain-stream character. It meanders beneath the hemlocks and hardwood trees that closely line the banks and passes through pools and riffles. As it leaves the mountain, the stream encounters another, smaller man-made pond, Frank Bentz Memorial Lake (**D**), before flowing off across the lowlands.

At first glance, no life is evident in the stream. However, look closely at a quiet pool and perhaps you will see a trout hiding in a shadow, water striders skating on the surface, or a water snake gliding by. Where the water moves swiftly, there may be even more inhabitants, though they are less noticeable. The stream is full of various life forms. Each has its own way of coping with the ceaseless current. Insects in their immature stages cling to rocks or hide between them. Trout, on the other hand, meet the current head on. With powerful movements, they push their streamlined bodies through the water with little resistance.

The most numerous members of the stream community are the algae that float in the water or coat the rocks, making them slimy and slippery. Individuals are impossible to detect with the naked eye, but long, silky filaments of algae often extend downstream from the rocks they are anchored to. These tiny algae are essential to all other life in their environment, in much the same way as green plants support life on land. Through photosynthesis, they manufacture their own food, thus supplying nourishment for higher orders of animals.

Feeding on them are countless insects in various stages of life. Mayfly and stonefly nymphs abound, as do caddisfly and blackfly larvae, all clinging to the streambed in areas of swift riffles. Dragonfly and damselfly nymphs live where the water moves more slowly. Look carefully where the water is still for mosquito larvae suspended just beneath the surface. (All of these insects spend most of their lives in immature stages in the water, emerging as adults only briefly to mate.) Waterpennies flatten themselves against rocks, while whirligig beetles sit on the surface of still water. Feeding on these small plants and animals are fish of all sizes, from little darters and sculpins to large trout. Bigger fish also feed on smaller ones. The food web expands to include larger green plants such as mosses and pondweeds, and other small animals like worms, crayfish, and snails.

Birds, turtles, snakes, raccoons, and other larger creatures, including humans, are also part of the web.

Three types of trout—eastern brook, brown, and rainbow—are found in the waters of Big Hunting Creek above **D**. Of the three, only the eastern brook trout is native to Maryland. Requiring cooler and cleaner water than brown or rainbow trout, the brook trout lives and reproduces only in the upper reaches of Big Hunting Creek. Brown trout, which were once stocked here, have been sustaining their numbers by natural reproduction since the 1970s. These hardier trout have less stringent environmental requirements. Rainbow trout are stocked for fishermen. While rainbows are easy to raise in a hatchery, they do not adapt well to streams in Maryland and rarely reproduce here.

Trout can live only in streams, such as this, with high water quality. Their growth and reproduction are based on numerous physical, biological, and chemical factors, of which the most important are water temperature, water transparency, and amount of dissolved oxygen in the water. The water must remain cool all summer; each species has its own temperature limit. The stream must be clear so that sunlight can penetrate, in order for the green plants, the basis of the food web, to grow. Oxygen is needed for respiration by all plants and animals, and it is consumed as material decomposes. Cold water can hold more dissolved gases than warm water, and cascading water, naturally aerated from constant contact with the atmosphere, contains much more oxygen than slow-moving or stagnant waters.

Development, for the most part, is detrimental to stream quality, but fortunately the upper reaches of Big Hunting Creek have been spared. The streamside forests protect the creek from the heat of the sun, so that the water is rarely warmer than 78°F. This protective ground cover also prevents topsoil from being eroded and adding silt to the water. This would not only decrease the water's transparency, but could directly suffocate the fish. From its headwaters to where it leaves the mountains, the land surrounding Big Hunting Creek has remained undeveloped. Because it avoids such pollution problems as those stemming from sewage, chemicals, and industrial heat effluents, Big Hunting Creek still provides excellent trout fishing in a virtually undisturbed setting.

Fishing is best during late April and May, although avid fishermen may venture out at any time of year. Anglers fly-fish for trout using synthetic flies that simulate real insects, but incorporate a hook. Wet flies, which sink below the surface of the water, resemble those insects in the immature stage. Dry flies, in contrast, float along on the surface and mimic the adult insects that either hatch directly from the stream or fall in from overhanging vegetation. All trout caught here must be returned to the stream, and only barbless hooks are permitted.

Remarks: *Fishing is best between Hunting Creek Lake and Frank Bentz Memorial Lake. Only fly-fishing, under a catch-and-release policy, is allowed. No fish may be kept. A fishing license and trout stamp are required. The creek is partly under the jurisdiction of the National Park Service.*

Other activities include hiking, camping, picnicking, swimming, boating (no motor boats allowed; canoe rentals available at the lake), hunting (be careful in deer season—see **#88**), *and cross-country skiing. The lake gets crowded in summer. An annual demonstration of making maple syrup is held in early spring. For more information contact Cunningham Falls State Park, Thurmont, Md. 21788, (301) 271-7574.*

54.
South Mountain

Directions: **Frederick and Washington Counties, Md. From Washington, D.C., take I-270 north about 45 miles to I-70. Go west on I-70 about 11 miles to Exit 42 for Myersville. Go north into Myersville and turn right onto Route 153 (Ellerton Rd.). Go 0.5 mile and turn west (left) onto U.S. 40. Go west about 3 miles. About 0.5 mile beyond the Pleasant Walk Rd. crossing and just before U.S. 40 crosses over I-70 is a small parking area on the left. The trailhead for the white-blazed Appalachian Trail is across the road just to the left of a driveway marked private property.**

Ownership: **National Park Service and Maryland Forest and Park Service.**

South Mountain runs some 34 miles across Maryland, extending both north into Pennsylvania and south across the Potomac River. Along its northern reaches, it forms the western boundary of the Blue Ridge Province (see **Blue Ridge**). Like Catoctin Mountain (**#52**), to which it is structurally related, South Mountain is a long, narrow ridge capped by resistant Weverton quartzite. These ridges lie on opposite sides of a large arching fold, or anticline, which has been pushed toward the west in such a way that both limbs of the

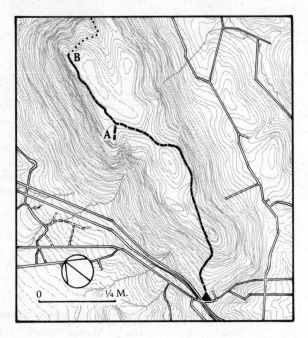

arch are angled, or dip, toward the east. Such a fold is termed an
overturned anticline. In a normal anticline, the two limbs dip in opposite directions away from the crest of the fold. (see **#95**).

The Appalachian Trail follows South Mountain's forested crest
through Maryland. Like Catoctin Mountain, South Mountain in the
southern part of Frederick and Washington Counties is a narrow,
linear ridge. Northward, however, the mountain broadens out into
a succession of knobs and flat-topped ridges. Hike north on the trail.
After the first steep half-mile, the trail levels off. Continue to Annapolis Rock (**A**) and Black Rock (**B**), which lie west of the trail, slightly
over 2 and 3 miles, respectively, from U.S. 40. The wide, flat-topped
area between Annapolis Rock and Black Rock is caused by minor
flooding within the arching Weverton quartzite. These two outcrops
interrupt the dense forest, composed mainly of chestnut oaks. Hickories, beeches, red maples, pitch and white pines, black birches, and
abundant mountain laurel also grow on this dry, rocky ground.
These open, windy ledges provide expansive views to the west, overlooking the rich farmlands of the Hagerstown Valley, which is part
of the Great Valley (see **#87**) and the mountains of the Ridge and
Valley Province farther in the distance (see **Ridge and Valley**).

Remarks: *Camping is permitted along the Appalachian Trail. The state-owned South Mountain Natural Environmental Area encompasses a narrow strip of land along the Appalachian Trail, designed to help preserve South Mountain's natural features. For more information, contact the Appalachian Trail Conference, P.O. Box 236, Harpers Ferry, W. Va. 25425, (304) 535-6331, or the South Mountain Natural Environmental Area, Gathland State Park, Route 1, Box 299A, Jefferson, Md. 21775, (301) 371-6630.*

Nearby Places of Interest

Devil's Racecourse: From the Appalachian Trail parking lot on U.S. 40, continue about 4 miles west on U.S. 40. Go north (right) 6.8 miles on Route 66 (on the west side, 0.6 mile north of I-70, is a trout hatchery—see #53). Turn south (right) onto Route 64, go 1.6 miles, then turn right onto Route 491, which leads up Raven Rock Hollow. (The large outcrop of quartzite that looms above the road to your left is Raven Rock.) After 2.4 miles, turn left onto Fort Ritchie Rd. Continue 0.7 mile, pull off the road, and park on the left. Devil's Racecourse is a few hundred feet to the left; a faint trail leads there.

Ownership: City of Hagerstown.

Devil's Racecourse is a large boulder field, some 200 feet wide, that extends about a quarter of a mile. Very little grows on these large, slightly rounded boulders nestled closely to each other; the field's barrenness contrasts starkly with the surrounding forest. Although glaciers did not cover this terrain, their presence to the north affected the climate here. Often under freezing conditions, water and ice worked their powerful forces against the mountain and created this boulder field. (See #118 for an explanation of the process.) Listen for mysterious sounds of running water, which betray the presence of a stream hidden beneath the rocks.

Washington Monument State Park: From I-70 just west of Frederick, take U.S. 40A west 11 miles. The park entrance is on the right. Or from the Appalachian Trail parking lot (see above), continue west on U.S. 40 about 4 miles to Route

66. Go south (left) on Route 66 for 4.4 miles to U.S. 40A. Turn left and go east for about 2 miles. The park will be on your left.

Ownership: Maryland Forest and Park Service.

This is central Maryland's best hawk-watching spot. The tower, the first monument to George Washington, offers an excellent vantage point and protection from the wind. The heaviest flights occur in the fall, when five to ten species in a day may be observed. Broad-winged hawks are most common in September, while sharp-shinned and red-tailed hawks pass overhead in October (see #5 and #78). In August and September, you can look down from the tower into the treetops, where migrating warblers (see #17) are active just after dawn. These birds can also be found along the edges of open areas. The park offers camping and picnicking; contact Route 1, Box 147, Middletown, Md. 21769, (301) 432-8065.

There are two other state parks and a county park on South Mountain: Greenbrier State Park, Route 2, Boonesboro, Md. 21713, (301) 739-7877, provides camping, swimming, boating, and picnicking. It is just north of Washington Monument State Park. The historic Gathland State Park (see Remarks above for address), to the south, has picnicking and primitive camping facilities. Pen Mar County Park, (301) 791-3125, near the Pennsylvania border, has an excellent scenic lookout.

55.
Maryland Heights

Directions: Washington County, Md. From Washington, D.C., take I-270 north about 40 miles. Go west on I-70 about 1 mile to the next exit. Take U.S. 340 southwest 15 miles. Turn left on Route 180, the last exit before the Potomac River; after 0.2 mile, turn right onto Sandy Hook Rd. Continue 1.2 miles and park in the pulloff by the trailhead (A). The trail has orange blazes.

Ownership: National Park Service.

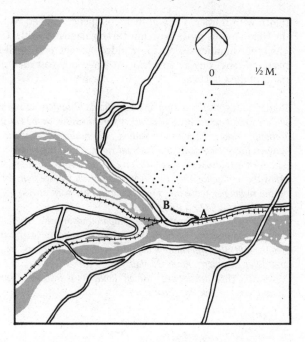

Elk Ridge is the northern extension of the main spine of the Blue
Ridge Mountains that runs through Virginia and West Virginia and
crosses the Potomac River into Maryland. It continues for several
miles before petering out about 2.5 miles southeast of Keedysville.
The Blue Ridge Province continues northward into Pennsylvania
following South Mountain just to the east (see **Blue Ridge**). The
structure of Elk Ridge is an anticline, or arch (see **#95**) similar to
that of South Mountain (see **#54**). The presence of these two parallel ridges along the Blue Ridge here may be due to a fault (see **#3**)
on the west side of South Mountain. The land on the west side of
the fault has been thrust up so that part of the structure of the
anticline is repeated. Elk Ridge, like Catoctin Mountain (see **#52**)
and South Mountain, is capped by the Weverton quartzite, a metamorphosed quartz sandstone. Where the Potomac River has carved
its way through this very resistant rock, cliffs loom above the water.
At Maryland Heights, the southern end of Elk Ridge, the cliffs rise
more than 1000 feet above the water. A rocky, moderately strenuous
trail traverses the slopes for half a mile to the second of two overlooks about halfway to the top (**B**). The terrific view takes in both
the Shenandoah River (to the left) and the Potomac River (to the

right), with Harpers Ferry at their confluence. It is no wonder that the Union troops chose to occupy this highland during the Civil War. The trail continues steeply to the ridgetop, where the well-marked, historic Grant Conway Trail takes a 2-mile loop past ruins and remnants of the Civil War.

Remarks: *Off-trail rock climbing here should be undertaken only by those with technical experience. All climbers should register at the Harpers Ferry National Historic Park ranger station. The main section of the park lies between the Shenandoah and Potomac rivers. To get there, go back to U.S. 340, turn left, and continue south, on U.S. 340. After crossing the Potomac below the confluence, then the Shenandoah, you will see signs for the park on the right. For more information, contact the park at Box 65, Harpers Ferry, W. Va. 25425, (304) 535-6371.*

Camping is available at private campgrounds nearby. There is a KOA campground opposite the park entrance on U.S. 340. For raft trips, boat rentals, and other information about recreation on the rivers, contact River and Trail Outfitters, Route 2, Valley Rd., Knoxville, Md. 21758, (301) 834-9950. They are located just off Route 340; instead of turning left toward Sandy Hook Rd., turn right.

Shenandoah
National Park

The 302 square miles of Shenandoah National Park encompass the ridge and slopes of the Blue Ridge Mountains. Rich vegetation, different on the mountaintops than
in the lowlands, shrouds the Blue Ridge. Animals such
as white-tailed deer, migrating and breeding songbirds,
and various salamanders abound. Because this is a national park, all plants and animals are protected, and no
collecting is allowed.

Skyline Drive, built in the late 1930s, begins in Front
Royal and winds 105 miles down the ridge to the Blue
Ridge Parkway, which continues south. Along Skyline
Drive are countless lookouts, trailheads for over 500 miles
of trails, and various park facilities (two visitors' centers
at 4.6 and 51.4 miles from Front Royal, large campgrounds, and three lodges). The road is open year round
(except during or right after snow or ice storms). Spring
wildflowers are at their best in April and May; the autumn colors peak in mid-October. The park is quiet and
enjoyable in winter, but be aware that most facilities are
closed.

An entry fee is charged. Backcountry camping here
requires a free backcountry permit, available from any
ranger station. Additional activities include many naturalist programs, picnicking, fishing (with a license), and
horseback riding. For more information contact Shenandoah National Park, Luray, Va. 22835, (703) 999-2266.
An excellent trail guide, which also includes cultural and
natural history, is *The Guide to Skyline Drive and Shenandoah National Park,* by Henry Heatwole; it provided portions of the following material (see **Bibliography**).

187

56.
Old Rag
Mountain

Directions: **Madison County, Va. From Washington, D.C., take I-66 west about 23 miles beyond I-495. Take U.S. 29 southwest 13 miles toward Warrenton, then take U.S. 211 west about 28 miles to Sperryville. Turn southeast (right) onto U.S. 522 and go 0.7 mile to Route 231. Turn south (right) and continue 7.6 miles. Following signs to Old Rag Mountain, turn right onto Route 601, which turns right after 0.3 mile. Follow this road another 2.9 miles. Park in the field on the left (A) or continue about another mile and park near the trailhead (B). See Remarks.**

Ownership: **Shenandoah National Park, National Park Service.**

Old Rag Mountain lies east of the main spine of the Blue Ridge (see **Blue Ridge**). The trail for this rewarding but very strenuous 8-mile hike crosses bold rock formations and winds around enormous boulders as it climbs some 2400 feet. The 3268-foot summit offers expansive views of the lofty Blue Ridge and the forests and farms of the adjacent foothills and valleys. This outlying peak has characteristics that differ from much of the rest of the park. Here, dry conditions give rise to scrubby woods that contrast sharply with the rich forests that prevail elsewhere in the park (see **#60**).

The mountain is composed of Old Rag granite, a white or light-gray massive rock widely exposed on its upper elevations. At 1.1 billion years old, this granite is among the oldest rocks exposed in the Appalachians. It crystallized from molten rock deep within the earth's crust under conditions of very high pressure and temperature. The molten material may have been thrust up from deeper in the earth or could have originally been part of older rock layers that were melted and then recrystallized. Hundreds of millions of years of uplift and erosion removed the overlying rocks and exposed the granite at the surface. Streams carved deep valleys into the granite; the hills, rising nearly 2000 feet higher, became rounded; and sediments were deposited in the lower stream valleys. The shape of this totally barren land was probably similar to that of the foothills that now lie to the east. From **B**, walk up the dirt road and turn left onto the blue-blazed Ridge Trail, which leads about 3 miles to the ridge-top.

The prominent outcrops attest to the granite's resistance to weathering. The rock surfaces, however, as the hiker will soon discover, are extremely rough. The coarse grains of quartz and feldspar—the prominent minerals—are each finely divided by tiny fractures, enabling water to etch them into relief. Large-scale fractures also cut through the granite. Boulders up to 10 feet in diameter litter the mountaintop where the rock is exposed to buffeting winds and water (**C**). Erosion enlarges the fractures, eventually breaking apart the rock. The blocks thus formed are then rounded into these boulders without being moved. Their sizes are determined by the spacing of the fractures. There is no clear evidence indicating when the jointing developed. It may have occurred when the Appalachian Mountains were thrust up, or it may be related to adjustments that took place deep within the earth's crust after the mountains were formed. The trail passes between the boulders, then crosses the ridge to the summit. Off the main trail near the summit are a number of large water-

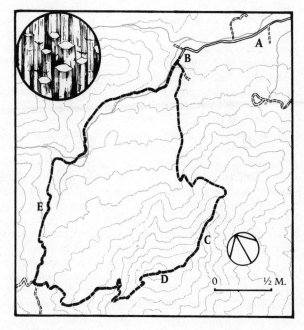

Inset: Columnar joints

filled holes known as "buzzard baths" (**D**). No one knows how they were formed—perhaps by the removal of softer material contained within the granite or by carving by a river.

A series of greenstone dikes or bands, cut northward through the granite. Amid the boulders (**C**), the trail leads through a passageway less than 3 feet wide that was once filled with greenstone. Most of the rock in this dike has been eroded from the top, leaving a natural stairway. This dark-green, fine-grained rock, called Catoctin greenstone, was originally a basaltic lava. As the basalt emplaced between the granite walls cooled, the rock contracted, forming columnar joints perpendicular to the walls. The columns are hexagonal or pentagonal in cross section. Those columns not yet eroded form the steps.

Some 600 million years ago, basaltic lava rose from the earth's depths and, through fissures such as these dikes, reached the surface. In episode after episode, the basalt spread out in sheets 100 to 200 feet thick on top of the eroded granite. At first, because of the hills, the lava was confined to the valleys. Eventually, it built up a broad plain that covered all but the highest peaks. The total thickness was probably greater than 2000 feet; near Big Meadows (**#59**), its remnants show evidence of twelve flows that today measure 1800 feet thick.

Beginning during this period of volcanism and continuing long afterwards, widespread subsidence, or gentle sinking of the crust, occurred. A trough developed, extending from Alabama to Newfoundland; sediments, eroded by streams flowing across the lava plain, were deposited in it. The area was subsequently covered by a sea. Over the 350 million years following the volcanic period, some 30,000 feet of terrestrial and marine sediments accumulated on top of the basalt. The increased pressures and temperatures caused by this sedimentation metamorphosed the basalt into the Catoctin greenstone. Elsewhere in the park, this resistant rock caps many of the peaks (see **#58**) and forms the cliffs and ledges over which the many waterfalls cascade (see **#60**). Some additional changes occurred when the rocks in this trough were squeezed and thrust up while the Appalachian Mountains were forming. The features we see today are the result of much later erosion.

The rugged upper reaches of Old Rag Mountain are barren or only sparsely vegetated by a small number of species. Although several fires and some clearing occurred in the 1930s, the sparseness of the vegetation here—so unlike the abundance elsewhere in the park— is largely due to the mountain's geology. The granite weathers slowly, producing only a thin, acid, rocky soil that is low in nutrients. Rainfall evaporates quickly, or it runs off the impermeable rock, carrying away much of the soil. Chestnut oaks, which tolerate these dry, rocky conditions, predominate here. Growing among them are bear and northern red oaks, black locusts, Virginia pines, and mountain laurels. Bigtoothed aspen, crack and pussy willow, pin or fire cherry, and sweet fern, species less commonly found in the park as a whole, also grow here. A more varied community exists in the protected areas. Northern red and scarlet oaks, tuliptrees, black birches, red maples, and white ashes grow along with pitch, white, and table mountain pines. Mountain laurel and serviceberry grow beneath them. Herbaceous plants, which are easily dried out, are scarce in the understory of the mountaintop forests.

Continue past the summit to the Byrd Nest Shelter 1. Turn right onto the blue-blazed Saddle Trail just before the shelter and proceed down the mountain to the Old Rag fire road. Go right for a short distance, then turn right again and follow the Weakley Hollow fire road back to the parking lot at Nethers.

The disparity between these sparse forests and the park's typically diverse woodlands is apparent on the return route through Weakley Hollow (**E**). The forest here is full of oaks, hickories, large stands of tuliptrees, and pawpaws, as well as a variety of other species, including cucumbertree, which is uncommon here on the east side of the park. Wildflowers (see **#60**) provide an added pleasure in springtime. Pennywort, golden saxifrage, and sweet pinesap are other less common plants that grow in the Old Rag Mountain vicinity.

Remarks: *Allow a full day for this difficult hike, which covers very rough terrain. Wear sturdy footwear and bring along food and water. This hike is popular; the trail is very busy on nice weekends at all times of year. The trailhead parking area fills early on such days. The Thorofare Mountain Overlook (Mile 43.3, near the Limberlost) affords a good view of the fractures that cut across the cliffs of Old Rag Mountain's north face. The late-afternoon sun highlights the north-trending joints.*

57.

The Limberlost

Directions: **Madison County, Va. Follow the directions for Old Rag Mountain (#56) to Sperryville. Continue west on U.S. 211 for 7 miles to Skyline Dr. at Thornton Gap, then go 11.5 miles south on Skyline Dr. Opposite Milepost 43**

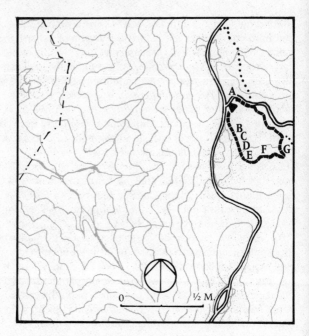

(just past Skyland), turn left onto a short, dirt fire road. Park at the end of the road (**A**). The trail begins on the south side of the road near the entrance to the parking area.

Ownership: **Shenandoah National Park, National Park Service.**

This easy 1.2-mile round trip on the Limberlost Trail leads through remnants of past settlements en route to one of Shenandoah National Park's most special places. In the boggy head of White Oak Canyon stands a dark, silent grove of stately old hemlocks. A walk to the Limberlost, one of the only places in the park that has never been disturbed by logging or clearing, is a trip into the past, providing a glimpse of a forest like those encountered by the early pioneers.

Gnarled, aged apple trees reveal the location of a long-abandoned orchard, now overgrown with ferns, sumacs, and Virginia pines (**B**). It serves as a reminder that many people once inhabited these hills. By 1840, the lower, more hospitable valleys were already settled, and new arrivals were forced up onto the hillsides and ridges. Where they settled was largely a function of geology. Abundant springwater, good soil, and manageable slopes occurred where basalt and granite form the mountains, as in this central section of the park. In contrast, metamorphic sandstones and shales underlie the southeastern part of the park; there, the thin, rocky soil that clings to the steep, dry slopes was unsuitable for farming.

As the population of mountaindwellers grew, the impact on the land from logging and farming also increased. The thin mountain soil could not sustain the intensive farming methods of the valleys, and more and more land was cleared as old fields wore out. By the turn of the twentieth century, the population reached its peak, while the land itself was deteriorating from overfarming, overgrazing, logging, and erosion. Game animals, which had provided some meat, had long since been hunted out. By the 1920s, most of the forests had been cleared. In addition, a blight caused the demise of the American chestnut trees so useful to the settlers (see **#30**). No longer able to eke out a living from the land, about half the residents left. Slowly the forest began to return (see **#59**). In 1935, Shenandoah National Park was established, and the remaining inhabitants moved away. Scattered vestiges of the past—old foundations, fences, and stone walls—lie hidden in today's dense forest.

The harsh weather, with which visitors must often contend, was another factor making life difficult for the settlers. Several large maple and oak trees (**C**), which stand to the left of the trail a short distance past the abandoned orchard, show signs of their own battles with the elements; repeated damage from ice and wind has caused these twisted, multiple trunks. The swampy area (**D**) just beyond, however, evinces the area's fertility. Shrubby alders, birches, and other trees grow in impenetrable thickets. Marsh marigold, false hellebore, boneset, and water hemlock bloom in the swamp.

Turn left, sharply, onto the Limberlost Trail at (**E**); the Crescent Rock Trail continues straight ahead. The hemlocks, whose shallow roots require readily available moisture, begin here. They increase in size and number as you approach the heart of the Limberlost (**F**). These straight, tall hemlocks, some as much as 36 inches in diameter, are about 300 years old. They were saved from destruction by the foresight of George Freeman Pollock, who founded the Skyland resort in 1894 and later became instrumental in establishing the park. White oaks grow scattered among the hemlocks and along the edges of the stand. Some of these grand trees are 400 years old, dating back to the 1580s. Small red spruce trees are also mixed in with the hemlocks, growing larger on the edges of the stand, where sunlight is more available. This area has never been logged; the occasional stumps are the remains of windfalls that were cut for safety reasons. Although mountain laurels thrive in the acidic soils and dense shade beneath the hemlocks, much of the Limberlost is barren of undergrowth. Wildflowers such as large-flowered trillium, wild lily of the valley, common wood sorrel, and Indian pipe, plus mushrooms, mosses and other deep-shade plants, dot the forest floor. Ferns grow where sunlight has penetrated the canopy.

The stream that the trail crosses drains from the swamp and is a source of White Oak Run. On the right just before the junction with the White Oak Trail is a large boulder of Catoctin greenstone (**G**), the metamorphic volcanic rock that underlies much of the park. Notice the obvious patterns of the columnar jointing, which developed as the original volcanic rock initially cooled (see **#56**).

Nearby Place of Interest

The steep White Oak Canyon Trail passes beside six waterfalls and is full of glorious wildflowers in springtime (see **#60**).

58.

Hawksbill Mountain

Directions: Madison County, Va. Follow the directions for Old Rag Mountain (**#56**) to Sperryville. Continue west on U.S. 211 for 7 miles to Skyline Dr. at Thornton Gap, then go 14.1 miles south on Skyline Dr. to the Hawksbill Gap parking area, an inconspicuous pulloff on the right with a large wooden trail map at Mile 45.6. The trail begins at the north end of the parking area.

Ownership: Shenandoah National Park, National Park Service.

Hawksbill Mountain, the highest peak in Shenandoah National Park, rises 4050 feet above sea level. This peak and nearby Stony Man Mountain, at 4011 feet, are the first mountains south of the Catskills

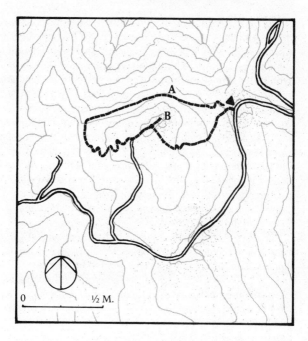

(see **#105**) to reach over 4000 feet. The nearly 360-degree pan-oramic view from the summit encompasses the long line of Blue Ridge Mountains, which drop steeply west to the flat farmland of the Shenandoah Valley, and roll gradually eastward in the green hills of the Piedmont (see **Blue Ridge** and **Piedmont**). In fall, hawks soar close overhead. This is the best vantage point in the park for watching the migration flights.

The moderately steep, 2-mile trail up Hawksbill Mountain paral-lels Skyline Dr. for a short distance; it then joins the Appalachian Trail and traverses the north slope of the mountain. After about a quarter-mile, it crosses several talus slopes (**A**). Above them loom the cliffs of Catoctin greenstone that cap the peak (see **#56**). Thou-sands of years ago, slabs of rock broke off the cliffs. These shattered, and the pieces, or talus, slid down to their present resting places here. The soil that has been gradually accumulating supports a vari-ety of ferns and mosses. More than six different kinds of lichen (see **#115**) cover the rocks. Yellow clintonia and Allegheny stonecrop, blooming in spring and summer respectively, highlight these natural rock gardens.

One of the animal inhabitants of these talus slopes is the Shenandoah salamander (*Plethodon shenandoah*). First discovered on Hawksbill Mountain in 1966, this endemic salamander has been found in only two other locations—Stony Man Mountain and the Pinnacles, both within the park—which have similar rock piles. Its habitat requirements are apparently very specific as it lives only on high, steep talus slopes that face north at elevations between 3000 and 3750 feet. Another factor now limiting the range of the Shenandoah salamander may be competition with the eastern red-backed salamander (*Plethodon cinereus*), a similar species that is very abundant throughout the eastern United States. It lives near the Shenandoah salamander but inhabits talus slopes more completely covered with soil, since it is highly sensitive to dryness; it does not fare well on dry talus slopes, and it may have pushed the Shenandoah salamander there from more hospitable areas.

The Shenandoah salamander is only one of several species with very isolated and restricted ranges in the high Appalachians. The Appalachian Mountains are considered to be the center of development for plethodons (small terrestrial woodland salamanders) and other members of the Plethodontidae family. During the Pleistocene Ice Age, which ended some 10,000 years ago, glaciers came within 200 miles of this area, creating a much colder climate than we have today. Salamanders, which require cool and moist habitats, had different distributions then. When the glaciers retreated, the climate grew warmer, perhaps even warmer than at present. Those species of plants and animals adapted to cooler conditions had to retreat to the north or to higher elevations to find suitable habitats. Salamanders, isolated on mountaintops by the deep valleys, were cut off from each other, and many species and subspecies evolved from the isolated groups. Researchers are still working to identify and classify the many varieties.

Seventeen species of salamanders inhabit the park. They will not be easily seen here, as most land-based salamanders spend daylight hours in the cool shade beneath the rocks. To look for salamanders, carefully turn over rocks or small logs; they may be hiding underneath. Do not walk on the talus slopes, as the loose rocks are unstable. Also, be sure to put back the rocks so as not to disturb the area. Although they outwardly resemble lizards, which are reptiles, salamanders are in fact amphibians, though a separate branch from frogs and toads. Unlike reptiles, which have scaly, protective skin, salamanders have not completely adapted to life on land. To keep their smooth skin moist, they live in damp and cool places. Because they are cold-blooded (like all amphibians), their respiration, circulation, and other metabolic rates increase with rising temperature and slow as the temperature drops. In summer, they keep out of the heat, and in winter they burrow beneath the surface or hide deep in a crevice to avoid freezing. Extended dry spells may also drive them underground. By hunting for insects, snails, worms, and other food at night or on rainy days, they can avoid the drying effects of direct sunlight.

Salamanders lay eggs in a nest, which the female protects. In aquatic species, gilled larvae hatch from the eggs. As they mature, lungs replace the gills; like all salamanders, they can also absorb oxygen through their skin. The larvae of the land-based salamanders, on the other hand, mature within the egg and emerge fully developed, and all members of the Plethodontidae family are lungless in all stages of life, absorbing oxygen solely through their skin and the linings of their mouths.

Continue past the trail to Nakedtop and bear left at the next trail junction. The summit observation platform (**B**) lies beyond the ledges and Byrd Nest Shelter 2. (On the way back down, the steep, 1-mile trail goes to the left beyond the shelter.) It is cold, windy, and moist on the top of the mountain. Plants typically found farther north grow here. The scattered balsam firs and large red spruces are southern outposts of these northern species. Other trees near the summit include red oak, black and yellow birch, and witch-hazel. All of them have been battered and broken by wind, rain, and ice, leaving them stunted and twisted.

In fall, large numbers of broad-winged hawks can be seen from the summit as they follow the Blue Ridge south toward their wintering grounds. In general, watch for them on the side of the ridge from which the wind is blowing. Red-tailed, sharp-shinned, and red-shouldered hawks, as well as kestrels, may also pass by, though in fewer numbers (see **#5** and **#78**). Throughout the year, common ravens often join the turkey vultures soaring on the rising air currents.

Remarks: *The Crescent Rock Overlook at Mile 44.3 offers a clear view of the greenstone cliffs on Hawksbill Mountain's north face.*

59.

Big Meadows

Directions: **Madison County, Va. Follow the directions for Old Rag Mountain to Sperryville. Continue west on U.S. 211 for 7 miles to Skyline Dr. at Thornton Gap. Go south 19.5 miles along Skyline Dr. to the Big Meadows area at Mile 51. Park by Byrd visitors' center, on the right. Big Meadows lies on the opposite side of Skyline Dr.**

Ownership: **Shenandoah National Park, National Park Service.**

Clearings like Big Meadows (**A**) are rare within heavily wooded Shenandoah National Park. The only other open, grassy areas are the picnic areas and the edges of Skyline Drive that, like the Meadows, are maintained by management. Although no official trails cut across Big Meadows, its 150 acres are open for exploring. Walk along the Rapidan fire road (**B**), on the southwest edge of the meadows, or wander freely through the grasses and flowers. Vague paths, trampled by visitors and deer, exist. Choose your own route rather than following them in order to avoid further damage to the meadow.

The bowl shape of Big Meadows, underlain by impermeable Catoctin greenstone (see **#56**), retains water welling up out of one of the many springs that dot the Blue Ridge. The swampy wetland thus formed near the center of Big Meadows persists throughout most of the year. Sun-loving plants thrive in the meadows—some 270 species have been recorded. While grasses and sedges dominate, hay-scented, cinnamon, bracken, and other ferns abound, along with blackberries, blueberries, and strawberries. With some 180 wildflowers, blooming mostly in summer and fall (see **#60** for spring wildflowers), Big Meadows has the greatest concentration of wildflowers found in any one spot within the park. Ox-eyed daisy, yarrow, black-eyed susan, and common milkweed bloom in summer, as do Turk's cap lily, northern evening primrose, beardtongue, and columbine. Other composites, such as various asters and goldenrods, together with stiff gentians and nodding ladies' tresses, splash the meadow with color in late summer and fall.

Large plants are noticeably missing from Big Meadows; the tall trees of the surrounding oak and hickory forest stop at the meadow's edge. A stand of hawthorns, red-panicled dogwood, red maple, and gray birch occupy the central, low wetland. Small trees—black locust, sassafras, sumac, and Virginia, white, and pitch pines—are scattered across the meadow.

Big Meadows provides food and shelter for a number of birds and several species of mammals. Because of its openness, this is a good place to look for nesting birds in summer. American goldfinches, chestnut-sided warblers, song and field sparrows, brown thrashers, gray catbirds, and rufous-sided towhees are often seen. Prior to nesting, American woodcocks execute their elaborate mating displays from mid-March to mid-April (see **#31**). Hawks and owls occasionally soar over Big Meadows in search of mice, voles, or other small mammals. Gray foxes and skunks often join the deer that come here to feed.

White-tailed deer are frequent visitors to Big Meadows and the roadsides of Skyline Dr., especially at dusk. Hunting and other pressures of civilization (see **#57**) during the nineteenth and early twentieth centuries obliterated the deer population in much of the region, but since then they have made a strong comeback. In 1936, after the park was established, fifteen deer were reintroduced into the southern section. Others wandered in from the Massanutten Mountains to the west. Today, the deer population is denser than one would normally find in similar, but completely undeveloped, woodlands.

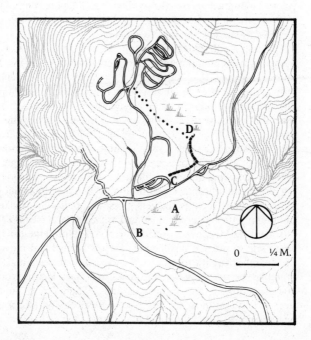

Under most circumstances, high population leads to depletion of food sources and starvation, with many deer dying in winter. This has not been the case here so far, because of the park's features, management, and location. Twigs, buds, and leaves of trees and shrubs are the mainstay of the deer's diet. In fall, they search the woods for acorns and other nuts. The roadside and open meadow, maintained by the National Park Service, provide plentiful grass from early spring through the fall, supplementing their diet and supporting the sizable population.

Hunting is permitted in the surrounding area, though not in the park itself, and undoubtedly plays a major role in controlling this poulation, since several factors combine to lead the deer out of the sanctuary offered by the park. Deer roam widely, but they tend to stay within a watershed. In the Blue Ridge Mountains, consequently, they are funneled down the mountain and beyond the boundaries of the park. Adjacent agricultural fields also attract the deer to the lowlands.

The deer herd here seems to be limiting its own numbers. At the age of two, does normally begin producing offspring and give birth to a single fawn. Each following year, they tend to have twins. In Shenandoah National Park, however, the rate of reproduction appears to be lower than the norm. Disease or other factors that have yet to be studied might also curb the population. Without these controls, the deer population would likely increase to numbers too great for the park's resources to support.

The origins of Big Meadows are not known. Perhaps it was cleared by fire, caused by lightning or set intentionally by Indians. We do know, however, that Big Meadows, which used to extend from Fishers Gap (about 1.5 miles to the north) to Milams Gap (an equal distance south) and over to the present campground, has existed for several hundred years. It is thought that Indians burned Big Meadows regularly. They came from the lowlands to hunt the deer and elk that gathered to feed in the clearing. They found that burning enhanced the growth of berry bushes, clearing out the larger plants without removing the soil. By destroying accumulated debris, burning also made collecting chestnuts in the fall easier. In addition, fires destroyed pests such as chiggers, ticks, and poisonous snakes. The mountain settlers later used the area as pastureland (see **#57**).

Today Big Meadows is maintained both to preserve the historic scene and to provide wildlife habitat. It is burned and mowed annually; otherwise the forest would encroach on the clearing. Slowly, brambles, berries, hawthorns, sumacs, and black locusts would overtake the grasses and shrubs. Sassafras, Virginia pines, and other trees would also move in. This pattern of succession (see **#41**) can be seen in the central thicket of trees that is allowed to grow, adding variety to the meadow habitat. Beneath these pioneers, hardwood trees could find the protection they need, and eventually became established, forming an oak, hickory, tuliptree, and ash forest in about forty years. After some 75 years without disturbances, Big Meadows would probably look much as the surrounding forest does today.

Until 1975, the National Park Service maintained Big Meadows solely by mowing, but this merely cut back the plants. Burning, on the other hand, sets back the process of succession and maintains the meadow ecosystem. Controlled fires provide additional benefits as well. Removing the natural litter lessens the chances of extensive and damaging fires. Burning releases nutrients to the soil and makes it more friable, promoting bursts of plant growth. Certain plants, such as conifers, need fires in order to reproduce (see **#63**). Some seeds must be exposed to intense heat before they will germinate; others require litter-free soil to grow. Potentially harmful disease organisms harbored in the litter are killed. Furthermore, some wildlife, white-tailed deer in particular, cannot survive in mature forests and require this sort of open habitat.

After exploring Big Meadows, return to Byrd visitors' center. From the northeast end of the parking lot (**C**), follow the "Story of the Forest" nature trail less than half a mile to the swamp (**D**); go past the horse trail and take the next trail on the right. Although water is plentiful in the park, this swamp, like the wet center of Big Meadows, is a rather unusual mountaintop habitat. It has dried somewhat in recent years, because the water supply has been tapped for development in the area.

Both the trail to the swamp and the swamp itself are a haven of wildflowers. Hepatica and various species of violets, watercress, cinquefoil, and pussytoes line the nature trail in April. In summer, after the marsh marigolds have come and gone, the swamp and vicinity are aglow with large blue flags and swamp roses. Blue-eyed grass is an iris, not a grass, that blooms only for one day, in the morning sun; if picked, the yellow-centered, purple flower will soon close. As summer draws to an end, other flowers open. This is the only place in the park where the brilliant red cardinalflower grows. Canadian burnet, with its tall stalks of tiny white flowers, also blooms, along with boneset and tall meadow rue. As fall approaches, the last of the wildflowers produce an array of colors: white cowbane (which is poisonous), yellow thin-leaved sunflowers, violet closed gentians, and purple New York ironweed.

Surrounding the shrubby swamp are numerous gray birch trees. These trees, quick to grow on poor soil and often found on abandoned farmland in New England, are here at the southern end of their range.

Numerous frogs, toads, and salamanders (see **#58**) inhabit the swamp. Nesting in the vicinity are a variety of birds—all those found across the road in Big Meadows, plus others, including several warblers, house wrens, and scarlet tanagers.

60.
South River Falls Trail

Directions: **Greene County, Va. From Washington, D.C., take I-66 west about 23 miles beyond I-495. Take U.S. 29 southwest about 70 miles to Ruckersville. Head west (right) on U.S. 33 for 14 miles to Skyline Dr. at Swift Run Gap. Go 2.9 miles north on Skyline Dr. to the South River picnic area, on the right at Mile 62.8. The trail begins at the far side of the parking area (A).**

Ownership: **Shenandoah National Park, National Park Service.**

The emergence of colorful wildflowers and the songs of migrating warblers announce the arrival of spring. The large and varied plant and bird populations of South River Falls Trail make it one of the finest places in the park to enjoy these spring attractions. Many of the thirteen hundred different kinds of flowering plants found in Shenandoah National Park grow here. Beginning in March with hepatica and bloodroot, an outstanding display of wildflowers continues and changes until late June, when the trees' leaves have spread and thrown a dark shade on the forest floor. The forest around South River is home to seven species of woodpeckers and is a prime spot for migrating and breeding woodland birds. Yet another enticement to walk this trail is the South River Falls themselves, which pour down into the deep valley below.

The trail switches back and forth down a steep slope through a forest of northern red and chestnut oaks, several hickories, tuliptree, and white ash. After a half-mile, the trail descends into a sheltered, stream-formed cove, continuing its 1000-foot drop in elevation. The moisture, depth, and fertility of the soil increase greatly, as evidenced by a shift in vegetation to a dense and diverse forest of "cove hardwoods." Sugar maple and basswood join the oaks and hickories.

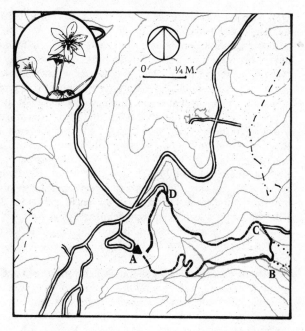

0   ¼ M.

Inset: Rue anemone

White oaks, yellow birch, hemlock, and eastern hophornbeam are among the other species to be found.

The underlying Catoctin greenstone (see **#56**) produces the fertile soil that covers the South River Falls area and much of the park. This rock is rich in iron and magnesium, as well as in calcium, sodium, and potassium; as it breaks down, these nutrients become available to the plants. The consistency of the soil is favorable as well; it is well-drained, yet it retains moisture.

The trail continues, following South River until suddenly, 1.2 miles from the start, the forest ends at the brink of a steep ravine (**B**). Here, South River plunges in its two-tiered waterfall over a ledge of Catoctin greenstone. At 83 feet, South River Falls is the third highest in the park. (Seventeen waterfalls in the park have been measured; the highest, Big Falls, drops 93 feet.) In summer, the tiny flowers of Michaux's saxifrage decorate the nearby rocky cliffs. Later, pale pink Allegheny stonecrop blooms along the ledges.

Follow the trail beyond the falls overlook to the left, then bear left again onto the dirt road. This brings you to the South River fire road (**C**). Turn left. This road climbs gradually up the slope for about a mile and a half. Continue to the junction with the Appalachian Trail

(**D**). Turn left once more onto the Appalachian Trail and walk three-quarters of a mile back to the picnic area.

In spring, particularly in late April and May, the entire forest floor along this route is a brilliant floral carpet (see **#36**). As the sun warms the ground, flowers begin to poke above last year's leaf litter. Soon, jack-in-the-pulpit, large-flowered trillium with its three petals and three leaves, and the wide umbrellalike leaves of mayapples appear. Look, too, for the small brown flowers of wild ginger growing close to the ground. After these plants have flowered, they remain erect and continue to be part of the ground cover. Others, in contrast, such as cut-leaved toothwort and rue anemone, wilt entirely soon after blossoming. The long, arching stems of both Solomon's seal and false Solomon's seal rise some 2 feet above the ground. Solomon's seal suspends its flowers in pairs along the stem. False Solomon's seal, a separate genus, sends out a spray of tiny flowers from the end of its stem. In May and into June, the dazzling azaleas are followed by an equally stunning show of mountain laurel.

A sharp observer will sight some of the sources of the forest's music. Woodland birds abound near the South River Falls, because of its plentiful food supply of insects, fruits, and seeds. Many birds hide in the excellent cover offered by the trees. Others take refuge in the more open edges of the fire road or along the banks of the stream. The extensive list of migrants, arriving in late April and May, includes Tennessee, magnolia, yellow-rumped, bay-breasted, and blackpoll warblers. But many other birds stay to breed. In fact, this area boasts one of the highest number of breeding species per acre in the park. Besides hooded, black-throated blue, Canada, Blackburnian, and worm-eating warblers, the nesting birds include American redstarts, which, like flycatchers, snatch insects while in flight; black-and-white warblers, creeping over tree trunks and limbs; cerulean warblers, which are uncommon; and the small northern parula warbler. Ovenbirds and Louisiana waterthrushes are present, both building their nests on the ground. Besides the warblers, look for red-eyed, yellow-eyed, and solitary vireos; wood thrushes; and veeries. You may glimpse vivid flashes of color as scarlet tanagers and rose-breasted grosbeaks dart among the trees. A complete bird list for the park can be obtained at one of the visitors' centers (see **Shenandoah National Park**).

Remarks: *Allow 3 to 4 hours for this nearly 4-mile round trip. Don't take shortcuts—because of the steepness, this is dangerous and will cause damaging erosion. Be careful along the high cliffs by the falls. After the spring woodland flowers have faded, others will be in bloom along the open edges of Skyline Drive and in Big Meadows (see **#59**).*

Ridge and Valley:
The Folded
Mountains

___

A long, wide band of mountains and high plateaus, the Appalachian Highlands, divides the eastern United States from the wide, flat lands of the Middle West. Dissecting the highlands like a high, narrow spine is a series of parallel ridges. From Lake George, New York, across the northwestern tip of New Jersey, west to Harrisburg, Pennsylvania, to just south of Birmingham, Alabama, they run for 1200 miles.

The layers of sedimentary rock that underlie the Ridge and Valley Province are like many layers of cloth that have been laid down one on top of the other upon a polished floor and then pushed from one side, creating a band of parallel wrinkles. At their highest, in Virginia and West Virginia, the ridges often reach 4000 feet, with some peaks still higher. The high ridges reach their northern terminus in the Shawangunk Mountains (pronounced *Shawn*-gum) near Kingston, New York, the northernmost site of the province in this volume.

Geologists have only recently discovered that the crust of the earth is apparently a series of plates that move, driven by forces within the earth. The continents sit on these plates, and there is strong geological evidence that the land masses of America, Africa, and Europe have collided at least twice to form one vast continent, only to break apart once more. It was the slow collision of continental plates, culminating in one final, violent upheaval approximately 250 million years ago, that supplied the crushing force necessary to fold and break the rock layers and heave them upward into the Appalachians of the

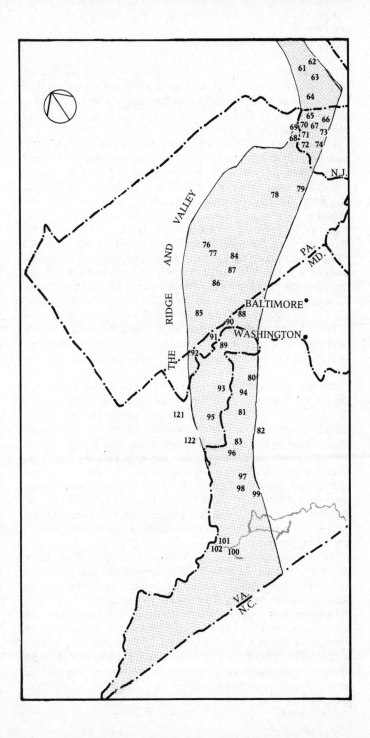

Ridge and Valley. The power of that collision was so strong that the rock layers were actually shoved westward many miles from their point of origin. Now, throughout the province, the rock layers form a series of undulating folds. The U-shaped curves, *synclines*, lie between bulging curves called *anticlines*.

The landscape of the province often belies the architecture of the folds beneath it. A high ridge may be part of a syncline, a sheltered valley part of an anticline. Erosion over perhaps 200 millions of years has carved away softer materials such as limestones, shales, and mudstones, leaving heights of very hard sandstones, quartzites, and conglomerates. When the mountains were first thrust up, they were jagged peaks, probably much like the Himalayas, and they towered above the land. Over 200 million years, they have been subdued and gentled by their rivers—the Hudson, Potomac, Delaware, Susquehanna, James, Roanoke, and New in our area, and farther south the Tombigbee, Tennessee, Cumberland, and Kanawha. The New River forms the southern boundary of this volume. It flows northward along the eastern flank of the mountains, crosses them south of Roanoke, and turns north again to join the Ohio River. The only north-flowing stream of any size in the region, the New River was once thought to be a link in the fabled Northwest Passage across the continent.

The last great natural forces to act on the landscape were the gigantic ice sheets that covered northern America at least four times in the past 2 million years. The glaciers spread southward from Canada, reaching as far south as northeastern Pennsylvania, covering the land with a mile-high wedge of ice. The glaciers scraped away the upper skin of plants, soil, and even rock. As the ice retreated, it left behind deposits of sand and gravel in the river valleys, and pockets and depressions in the bedrock, which became bogs, swamps, and lakes like Sunfish Pond and those in the Shawangunk. The soils in the northern glaciated sections have developed largely from glacial deposits. Those to the south developed in place from the underlying bedrock.

The mountain heights of the Ridge and Valley produce abrupt changes in climate. As elevation rises, temperature drops and rain and snow increase. Soils tend to be poorer, due to the leaching action of rainfall. Vegetation and birdlife on the ridgetops of Virginia have as much in common with the forests of New England as with the Piedmont Province just a few miles to the east. Many species of northern birds, like the Canada warbler, the least flycatcher, and the winter wren, extend their breeding range southward in a finger along the mountains; conversely, some southern species like the barn owl and prothonotary warbler are absent from much of this area.

The mountains of the Ridge and Valley are a major flyway for autumn migrations of many species of warblers, thrushes, hawks, and other birds. One of the great spectacles is the annual hawk migration, which can be observed at many points along the ridges, such as Hawk Mountain in Pennsylvania and Sunrise Mountain in New Jersy.

The variety of habitats in the Ridge and Valley Province, from lowland woods to open fields to dry ridgetop forests, shelter a vast array of plants and animals—about 3000 higher plants; 390 kinds of birds breeding or wintering here; 106 species of reptiles and amphibians, some of which occur only in small, isolated communties; and 263 species of native fish.

The ranges of plants and animals of the Ridge and Valley Province give clues to climatic changes and the movements of the continents. Some organisms found here also occur in Europe or Asia—or at least their nearest relatives do. This distribution is probably the result of ancient migrations that took place when the continents were joined. The bitter climate that came with the glaciers brought many Canadian and New England species southward, where they have survived in the mountains and in cool bogs of the area. The ice ages were followed by a warm and dry period, during which many grasses moved eastward from the western plains and prairie states. There are also endemics—communities of plant or animal species that exist only in a small area, such as the unique plants of the shale outcrops at Green Ridge State Forest.

Throughout most of the region, the mature forests of the slopes and gentler ridges are made up of mixed oaks. High ridges are crowned with a canopy of chestnut oaks. As one descends, bear, black, northern red, and scarlet oaks share the canopy along with hickories, red maple, and a variety of pines. Shrubs of the heath family like blueberry, huckleberry, mountain laurel, and rhododendron have adapted to poorer soils and dominate the understory.

On the richer soils of the valleys, fewer wooded tracts remain, for here the settlers cleared the land for farms and pastures. White-oak stands are common on deep, well-drained soils, sometimes forming extensive forests. From Virginia southward these stands often blend into a type of forest, called cove hardwood forest, known for its lush diversity. Made up of tuliptree, basswood, northern red oak, American beech, red and sugar maples, yellow and black birch, yellow buckeye, silverbell, and many other species, the trees grew tall in the rich soils of the sheltered valleys. Only scattered examples of these cove forests remain. North of West Virginia, the forests grow more like those of the northeast. Hemlock and yellow and black birches become more common, especially in the ravines.

The highest ridgetops, exposed to the elements and poor in soil, are often colonized by pines and chestnut oaks. In the Shawangunks it is pitch pine that covers the tops of the mountains. In Virginia you may find shortleaf, pitch, table mountain, Virginia, and some white pines. Fires, started by lightning or careless humans, drought, insects, and other forms of disturbance probably help keep other trees from shading out the light-loving pines.

There are wetlands, too, from the mountain bogs and lakes most common where the glaciers have made their mark, to the floodplains of the rivers and streams like those along the Delaware. In the northern section the floodplain forests are usually dominated by elm, ash, and soft maples (red and silver). Southward, black willow, sycamore, river birch, and cottonwood become more prominent.

Before the settlers came, the forests of the Ridge and Valley Province were prime hunting lands, where bears, cougars, wolves, elk, wild turkey, and other animals were abundant. The settlers farmed the lowlands and timbered the forests, moving gradually westward from the Coastal Plain and the Piedmont. Black bear, bobcat, and white-tailed deer are still found here along with beaver, river otter, muskrat, and mink in and around the streams and rivers. The wolf, cougar, and elk are long gone.

Human activity continues to shape the vegetation and wildlife of the region. Along the grassy borders of the roads and edges of fields, redcedar, Virginia pine, and smooth sumac are quick to invade. In old fields or pastureland left to themselves, successive invasions of vegetation occur. Asters and goldenrod and other forbs give way to tawny broom sedge. Later, blackberry, catbriar, and other vines invade, only to be followed by sassafras, persimmon, redcedar, and pine. Perhaps 50 to 100 years later, various oaks, beeches, hickories, maples, and other large hardwoods may return.

Timbering has also shaped the forests. The cuttings encourage species that grow best in abundant sunlight, and usually eliminate species with very special requirements. The forests are rarely given enough time to regenerate between cuttings. It takes hundreds of years for a stable community to establish itself, one made up of species whose seedlings can survive in the shade of the canopy and can tolerate the chemical toxins given off by their neighbors.

Scattered across the face of the province are a few pockets of old forest. Some, like the hemlock stands of Alan Seeger Natural Area and Ricketts Glen, are nearly virgin stands. Here, among these vast trees that have never been cut or burned, one can catch a sense of the forests that used to be.

—H. R. DeSelm

The Shawangunks

West of New Paltz, N.Y., a wall of white cliffs and forested uplands strikes northeast and southwest across the horizon for many miles. It rises abruptly from the rolling plain, over 2000 feet at its highest point.

The white cliffs of the Shawangunks (pronounced *shawn*-gum) are made of conglomerate, a coarse mixture of quartz pebbles and a sandy matrix. It is formed from debris of mountains that stood beside a vast sea that covered much of the continent about 420 million years ago. Erosion picked apart the quartz-bearing rocks that formed those peaks, and steep mountain streams carried the pebbles down to rest at the edge of the sea. In that trip the pieces of quartz became rounded as the water rolled them along. The smooth round stones were incorporated into other sedimentary layers and, over millions of years, became compacted into the very hard, resistant rock one sees today.

Beneath the Shawangunk conglomerate lie softer and older sedimentary deposits, layers of shale thousands of feet thick, derived from muds that collected at the bottom of an earlier sea. We know the shales were deposited on an ocean floor because the formations contain the fossils of marine animals.

About 250 million years ago, as the plates of ancient continents pushed against each other, the beds of conglomerate and other sedimentary material were thrust upward toward the west. This period of mountain-building is known as the Allegheny Orogeny (see **Ridge and Valley**). Subsequently, the softer material on top eroded away until the Shawangunk escarpment was uncovered. The ridge here is a monocline—that is, a fold in the earth's surface, shaped like a step.

61.

Bonticou Crag

Directions: **Ulster County, N.Y. From New York City take I-87 north about 80 miles to Exit 18 at New Paltz. Turn west on Route 299 across the Wallkill River. Take the first right at the sign for Lake Mohonk and go northwest on Springtown Rd. (Route 7). Go 0.5 mile and bear left on Mountain Rest Rd. Follow it 3.5 miles to the gatehouse of the Mohonk Mountain House. Turn left into the parking area. Day visitors are charged $4 per adult and $2 per child to park here as of 1983. Cross the carriage bridge over Mountain Rest Rd. Bear left immediately on Spring Farm Rd. The other branch of the Y is Bonticou Rd. You will return by this road.**

Ownership: **Mohonk Preserve, Inc.**

Spring Farm Rd., an old carriageway, passes through a mixed hardwood forest of red and chestnut oak and red and sugar maples. Stay right where a trail branches off to some service buildings. En route to the crag are some small depressions, probably the result of glacial carving (see **#72**). These become small ponds in early spring as the snow melts. During the first warm spell, usually in February, a variety of salamanders gather at the pools to breed. Species found here may include the northern dusky and the red-backed (see **#58**). If you are walking or skiing here at that time, look for their clusters of jellylike eggs in the water.

After about a mile turn right at the sign for Bonticou Rd. Along the road look at the layers of shale that have been uncovered on the hillside to your right. The shale was originally deposited as clay particles in horizontal layers. You can still see the layers of shale, but they are no longer horizontal. As you move along the road, you will see that first the layers tilt at an acute angle in one direction, become vertical, and then tilt in the opposite direction. This is graphic evidence of the tremendous pressures which were exerted during mountain building (see **Ridge and Valley**).

The Bonticou Crag is a mound of huge chunks of Shawangunk conglomerate, 1100 feet high. It has been weathered and broken up into a fantastic ruin of giant building blocks. Ice, water, and chemical changes have all had a part in this process (see **#118** and **#16**). Look for a path leading off to the left to the base of the crag. A pathway up the rocks has been marked with blue blazes, but it should be traversed with great care. You can clearly see the material that makes up the rock—the rounded quartz pebbles and the sandy matrix. In places you will find surfaces on the rock that were polished smooth by the Wisconson glacier as it dragged rock against rock about 20,000 years ago.

On the exposed bedrock atop the crag, the vegetation is sparse, consisting almost entirely of pitch pines, a few gray birches, lowbush blueberries, mosses, and lichens. Pitch pine is a southern species that has traveled north. It is abundant in the Pine Barrens of New Jersey, where it lives in severe conditions similar to this: dry, infertile soil and frequent fire. Trees that on better soils would outdo pitch pines in the competition for nutrients, water, and light cannot grow here.

The southern slope of Bonticou is a favorite sunning spot for timber rattlesnakes. Snakes are so-called cold-blooded creatures. Their bodies' metabolism is totally dependent on the outside temperature. They bask in order to increase the rate at which chemical reactions take place in their system. Growth and reproduction must take place in the warm summer months. When temperatures drop, the snakes must hibernate, their metabolic rate slowing down to very low levels.

To return, continue around the loop past ski runs and a golf course to the Gate House.

Remarks: *It is about 3 miles to the crag and back on a fairly flat road. Do not forget sturdy rubber-soled shoes if you intend to climb the rocks. If you go looking for snakes, move slowly and look where you step. A snake will move away if given the opportunity.*

62.

Rock Rift Crevices

Directions: **Follow directions for Bonticou Crag (#61).**

Ownership: **Mohonk Mountain House; Mohonk Preserve, Inc.**

Start the walk on the one-way "in" road to the hotel. Take the carriage road to the right marked "Walkers' Trail to Mohonk Mountain House" and "Glen Anna." At the T, go right on North Lookout Rd. Glen Anna is a beautiful hemlock ravine that has never been timbered. The trees are over a hundred years old. Along the North Lookout Rd. an ice storm in 1977 caused tremendous damage. Because of their brittle wood and shallow root systems, hemlocks are particularly vulnerable to ice storms (see **#67**). You should be able to see a few of the fallen trees. In the sunny patch now opened up in the canopy, various hardwood species are sprouting.

Where North Lookout Rd. ends go left on Rock Rift Rd. A sign to the Rock Rift Crevices will shortly appear on the right. A series of red blazes leads you through a maze of enormous slabs of rock, tilted on end, forming caves, canyons, and narrow passageways. Underneath the tough cap of conglomerate, the brittle shale has been slipping away, dislodged by water seeping through it for thousands of years. As it slides out from under the conglomerate, the shale literally leaves the harder rock hanging. The conglomerate is durable, but it cannot long resist the force of gravity. It breaks off in the huge chunks you see here.

As you scramble through the clefts, look carefully at the seams in the rock face. You will see that the inner surfaces of the cracks are smooth. This is an example of *slickensides*. It occurs as the two sides of a fault rub against and polish each other (see **#3**). At the bottom, turn right and right again to return to North Lookout Rd.

Remarks: *It is an easy, moderately steep 20-minute walk along well-marked carriage roads to the crevices; once there, the going is rougher as the trail winds in and out of the huge boulders. Wear rubber-soled shoes. Allow another 20 minutes to explore the trail through the crevices.*

63.

Millbrook Mountain
and Gertrude's Nose

Directions: **Ulster County, N.Y. From New Paltz, take Route 299 west 5.5 miles. Turn north (right) on U.S. 44; go 1.4 miles to Trapps Bridge, where U.S. 44 passes underneath the old carriage road. Park on the south (left) side of the road.**

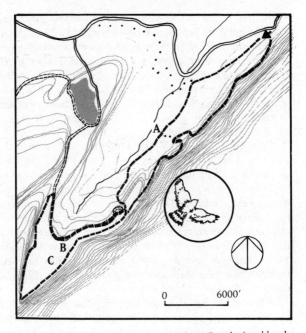

Inset: Broad-winged hawk

Ownership: **Mohonk Preserve, Inc.; Minnewaska State Park, New York Office of State Parks and Recreation.**

This is a full day's expedition, 5 to 6 hours, which will take you along the brink of the escarpment, 1000 feet above the floor of the Great Valley and out to a sharp promontory of rock, Gertrude's Nose. The views are spectacular. In fall, hawks migrate along the ridgetop; in summer, turkey vultures roost on the crags and soar out over the valley. The black huckleberries and blueberries are delicious in July.

Walk southwest (over the bridge and to the left) along the carriage road for about 1 mile. Go south (left) on the blue-blazed trail (**A**), passing through a forest that began to grow up in the mid-nineteenth century, when farms here were abandoned for richer lands in the West. As you ascend toward Millbrook Mountain, the soil becomes increasingly dry, resulting in distinctly different types of forest. The general rule that soils become drier as the altitude increases is especially true here on the Shawangunk, where the soil covering the hard conglomerate is very thin. Furthermore, the conglomerate itself is impermeable, causing water to run off.

The trail begins in upland forest dominated by sugar maples and eastern hemlocks, representatives of northern forests. The trail soon moves into a younger second-growth woodland of mixed hardwoods, where sugar maples, red maples, oaks, ashes, beeches, and hickories make up the canopy. Here, in the shallow valley behind the ridge, soils and nutrients have been carried down from the slopes above. Moisture collects here and enables this mixture of hardwoods to grow, as well as a thick shrub layer of lowbush blueberry and black huckleberry.

After about 1 mile a red-blazed trail (**B**) comes in from the southeast. Continue to the blue trail. Just beyond is an abandoned farm site, marked by an old springhouse and the remnants of stone buildings. There is a large colony of ground cedars here, plants that flourish in moist, semishaded areas—often where existing vegetation has been disturbed by farming, fires, or logging, for example.

As the trail rises, red oaks and chestnut oaks predominate; then the red oaks give way to pitch pines mixed with chestnut oak. Vireos, tanagers, and woodland warblers—yellow-rumped, black-throated blue, and black-throated green—are found here throughout the summer.

Over the next half-mile, the trail rises 300 feet and ends at a red-blazed trail running southeast-to-northwest. Turn southeast (left) along the Red Trail, climbing another 200 feet to the top of Millbrook Mountain. The mountain ends in an escarpment that plummets 350 feet to the jumble of rocks below. This is one of the highest sheer drops east of the Mississippi. At the base of the cliff lie huge chunks of conglomerate, many the size of a schoolbus. As at the Rock Rift Crevices (**#62**), the softer shale underneath the ridge has eroded away, causing the rock to break under its own weight. Turn southwest (right), again following the lip of the escarpment.

On top of Millbrook Mountain, conditions are very dry. The trees are smaller and farther apart. Scrub oak, chestnut oak, and pitch pine make up the forest canopy. Beneath them grow mountain laurel, highbush blueberry, lowbush blueberry, and black huckleberry. Evidence of a recent fire highlights the special adaption of the vegetation to its environment. In the past the area was frequently burned to ensure good crops of huckleberries and blueberries. These shrubs need abundant light. Lightning fires are also common along the exposed ridgetops. Pitch pines and chestnut oaks can survive many fires because their bark is thick and insulates the living tissues. If fire kills the upper portions of the plant, these trees sprout again from their roots. Pitch pines also have the rare ability to sprout new needles directly from the bark of the branches and trunk; this enables them to quickly resume food production and storage. All the species on the summit thrive in abundant sunlight, and the frequent fires help keep the forest from becoming too shaded.

After about a mile and a half, the Red Trail leads out onto Gertrude's Nose. At times, the trail is very close to the cliff edge, so be careful. The promontory is even more vulnerable to the elements. As you approach the tip of the nose, you pass through a pine barren where only stunted pitch pines, some scrub oak, mountain laurel, and blueberry bushes manage to grow. Just a few feet farther out, the pitch pines disappear and there is a band of mosses and stunted shrubs. This is only a few feet wide. Beyond it, the rocks are covered with lichens. Finally, at the very edge of the precipice, there is only bare rock with perhaps some microscopic forms of life.

When the last glacier retreated northward some 10,000 years ago, the entire surface of the ridge and the valley below must have borne a strong resemblance to the barren tip of Gertrude's Nose. The large boulders scattered about are glacial erratics, flotsam carried here by the ice sheet and left behind when it retreated.

Over the thousands of years that followed, most of this bare rock was transformed through infinitesimal stages into forested slopes. This process is known as primary succession (see **#41**). The change in vegetation from the tip of Gertrude's Nose to the forested valley below, as it exists today, suggests the course of that evolution. First, microscopic plant life colonized the stone, laying a thin sheath of organic nutrients over the surface. Then followed the lichens, and more organic material was caught in cracks and crevices (see **#115**). Gradually the rock itself changed. Acids from decaying plant material, gases in the atmosphere, and rainwater (itself slightly acid) all reacted chemically with the surface of the conglomerate, breaking it up. During the cold winters, water alternately freezing and thawing also worked in the tiniest fissures in the rock, wedging them apart (see **#118**). This process is still at work. Scattered across the surface of Gertrude's Nose are small pockets of gravel representing one stage in the development of rock into soil.

A thin layer of soil capable of retaining small amounts of moisture thus came to cover the mountain. The ground cover was similar to that at (**C**), made up of mosses and low shrubs. The root systems of these plants helped to anchor the thin soil and kept it from washing away. Their shade helped retain moisture. Beneath the soil, the rock continued its disintegration, while from above, decaying vegetation added nutrients to the soil. As the soil grew richer in moisture and nutrients, the first trees began to appear. Those early forests were made up of northern conifers, for the climate continued to be cold long after the ice retreated northward. Gradually, as the climate warmed and the soils developed further, oaks, hickories, maples, beeches, and other hardwoods began to appear on the richer slopes and in the valleys below.

The journey from the rocky outcrop to the richer woods of the valley floor illustrates a basic principle of the natural world. Over time, habitats are moderated; very wet places become drier and very dry places become more moist. A lake shrinks gradually, as marsh species and organic debris fill it in; eventually, the open water becomes a shrubby swamp and then a woodland. Dry, barren rock is colonized by succeeding generations of plantlife, each creating a habitat moister and more hospitable to other plants (for a discussion of secondary succession, see **#41**). The extremes are harsh; few plants grow in the middle of a lake or on the open rock. A moderate habitat—not too moist, not too dry—is where the greatest variety of species will flourish.

Conditions on the tip of Gertrude's Nose are severe. It will be thousands of years before this point of rock is also clothed in forest.

Look into rocky crevices along the cliffs for the mountain sandwort, a species that can survive in inhospitable regions where other plants fail. The mountain sandwort is a northern species. In the United States, it is found on rocky mountain ledges from New England to Georgia. As the Wisconsin Glacier moved south 20,000 years ago, it brought the seeds of northern species like this with it. In the cold climate that the ice created along the eastern seaboard, the mountain sandwort took hold; it persisted even after the climate grew warmer. The poor soils of its mountain habitat are similar to the nutrient-poor soils of the tundra on which it originated.

From the tip of Gertrude's Nose, walk north (right) along the Red Trail. On the southwest side of the point is a steep ravine, the Palmaghatt Kill, caused by a large fracture and cut by a stream. Because of its rugged terrain, this ravine was never logged. Some virgin stands of timber line the walls and floor of the valley—hemlocks, white pines, oaks, red maples, sugar maples, and blackgums. In summer, listen for hermit thrushes singing from the forests below.

Follow the right-hand prong of the Red Trail to Millbrook Dr. Turn east (right) and walk about half a mile back to the edge of Millbrook Mountain and the intersection of the Red and Blue trails. Either retrace your path or follow the Blue Trail as it skirts the escarpment 3 miles back to Trapps Bridge.

Remarks: *A long, sometimes steep hike of about 11 miles over rough terrain. Wear sturdy shoes and take water. Think twice about going if you are nervous about heights. A ranger may stop you to collect a minimal hiking fee. Camping at Lake Minnewaska State Park.*

*Nearby Places
of Interest*

There are three spectacular lakes in the area. Each is rimmed with white cliffs of Shawangunk conglomerate. Mohonk Lake is on the property of the Mohonk Mountain House. For further information contact the Mohonk Preserve, Inc., Mohonk Lake, New Paltz, N.Y. 12561, (914) 255-0919. Lake Minnewaska, just off U.S. 44 west of New Paltz, is also privately owned. Hikers must pay a fee to see both these lakes. There is no charge, though, to visit Lake Awosting in Minnewaska State Park, on U.S. 44 west of Lake Minnewaska; you can also camp at the park.

Also of interest are the Ellenville Ice Caves; continue west of Minnewaska along U.S. 44 about 4 miles, then southwest on U.S. 209 about 7 miles to Ellenville, then south on Route 52 to the signs for Ice Cave Mountain. Circulation of warm humid air into the cold caves each spring causes ice to form (see #85).

64.

Bashakill Wildlife Management Area

Directions: Sullivan and Orange counties, N.Y. From New York City, take I-87 to Exit 16, about 50 miles. Go west on Route 17 to Exit 113, about 30 miles. Turn south (left) on U.S. 209 and go 1.9 miles. Turn east (left) onto Haven Rd., drive 0.8 mile to South Rd. and turn south (right). After 2.4 miles, turn right onto a dirt road and park, after 0.1 mile, at its end (A). An abandoned railroad bed runs the length of the wetland and serves as a trail.

Ownership: New York Division of Fish and Wildlife.

Between the Shawangunk Mountains (see **Shawangunks**) to the east and the Catskill Mountains (see **Catskill Mountains**) to the west lie the largest wetlands in the nearly 300 miles that separate

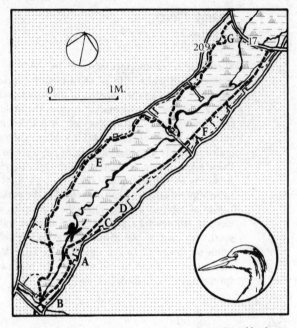

Inset: Great blue heron

New York City's Jamaica Bay and the Montezuma National Wildlife Refuge west of Syracuse. Because of its size and location, the Bashakill Wildlife Management Area, 5 miles long and less than a mile across, offers an extraordinary diversity of habitat and plant and animal life. Over 180 birds, 38 mammals, and nearly as many reptile and amphibian species take advantage of the various habitats—marsh and open water, upland and swamp woods, old fields, and abandoned orchards.

Facing the wetlands, turn left and walk downstream to its southern end where two streams, the Bashakill and the Pine Kill, meet (**B**). The main channel of the Bashakill meanders through the broad valley. The Pine Kill is a tributary that rushes off the western hills. This steep, quick-flowing stream is full of rock and soil—much of it gravel deposited during the most recent period of glaciation, which ended 15,000 to 10,000 years ago (see **Ridge and Valley**)—eroded from the highlands over which it runs. The amount of sediment carried by a stream depends largely on the volume of water and on its velocity, which is a function of the steepness, or gradient, of its channel. As it runs down the hillside into the Bashakill, the Pine Kill is slowed abruptly by the drastic change in slope. It can no longer carry its load of sediment, and the larger pieces drop to the stream's bottom. The natural gravel dam thus deposited at the confluence of these two streams is the key to the wetlands' existence, slowing and backing up the water of the Bashakill. Any disturbance of the gravel would lead to the destruction of the marsh. Although you can't see the gravel, you can see evidence of the dam in the water's flow, where the flat surface is broken into shallow riffles. Below this point, the Bashakill becomes a more typical mountain stream, flowing through pools and tumbling over rocks.

Large volumes of water move slowly through the 1333-acre marsh. The high waters of early spring and late fall give it the appearance of a shallow lake. With the onset of summer, the scene is transformed, mostly by arrow arum and pickerel weed, into a thick, nearly impenetrable green carpet. Floating yellow bullhead and white water lilies speckle the green surface throughout the summer. Birds, turtles, beavers, and muskrats rest and nest on the floating mats of vegetation. The rare river otter has been seen at the marsh. Beaver and muskrat build their houses in the marsh's edges and make sluiceways—also used by waterfowl—through the plants. These passageways become evident as the vegetation dies in the fall.

From the stream's southern end, retrace your steps to **A**, where there is evidence of the resident beavers. Although beavers often build dams to create a pond, the natural gravel dam here has made this unnecessary. Look near the water's edge for a beaver lodge built of branches, mud, and clay. The walls are 2 to 3 feet thick at the base. The top of the lodge is loosely woven to allow ventilation. On cold winter days, steam rises from the lodge like smoke from a cabin. The opening is below water, which protects the young against predators and allows the animals to come and go in winter when the water is frozen. The den though, is up above the water, and as the water level rises, the beavers will scrape away at the ceiling and add new material to the floor.

Beavers are the largest aquatic rodents in North America, with bodies 25 to 30 inches long. The flat, hairless tail adds another 9 or 10 inches. Through evolution, the beaver has gradually developed an extraordinary range and number of physiological features which enable it to survive. Its large lungs and large liver allow it to stay submerged for 15 minutes without running out of oxygen. It is able to shut its lips behind its large incisor teeth so that it can gnaw under water. Its nose and ears are equipped with valves which automatically close as the animal submerges. The large webbed back feet are used for swimming and for spreading water-repellant oil on its fur. The agile front feet are used like hands to pick up and hold stones and sticks and mud. The tail is particularly useful, for it has several functions. In the water it works as a rudder. It is also a thermostat, helping the beaver regulate its body temperature. During the summer beavers build up stores of fat in the tail, which help it survive the winter. By slapping the tail on the water, beavers alert each other to danger.

The average size of a family is around six to seven individuals, including the adult pair, which mates for life, yearling offspring, and the new litter of kits. When the young beavers are two years old, they are driven out of the lodge. Because of their large size and strength, beavers do not need to produce large litters in order to maintain their numbers. Although the colony becomes less active during the cold weather and spends a great deal of time huddling together for warmth, the animals do not hibernate. Beavers are basically nocturnal animals. Your best chance of seeing them is in early morning, though they will venture out during the day in the summer and occasionally in other seasons.

Continue north along the trail. At **C**, by another parking area, is a muskrat lodge. Named for its strong scent, the muskrat is a smaller relative of the beaver, weighing only about 3 pounds. Muskrat lodges are not always as small as this one—sometimes they measure 10 feet in diameter and 4 feet high. Generally, the lodges rest on high, moist ground; the muskrats then dig a plunge hole and channel to the water.

The boundary between marsh and upland here is indistinct; water spills beyond the marsh proper, creating wet meadows and hardwood swamps at its periphery. A broad assortment of plants grows in the 842 acres of transition zones and uplands. Red maples, gray birch, and various oaks dominate. A wide variety of shrubs and ground cover grows beneath them. From spring through fall, a multitude of wildflowers paint the uplands and the marsh margins with splashes of color. Wood duck and other birds and mammals—including white-tailed deer, gray fox, and mink—seek cover in the woods. Abandoned orchards and old fields in various stages of succession attest to the past agricultural uses of the land. Some of the fields are mowed periodically to help maintain varied habitats for the wildlife. Most of these habitats can be found near the abandoned Melrose Farm (**D**).

The Bashakill Wildlife Management Area is a bird-watcher's delight. Great blue herons have established two rookeries at the marsh. With the aid of a spotting scope, both are observable from the trail. One rookery is located in a large stand of dead trees midway down the marsh at **E** and can be seen as you continue north along the trail. At the time of this writing, it is reported that this heronry has at least four nests. Look near the treetops for large nests built out of sticks.

Eighty species of birds come here to breed, of which nearly twenty are warblers (see **#17**). Along with the common prairie and golden-winged warblers, blue-winged and the less common hooded warblers can be found. Several other warblers, such as the Cape May and uncommon mourning warblers, are migratory. A good place to look for warblers, particularly in spring, is the woods a mile and a half past **D** at **F**. Other breeding species include Virginia and sora rails, gallinules, and the grasshopper sparrow in its only Sullivan County location. Substantial numbers of American bitterns nest here, as do a lesser number of least bitterns.

Bashakill is at its busiest during April and May, when spring migration is underway. Ospreys pass through on their journeys north. The northern shrike, not often seen in this area, has been noted in early spring, en route to breeding grounds in the far north. In fall, migratory waterfowl pause at the marsh. Broad-winged and red-tailed hawks can be seen, soaring above the adjacent ridges en route south (see **#5** and **#78**).

Because the marsh freezes over, few birds come here expressly to winter, but nearly sixty species are year-round residents. The frozen marsh and the islands, where great horned, barred, and screech owls roost year round, can be explored on snowshoes or skis. Bald eagles winter in the area, generally on reservoirs some 15 miles away, where the water remains open. They often appear when the marsh thaws in early spring, but some have been seen here as late as June.

Purple loosestrife, an exotic plant from Europe with little food value for wildlife, grows abundantly in the northern portion of the marsh. It poses a threat to the other marsh vegetation, as it grows in both shallow and deeper water. By following the trail toward the northern end of the wetlands, you may be able to see some members of the second heron rookery, located in the northwest corner (**G**) in a stand of white pines. Again, a spotting scope will be needed to see the fifteen reported nests.

The Bashakill harbors more than 30 species of fish. Common ones like chain pickerel and largemouth bass keep company with some more unusual species. For example, the iron-colored shiners living here are the northernmost population of the species and the only confirmed population in New York, while the Bashakill's blue-spotted sunfish population, also at the northern edge of its range, is the largest in the state. One reason for the presence of these unusual fish may be the proximity of the Bashakill to the Delaware River. The fish can swim up the Delaware into the Neversink River and then make their way into the Bashakill. Another factor is that people have introduced various species in order to be able to fish for them here. From the northern end of the marsh, follow the trail back to your car.

Remarks: *This trail, about a 10-mile round trip, is level and easy to follow. Sections of it may be wet at times. By parking in one of the many other parking areas, the walk can be shortened. In addition, the close proximity of the marsh and trail to the parking lots makes them accessible to handicapped persons. Another trail runs along the western side of the marsh, following the old Delaware and Hudson Canal towpath. Boats can be launched at* **A** *as well as other parking lots, but rentals are not available. Only oar-powered or electric boats are permitted.*

Fishing (with a license), hunting, and trapping are allowed. Hikers should be wary during big-game hunting season, as hunting is permitted on all state lands in New York. The exact dates for the season vary yearly, but fall between mid-November and mid-December. However, hunting is not allowed on Sundays in most parts of the state. It is safest not to venture out during hunting season. For more information, contact the Department of Environmental Conservation at 21 South Putt Corners Rd., New Paltz, N.Y. 12561, (914) 255-5453.

65.
John D. Kuser
Natural Area

Directions: **Sussex County, N.J. From New York City drive west on I-80 about 40 miles to Exit 34. Take Route 15 northwest about 16 miles. Turn north (right) onto Route 94 and drive about 8 miles. Turn northwest (left) onto Route 23 and drive about 13 miles to High Point State Park Office. Turn right and bear left at each junction to reach the cedar swamp.**

Ownership: **High Point State Park, New Jersey Division of Parks and Forestry.**

This site contains a bog of Atlantic white-cedar, a species rarely found west of the wetlands of the Coastal Plain. Also in the bog is black spruce, a species that reaches its southern limit here. In the shade of the trees, few plants other than mosses, ferns, and some insectiverous bog plants grow.

A trail begins at the parking area and encircles the bog. Bear left. The white-cedars you see to your right are a light-loving species and cannot regenerate in their own shade. The young red maples now growing in the bog may eventually take over the canopy. Perhaps because of their intolerance to shade or perhaps because the seedlings require other special conditions to sprout, cedar stands are made up of trees of roughly the same age. Any difference in size is the result of competition and of differences in conditions around a given tree. (The ground, for example, might be somewhat drier or rockier in one spot than in another.)

In and around the edges of the bog are a number of plants of northern origin. They include goldthread, named for its bright yellow roots, northern jack-in-the-pulpit (which closely resembles its southern relative), corn lily, striped maple, and mountain holly. Many of these species have a range that extends to the south by way of the Appalachian Mountains. Their distribution reflects the cold

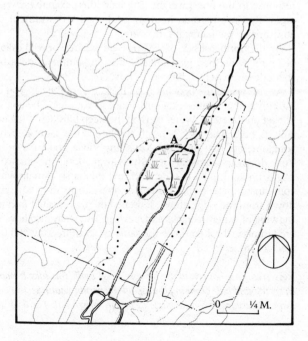

climate that existed during the more recent glacial advance. As the ice sheet retreated 15,000 to 10,000 years ago, these plants were probably distributed widely. Now, they are confined to the rigorous, cooler climates of the mountains.

Bog soils are very wet and very acidic (see **#120**). High acidity prevents plants from extracting needed nutrients from the soil and thus severely limits the number of species that may grow in bogs. Insectivorous plants—pitcher plants and sundews—circumvent this problem by trapping bugs in order to obtain nitrogen. Nitrogen is one of the most important nutrients for all plants and is also one of the least available in bogs.

Pitcher plants grow in the shape of a cup, which collects rainwater. An insect is attracted into the cup by the sweet scent, and the bright red markings on the leaf guide it down into the water. Once it is inside, the bug cannot escape because the cup is lined with sharp hairs pointing downward. The hapless bug eventually drowns and drifts to the bottom of the cup, where enzymes released by the plant digest the insect. The plant then absorbs the nutrients into its cells.

The small round-leaved sundew is covered with glandular hairs, each tipped with a clear drop of sticky fluid. An insect lands, gets stuck, and is enfolded by other glandular hairs, which move in response to the bug's weight. The hairs then excrete enzymes that digest the insect inside its own hard shell. The nutrient soup is absorbed by the hairs into the plant.

On the northeast side of the bog is an expanse of wild calla (**A**), a beautiful white bog plant that blooms in summer, and a bank of rhododendron, which flowers in July.

As you round the bog and head back toward the car, you can see the rising slope of the Kittatinny Ridge to your left. The bog sits in a pocket on the ridge. Water runs off the steep hillsides to the east and collects here. The rock beneath the bog is the same impermeable conglomerate that lines the Kittatinny Ridge and runs from New York down to Alabama (see **Shawangunks**). The surface of the bog is broken up by boulders. During the harsh climate which accompanied the last glacial advance, these rocks may have tumbled down from the ridge above, loosened by the repeated freezing and thawing of water in cracks and crevices. They may also have weathered in place, broken up by the same cycles of freezing and thawing (see **#118**).

Remarks: *An hour walk on an easy, level path, this hike is most lovely in spring and fall. Camping is available by permit within High Point State Park. Reservations can be made in person or by mail. For details contact the park at R.R. 4, Box 287, Sussex, N.J. 07461, (201) 875-4800. The park offers many miles of hiking trails, swimming, and fishing (with a license).*

66.

Tinsley
Geological Trail

Directions: Sussex County, N.J. From New York City, take I-80 about 38 miles west to Exit 34. Turn northwest on Route 15; go 20 miles to junction with U.S. 206. Continue northwest on U.S. 206 for 6 miles to Route 636. Turn right and go 0.2 mile. Turn north (left) at the sign for Sunrise Mountain Rd. and travel 3.7 miles to the head of Tinsley Trail. Park car on the right. A yellow-blazed trail begins to the west (left).

Ownership: Stokes State Forest, New Jersey Division of Parks and Forestry.

As the last ice sheet, the Wisconsin Glacier, moved across northern New Jersey, it towered high above the Kittatinny Ridge that rises above you to the east of Sunrise Mountain Rd. The power of the ice sheet was immense; it changed the face of the land irrevocably. Boulders were swept along for many miles, tons of rock were scraped from the surface of the earth, scars were gouged in the rock below. As the ice melted, it dropped the materials it had carried, leaving a thick blanket of soil and rock behind. The results can be seen along the Tinsley Trail. There are few places in the Mid-Atlantic region where the record of the glacier is so clear.

The forest along the trail is second-growth, having been cleared for farming, logging, and charcoal production up until a century ago. None of the trees grows very tall, as the poor soil and the rocky ground left by the glacier are inhospitable. As a result the trees are vulnerable to diseases, and many have rotted from within. White, red, black, and chestnut oaks are dominant, together with red maples. Black and yellow birches, sugar maples, beeches, and hickories are also present. These forests were once filled with chestnut trees, but in the early 1900s a severe chestnut blight introduced from

Europe decimated the forests and persists to this day. Although the trees will sprout—you can see one about 70 feet from the head of the trail (**A**)—they very soon show signs of disease (see **#30**).

At **B**, just a few yards down the trail, the hillside to the left of the trail is covered with a jumbled pile of rocks. This is called *talus*. Here it consists of large pieces of Shawangunk Conglomerate, a hard rock formed from pebbles and sand deposited by quick-flowing mountain streams at the edge of a sea about 420 million years ago (see **Shawangunks**). Subsequently covered by layer upon layer of sedimentary rock, the conglomerate was pushed up into a mountain range. The mountains were eroded away and the land was once again raised and then eroded by water, wind, and glacial ice until the ridgetop of Shawangunk conglomerate was laid bare. As the last glacier began to recede about 15,000 years ago, water seeped into the crevices of the conglomerate, where it froze and expanded, breaking apart the rock (see **Ridge and Valley**). As the ice sheet drew back, the loose boulders fell off of the Kittatinny Ridge and came to rest here.

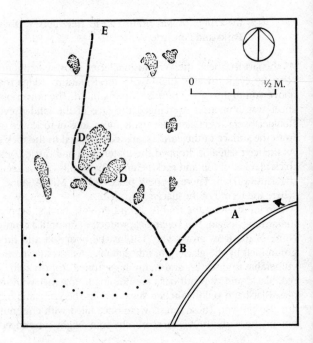

The Tinsley Geological Trail, marked with red circles, branches off to the right just below the talus slope. The turn is hard to see. Look for a red arrow on the left side of the trail. Scattered along the path are red and black rocks of nepheline syenite, a coarse volcanic stone which came from a valley east of the Kittatinny Ridge. The glacier picked up these stones and transported them across 4 miles and up over the 220-foot ridge. In the middle of the trail at **C**, a large hunk of the rock sits in a cage to protect it from theft.

The glacier did not withdraw in one continuous sequence. The ice sheet melted, halted, withdrew again. Even as the southern edge was retreating, new ice formed at the center of the glacier and moved south, carrying rocks and sediments with it. At each resting place in the glacier's retreat, vast amounts of rock, gravel, and finer materials were left behind, forming a thick covering of debris called a *recessional moraine.* Within these moraines, great blocks of ice were sometimes trapped and separated from the sheet of the glacier. As the block melted, the water filtered away, leaving behind a basin lined with glacial deposits, or till. At **D**, a number of these basins or kettles are found along both sides of the trail.

The rock at the bottom of the kettles has been bleached white. This is due to the decomposition of oak leaves that fall into the depressions. In spring, the kettles fill with water from melting snow and rain. The decaying leaves give off carbon dioxide, which combines with water to form a weak acid. Tannin, which contains the brown pigment in the leaves, also forms an acid. These acids "clean" the surface of the rock. Organic material, from drifting leaves and from the sedges and mosses that grow in the wet soil in the kettles, has begun to fill in the holes. Eventually, they will be almost indistinguishable from the surrounding terrain.

The boulder field (**E**) is also part of the recessional moraine. These rocks were carried off the ridgetop by the glacier and left behind, embedded in tons of soil and rocky debris. Gradually, the boulders were forced to the surface in the same way that rocks are continually stirred up to the surface of a farmer's field; water seeps down under the stones, then freezes and expands, lifting the rocks a fraction of an inch at a time. As the water melts again, fine silts from above are washed underneath the stones, which then cannot settle back to their original level. Over thousands of years, this process has lifted these rocks to their present position.

Remarks: *The trail traverses gently rolling terrain. Wear sturdy shoes for scrambling around on the rocks. The walk takes less than an hour. Camping in Stokes State Forest; the office is on U.S. 206. There are rattlesnakes in the area, but they are shy. In summer, pay attention to where you step* *(see #72). Take bug spray in warm weather. For further information* *contact Stokes State Forest, R.R. 2, Box 260, Branchville, N.J. 07826.*

Nearby Places of Interest

Birding at Stokes State Forest: From the trailhead of the Tinsley Geological Trail, continue north by car for 1.4 miles to Sunrise Mountain. From the parking area walk south (right) on the well-trodden path that follows the ridgeline. From several points along the path, there are excellent lookouts for hawk-watching from September to November. The ridge is so high that the birds are often at eye level. As you walk along, you will see that the surface of the rocks is often polished smooth. This was done by the Wisconsin glacier as it moved over the ridge.

The outlet stream of Culver's Lake is famous for warblers during the spring migrations from mid- to late-May, especially when the black flies are hatching. To reach it go south on U.S. 206 about 2 miles beyond the state forest office and turn west on Route 521 about 100 yards beyond Route 630 and just before the Dairy Queen. Take the first left and park just before the bridge. The lake itself is often dotted with migrant waterfowl.

Remarks: Dress warmly for hawk-watching. The winds can be cold.

67.

Tillman's Ravine Natural Area

Directions: Sussex County, N.J. From New York City, take I-80 about 40 miles west to Exit 34. Head northwest 20 miles on Route 15. Continue northwest on U.S. 206 for 8.5

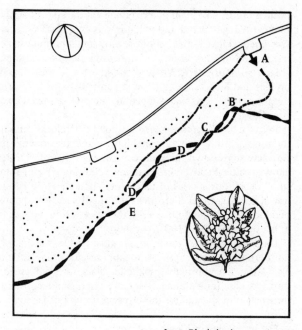

Inset: Rhododendron maximum

miles to Struble Rd. 0.3 mile beyond the forest office. Turn left at the sign for the Kittatinny Boy Scout Reservation. Go west 4.3 miles. Park on the left in the Upper Falls Parking Area.

Ownership: **Stokes State Forest, New Jersey Division of Parks and Forestry.**

Tillman's Ravine is a lovely, secluded area combining tall hemlocks, some 150 years old, and curious rock formations that provide clues to the history and the future of the site.

Beginning at **A**, the well-marked trail leads northwest almost immediately into the ravine. Hemlock ravines such as this are noted for their dense shade, provided by mature trees, and for the acidity of their soils, to which both the underlying stone (sandstone in this case) and the hemlocks themselves contribute. The needles of these trees fall, creating a deep layer of litter on the forest floor. As they break down, organic acids are released to the soil.

Rising from springs on the Kittatinny Ridge, Tillman's Brook cuts through reddish shales and sandstones. These sediments were deposited on the vast plain of a river delta at the edge of an inland sea that existed here about 420 million years ago. The sedimentary rock was lifted, cracked, and bent in several long and intense periods of mountain-building during the upheavals that created the Appalachians (see **Ridge and Valley**). Stand between the first and second bridges and look at the northwest bank (**B**) for a fold, or bend, in the rock layers. This fold, shaped like an arch, is called an anticline (see **#95**).

Because the soil in the ravine is thin, the hemlocks cannot anchor themselves firmly, and they are highly vulnerable to windstorms. At **C**, a few steps down the trail, you can see where fallen trees have allowed sunlight to enter, enabling yellow birch and some other small deciduous species to take root. Rhododendron is one of the few species that can flourish in the shady, acid conditions of the hemlock ravine. On both sides of the creek, extensive stands bloom in late June (**D**; see **#100** on acidity).

The cool hemlock woods are an ideal nesting habitat for certain northern birds. From spring into summer, look and listen for warblers—the Blackburnian, magnolia, black-throated green, black-throated blue, and Canada—solitary vireos, and northern waterthrushes. It is unusual for these species to nest as far south as New Jersey.

The brook flows along a fracture in the crest of a large anticline. After the last glacier began its retreat about 15,000 years ago, gushing streams of meltwater poured forth, seeking the easiest route to the sea. One stream found its way into the fractured fold of Tillman's Ravine. Where the main trail turns sharply right, take a short detour to **E**. Here the brook eroded a deep trough, so that today the two planes of the fracture rise sharply on either side of the stream as it runs down over the falls. The steep-sided valley is typical of a young stream.

At the falls, the stream has created a series of potholes. The land drops away more steeply here, and the water moves with greater force. It is the downward pull of gravity which moves a stream to the sea, but as water runs across the land much of that downward force is spent in horizontal motion. As a stream course steepens, the path of the water and the direction of the pull move closer. Thus, the strength of the downward pull increases. In a waterfall there is no horizontal movement at all. The water plunges directly downward; the full power of gravity's vertical pull is in play. As the water strikes the bottom of the falls, it swirls sand and pebbles against the bedrock. On each ledge, this swirling action wears away a bowl, which gradually deepens. Three stages of the process are visible. A horseshoe-shaped basin at the bottom of the falls is an old pothole;

the stream has finally broken through the outer lip. Up one step is a deep, rounded pothole, the Teacup—roughly 6 feet in diameter. At the top of the falls is a lip of stone just beginning to wear away. As you can see from these three potholes, the position of the falls is very gradually moving farther upstream. Return to the trail and follow it up hill back to the parking area.

Remarks: *This is a half-hour walk over easy terrain. Camping at Stokes State Forest. For further information contact Stokes State Forest (see #66).*

68.
Delaware River
from Bushkill
to the Water Gap

Directions: **Monroe County, Pa.; Sussex and Warren counties, N.J. From New York City take I-80 west to the Delaware Water Gap. Cross the toll bridge; take U.S. 209 north 13 miles to Bushkill Access, 1.5 miles beyond the town of Bushkill. Park on the right. Canoes can be rented in the village of Delaware Water Gap and many other places along the river; they are delivered to your access point and picked up at the landing point. If you bring your own canoe, leave one car by the landing point, in the Kittatinny Point Information Station parking lot. To reach it, take the last exit before the bridge on the New Jersey side, marked for Millbrook and the information station.**

Ownership: **Delaware Water Gap National Recreation Area, National Park Service.**

As the Delaware River flows southward, it moves back in time through older and older rock formations, each mile representing millions of years of geological history. Mountains rise up to the east and to the west; cliffs swing into view; small streams marked by dark-green bands of hemlock rush down to the river; islands slip by. Finally, the river comes to the gap itself, sliding swiftly and smoothly through the cleft it has chiseled there.

Many of the points of interest along the way are accessible from the roads on either side of the Delaware, but traveling down the river itself will give you not only a wonderful view but a unique understanding of the genealogy of this vast geological panorama and of the power of the river to mold and change the landscape.

As you canoe southward, the river will guide you through a series of ridges and valleys. The entire region is made up of layers of sedimentary rock 35,000 feet thick laid down in rising and falling seas over a span of 200 million years during Paleozoic times 250 to 575 million years ago (see **#111**). Then, during a period of great upheaval, these sandstones and shales were crumpled into high mountain peaks and compressed into dense quartzite and brittle slate. These ancestors of the present Appalachians were worn away over yet more millions of years. Water was the chief destroyer of the mountains. It broke up the rock through endless cycles of freezing, thawing and freezing within cracks (see **#118**). Water disintegrated the rock by reacting chemically with its mineral components. Rivulets, brooks, and streams carried down pebbles, rocks, and finer sediments. Swept along by the current, this debris cut away at the mountains, grinding them down.

As the weight and pressure of these mountains was removed, the earth beneath them rose as though mounted on a slow-moving spring. A new highland rose, only to be sculpted and shaped by erosion in its turn. The Delaware River began its work sometime in this period, cutting first through the soft, young rocks that covered the landscape at the time, and then carving into the older, tougher formations.

The river is wide and gentle where the trip begins (**A**), bordered by rolling hills. The forested slopes are well watered but not wet, covered with a forest of mixed hardwoods: white, black, and red oaks, beeches, maples, and hickories. This forest was last cleared around the turn of the century. On the floodplain along the banks of the river, sediments carried downstream and washed off the slopes collect in a thick, nutrient-rich layer of moist soil (see **#44**). Here silver maple, sycamore, and river birch predominate.

About half a mile below Bushkill Access, beach the boat where Bushkill Creek comes into the Delaware (**B**). The water in the creek is a dark orange-brown due to the stream's high tannin content. Hemlocks in particular produce enormous amounts of tannin or tannic acid (see **Catskill Mountains**).

Forming a high bank between the Bushkill and the Delaware is a thick glacial deposit of fine brown silt carried along by the ice sheet and deposited here when the ice melted. This rich moist soil, and the shelter provided by the ridge to the south are ideal growing

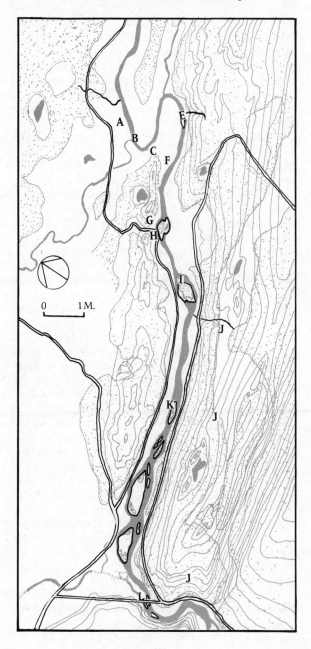

conditions for the huge sycamores and clumps of ostrich fern 5 feet high. Here and on many of the islands in the river, this fern is abundant, but it is uncommon elsewhere in the region.

Once back in the canoe, paddle across to the other side of the river. The rocks by the shore are pocked with circular depressions, some with a pebble still inside. The river swirls these stones inside cracks in the rock until a circular pocket has been whittled into the surface.

Paddle back toward the western shore as the river begins to curve around and through the high ridge of the Wallpack Bend (**C**). Look at the trees on the west bank to your right. An ice line below which no branches can grow is clearly visible on the trunks.

Now the river cuts sharply northeast through the ridge. The Wallpack Bend rises steeply to your right, its flanks covered with large hemlocks and dense rhododendron. Because the slope is so precipitous, this stand may never have been logged.

The river was well established by the time the glaciers began to grind their way across the land about 2 million years ago, but the outlines of the Wallpack Bend were still hidden by younger rocks. The ice sheets scoured off layer after layer of surface rock (see **Ridge and Valley**). As each glacier retreated, tons of water bearing new loads of sediment flowed into the Delaware, giving it renewed cutting power. Finally, when the last ice sheet melted back, all traces of the upper, softer rocks had been removed. Two resistant ridges, the Wallpack Bend (**C**) and the Kittatinny Ridge (**J**), which is traversed by the Water Gap, lay exposed, breached by the Delaware River.

Along the precipitous west bank of the Wallpack Bend is a formation of five lumps of rock called the Five Loaves of Bread (**D**). These "loaves" were created by erosion. The outer layers have been gradually removed, leaving these rounded shapes behind. Along this bank are huge boulders brought down from the ridge above by a process called "plucking": the ice beneath the surface of a glacier melts and refreezes; as it does so, water surrounds chunks of rock and then turns to ice, connecting these boulders with the ice sheet. Then, when the glacier moves forward, these chunks are carried with it. This phenomenon occurs most often on the slope of a ridge where the glacier progressed downward. Here, the glacier moved up over the northern side of the ridge at Wallpack Bend and down the southern side where the boulders were eventually dropped by the edge of the water.

Two and a half miles from the loaves is Sambo Island (**E**). Here ledges of High Falls sandstone (N.J.) or Bloomsburg Formation (Pa.)—younger than the Shawangunk conglomerate that forms the top of the ridges—come down to the water. Their red color indicates the presence of iron in the stone. Along fractures in the rock, small ferns and mosses have taken hold. The cracks provide shelter from flood-waters and trap soil and debris. The roots of these plants work away at the rock surface, breaking it up and contributing to its transformation into soil (see **#63**).

Moving down the quiet river another 2 miles, you will come to the Shadrocks (**F**), a sheer rock face that plunges into a deep pool on the western bank. The name derives from the shad which run up the river every spring to spawn and are caught at the rocks in great numbers. The surface of the rock face has been smoothed by the scouring action of running water. The flat expanse of rock was probably the surface of contact between two different rock formations. The outer formation was softer and has been eroded away by the river. This is a good place to go swimming. You can land your canoe to the south of the rocks.

Make a stop 1 mile farther downstream on the west (right) bank, opposite Depew Island. A spring bubbles up through limestone formations here (**G**). Cress, spearmint, and a variety of mosses flourish. Around the spring are pockets of very fine red clay, another glacial deposit.

A little farther on, also on the west bank, sits Indian Rock (**H**). This boulder is huge, too big to have been carried by the river, and it comes from a formation unlike any of the surrounding rock. It is very likely that this is a glacial erratic, a stone transported by the ice from somewhere else. At its foot is another good swimming hole.

Now the river runs a mile to Poxono Island (**I**). In the 8.5 miles between Poxono and the Water Gap are many islands both small and large, all formed in the following way. It is a general rule that the faster a river flows, the more material it can carry. Along this section of the Delaware, it is a *braided stream,* which means that it carries more sediments than it can handle, being shallow and slow-moving for much of its length. It is always ready to deposit some of its burden, and whenever a boulder or dead tree falls into the water, or currents create an irregularity in the streambed, an island may begin to form. As the river flows around an obstacle, the current slows. Some material is dropped out. Roughly two-thirds of any of the older islands, is comprised of large stones. Carried downstream by high water during spring floods, these heavy rocks are deposited first by the river whenever it slows for some reason. Little grows on these rocky points but shrub willows. On the downstream side of this rocky barrier, the current eddies and slows down, and the finer sand and silt are deposited. Much of this material is glacial debris, the rest is the result of erosion of the ridgetops. In the rich soils on the downstream end of the islands, sycamores and river birches flourish. Over the years, the islands slowly shift, some grow, some shrink. All of these islands are open to the public. They make good lunch spots or camping places (for canoeists only; see Remarks).

The Delaware's course is not stable; it is continually changing. At one time it flowed on both sides of Poxono Island. Gradually, the eastern channel became filled with river sediments and the water was forced into the western channel. This increased flow has begun to eat away at the western bank, revealing layers of sediment previously laid down by the river. A powerful flood could change the geography at this spot by cleaning out the eastern channel all over again.

Below Poxono Island, the Kittatinny Ridge (**J**) looms up on the bank. This ridge originates in New York State as Shawangunk Mountain (see **Shawangunks**) and runs throughout northwest New Jersey into eastern Pennsylvania, where it is known as Blue Mountain. The same ridge of quartzite is found as far south as Alabama. At intervals dark lines of hemlocks stand out against the lighter green of the hardwoods, marking the moist and shaded ravines of the small streams that drain into the river (see **#69**).

Tocks Island (**K**), a small, narrow, and rather insignificant island 2.5 miles below Poxono Island, has become the symbol for a great and bitter debate over development in the Delaware Valley. There are many who advocate building a dam, which would flood thousands of acres with a recreational lake; this would also provide cooling water for proposed nuclear plants farther down the Delaware. The project has been supported by construction interests and utilities; environmentalists have been equally determined to prevent it. At present, although the dam has been authorized, the river is protected by the National Wild and Scenic Rivers Act. New state water plans in Pennsylvania and New Jersey have reassessed local needs and conclude that there is no immediate call for a dam. As electric power needs have fallen off, the proposed nuclear plants have been shelved. Any new campaign to build the dam seems unlikely until after the year 2000.

From Tocks Island the river is wide and shallow, flowing about 4.5 miles to pass under I-80. Just above the bridge at (**L**), the formations on the eastern shore show extreme contortion. Some of the rocks have clearly been stood on end by the upheavals of mountain building, as the layering of the rock is vertical rather than horizontal. Here, the river is beginning to cut into the Kittatinny Ridge (**J**).

Beyond the bridge the river begins to curve into the Water Gap. As the canoe moves into the gap itself, the river narrows to only 300 feet wide. Forced through a smaller passageway, the water picks up speed and the channel deepens to 60 feet. Like the great curve of the Wallpack Bend, the Delaware twists through the high wall of the Kittatinny Ridge. First the western rampart, Mount Minsi, towers up straight ahead. Then the river swings east, and the sandstone and quartzite layers of the eastern flank stand like a great wall before you. Mount Tammany, as this section of the ridge is called, is 1527 feet high. The twisted and broken planes of rock show clearly the power of the slow, grinding upheaval that occurred between 230 and 200 million years ago, raising the great chain of mountains that in time were eroded into the Appalachians (see **Ridge and Valley**). Below the gap the river widens again as it crosses softer, older slates.

On the east bank at the head of the gap is a broad beach just below the Kittatinny Point Information Station. This is the takeout point. If the winds are blowing upstream, canoeing against the current is not too difficult, and you may want to canoe farther into the gap before returning to the beach. At other times the current may be too strong.

During the fall, the Delaware is a good place to see migrating hawks, ducks, and geese. The hawks soar on the updrafts that rise off the mountains and on the thermals over the open flatlands to the east and west. Geese use the river as a navigational landmark, and local biologists believe that they use the gap itself to get their bearings. Common loons, black duck, mergansers, mallards, common goldeneyes, buffleheads, wood ducks, and pied-billed grebes are regularly observed. Great blue herons and green herons frequent the banks of the river in spring, summer, and fall. Deer are often seen on the islands early in the morning.

Remarks: *The trip to the Water Gap is 16 miles and can be made in one long day of about 7 or 8 hours, including generous time for fishing or swimming. There are other takeout points along the way. Camping for canoeists is permitted on designated islands. Spring, early summer (when the rhododendron are in bloom), and fall are beautiful seasons to see the river and less crowded (especially during midweek) than full summer. Take sunscreen and a hat, as the glare off the water can be fierce. Mosquitoes are usually bothersome only at night. Take something to drink; do not drink the river water. Canoeing is easy all along this journey. There is no whitewater. In some places where the river is deep, swimmers should be careful of stronger currents. Life jackets must be worn when boating. If you canoe into the gap below Kittatinny Beach, be aware that motorboats also use this stretch of river. Their wake can upset a canoe. For information on camping and guided canoe trips contact the Delaware Water Gap National Recreation Area, Bushkill, Pa. 18324, (717) 588-6637.*

69.

Dingman's Falls

Directions: **Pike County, Pa. From New York City go west 75 miles on I-80 to the Delaware Water Gap. Cross the bridge and turn north on U.S. 209. Go 23.5 miles to Dingman's Ferry. At Dingman's Ferry on U.S. 209 go west (left) at the sign for the falls. At 0.4 mile go right; at 0.2 mile bear left, following signs for the falls; park by the ranger station. The trail begins to the left in the picnic area.**

Ownership: **Delaware Water Gap National Recreation Area, National Park Service.**

Dingman's Falls is a cool, shaded glen of tall eastern hemlocks, some over 200 years old. It is a place of few birds or animals, its silence broken only by the rushing of two waterfalls. All along the Delaware River are ravines much like this one, where small streams have eroded steep pathways down to the river. These moist clefts are a perfect environment for hemlocks. This short, easy trail winds through the ravine past waterfalls and rhododendrons that bloom in late June or early July.

As the hemlocks grow, they change the environment of the forest floor. Acids from the tannin in their needles and from the decay of organic material collect in the soils below, and the shade deepens as the branches spread into a dense canopy (see **#67**). Because few other plants are adapted to these conditions, mature hemlock stands are usually open beneath the canopy. Ferns, however, are well suited to the moist shade of these woods. Along the trail you can find spinulous and marginal wood fern, Christmas fern, and lady fern. The hemlock-rhododendron combination is the climax stage of vegetation in the ravine (see **#41**).

The limited number of plant species in this hemlock-dominated environment in turn limits the wildlife population. Woodpeckers of various sorts venture in to feed on the carpenter ants that attack the trees. Red, gray, and southern flying squirrels inhabit the ravine, although flying squirrels, being nocturnal, are rarely seen. Other small mammals include the smoky shrew, long-tailed weasel, boreal red-backed vole, and porcupine.

At **A**, just before the first bridge, spikenard, a tall plant with a

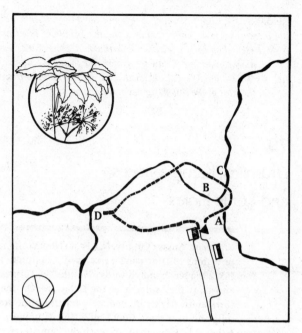

Inset: Spikenard

showy spring blossom, grows abundantly. It has found a niche here because it can grow in the deep shade and acid soil under the hemlocks. In more favorable, sunny spots it is crowded out by other plants.

Sunlight shines through along the stream (**B**), and a variety of hardwoods have taken root: yellow and blackbirch, basswood, sycamore, and beech. Brook, brown, and rainbow trout, sunfish, and dace are all found in the stream.

The ravine is carved out of brittle shales laid down in the middle Devonian period, about 388–385 million years ago. The rock is full of fractures and faults. A few steps beyond the stream, Silver Thread Falls tumbles 80 feet along the line of one such fracture (**C**). Several hundred yards on, the trail leads to the base of Dingman's Falls (**D**). On the wet rocks to your left a microclimate has been created that differs radically from the hemlock woods. Sunny rock ledges, heavily misted by the falls, support a wide variety of plants. Some of the more visible ones are maidenhair spleenwort, long beech fern, fragile fern, liverworts, rockcress, and St. Johnswort.

Remarks: *This is an easy half-hour walk along the half-mile trail. Camping at many private campgrounds along the Delaware River and on the New Jersey shore of the river at Worthington State Park. For further information contact the Delaware Water Gap National Recreation Area (see #68). Dingman's Falls is about 10.5 miles upstream from Bushkill Access, the start of the canoe trip down the Delaware.*

70.

Drumlins, Kame Terraces, and Kettle Holes

Directions: **Sussex County, N.J. From New York City follow directions to Dingman's Ferry (#69). Continue north on U.S. 209 a few hundred yards to Route 739. Turn east (right) and cross the bridge over the Delaware. On the far side turn south (right) immediately on Old Mine Rd. Go 0.8 mile and bear right. Go 0.2 mile. The drumlins rise up on either side of the road. To reach the kame terrace and the kettle holes return to Old Mine Rd. and go north 1.3 miles. Turn west (left). This road is not maintained. You may want to park here. Go 0.7 mile and turn north (right). Go another 0.7 mile. There is a large kettle hole to the left of the road. You can park your car on the shoulder. There is another kettle hole on the right side of the road 0.1 mile farther along.**

Ownership: **Delaware Water Gap National Recreation Area, National Park Service.**

These three features are topographic autographs left behind by the last glacier. *Drumlins* are smooth, rounded hills, elongated along the axis of the glacier's path. Made up of highly compacted glacial debris, clay, and rocks, they are often in the shape of the bowl of an inverted spoon, the pointed end aiming south, in the direction of the glacier's flow. Drumlins are formed hundreds of feet beneath the surface of the glacier, under millions of tons of moving ice. They are best seen in the spring and fall when vegetation does not obscure their shape.

Kames are also molded out of glacial deposits, but they are formed from sands and gravels carried by the meltwaters of the glacier, like

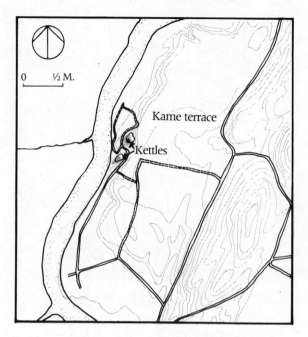

the islands found in the river itself. In one place along the river, this material was bounded by the valley on one side and melting glacier on the other and became a terrace, rather than a hill. In the terrace are circular depressions called *kettle holes,* created when lumps of glacial ice buried in the terrace melted away (see **#66**).

71.

Raccoon Ridge

Directions: Warren County, N.J. From New York City take I-80 west about 64 miles to Exit 12. Follow Route 521 north 5 miles. Turn west (left) on Route 94; go through Blairstown to Walnut Valley, 4 miles. Turn north (right) on Walnut Valley Rd. and drive to the end at the entrance to the Yard's Creek Pumped Storage Station. Register and park

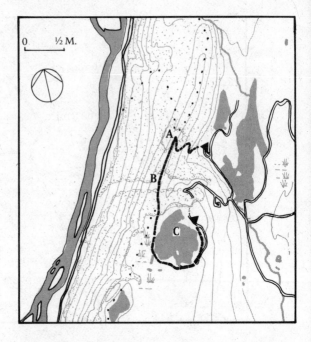

at the gate. Ask if you can walk up via the Boy Scout Camp; from there, walk along the lower reservoir, past an old building on the left. Just beyond take the dirt road that goes left by a tree marked with an Appalachian Trail sign. This will lead you up to the ridgetop, a steep hike of 30 minutes. Turn left at the top along the white-blazed Appalachian Trail. You will come immediately to Little Raccoon Lookout (**A**), a clearing from which you can look west, north, and east. A quarter-mile farther south is Big Raccoon Lookout (**B**), an opening that provides a broader panorama of the region. If you are sent to the visitors' picnic area, walk from there up the road about 1 mile to Yard's Creek Reservoir (**C**); bear left around the reservoir a mile and a quarter and pick up a trail going northwest (left). This trail joins the white-blazed Appalachian Trail in about a quarter of a mile. Turn northeast (right). You will cross under the power line and reach Big Raccoon Lookout (**B**) after a few minutes' walk.

Ownership: Jersey Central Power and Light Co. and Public Service Electric and Gas Co.

The two clearings at Little and Big Raccoon lie along the Appalachian Trail on top of the Kittatinny Ridge, the same ridge that forms
Hawk Mountain (**#78**) in Pennsylvania and the Shawangunks (see
Shawangunks) in upstate New York. The same spectacular flights
of broad-winged and other hawks soar over Raccoon Ridge in fall,
but this less-popular area is free of the crowds that visit Hawk Mountain. The reservoir to the east of the ridge is a collecting point for
diving ducks, dabbling ducks, brant, and Canada geese. The woods,
fields, and brushy area along the road are good locations for spotting
migrant landbirds. Bluebirds are particularly common. Flights of
evening grosbeaks, cedar waxwings, and pine siskins can also be
quite spectacular.

At the top of the ridge is a forest of hickory, stunted by sharp
winds and the dry conditions here. This stand is unusual, for on
most of the Kittatinny Ridge, chestnut oaks are the dominant species, with other oaks, black birch, and hickories as less important
constitutents. Some disturbance such as logging or fire may account
for this cluster of hickory. From the ridge on a clear day, you can see
three states—New Jersey, Pennsylvania, and New York. Mountains
as far away as the Poconos, Catskills, and Shawangunks are visible.

Remarks: *This is a moderately strenuous hike of 4 to 5 miles. Little
Raccoon is often a better vantage point on days with low cloud cover, when
the birds fly close to the ridge. On clear days the birds tend to fly high, and
Big Raccoon is better. You can reach the lookouts from Sunfish Pond by
walking about 1.5 miles along the Appalachian Trail (see **#72**). Nearest
camping is at Worthington State Park. Other activities in the area include
canoeing on the Delaware, fishing, swimming, and hiking (see **#68**).*

72.
Sunfish Pond

Directions: **Warren County, N.J. From New York City go
west on I-80 about 75 miles to the Delaware Water Gap.
Take the last exit before the bridge, marked Millbrook-
Flatbrook and "Delaware Water Gap Information Station." Bear north (right) on Old Mine Rd. for 3 miles. Park
car on the left. Across the road, pick up the blue-blazed
trail.**

Ownership: **Worthington State Park, New Jersey Division
of Parks and Forestry.**

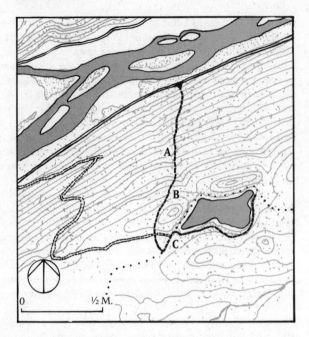

High on top of the Kittatinny Ridge is a blue lake, Sunfish Pond, a relic of the Wisconsin Glacier, which reached its farthest extent about 18,000 years ago. The Appalachian Trail, which is heavily traveled in this area, passes along the eastern side of the lake.

Walk up through the forest of young sugar maples and oaks. Pileated woodpeckers and barred owls are found nesting here. Lilac bushes, not native to this area, and piles of rock are all that is left of a hotel that stood here until the 1950s (**A**). Great numbers of warblers pass through this National Natural Landmark during the spring migrations.

A grove of hemlocks at (**B**) is a surprise. Although these trees are usually found on north slopes and in damp ravines along the Delaware, they will catch hold even on a dry mountain ridge if the young trees can take root in a sheltered hollow that collects some moisture.

At the top of the ridge, the Blue Trail joins the Appalachian Trail. Turn north (left) and follow the white blazes. Large boulders litter the ground (**C**). These rocks were picked up by the glacier as it moved south. As the ice moved over the ridgetop, the rocks it carried gouged out a hollow, which later filled with water and became

Sunfish Pond. When the glacier melted, these rocks were left behind. The finer debris —sand, silt, and clay—was washed down the mountain to help form the rich river-valley soils, leaving the boulders behind. Chestnut oaks dominate the dry, rocky ridgetop.

Bears, opossums, and porcupines are found in the forests, as well as two shy and unusual poisonous snakes, the timber rattlesnake and northern copperhead. The timber rattlesnake is best identified by the rattles on its tail. This snake will retreat if given warning. The northern copperhead is a reddish-brown color with a coppery head and bands of darker red-brown on its back. Neither snake is aggressive but will probably bite if you step on it. The copperhead is especially lethargic. You may spot a snake basking in the sun on a spring or summer day. Like all reptiles, snakes are dependent on outside sources of heat to stay active. When the weather is cold, their metabolism slows down and they hibernate.

Remarks: *The path to the lake is wide and occasionally steep. Allow an hour and a half to go up and an hour to go down. You can hike all the way around the lake, a walk of 1.5 miles. An alternate route is to descend by the Appalachian Trail. As you retrace your steps from the lake, do not turn off the white trail. It will take you to the Kittatinny Information Station at the Delaware Water Gap (see #68). Parking is available at the Rest Stop Exit, just south of the bridge on I-80. The mile trail is very steep over the final descent. For snakebite, the best defense is to be alert. Don't put your hand under rocks or logs; stay on the paths. Wear sturdy hiking boots, not sneakers. If you are planning to do long-distance hiking in snake country, take a snakebite kit and learn how to use it properly. Many people do themselves unnecessary injury trying to treat snakebite. If you have been bitten, don't panic. Identify the snake if at all possible. Keep movement to a minimum, and get to a doctor.*

73.

Big Spring

Directions: **Sussex County, N.J. From New York City take I-80 west to Exit 27, about 50 miles from the George Washington Bridge. Take U.S. 206 about 10 miles north to Springdale; go west (left) on Fredon Rd. (Route 618)**

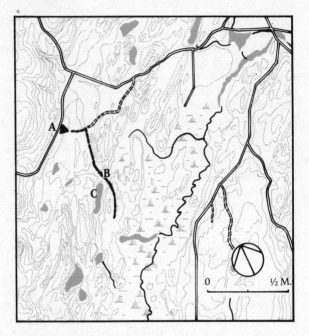

1.3 miles to Springdale Rd. Turn south (left) and go about 0.5 mile. There is a small parking area (A) and a sign on the east (left) side of the road. A dirt road leads into the wildlife management area.

Ownership: **Whittingham Wildlife Management Area, New Jersey Division of Fish, Game, and Wildlife.**

The moist woods, rocky limestone ravines, and swamps of Big Spring are rich in botanical species—from abundant spring wildflowers, to diverse trees of the canopy, to ferns nestled in the limestone rocks. The emerging forest of sugar maples and mixed hardwoods at Big Spring is a remnant of a forest type that once covered large sections of the state before the European settlers cleared the land. Today the area around Big Spring is still heavily farmed.

At the parking area (**A**), pale jewelweed grows profusely in summer, a sign of the basic, calcium-rich soils that exist here. Like the cliff at Johnsonburg (**#74**), Big Spring lies in the Kittatinny Valley on top of limestone formations. Here, on the gently rolling land, soils rich in calcium have developed; much of the area is very fertile. Soils derived from limestone are called *basic* or *alkaline,* as opposed to the *acidic* soils found in most of the Mid-Atlantic region. The *pH scale,* from 0 to 14, is used to measure acidity and alkalinity, with 7 being the central point of perfect neutrality. Neutral soils are those with a pH of 6.5 to 7.4; below 6.5, acidity increases, and above 7.5, soils are increasingly alkaline. On calcium-rich or *calcareous* soils, such as those at Big Spring, pH values generally range between 7 and 8. This means that even though these soils are alkaline, they are still close to the neutral range for pH. In the neutral range a plant is able to take in the widest spectrum of nutrients from the soil, making neutral soils the most fertile. The alkalinity of the soils at Big Spring is constantly being countered by rainwater, which leaches calcium and other nutrients deeper into the soil, and which supplies weak carbonic acid to the soil. Carbonic acid forms as hydrogen atoms in the rainwater combine with carbon dioxide in the atmosphere (see **#100**). On the other hand, the deep roots of the trees are constantly drawing up nutrients that have been leached from the upper soil layers. The nutrients are placed back on the soil surface in the fallen leaves. As a general rule, smaller plants are much more sensitive to changes in pH than trees, though certain species of trees such as the hemlock are often an indicator of acid soil.

Go through the first gate and follow the track out across the fields a quarter-mile to the band of trees; here the dirt road turns right and after about a half-mile passes through a wooden gate. Just beyond the gate is a small clearing on the right (**B**). Around the edges of it are a number of black walnuts. This species is typically found in the sugar-maple–mixed-hardwood forest of the Kittatinny Valley. Open patches such as this are kept clear by the Division of Fish, Game, and Wildlife. In these old fields and around the edges of the cultivated fields grow a variety of summer flowers, which attract butterflies. Wild bergamot and black-eyed susan are two such plants. Many species of butterflies gather here in summer, including spicebush, black, and tiger swallowtails, great spangled fritillaries, wood nymphs, satyrs, and skippers. Look for the hummingbird moth too, an odd diurnal species that feeds and flies like the bird it is named after, using a long tubelike proboscis instead of a bill to feed on the nectar of flowers.

Turn right off the road and walk straight through the clearing into the woods a few hundred yards toward a long marshy pond (**C**), one of many in the area. Dependent largely on rainwater, these ponds are full in spring and very low in summer or times of drought. The pond basins were formed primarily by the scouring action of the ice sheets as they moved slowly over the land during the Ice Ages (see **#72**). Alongside the pond, the hillside is blanketed with a layer of broken rock called talus (see **#66**). Large chunks of limestone provide a habitat for narrow-leaved spleenwort and walking fern, two ferns found in calcareous outcrops.

The shallow waters of these ponds are breeding places for amphibians, including several interesting species of salamanders. The long-tailed salamander, a very thin yellow salamander with strong black herringbone markings on its long tail, is found in pools in this limestone belt of northern New Jersey, and from southern New York south through the mountains of West Virginia. The spotted salamander is found throughout most of the Mid-Atlantic except for the Coastal Plain in New Jersey and the Delmarva Peninsula. The Jefferson salamander, on the other hand, has a range which touches only the northwestern tip of New Jersey and southern New York and the upland regions of Pennsylvania, Maryland, Virginia, and West Virginia. It is a large dark-colored salamander with long toes and bluish flecks on its sides. Found throughout the entire Mid-Atlantic region is the northern red salamander; its reddish orange back is dotted with black spots. The best way to see these salamanders is to overturn rocks, logs, and other debris by the ponds during or just after wet weather in spring. In the event that you might scare up a snake, turn rocks over with a stick. In early spring, the salamanders begin to move around with the first warm rains, migrating to these traditional breeding ponds at night to lay thousands of eggs in only a few days.

Another amphibian to watch for in early spring is the gray treefrog. Both the northern and southern species of the gray treefrog are found throughout the eastern United States. They are virtually indistinguishable except for their songs, one trill being slightly higher and slower than the other. At Big Spring, the slower trill of the northern species is heard from April to June. Treefrogs are especially adapted for climbing, with long limbs and toes equipped with sticky pads. Depending on temperature, humidity, light, and diet, treefrogs can vary from green to pearl gray to brown. Treefrogs have black pigment in their skin cells, which are connected to the nervous system. As the nervous system receives different stimuli through the eyes or through physiological changes in the frog, these clusters of black pigment change shape. While it is generally true that frogs living in and around dark cold waters have dark skin, the changes in color are not easy to predict or explain. Some species, such as the spring peeper, change very rapidly, in about 10 minutes; other species take much longer. The gray treefrog is large for a treefrog, about 2 inches long and warty above with bright orange patches under its back legs. It can sometimes be seen on the ground near the water during the breeding season in early spring, but its excellent camouflage makes it difficult to see.

Around the ponds you may find nesting northern waterthrushes and cerulean and prothonotary warblers. Pileated woodpeckers, eastern bluebirds, and wood ducks also nest at Big Spring. River otters have occasionally been sighted here; apparently they are making a comeback after many years of absence.

By the shore of the pond there are large sycamores, green ashes, and many silver maples, the roots buttressed for support in the soft, wet muck. On the higher ground a younger forest of sugar maple mixed with a great variety of other species makes up the canopy. White, red, and black oaks, red maple, basswood, white ash, tulip-tree, chinkapin oak, black birch, and various hickories are prominent. The shrub layer is also diverse and lush, including spicebush, bladdernut, northern prickly ash, and shadbush. Flowering dogwood is a common understory species. The diversity and lushness of the vegetation here reflect the fertile, well-watered conditions.

The display of spring flowers in these woods is outstanding, Look for the showy white flowers of bloodroot, the curiously shaped blossoms of Dutchman's breeches, red columbine, purple round-lobed hepatica, delicate white rue anemone, and many others.

Return to the dirt road and turn southwest (right). The road bears right, uphill through upland woods. Follow it to the end, about a half-mile, turn northwest (right) off the road into the woods, and clamber a few yards down into a narrow dell. Be careful of the old wire fencing. Among the limestone boulders you will find an extensive stand of Goldie's fern, its large, golden-green fronds arching backwards. It is found in only a few locations in the region. Nearby are maidenhair spleenwort and walking fern, which also are associated with limestone (see **#74**). In middle to late summer cardinal flowers bloom along the stream.

If you turn to the left and follow the ravine southwest, you will emerge out into black-ash swamp, a huge trackless area difficult to explore. To return to your car, backtrack along the road.

Remarks: *This walk of about 3 miles is on easy terrain. A compass and binoculars are recommended. Wear sneakers. Nearest camping is at Jenny Jump State Forest south of I-80 off Route 519. For an interesting canoe trip, put in at the bridge in Springdale and paddle south into the freshwater marsh and swamp. These wetlands support an array of birds. Ospreys and great blue herons pass through the area on migration in April and May and from August to October. Ring-necked ducks, hooded mergansers, and blue- and green-winged teals are also found here in spring and fall. This area is open to bow-and-arrow hunting in October and November and to*

*shotgun hunting for one week in December. Use it carefully or on Sundays,
when no hunting is allowed. Spring is an excellent time to explore the area.
In summer Big Spring can be hot and buggy. For further information
contact the New Jersey Division of Fish, Game, and Wildlife, CN 400,
Trenton, N.J. 08625, (609) 292-2965.*

74.
Johnsonburg
Limestone Cliffs

Directions: **Warren County, N.J. From New York City take
I-80 west about 55 miles to Exit 19. Coming off the exit
ramp, cross over Route 517 and drive into Allamuchy. Take
the second left, Johnsonburg Rd., which goes northwest.
(In Quaker Church the road jogs right.) After 7.5 miles
turn northeast (right) onto Route 519 and drive into Johnsonburg, 0.2 mile. At the intersection of Routes 519 and
661, continue straight on Route 661 and drive 0.2 mile,
crossing under the railroad tracks. Turn west (left) immediately on Kerrs Corner Rd. and drive 0.3 mile to a rough
dirt road on the left leading up to the old railroad station.
Park by the station and walk westward (right as you face
the tracks) about 0.5 mile along the tracks until you come
to a cliff on your left.**

Ownership: **Private.**

Neatly displayed on this limestone cliff are several ferns unique to
limestone outcrops. Because of the special conditions under which
they grow, these are rarities to most of us. The limestone formation
exposed here is part of the Kittatinny Valley, which lies between the
Kittatinny Ridge to the west and the New Jersey Highlands to the
east (see **#68** and **#50**). The valley is lower than the surrounding
ridges because it lies over shales and limestones, more easily eroded
than the rocks of the ridges. These formations are very old, dating
back to the Ordovician and Cambrian periods, approximately 450 to
570 million years ago. In Pennsylvania, the Kittatinny Valley opens
up into the wide expanse of Great Valley (see **#87**).

The community of ferns clinging to the cliff flourishes because these species have adapted to the special conditions here. Moisture is intermittent, held only by minute pockets of soil that collect in the cracks and crevices. These pockets of soil offer little anchorage and few nutrients to plants. The ferns must also be able to cope with the disadvantages of growing on limestone. Just as acid soils prevent a plant from absorbing certain nutrients, the alkaline conditions of the limestone cliff also inhibit the absorption of certain nutrients (see #73 and #100 on acidity and alkalinity).

Walk slowly along the railroad tracks, scanning the left cliff face carefully. These ferns are small and easy to overlook. You should be able to find purple cliff brake, a bluish-green evergreen fern with striking, glossy purple stems. There is also wall rue, which has tiny fan-shaped leaves, not like a fern at all. It apparently withers in dry periods but comes back to life with rain, like the resurrection fern to the south. Occasionally you may see Scott's spleenwort, which is very uncommon. It is a cross between ebony spleenwort and walking fern, another fern of limestone outcrops, and it grows only where these two species are found. Its leaves tend to have short leaflets at the base and an elongated tip, but there is considerable variation from one plant to another. Fragile fern is common on the cliff. Not confined to limestone, it grows on any rocky cliff, keeping to shady crevices. Fragile fern wilts during the summer, but grows again during the fall.

As you walk along the tracks listen for the song of the worm-eating warbler.

Remarks: *To reach the foot of the cliff you must scramble through wild raspberry bushes and over loose rocks. Wear sturdy shoes. The best time to visit this area is from April through June to see the ferns at their peak. Nearest camping is at Jenny Jump State Forest, a few miles south of Exit 20 on I-80. Activities include hiking at Jenny Jump and along the Delaware River just to the west, canoeing and fishing with a license in the Delaware. Boat rentals available all along the Pennsylvania side of the river.*

75.
The Tubs
Natural Area

Directions: **Luzerne County, Pa. From Scranton take I-80 southwest about 14 miles to Exit 475 for Bear Creek and Route 115. Turn southeast and go 1.5 miles. Just past the median barrier turn sharp right on the old East End Blvd. Park the car and walk down about half a mile to a dirt path, which leads left to the base of the falls.**

Ownership: **Luzerne County Park Department.**

Here on the outskirts of Wilkes-Barre, Wheelbarrow Run drops through a series of cauldrons, smooth basins hollowed out of the bedrock, shadowed by hemlock and mountain laurel. The largest pool, at the top of the falls, is about 30 feet across. The Tubs were formed by torrents of water released as the last glacier melted over a period of thousands of years. In the warm summers, great cascades of meltwater, bearing tons of gravel, sand, and boulders, spilled over the edge of the ice sheet or down through a crevasse within the glacier. Finding its way to the bedrock, the deluge of water swirled the abrasive material it carried around and around, hollowing out the bedrock into a series of potholes (see **#67**). Follow the rough path which leads upstream along Wheelbarrow Run. In one of the upper basins there is still a large boulder with which the water worked the stone. When the ice sheet finally withdrew to the north, the volume of water decreased. The shape of the potholes has remained essentially unchanged for thousands of years.

Remarks: *Spring and fall are good seasons to visit; the site can be very crowded in summer. The nearest camping is at Hickory Run State Park. (see **#118**). Across Laurel Run at the bottom of East End Blvd. is Mountain Park, with a number of paths. It overlooks strip mines on the northeastern slope. For further information contact the Superintendent, Department of Parks and Recreation, Moon Lake Park, Hemlock Creek, Pa. 18621, (717) 675-1312.*

76.

Bear Meadows
Natural Area

Directions: **Huntingdon County, Pa. From the intersection of U.S. 322 and Route 26 in State College, go east 5.8 miles on U.S. 322 to Bear Meadows Rd., just opposite a golf course. Go south (right). After 1.5 miles bear left at the fork on Bear Meadows Rd. Go 3.0 miles to a right turn. Drive past it another 0.5 mile and bear right. Park at the bridge just ahead. A sign indicates the natural area. From your car walk up the road a few yards and turn right along an old road that follows the southern side of the bog. After a few hundred yards a short trail, on your right, leads to a wooden observation tower at the edge of the bog (A).**

Ownership: **Pennsylvania Bureau of Forestry.**

From the observation tower, look out over a high and wide meadow of sedges, cotton grass, northern conifers, and bog shrubs surrounded by ridges. This National Natural Landmark is one of the few peat bogs found in the Ridge and Valley Province. Bogs are common on the plateaus to the north and west, where glaciers scoured out many basins in the horizontal layers of rock. In the Ridge and Valley Province, where the rock has been compressed and contorted, broken, and faulted and where the glaciers did not reach, there are few such bowls where water is held.

As you stand on the observation tower, the bog looks more like a wet grassland than the bogs of the pine barrens or those of the north (see **#120**). It is believed that this relatively shallow peat bog began to form after beavers dammed up the outlet to Sinking Creek, which now drains the bog. Pollen specimens taken from the bog indicate that it is over 10,000 years old. These pollen specimens have allowed scientists to partially reconstruct the forests that grew here in the shadow of the glacial ice sheets and which changed as the climate warmed. First a spruce forest, such as that in the far north of Canada, covered the region. This was followed by a pine forest, which eventually became a mixed deciduous forest. A few northern species remain in the bog, such as the black spruce and the balsam fir. These trees can be seen from the observation platform. The fir is narrow and pointed at the top, its needles flat and aromatic. The black spruce has a more irregular crown; its needles are four-angled and spread out from all sides of the twig. The northern bog species found here, such as the spruce, fir, cotton grass, goldthread, and sundews, are able to flourish in part because the temperatures in the bog are much cooler than those on the surrounding ridges. This is because cold air, denser and heavier than warm air, sinks and remains trapped in the valley. Temperatures here can be below freezing for nine months of the year.

Other tree species invading the meadows are hemlock, white pine, and blackgum. Mats of sphagnum and sedges and cotton grass are found throughout the bog, with occasional patches of round-leaved sundew. The common shrubs at the edges of the bog include blueberry, alder, and virbunums. Pitcher plants grew in the bog 10 years ago but have since disappeared, victims of overzealous collectors. All the species found at Bear Meadows are well adapted to the acidic conditions of a bog (see **#120** for more discussion on bog vegetation).

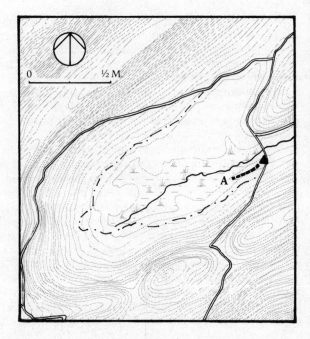

Remarks: *The peat is not very thick here, only about 7 feet, but this is enough to make walking treacherous in places. Also be advised that it is easy to lose your sense of direction in the bog. If you intend to go into the bog, take a compass; wear rubber boots or old sneakers. A hiking trail encircles the area. Nearest camping is at Greenwood State Park, south of Bear Meadows along Route 26. Mosquitoes may be fierce in summer.*

77.
Alan Seeger
Natural Area

Directions: **Huntingdon County, Pa. From State College, take U.S. 322 east and south 18.1 miles to the Laurel Creek Reservoir and turn west (right) on Stone Creek Rd. Go 0.1 mile and turn right again. Drive 7.3 miles to the parking area by the intersection of Seeger and Stone Creek roads. The well-marked trail begins by the parking area.**

Ownership: **Rothrock State Forest, Pennsylvania Bureau of Forestry.**

A stately grove of hemlocks and an impenetrable tangle of rhododendrons shade the streambed of Standing Stone Creek. Like the stand at Ricketts Glen (see **#113**), this remnant of virgin forest hints at the forests of tall trees that once covered North America. Pockets of hemlock, white pine, and rhododendron were once common along watercourses throughout the Ridge and Valley Province, but most of them were decimated to produce charcoal in the nineteenth century and tannin in the early twentieth. (Tannin was used to cure leather.) It is not clear why this area survived, for it was surrounded by logging operations.

The trail begins on slightly higher ground (**A**), where white oaks, white pine, pitch pine, red maples, and an understory of flowering dogwood are the principal species. Rhododendron is absent. These trees are much younger than the hemlocks farther down the trail, this area having been cut once in the late 1800s.

About halfway around this half-mile trail, along the banks of Stone Creek, are the largest and oldest hemlocks. Age estimates of over 500 years for these are conservative; a much smaller tree that fell over along the millrace (**C**) was determined to be 500 years old. Notice that the hearts of some of the hemlocks have rotted. These trees can continue to survive as long as the outer layer of bark, which contains the living tissue responsible for the transport of water and nutrients, remains healthy. The path winds through a tunnel of high rhododendron bushes, which grow well in the damp, acid soils in the shade of the hemlocks. The height of the blooming period is early July. Few other plants can grow under the heavy canopy, but mushrooms such as the deadly amanita can be seen. The amanita is a stark white mushroom with a long and delicate stalk. It has a distinctive fringed collar around the middle of the stem and is very poisonous. Do not touch it.

The hemlocks that have been preserved here indicate the transition from the oak forests of the Ridge and Valley Province to the hemlock and white pine forests of the Appalachian Plateau (see **Appalachian Plateau**). Note the difference between the gentle topography of this site and the steep north slopes on which the isolated hemlock stands are found farther south (see **#47**).

Remarks: *The hike is all on flat ground. An interesting side trip can be made to an old narrow-gauge railway grade. At* **C** *turn north (left) and cross Stone Creek Rd. on the blue-blazed Greenwood Spur Trail. This runs into the railroad grade just across the road. The Greenwood Spur runs from Greenwood State Park to the Mid-State Trail. For further hiking information write the Keystone Trails Association (see* **Susquehanna River Gorge***). For a map of trails in the Rothrock State Forest, write to Pennsylvania Bureau of Forestry, 3rd and Reily Sts., Harrisburg, Pa. 17120. Nearest camping is at Greenwood Furnace State Park along Route 26 south of the natural area. There is lake fishing with a license, swimming, and boating. The lake is used for ice-skating during the winter.*

78.
Hawk Mountain
Sanctuary

Directions: **Berks County, Pa. From Philadelphia, go north on the Northeast Extension of the Pennsylvania Turnpike about 37 miles to I-78. Go west about 17 miles to Exit 11. Turn north (right) on Route 143 and go 3.8 miles. Turn** west (left) toward Eckville, following signs for the sanctuary. Drive 6.6 miles along this road and turn left into the parking area for visitors' center. From New York City take the New Jersey Turnpike south to Exit 14, Newark. Then go west on I-78 and U.S. 22 to Allentown, about 110 miles in all. From Allentown continue west about 16 miles to Exit 11, Route 143.

Ownership: **Hawk Mountain Sanctuary Association.**

The North Lookout of Hawk Mountain balances on the knife edge of Blue Mountain. To the north, the land drops away 1000 feet to the valley of the Little Schuylkill River and farther away the mountains of the Ridge and Valley Province ripple along the skyline. Southward the rolling and more ancient hills of the Great Valley stretch to the horizon. From September through November hawks hold dominion. An average of twenty thousand birds of prey, about fifteen different species, follow the line of the ridge, many of them at eye level, from the thousands of broad-winged hawks in the warm days of early fall to the golden eagles riding the November gales.

Blue Mountain or Kittatinny Ridge is the same formation that runs across the Delaware Water Gap (**#68**) and on up into New York, where it becomes the Shawangunks (see **Shawangunks**). The upper layer is known as the Tuscarora sandstone here, but it was formed about 420 million years ago in the same seas as the Shawangunk conglomerate to the north. It was thrust upward in the same gargantuan upheavals, exposed by the same millions of years of erosion. This region was not covered by any of the four glacial advances that sculpted the lands to the north. The ice sheets, which stopped in northern Pennsylvania, did change the climate here, though, bringing the severe temperatures characteristic of a subarctic region. From the parking area, take the well-marked trail a few hundred yards to the South Lookout. Below you is the River of Rocks, a field of great boulders that were broken off the cliffs above through the stress of water freezing and thawing over and over again in the bitter climate that accompanied the glaciers (see **#118**).

Continue up the rocky, sometimes steep trail for three-quarters of a mile to the North Lookout. From here you have a clear view in three directions.

The magnificent hawk flights along the Kittatinny are a direct result of the topography of the Appalachians. This mountain chain runs the length of the eastern United States, curving from northeast to southwest. Autumn wind patterns along the ridges allow the hawks to conserve energy by gliding and soaring through much of their journey. The prevailing northwesterlies of fall strike the ridges and sweep upward. These rising air currents give the birds lift; they spiral upward and then glide southward, gradually losing altitude. By repeating this pattern over and over, the hawks can move southward many miles a day. The Kittatinny Ridge is the southeastern-most highland. The wide sweeping view from the North Lookout makes Hawk Mountain one of the best sites in the East for observing the migrations.

The stream of hawks along the Kittatinny comes only in autumn. During the spring migrations, the birds do not follow the ridge line here, for then there are no strong and steady winds to create up-drafts.

The migrations over Hawk Mountain are similar to those over the Montclair Hawk Lookout (see **#5**). The birds that fly along the Kittatinny come from New England, the Great Lakes region, and Canada. Merlins, kestrels, and the uncommon peregrines—hawks that follow the coastline—are relatively few here. One of the earliest migrants, the bald eagle, passes over in August. Golden eagles, a rarity along the coast, are seen here in small but significant numbers every year in the cold winds of November. The rough-legged hawk of the Arctic and the goshawk of the northern forests are seen occasionally, but their numbers are cyclic. Their passage depends on the supply of prey in their northern hunting grounds. In some years the number of rodents decreases dramatically and the birds head south in search of better hunting.

Different wind patterns produce different lines of flight along the ridge. In early fall the weather is still mild and calm. On warm, sunny days abundant thermals rise off open fields on either side of the Kittatinny, making favorable conditions for great fights of broad-winged hawks (see **#5**).

By October most broadwinged hawks have moved south. Now the winds blow more briskly, coming more from the northwest. This is the best month for seeing the greatest variety of hawks. Sharp-shinned, Cooper's, red-tailed, and red-shouldered are the most common species. Ornithologists who have monitored the migrations since the sanctuary was established nearly 50 years ago have found that a certain combination of weather conditions produces the prime days for hawk watching. First, a low-pressure system moves across New England. On its heels a cold front flows down from Canada, accompanied by steady winds out of the northwest. Several good days of hawk flights should follow, as the birds track the north slope of the ridge, gaining uplift from the northwest winds that strike the mountain and rise up and over it. The North Lookout is best in this weather. As the winds become stronger, the birds fly closer to the ridgetop, where the turbulence is less. They seldom fly in fog or rain.

Hawk Mountain, a National Natural Landmark, is also well worth a trip in spring. Though spectacular hawk flights do not occur, waves of warblers pass through, peaking in early May. Thirty-eight species have been recorded, of which seventeen have nested at the sanctuary.

Remarks: *The walk to the North Lookout takes an hour and a half, round trip. Binoculars are a necessity. It is rocky but not too difficult. The sanctuary is open all year round. A naturalist is on duty at the lookouts from September through November. Fall weekends are extremely crowded. There is an admission charge for non-members. You can hike on trails through the sanctuary, including the Appalachian Trail. There is good cross-country skiing during the winter. For further information contact Hawk Mt. Sanctuary, Route 2, Kempton, Pa. 19529, (215) 756-6961. Camping at Blue Rocks Campground through October 31st. The campground is on Route 143 between I-78 and Albany, Pa.*

Caverns
of the
Great Valley

All along the Great Valley of the Ridge and Valley Province run formations of limestone and dolomite often hundreds of feet thick. Within them are countless caves, small chambers, passages, and vast halls. Some of these are decorated with banners and spears of stone, sculpted columns, and still pools reflecting delicate spires and buttes.

From approximately 575 to 250 million years ago, this region was repeatedly covered by a shallow sea. During those millions of years, thick beds of sediment accumulated, rich in calcium and carbon from decayed marine algae. The sediments hardened over time into limestone and dolomite (limestone is made up of calcium carbonate, while dolomite contains calcium carbonate and magnesium). As the seas advanced and retreated, the composition of the sediments changed, and interlayered between the formations of carbonate rocks are beds of sandstone, shale, and other sedimentary strata (see **#111**).

Then followed an age of turmoil, when the plates of the earth's crust collided, ground together, and raised up the towering ancestors of the Appalachians (see **Ridge and Valley**). The sedimentary rocks were fractured, heaved upward, and tilted at varying angles.

For millions of years, the limestone and dolomite formations lay below the water table. Then, over time, the land was lifted, and the water table dropped. Meanwhile, erosion stripped away much of the overlying rock. Now groundwater could seep through fissures and along the joints or planes of fracture in the layers of rock. Groundwater often carries carbonic acid, a weak acid formed as water combines with carbon dioxide from the atmosphere or from the soil, where it is given off by decaying organic material. As acidic water worked its way through the carbonate rocks, the carbonic acid combined with the calcium, dissolving the rock and enlarging its cracks and openings. Gradually, passageways and caverns took shape as the water moved slowly downward.

The water table continued to fall, and air seeped into the caverns. The layers of rock and soil above the caverns trapped rainwater and melting snow like a sponge, so that water dripped and trickled along ceilings and walls. Now, the decoration of the caves began. It still continues, for all the caverns described here are "alive," the formations still growing.

It is virtually impossible with today's technology to date these stages of cave development. There is speculation that much of the shaping of northern caverns took place during the glacial ages, when vast amounts of meltwater flowed over the northern United States. As the glaciers stopped far to the north of the Virginia caverns, though, it is unclear how these caves could have been affected.

The icicles, ribbons, cascades, and columns of stone that festoon the caverns are made of the mineral *calcite*, a crystalline form of calcium carbonate. As water bearing calcium carbonate drips from the ceiling or flows along a wall, minute amounts of carbon dioxide are released to the air. A corresponding amount of calcite is deposited. These formations accumulate very slowly. It may take two centuries for a cubic inch of stalactite to grow. Temperature is an important factor in the process. The colder the water is, the more carbon dioxide it can hold and the more calcium carbonate it can absorb. On the other hand, as temperatures drop, the bacteria that break down vegetation and release carbon dioxide become less active.

The most familiar formations are *stalactites*, which hang from the ceiling, and *stalagmites*, which grow up from the floor. Stalactites begin as delicate, hollow tubes of stone called *soda straws*. The calcite forms as a ring around the outer edge of a bead of water. The water continues to drip down the middle of the tube until the tube clogs. The tube might be only 2 inches long before this happens, or it might be 6 feet. Moisture then seeps down the outside of the tube, thickening and lengthening it. Stalagmites grow underneath stalactites, where the dripping water strikes a firm, level surface. When the two formations join, they become a column.

Calcite deposits come in an extraordinary variety of shapes: coiling growths of stone called *helictites; rimstone,* a thin, icelike sheet that forms along the edge of cave pools; three-dimensional stars of *anthodite crystal;* odd, rumpled bumps known as *popcorn.* The deposits are often colored with iron, copper or other minerals.

From time to time, the caverns may be flooded during periods of very high water. Silts and clays are carried in and deposited, sometimes filling entire caves. Flowstone may form on top of the sediments, only to be left as a dangling shelf when new floods sweep through the caverns and remove the sediments. Changing levels of sediments can also cause major falls from the roof and walls of the caverns, as tons of rock are suddenly left unsupported.

The last stage of a cavern's life occurs when the layers of rock above have eroded to a thin shell, and little water seeps through the walls. The formations dry out, become brittle, and break. Eventually, the roof falls in, and the cavern becomes just a hole in the ground. These *sinkholes,* as they are called, are typical of limestone regions.

79.

Lost River

Caverns

Directions: **Lehigh County, Pa. From Philadelphia go northwest about 25 miles on the Northeast Extension of the Pennsylvania Turnpike, Route 9, to Exit 32. Take Route 663 east (right) about 2 miles and turn northwest (left) on Route 309. Go about 7 miles to Center Valley and turn north (right) on Route 378. Go about 6 miles and turn east (right) on Route 412. Drive 4.5 miles east then south into Hellertown; turn left at the light. The turn is marked by a large sign for the cavern. The parking area is 0.6 mile down the road on the right, just beyond a blind curve.**

Ownership: **Private—the Gillman family.**

Glistening crystals of anthodite flowers and the peculiar twisting shapes of helictite are the highlights of this small group of caverns. The caverns lie in the Lehigh Valley, part of the Great Valley, which stretches from Georgia to New York (see **Ridge and Valley**). Beneath the surface soils of the valley lie formations of dolomite and limestone. These rocks are largely made up of calcium carbonate or calcite, a mineral that is easily dissolved by groundwater, which is slightly acidic. The Great Valley forms a long trough between the more resistant rocks of the Blue Ridge on one side and the Appalachians on the other (see **Caverns of the Great Valley**).

Crystals of anthodite may contain gypsum or aragonite, which are minerals made up of calcium and other materials. The large size of the crystals indicates that they grow slowly; their rarity indicates that special conditions must exist for their formation. Geologists have not determined what these conditions are (see **#80**). Helictites are also mysterious. They are apparently stalactites which have started to curve and curl. Another puzzling and interesting feature of these caverns is that there are fewer stalactites than stalagmites. Usually, stalagmites only form underneath growing stalactites, which hang from the ceiling. The stalactites which do exist here tend to be small. The brownish stains on the cave formations are caused by the oxidation of iron which is contained in small amounts in the formations here. The grayish stains indicate the presence of zinc.

The "lost river" for which the caverns are named apparently has no exit near the caverns. Attempts to trace its path have failed. During the long drought of 1981–82, the river disappeared, allowing access to another cavern full of interesting formations, including a number of anthodite flowers. In the spring of 1983 the waters returned as heavy rains raised the water table, and the passageway to this cavern was once more covered by many feet of water.

A few creatures live in the cave, most of them insects. They include grasshoppers, spiders, and a few salamanders.

Remarks: *The caverns are open for guided tours every day except Christmas and New Year's Day from 9:00 a.m. to 7:00 p.m. The tour is an hour long. Admission is charged. Camping is available for trailer units at the caverns. For tent camping there is a private campground at Moyers Lake in Coopersburg, 6 miles south of Allentown on Route 309. For further information call (215) 838-8767 or write Lost River Caverns, P.O. Box 103, Hellertown, Pa. 18055.*

80.

Skyline Caverns

Directions: **Warren Co., Va. From Washington, D.C., take I-66 west about 65 miles to U.S. 340 at Front Royal. Follow U.S. 340 south about 5 miles (1 mile south of Skyline Drive) to the caverns, located on the left.**

Ownership: **Private.**

Skyline Caverns, discovered by scientists in 1937, is one of the largest systems of caverns in the Shenandoah Valley. Many miles of passageways have been explored.

The outstanding feature of this relatively young cave is the room of anthodites. Delicate white needles radiate out several inches in all directions to form these unusual, exquisite, flowerlike structures. Exactly how and why these mineral flowers occur is somewhat of a mystery. Unlike most cave formations, which are composed of calcites, anthodites are made of aragonite, a similar, although less common, calcium carbonate mineral. The room whose ceiling is adorned with anthodites was cleared of the clay that had filled it and is kept at a temperature of 56°F, 2° warmer than the rest of the cave. It seems that these structures require a specific, narrow range of temperature, and of physical and chemical conditions, in order to form.

Another prominent feature is Rainbow Falls, where one of the three underground streams drops 37 feet.

Remarks: *Open year round; hours vary seasonally. Call for information, (703) 635-4545. The entry fee (1983) is $6 for adults and $3 for children ages 7 to 13. The guided tour lasts about 1 hour.*

81.

Shenandoah

Caverns

Directions: **Shenandoah County, Va. From Washington, D.C., take I-66 west about 75 miles, then take I-81 south about**

30 miles to Exit 68. Following the signs for Shenandoah Caverns, turn left after leaving the highway, then right onto Route 730 after 0.3 mile. The caverns are 1 mile up this road.

Ownership: Private.

Shenandoah Caverns, one of the many commercial caves dotting the Shenandoah Valley, offers spectacular displays of a variety of cave formations. Along with stalactites, stalagmites, and columns, some majestic draperies, formed by flowing rather than dripping water, can be seen. Flowstone formations that look like bacon strips decorate many of the ceilings.

The chambers of the cave lie in an S-shaped pattern. The two limbs of the S indicate the main channels of the underground streams which carved the cave. The connecting passageway lies along a fault line. This zone of weakness in the otherwise massive limestone influenced the pathway of the water's flow.

Remarks: *Open year round; hours vary seasonally. Call for information, (703) 477-3113. The entry fee is $4.50 for adults and $2.25 for children ages 8 to 14. Guided tour takes about 1 hour.*

82.
Grand Caverns

Directions: Augusta County, Va. From Washington, D.C., take I-66 west about 75 miles. Take I-81 south about 64 miles to Exit 60. Turn east (right) on Route 256 and follow signs to Grand Caverns, about 7 miles.

Ownership: Upper Valley Regional Park Authority.

This is a National Natural Landmark, and one of the most spectacular and well-presented of the Shenandoah Valley caverns. Throughout the caves are unusual "shield" formations: thin, paired slabs of rock which jut out from the ceilings, walls, and floors. Although shields are abundant here, they are unknown in any other caves of the valley. Geologists suspect the shields are created from the action of water seeping through threadlike cracks in the rock. Calcium carbonate deposits in the water gradually accumulate along each edge of the crack, extending outward in a brittle, semicircular formation. Over time the shields themselves become garlanded with stalactites and fantastic stone draperies as water continues to seep over them.

Another unusual feature is the high, narrow shape of the caverns themselves. Here, the layered beds of limestone were heaved up on end as the mountains in this area were created, so that they lie on a nearly vertical axis. Where one layer of limestone meets another, a weak place occurs, and where the rock has been compressed by pressures within the earth and then released, joints or fissures develop. Water flowing through the cave or seeping down from above can erode the rock more easily at these junctions, producing, in time, the vaulted chambers one sees here. Elsewhere in the valley the limestone beds were not tilted so severely; water eroded the rock on a roughly horizontal plane, producing broader, more open caves.

Remarks: *Entry fee. Caves open from March to November. Call to confirm opening and closing schedules: (703) 294-5705. Guided tour of about 1 hour. Camping at Natural Chimneys State Park (see* **#83**).

83.
Natural Chimneys
State Park

Directions: **Augusta County, Va. From Washington, D.C., take I-66 west about 75 miles. Take I-81 south about 59 miles to Exit 61. Turn west (right).**

Ownership: **Upper Valley Regional Park Authority.**

Wander among these majestic rock towers, the tallest of which is 120 feet high. They are the ruins of a vast block of limestone that covered the area over 500 million years ago. The North River pared away much of the rock, sculpting out great cliffs of limestone. Then, water, seeping down through vertical cracks in the limestone and eroding it, isolated these columns from the main body of the rock. The columns were more resistant to erosion because of a hard cap of chert. Although it is a sedimentary rock, chert is very resistant. It is more durable than limestone because it contains the mineral silica. As this chert was deposited on an ocean floor, it may have come from plankton or from seawater. Beds of sandstone in the limestone have also strengthened the columns. Sandstone is not broken down by carbonic acid the way limestone is (see **Caverns of the Great Valley**).

Remarks: *Camping is available at the park.*

84.

Hoverter and Sholl Box Huckleberry Natural Area

Directions: **Perry County, Pa. From Harrisburg, travel north along U.S. 22 and 322 about 23 miles. Turn southwest (left) on Route 34 and drive 8 miles to New Bloomfield. Turn southeast, still on Route 34, and drive 1.5 miles. Turn right onto Huckleberry Rd. and drive another 1.5 miles to the natural area. Park by the road. A large sign marks the beginning of the trail.**

Ownership: **Tuscarora State Forest, Pennsylvania Bureau of Forestry.**

Beneath a canopy of pines and oaks, a small, bushy evergreen shrub covers several acres of the forest floor of this National Natural Landmark. Although it looks quite ordinary, box huckleberry is in fact one of the oldest living things on earth. What appears to be many different plants is actually just one. It spreads over the ground by a system of runners. By measuring the rate of growth of the runners, scientists calculate that this plant is about 1200 years old. Another colony along the Juniata River is estimated at 13,000 years old, perhaps the oldest living thing in the world. Unfortunately, that site has been nearly destroyed by highway construction.

Related to blueberries and other heaths, box huckleberry grows on sandy, acidic soils. In May, it blossoms with small, pink or white flowers. Later in the summer, it bears edible blue berries which are eaten by ruffed grouse and other wildlife.

Box huckleberry is a rare plant, known only in Pennsylvania and six nearby states: Delaware, Maryland, Virginia, West Virginia, Kentucky, and Tennessee.

Remarks: *Stay on the path to avoid damaging the plant. A quarter-mile nature trail leads through a woodland of mixed oaks and white pines. Camping is available at Col. Denning State Park, (see #87) and at Sprout's Campground 1 mile east of Millerstown on U.S. 322 and 22.*

85.
Trough Creek
State Park

Directions: **Huntingdon County, Pa. From Harrisburg, travel west about 80 miles on I-76, the Pennsylvania Turnpike, to Exit 12. Take U.S. 30 west toward Everett. Go 8 miles to Route 26. Turn north (right) and go about 30 miles to Entriken. Turn east (right) and drive 5.2 miles on Route 994. Go north (left) on Trough Creek Dr. 1.7 miles to a T junction. Turn left and drive to the end of the road. Park here.**

Ownership: **Pennsylvania Bureau of State Parks.**

Trough Creek runs along the bottom of a narrow steep-sided gorge. Stands of hemlock and rhododendron cover the precipitous slopes. In early July the rhododendron is covered with white blossoms. Although this valley lies in the midst of the undulating and contorted topography of the Ridge and Valley Province, the layers of rock exposed throughout the gorge are horizontal. Trough Creek has cut its way down hundreds of feet into the flat layers of rock at the bottom of a syncline, a U-shaped fold. The entire province is a series of wave-like folds, the synclines forming the troughs, and the arching folds called anticlines forming the crests (see #95). The scale of this syncline is huge. You cannot see any remnant of the sides of the syncline because millions of years of erosion have removed them. The odd geological features of the park, the ice mine and the hanging rock perching improbably at the edge of a cliff, are the result of weathering and erosion of the horizontal rock layers.

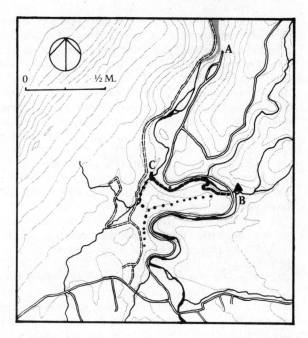

The ice mine lies at the end of the road at the base of a rocky hillside (**A**). The stony slope is the result of weathering in the horizontal rock layers. Water seeping down into cracks in the rock, and then freezing and expanding, broke the rock apart and sent it tumbling down the hillside (see **#118**). The opening itself was probably dug during mining exploration early in the century.

Ice builds up at the mouth of the hole in spring and early summer because of the configuration of the hillside and the flow of air in and out of the cave. During the winter, cold air sinks into the crevices and openings between the rock and into the opening at the base of the slope, cooling the rocks. The steep-sided slopes receive little of the winter sun's warmth. As spring comes, the current reverses and cold air spews out of the cave. Meltwater from the winter snows runs down the slope. The water freezes as it comes in contact with the rocks at the mouth of the mine, cooled by the very cold air coming from the opening. As the warm weather progresses, ice continues to form on the rocks as the cold air and the warm, humid spring air meet. By midsummer, temperatures in the cave have risen enough so that ice is no longer forming, though the cave remains cool into August.

Now you can either cross over Trough Creek and follow the red blazes of the Brumbaugh Trail up onto Terrace Mountain then south along the ridge and back down into Trough Creek to Raven Rock, a hike of two and a half miles; or drive back along the road to the Copperas Rock Parking Area. From the car, walk to Copperas Rock (**B**), which is situated at a bend in the creek. Here, you can see the beginnings of the process that created Raven Rock (**C**). As the stream winds its way through the horizontal layers of the bottom of the syncline, it cuts into the formations, creating overhangs. Interspersed with massive layers of sandstone are softer, crumbly layers of shale. The shale erodes more rapidly than the sandstone blocks that sandwich it. Eventually, the big chunks of sandstone of the upper layer may come to rest on the lip of the sandstone ledge below, just as Raven Rock rests at the edge of a cliff.

To reach Raven Rock (**C**) walk across the road from your car and go west about 100 yards on Copperas Rock Trail, which is well marked. Then turn right onto the Rhododendron Trail as it follows the stream. Rhododendron Trail becomes Raven Rock Trail, crosses Abbot Run, and after about three-quarters of a mile climbs up the other side to the balancing rock. Make a short detour up Abbot Run to see the falls in early spring. Although Raven Rock seems to be precarious, it has probably rested here for thousands of years. From here retrace your steps or continue on this trail, which will eventually lead you down to the creek and a small suspension bridge. Cross the bridge, and turn right to return by the road to your car.

Remarks: *Camping facilities are available at the park. Other activities include hiking, swimming, and fishing with a license for rainbow, brook, and brown trout. At Raystown Lake just to the west of the park there is boating, fishing, and swimming. The best time to see the ice mine is in early summer. The best views from Terrace Mountain are when the trees are bare.*

86.
Frank E. Masland
Natural Area

Directions: **Perry County, Pa. From Harrisburg drive southwest on I-81 about 23 miles to Exit 14. Drive north on Route 74 for 16 miles to Alinda and turn west on Route**

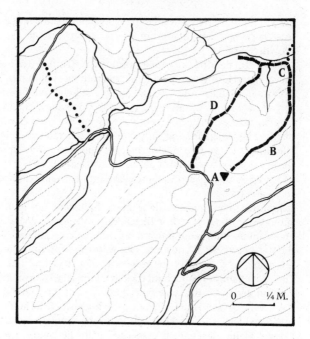

850. Drive west through Landisburg and continue on Route 233 for about 4 miles. Turn right onto Laurel Run Rd., which becomes a rough, bumpy dirt road, and go 8 miles to a Y intersection, bear right, and continue 0.3 mile to the sign for the natural area. There is a small parking area at the head of Turbett Trail (A), an old road that begins right by the sign for the natural area.

Ownership: Tuscarora State Forest, Pennsylvania Bureau of Forestry.

This 1270-acre woodland of tall oaks runs from the ridgetop of Bowers Mountain, northwest of this area, to the spine of Middle Ridge to the southeast. Laurel Run, a small, energetic trout stream, flows through the middle of it. The quiet is occasionally broken by the echoing cries of a pileated woodpecker, the insistent drumming of a hairy woodpecker, or the rasping call of a great crested fly-catcher. Situated amidst timberlands which have been cut again and again, this natural area stands out as perhaps the oldest second-growth forest on state forest land. (Woodlands that have been cut at least once—perhaps many times—are still referred to as second-growth forests.)

From the parking area hike northeast on Turbett Trail about 1 mile to Laurel Run; turn west (left) on a path that follows the stream.

Once this land was covered by an oak-and-chestnut forest which spread over much of the Ridge and Valley Province. The extensive logging of the nineteenth century was followed by the chestnut blight, which began in the early 1900s and killed off virtually every chestnut by 1930 (see **#30**). The chestnuts have been replaced in these woods by a variety of oaks. No trees have been cut since the 1930s when the Civilian Conservation Corps did some clearing along roads and trails.

From the parking area, the Turbett Trail starts out high on the shoulder of Middle Ridge, which, along with Bowers Mountain, is an anticline—that is, an upward bulge in the layers of rock beneath the soil (see **#95**). If you walk southeast (right) from the trail up a few yards to the top of the ridge (**B**), you will find outcrops of Tuscarora Sandstone, the hard rock that forms the spine of the ridge. The canopy on the dry ridgetop is dominated by white and chestnut oaks. Witch-hazel is prominent in the understory. In autumn, the bright red leaves of blackgum gleam in the brown woods. On the Coastal Plain, blackgum is associated with the canopy of swamp forests (see Mid-Atlantic coastal volume). In the uplands of the Ridge and Valley, though, it grows on well-drained and dry sites but is generally smaller and confined to the understory. American chestnut sprouts are also abundant in the understory (see **#30**). Although the trees on top of the ridges are the same age as those farther down the slopes, they are stunted by the less favorable conditions here.

Return to Turbett Trail and continue walking northeast. Here, red, black, and scarlet oaks, red maple, and black birch are added to the white and chestnut oaks of the ridgetop. Shrubs along the upper part of the trail are mostly huckleberry and mountain laurel. The forest is open, the shrub layer sparse. This is typical of these oak forests, perhaps because soils tend to be thin and dry over the slopes and ridges. The trail follows an old roadbed that is covered with moss in some places. Very primitive plants, mosses and liverworts were the first forms of plant life to move from the sea to the land over 400 million years ago. They are a transitional stage from aquatic to terrestrial species, for they must still rely on water to complete reproduction. The "leafy" plant that we recognize as moss carries female and male sexual organs, the *antheridia* and the *archegonia*. The sperm cells must swim from the male organ to the female organ, relying on rain or dew to supply the medium of transport. Having no real roots, leaves, specialized cells to transport water and nutrients, or strong structural tissue, mosses are unable to grow very high. Because mosses draw in nutrients through the surface of the plant and not through roots, they can colonize bare rock and soil, playing a major role in the process of primary succession (see **#63**).

Close to Laurel Run, the canopy changes again (**C**). Red and white oaks, tuliptrees, hemlocks, red maples, blackgum, and a few white pines are the chief species growing on the damper soil. Here the largest trees are found, many well over 100 feet tall. In the understory, mountain laurel grows thickly. Its large white and pink blooms are at their peak in early June.

Fifteen species of birds compete for nesting holes in the trees of these woods. Many of the world's species of birds are hole nesters, including those which dig holes in the ground like the bank swallow. Digging out a hole or using a natural cavity solves two vital problems for breeding birds: how to protect both the eggs and the baby birds from weather and from predators. Birds nesting in cavities commonly have white eggs, for camouflage is unnecessary. But there are disadvantages to hole nesting as well. Competition for sites is very fierce, especially among species like the great crested flycatcher which do not have bills powerful enough to excavate their own holes. They must rely on natural cavities in old or dead trees or on abandoned woodpecker holes. Some bird populations are limited by the lack of nesting sites. Woodpeckers, however, have the advantage of being able to make their own nesting holes. Equipped with heavy, hard, sharply pointed bills and thick skulls, they can use their beaks as jackhammers without injury to their brain. Hole-nesting species have developed a wide range of calls and behavioral signals to indicate to each other an urge to feed or to enter the hole and rest. Most of these species are primarily insectivorous. Some, like the great crested flycatcher, take insects on the wing; the woodpeckers, on the other hand, have exceedingly long tongues which enable them to catch insects inside trees and under bark, once their strong beaks have drilled a hole through the bark. The long, sharp toes and stiff tail feathers of woodpeckers enable them to rest on the trunk of a tree propped at the right angle to feed and drum.

Retrace your steps to the car. To make a circuit of the area walk in on Deer Hollow Trail (**D**) all the way to the stream. The trail peters out just before the brook. Then turn right along Laurel Run until the Turbett Trail comes in from the right.

Remarks: *Other activities include hiking along many miles of trails in the area. Just to the east is the Tuscorora Trail which goes from the Appalachian Trail to the east down into Maryland and West Virginia. Write the*

Keystone Trails Association for further information about hiking in Penn-sylvania (see **Susquehanna River Gorge***). Fishing for native brook trout in Laurel Run is permitted with a license. The circle route described above is easy walking and will take about an hour and a half. Amphibians and reptiles are protected here; do not collect them. There are timber rattle-snakes in the woods.*

87.
Flat Rock
Trail

Directions: **Perry and Cumberland counties, Pa. From Har-risburg take the Pennsylvania Turnpike, I-76, west about 45 miles to Exit 15. Take Route 997 northeast for 12 miles to the end. (There are three sharp turns that may not be marked: after 1.6 miles turn left, after 7.0 miles turn right, and after 7.6 miles turn left.) Turn north (left) on Route 233 and go 3.1 miles to the sign for Col. Denning State Park. Turn to the right and park by the nature center.**

Ownership: **Pennsylvania Bureau of Forestry.**

The Great Valley of the Appalachians extends from New York to Georgia, over 1000 miles. Known as the Kittatinny Valley in New Jersey, the Shenandoah Valley in Virginia, and the Cumberland Valley here, its rich soils have been prized for farming since colonial times (see **Ridge and Valley** and **#73**). From the overlook at Flat Rock, one of the few natural vistas in the wooded hills of Pennsyl-vania, you look southward over the expanse of the valley all the way to South Mountains, 20 miles away.

The trail to Flat Rock begins by the nature center (**A**) and climbs steeply out of hemlocks and rhododendrons up into open forests of white, red, black, scarlet and chestnut oaks, red maple, and black birch which are typical of the Ridge and Valley Province (see **#86**). Witch-hazel is abundant in the understory. Other species include striped maple, blackgum, and some flowering dogwood. The shrub layer is dominated by lowbush blueberry and mountain laurel. After a mile the trail levels out and joins several other trails at an intersec-

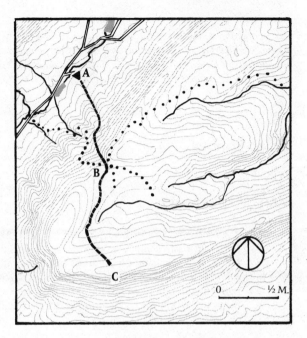

tion called the wagon wheel (**B**). Keep straight across the intersection and walk about another mile to the rock (**C**). On a warm, sunny day the woods may be still but there will always be a breeze hitting your face as you come out to the overlook. This is caused by warm air rising up off the valley floor.

The ridge on which you stand is supported by the tough, resistant Tuscarora Sandstones that have withstood erosion better than the softer limestones and shales which lie beneath the soils of the Great Valley. This is the same formation found at Hawk Mountain and farther north along the Kittatinny Mountain. It is the breaking down of these softer, mineral-rich rocks and the ample supply of moisture in the valley which are largely responsible for the good agricultural soils there.

Remarks: *The walk up and back will take at least 2 hours; the first part of the climb is very steep and slippery. Good hiking shoes are very helpful. Be careful at the edge of the rock; the fall is abrupt. There are a number of other hikes in the area. For a map of other trails in the Tuscarora State*

Forest, write to Pennsylvania Department of Environmental Resources, Harrisburg, Pa. 17120. Other activities at the park include swimming, fishing with license, and ice skating in winter. Year-round camping is available at the park. For further information contact Colonel Denning State Park, R.D.3, Box 293, Newville, Pa. 17241, (717) 776-5272.

88.

Indian Springs Wildlife Management Area

Directions: **Washington County, Md. From Hagerstown, take I-70 west to Exit 18 for Clear Spring. Turn right and follow Route 68 north 0.5 mile across U.S. 40 and to the end. Turn right onto Broadfording Rd. and go 0.6 mile. Turn left onto Blairs Valley Rd.; go 2.7 miles to Blairs Valley Lake. Park on the left by the lake.**

Ownership: **Maryland Wildlife Administration.**

Indians Springs Wildlife Management Area encompasses 5600 acres in several tracts of land. It includes forested mountainsides of oaks and hickories, agricultural fields, stream valleys, the man-made Blairs Valley Lake, and a man-made pond. The management mows and plants sources of foods in the valleys, cuts clearings in the woods, controls burning, manages agriculture, and places nesting structures in order to create and maintain wildlife habitats for deer, rabbits, squirrels, wild turkeys, quail, and pheasants. The area also offers excellent bird-watching. The varied population is at its most outstanding during spring and fall migrations. Counts of as many as thirty species of warblers in a single May day are not unusual. Birds are plentiful by the lake and the pond. Surrounding these two bodies of water are many logging roads, which you can explore on foot.

In spring and fall, migrating loons and diving ducks settle on Blairs Valley Lake, created in the late 1960s. Northern ravens nest on the ridge behind the lake, while rough-winged swallows and belted kingfishers nest on the slopes. Buildings provide nesting spots for barn and cliff swallows; eastern bluebirds and tree swallows make use of bluebird boxes; and over one hundred pairs of purple martins inhabit martin houses, white boxes set on high poles. American bitterns and soras hide in the marshy area below the dam. Many songbirds breed in the stream valleys and hedgerows. Look for both yellow and yellow-throated warblers, warbling vireos, yellow-breasted chats, northern and orchard orioles, and blue grosbeaks.

To get to the small pond, which offers terrific birding, go back down Blairs Valley Rd. 0.4 mile to Hanging Rock Rd. and turn right. Bear left at the fork in the road after 1.9 miles. After another 1.4 miles, turn right over a small wooden bridge onto Catholic Church Rd. This road ends in 4.2 miles at Indian Springs Rd. Turn right onto Indian Springs Rd., and immediately take the left fork onto Mooresville Rd. White-eyed vireos, yellow-breasted chats, and a good number of warblers—worm-eating, black-and-white, golden-winged, prairie, and Kentucky—breed here. Continue 0.6 mile on Mooresville Rd. A mailbox on the left is labeled "R. Shank"; turn right and park just ahead on the left by the pond. A self-guiding nature trail (pamphlets are available at the trailhead, by the large sign to the left) leads through the surrounding area, where cedar waxwings and pine, cerulean, Kentucky, and yellow warblers nest. Blue-winged warblers, northern waterthrushes, and olive-sided flycatchers migrate through here. Rusty blackbirds appear in early spring. Red-breasted nuthatches winter in the pines.

To return to the highway, go back down Mooresville Rd. to Indian Springs Rd. Turn right and drive 3.7 miles to U.S. 40. Route 68 is 4.2 miles to the left. Turn right onto Route 68 to reach I-70. Or turn right onto Mooresville Rd. after leaving the pond. Go 0.7 mile and turn left onto Pectonville Rd. This leads to the junction of U.S. 40 and I-70 in 2.6 miles.

Remarks: *There are many logging roads, open for foot travel, throughout the area. Explore freely. Be sure not to block traffic if you stop along the paved streets. Much of the land you will drive by is privately owned; do not trespass without permission. Fishing (with a license and trout stamp) is allowed; the lake and pond are both stocked. Hunting and trapping are both permitted, so hiking during deer season can be dangerous. The dates for deer season in Maryland vary yearly, but it falls between mid-November and mid-December, excluding Sundays. For more information contact the District Wildlife Manager at Indian Springs Wildlife Management Area, Route 1, Box 118, Big Pool, Md. 21711, (301) 842-2702. Much of the information for this article was obtained from "Washington County Offers Scenic Landscape and Unsurpassed Birding," by Claudia Wilds in* Audubon Naturalist News, *May 1982. Camping is available in summer at the historic Fort Frederick State Park. For information, contact the park at P.O. Box 1, Big Pool, Md. 21711, (301) 842-2504.*

89.

Paw Paw

Tunnel

Directions: **Allegany County, Md. From Hagerstown, take I-70 west about 28 miles to Hancock. Take Exit 1 and head south on U.S. 522 into West Virginia. After about 6 miles, turn southwest (right) onto Route 9 in Berkeley Springs, W. Va. Go about 20 miles southwest to Rt. 29 and turn north (right). Go about 4 miles to Paw Paw, W. Va., and cross the Potomac River into Maryland (where Route 9 becomes Route 51). Go 0.4 mile beyond the bridge and turn right into the Chesapeake and Ohio Canal parking area. Walk up to the towpath, turn right, and continue to the Paw Paw Tunnel.**

Ownership: **Chesapeake and Ohio Canal National Histori-cal Park, National Park Service.**

The Paw Paw Tunnel on the Chesapeake and Ohio Canal (see **Chesapeake & Ohio Canal**) follows the axis of an arch in the rocks. The builders planned this, for the natural rock arch gave structural support to the tunnel. This was important because the shale through which it runs is weak. The arch helped prevent cave-ins both during and after construction. The fold can be seen clearly at each end of the tunnel (**A,B**). Shale breaks easily, and inside the tunnel, you can see spikes that were driven through the brick lining into the rock to hold the layers of shale in place.

The tunnel itself is five-eighths of a mile long, with deep cuts on both ends. Building the tunnel enabled the canal to bypass the 6- or 7-mile stretch of river around the large Paw Paw Bends. (The parallel bends in this stretch of the river are controlled by the structure of the rock; see **#94.**) In addition to saving distance, the canal builders were also able to avoid difficult terrain where cliffs run directly down to the river. Otherwise, their chief options would have been to cut the canal and towpath into the cliffs or to cross the river into West Virginia. The decision to build the tunnel was questioned throughout the construction period, which lasted from 1836 to 1850. Progress on the hand-dug tunnel was often interrupted by both building and labor problems. Finally completed, it was used until 1924. This re-markable tunnel was restored in 1966 for foot travel. At its northern

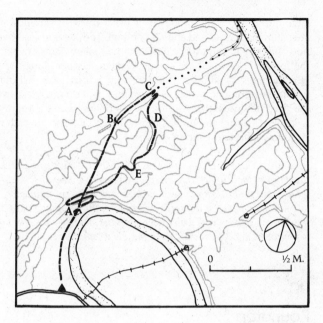

end (**B**) is a high wall of shale kept wet by one of the many local springs. A set of steps once led to the spring, a favorite spot for picnicking and watching the barges go by. The ropes with which mules pulled the barges wore horizontal grooves, still visible, into this wall as well as across the wooden railing.

Between the end of the tunnel and the river, many wildflowers bloom both in the swampy canal bed and on the drier banks and towpath. Just beyond the tunnel, the canal bed is used as roadway for repair vehicles, so flowers there are few. Farther along the canal, bluets, jack-in-the-pulpits, columbines, hairy beardstongue, and phlox bloom on the banks, while blue flags and cattails may line the canal bed in spring. These are replaced in summer by wild rose, Queen Anne's lace, butter-and-eggs, and leatherflower. In early fall, brilliant red cardinalflowers burst forth in the canalbed and jewelweed blossoms on the banks. This is a good place to look for warblers (see **#17**), thrushes, and other migrating songbirds in spring.

At **C**, turn right and take the unmarked Tunnel Hill Trail over the hill. The trail begins along an old tunnel construction road. The digging of the tunnel produced some 218,000 cubic yards of waste material. This debris was carted along the road and dumped away from the tunnel (**D**). Scattering it kept the piles from becoming too large and reduced the problems of water-caused landslides in an area of many springs and abundant runoff. The piles are less obvious now that Virginia and white pines, whose shallow roots can cling to the loose, rocky soil, have colonized them. Farther along the trail (**E**), the forest is composed of white and scarlet oaks, red maple, sumac, flowering dogwood, and sassafras. Soil is rapidly carried off the steep hillside so that, even in these forested areas, the vegetation is sparse. Continue down the hill. The trail rejoins the towpath near **A**; follow it back to your car.

Remarks: *This moderately strenuous loop is about 2 miles long and climbs steeply over the Tunnel Hill Trail. A flashlight is helpful when going through the tunnel, both to avoid puddles and to observe its interior. It is safe without a light, for a sturdy railing guards the well-maintained path. In winter, a wooden wall with a door covers the southern end of the tunnel to protect the bricks from cracking in the cold weather.*

90.
Roundtop

Directions: **Washington County, Md. From Hagerstown, take I-70 west about 25 miles to Exit 3. Follow Route 144 west 1.4 miles into Hancock, then turn south (left) onto Canal Rd. Cross the railroad tracks and go 0.1 mile to the tow-path parking area. Walk west (right) along the towpath about 3 miles to Roundtop.**

Ownership: **Chesapeake and Ohio Canal National Histori-cal Park, National Park Service.**

Approached from the east, Roundtop is the most prominent feature above the towpath (see **Chesapeake & Ohio Canal**), with Tonoloway Ridge stretching out behind it. The same forces that contorted the rocks of the Ridge and Valley Province into large-scale anticlines and synclines (see **Ridge and Valley** and **#95**) also folded the rock layers of this mountain into many beautiful, smaller arches, easily observed at close range. A particularly outstanding fold just above the towpath is known as Devil's Eyebrow. Layers of red sandstone and shale (called *red beds*) form a sizable arch, the center of which was removed either intentionally or by erosion. Because of this gap (which gives the structure its name), the fold looks like a giant eye from a distance.

Just beyond Devil's Eyebrow are the ruins of the Roundtop Cement Mill. From 1837 until the early 1900s, "natural cement," or limestone, was dug from the mountain and fired in these kilns. Much of the cement and mortar used to build the C&O Canal was produced here. The limestone was mined from the rocks which lie above the red beds by the canal. Interlaid with shales, these gray rocks are spectacularly folded. Climb carefully a short distance from the towpath up the hillside to the abandoned railroad tracks above the cement mill (there is no trail). More than ten folds are exposed along the railroad cut, ranging in size from several feet to over 30 feet. A fault (see **#3**) runs through Roundtop and breaks some of the folds. The limestone was mined in this vicinity. A number of mines and caves exist here; they are dangerous and should not be explored.

Remarks: *The towpath is level; the walk to Roundtop is easy and pleasant. Note that the land to the north of the railroad tracks (above them) is privately owned. This access to the C&O Canal also provides a boat launch to the Potomac River.*

Hancock lies at the narrowest part of Maryland. Pennsylvania is less than 2 miles to the north, and West Virginia lies on the other side of the river.

91.
Green Ridge
State Forest

Directions: **Allegany County, Md. From Hagerstown, take I-70 west about 28 miles to Hancock, where I-70 turns north. Continue west on U.S. 40 about 14 miles. Go north (right) on Orleans Rd. 0.2 mile to Scenic U.S. 40. Turn west (left) onto it and drive 1.5 miles to the top of Town Hill. Park opposite the abandoned inn on the right.**

Ownership: **Maryland Park and Forest Services.**

Narrow, forested ridges and valleys cut by streams and crossed by dirt roads and hiking trails characterize Green Ridge State Forest, the second largest state forest in Maryland. The ridges rise more than 1500 feet above the level of the Potomac River, providing excellent views of the surrounding land from numerous overlooks. A large variety of trees grow here, and many wildflowers bloom before the trees are in full leaf. The forest is young—the area was cut, burned, and cleared for agricultural fields until the 1920s. As it slowly reaches maturity, wildlife habitats are improving. Deer, squirrels, and red foxes roam the woods, while beavers and muskrats live by the water (see **#64**). Wild turkey (see **#98**), ruffed grouse, and quail are among the gamebirds that also inhabit this forest. Over 200 species of birds have been recorded. Bird enthusiasts will find a visit to the forest worthwhile, particularly in spring.

Of the fifty-nine species of trees found here, seven different types of oak and four of hickory predominate. Other trees include maples, pines, hemlocks, and aspens, as well as tuliptrees, sycamores, and ashes, which grow along the valley bottoms. In fall, the forest glows with color.

In spring, waves of migrating warblers (see **#17**), thrushes, fly-catchers, tanagers, and finches pass by. One is apt to see yellow-throated, warbling, and red-eyed vireos; and prothonotary, Kentucky, cerulean, parula, pine, and hooded warblers. Nesting species include golden-winged and black-throated green warblers, black-billed cuckoos, least flycatchers, and both black-capped and Carolina chickadees. The ridgetops tend to become dry by July and the resident birds move down the hillsides. Some hawks may be seen during fall migration (see **#5** and **#78**); pause on the successive ridge-tops while driving west on Scenic U.S. 40 to watch the skies for passing raptors. Only a few birds remain here in winter.

Stop at the crest of Town Hill. Enjoy the views, but also peer into the tops of trees growing on the slope below for waxwings, finches, and warblers. At the southern end of this area is Tower Rd. A walk along this dirt road may yield great quantities of woodland birds in spring migration.

Continue about 4 miles west on Scenic U.S. 40. Just before the junction with U.S. 40, after crossing Fifteen Mile Creek, watch for a very small picnic area on the left. Park there, then walk down the road to the sparsely vegetated rock outcrops on the right. While it may look insignificant, this crumbly rock houses a unique plant community—one of the small desertlike shale barrens that are found within the rich, moist Appalachian Mountains. A zone of scattered shale barrens extends from southern Pennsylvania through Maryland and into western Virginia and eastern West Virginia. The barrens here occur where shale—a rock deposited as sediments on the bottom of a sea in the Devonian period some 380 million years ago—crops out on south-facing slopes. In other places, these communities are found on older rocks. Because the shale barrens are maintained by constant erosion, they occur where roads or streams undercut the thinly layered rock. Although shale easily breaks down, most of the resultant soil washes off the steep slope, leaving behind a cover of shale flakes. Annual rainfall is 25 to 30 inches, but most of this water is unable to penetrate through the loose shale to reach what soil does exist, and it runs off. Some water does reach beneath the surface. However, it seeps deeply into fractures in the rock and remains unavailable to the plants.

On many shale barrens stunted and twisted redcedars, chestnut oaks, and Virginia pines manage to survive where some soil has accumulated. A sparse cover of herbaceous plants clings to the slopes. In most cases, these are limited to this particular habitat. Some are endemic (found only on shale barrens in the mid-Appalachians), while others are disjunct species, the closest populations of which grow under similar conditions in Texas and the southwest. In general, these shale-barrens plants include Kate's mountain clover, showy yellow buckwheat, white-haired leatherflower, and large-flowered evening primrose. Some other plants to look for are dwarf bindweed, moss phlox, and dwarf hackberry. Prickly-pear cactus is a common, more obvious member of this community. Only some of these species are usually found at any specific shale barren, and those present will vary in abundance from site to site. Chestnut oaks, Virginia pines, moss phlox, and dwarf hackberry are fairly common here.

All these plants have specialized in order to adapt to this environment. Their seedlings must tolerate low surface moisture and a ground temperature sometimes reaching 140°F. Small, hair-covered leaves help protect the plants from desiccation, and deep roots reach whatever water is available. With space enough to accommodate their roots and conditions too harsh for competing plants, these uncommon plants will colonize the shale slopes. Under slightly better conditions, however, other, more competitive plants will prevail over the shale-barrens community.

These habitats and the plants found on them are extremely fragile and quite rare. In order to preserve these unique environments, stay off the easily crumbled rock and do not pick any of the plants. This shale barrens, like many others, can be studied from the road.

If you wish to explore some of the back roads of Green Ridge State Forest (a potentially worthwhile venture for bird-watchers), continue on Scenic U.S. 40 to the bottom of the hill, turn left, and cross U.S. 40 to Fifteen Mile Creek Rd. Stop at the forest headquarters to obtain a map. Green Ridge Rd. is easy to follow and emerges on Route 51 about 6 miles west of the Paw Paw Tunnel (see **#89**). Just over 2 miles down Fifteen Mile Creek Rd., Green Ridge Rd. bears to the right. This is a good place to look for warblers in the treetops. Green Ridge Rd. goes along the level ridgetop for about 10 miles and offers excellent views of the ridges and valleys to the west.

Remarks: *Activities include picnicking, hiking, camping (a free permit must be aquired at the forest headquarters), fishing (with a license and trout stamp), and hunting (be careful during deer season—see **#88**). For more information contact the Forest Manager, Green Ridge State Forest, Star Route, Flintstone, Md. 21530, (301) 478-2991.*

92.
The Narrows

Directions: **Allegany County, Md. From Hagerstown, take I-70 west about 28 miles to Hancock. Continue west on U.S. 40 for 38 miles; take Exit 44 just east of Cumberland to follow U.S. 40 west. Turn right onto Baltimore Ave., then right again after 0.7 mile onto Henderson Ave. (U.S. 40). Continue 0.6 mile; turn right into Valley St. and go one block (0.1 mile), then turn left onto Columbia St. At the end of this street (0.4 mile), turn right onto Piedmont Ave. Take the first left turn (0.3 mile); this road climbs steeply past a sign for Lover's Leap. Drive 0.7 mile to the end of the road, just past the Artmor Plastics Co. building, and park. The precipitous overlook is known as Lover's Leap. U.S. 40 west continues through the Narrows (see Remarks).**

Ownership: **The Narrows: Allegany County; Maryland Forest and Park Service; and private. Lover's Leap: Artmor Plastics Co.**

Where a stream has carved a course through a mountain ridge, it is known as a water gap. These are common in the Ridge and Valley Province of the Appalachians. Water gaps on the magnitude of the Narrows at Cumberland are spectacular sights. The course of Wills

Creek was established millions of years ago when the valley floor was composed of soft, easily eroded limestone and shale formations which occur above the Tuscarora sandstone. As erosion gradually lowered the land surface toward its present level, the stream encountered the hard ridge of Tuscarora sandstone lying across its path. With continuing erosion, it chiseled out a deep and narrow passageway through the mountain. The highest point, on the north side of the Narrows, is about 1530 feet above sea level. The steep walls, rising 800 feet from the water's edge, can be seen from Lover's Leap, perched high on the edge of the Narrows.

Wills Mountain is a large anticline, or arch (see **#95**), in the folded Ridge and Valley Province (see **Ridge and Valley**) extending from central Pennsylvania south along the Virginia–West Virginia border. This huge arch of rocks, which are over 400 million years old, is well exposed here. The upper 380 feet are cliffs of Tuscarora sandstone, the tough massive quartz sandstone that caps the mountain. Below it lie 400 feet of the Juniata shale and sandstone. Obscured to a large extent by the talus slopes that extend some 500 feet up the sides, this dark red rock is visible toward the eastern end of the gap, where the arch slopes gently downward. As is typical of this folded belt of mountains, the western limb plunges steeply. The Tuscarora sandstone disappears beneath the surface at an angle from the horizontal, or *dip*, of 72 degrees.

Remarks: *Lover's Leap, which overlooks the Narrows, is open only Monday through Friday from 9:00 a.m. to 5:00 p.m. U.S. 40 is a congested, narrow road; once you have entered the Narrows it is impossible to stop. To view the Narrows from the bottom, stop at one of the adjacent commercial establishments. There are no trails.*

Nearby Place
of Interest

Rocky Gap State Park, 7 miles east of Cumberland off U.S. 40, offers hiking, picnicking, swimming, boating (rentals available; only electric motors permitted), camping, fishing (with a license), and hunting in certain areas (be careful during deer season—see **#88**). Sledding and ice-skating are popular activities in winter. For more information contact the park at Route 1, Box 53, Flintstone, Md. 21530, (301) 777-2138.

93.
Greenland Gap
Nature Preserve

Directions: **Grant County, W.Va. From Washington, D.C., take I-66 about 65 miles west, then take I-81 northeast about 10 miles. Follow Route 37 north around Winchester to U.S. 50; take that west about 40 miles to Romney, W.Va. Continue west on U.S. 50 another 20 miles, then turn south (left) onto Route 93. Drive 11.8 miles; turn east (left) onto Greenland Gap Rd. (Route 3) just before Route 93 intersects with Route 42. The road forks immediately; bear left and cross the narrow bridge. After 1 mile, turn right, continuing into Greenland Gap. Park in pulloffs along the road or by the preserve sign 1 mile beyond the turn. Be sure not to block traffic, and be careful of passing cars. You can drive slowly through the gap and enjoy the scenery or take an hour's walk along the road (see Remarks).**

Ownership: **The Nature Conservancy.**

Greenland Gap Nature Preserve encompasses a 1-mile-long water gap where the North Fork of Patterson Creek cuts through New Creek Mountain. Its tall, steep walls are capped by sandstone cliffs and are covered below by extensive talus slopes of this sandstone. Within the narrow valley are several distinct plant communities, influenced by environmental factors such as the underlying rock, elevation, slope, and exposure to the sun. The dry mountain crests and south-facing slope sharply contrast with the cool and moist streamsides and north-facing slope. This scenic area provides a chance to examine how these factors interact. If you are lucky, one of the feral goats, released years ago, that roam the area may appear.

Greenland Gap is structurally related to the Narrows in Cumberland, Md. and Seneca Rocks (see **#92** and **#95**) as New Creek Mountain is part of the Wills Mountain anticline. This giant arch of rock is asymmetrical—it slopes more gently to the east than to the west, the peak of the arch lies west of center. The forces that folded the rock layers also caused faults (see **#3**) such as the one that can be seen high on the cliffs toward the gap's eastern end.

Although the geology is the same on either side of Greenland Gap, the microclimates, or localized climatic conditions, and vegetation are strikingly different (see diagram). The south side is completely covered with a hemlock-and-northern-hardwood forest where the black-throated green warbler is at home. Mixed in with the predominant hemlocks are sugar maple and yellow birch. Beneath them grow American yew, red elderberry, and striped and mountain maple. Ferns and mosses cover much of the talus. This kind of community is usually found in mountains at elevations between 2500 and 4000 feet, but here it occurs at only 1400 feet. Mostly original, the forest thrives here because the north-facing slope, always in the shade, provides cool and moist conditions.

Greenland Gap viewed from the east.

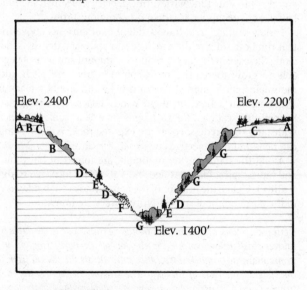

A: Oak, Pine, Heath, Scrub
B: Chestnut, Oak
C: Yellow Pine
D: Exposed Talus
E: White Pine
F: Talus Aggregation
G: Hemlock, Northern Hardwoods

Hemlocks and hardwoods also line both sides of the stream, where Louisiana waterthrushes, kingfishers, and tufted titmice can be found. Sunlight penetrates on the north side, allowing other hardwoods, including red oak, bitternut hickory, tuliptree, and basswood, to grow. Greenbriers provide berries in fall for the resident grouse and wild turkeys.

The dry, south-facing slope (on the north side of the gap) is sparsely vegetated. The only plants growing on the wide-spread talus piles are various forms of lichen (see **#115**). Between stretches of bare rock are open stands of red maple, black, red, and chestnut oaks, black locust, and blackgum interspersed with white pines and hemlocks. This forest merges into the next community, which reaches up to the base of the cliffs. The American chestnuts that were dominant have been replaced by chestnut oaks (see **#30** for discussion of chestnut blight). Pitch pine, red maple, black locust, and blackgum are also present. Blueberries, huckleberries, deerberries, mountain laurel, and greenbrier are the most common shrubs.

Turkey vultures and hawks ride the air currents above the cliffs that rim both sides of the gap. The sun and wind dry the sandy soils along the edge of the gap, limiting the amount and type of vegetation able to grow there. The most common trees are pitch and table mountain pines; gnarled chestnut oaks and shrubby black birches also maintain a hold on these windy edges. Poverty grass grows beneath the scattered trees. Lichens, as well as some mosses able to withstand the dryness, cover the exposed rock. Wild bleeding heart can be found in protective crevices in the cliffs.

Along the flanks of the mountain are forests of oaks, hickories, and pines typical for the Ridge and Valley Province (see **Ridge and Valley**). Unlike the interior of the gap, the adjacent land was cleared in the past and these second-growth trees are immature.

Remarks: *Walk along the road (a nature trail guide is available from the sources listed below) or hike to the top of the north rim via a rough, unmaintained, unmarked trail that starts across the stream from the sign and follows the edge of the gap. The stream is stocked with trout, and fishing (with a license and trout stamp) is allowed. Stay off the talus slopes; they are unstable and can be dangerous. Although it is unlikely that you will see them, watch for rattlesnakes and copperheads. Don't miss seeing the falls at Falls Gap on the left, less than 1 mile past the Greenland Gap Nature Preserve sign. For more information, contact the preserve steward, Robert Snyder, Lahmansville, W.Va. 26731, or the Nature Conservancy, West Virginia Field Office, 1100 Quarrier St., Charleston, W.Va. 25301, (304) 345-4350.*

94.

Woodstock Tower

Directions: **Shenandoah County, Va. From Washington, D.C., take I-66 west about 65 miles to I-81. Go south on I-81 about 20 miles to Exit 71 for Edinburg. Go east on Route 675 for 0.8 mile. Turn left and go north on U.S. 11 for 0.6 mile, then turn right and continue east on Route 675. Drive 5.9 miles to Route 678, and turn left. Go 7.4 miles to Route 758, and turn left again. This road, which becomes dirt, leads to Woodstock Tower in 3.9 miles. Park by the sign on the left and walk along the short, level trail to Woodstock Tower. You must then climb steps to the top in order to see the Seven Bends of the Shenandoah.**

Ownership: **George Washington National Forest, U.S. Forest Service.**

For the 14 miles between Edinburg and Strasburg, Va., the North Fork of the Shenandoah River winds back and forth across the valley floor in giant, parallel loops. Rising steeply on the east side of the valley is Powell Mountain, a ridge of the Massanutten Mountains, atop which stands Woodstock Tower. The tower provides a superb view of the Seven Bends of the Shenandoah, as these spectacular meanders in the river are called. The loops take the river on a journey 3.2 times as long as the direct distance down the valley. That the Shenandoah meanders is not unusual, for most rivers follow a sinuous path. These, however, differ from typical meanders because they are largely controlled by planes of weakness within the bedrock beneath the water.

Exactly why meanders develop is not fully understood. It appears that streams take the path of least resistance as they travel from point to point. Whether a stream meanders or breaks into many small, branching channels depends on a number of hydraulic factors, such as the amount and size of sediment carried by the stream; the slope, width, and depth of the stream; and the quantity and velocity of water. Long, straight stream channels are uncommon, regardless of the terrain. Instead, water tends to flow in fairly regular, broad, and semicircular curves which, apparently, are often the most efficient means of transporting sediment. Just as streams that flow over alluvium, or water-deposited sediment, typically meander, so do streams that are dissolving their ways through limestone caverns, meltwater streams on glaciers, and the water within the Gulf Stream.

Even in the straight section of a river, the water follows a sinuous route. The *thalweg*, or line of maximum depth, which generally coincides with the strongest current, crosses back and forth across the river. Where it approaches one side of the stream, bars and sand and mud, called point bars, build up along the opposite bank. This pattern alternates from side to side along the length of the river. Because stream velocity increases along the outside of a bend, the swift current erodes that bank. On the inside of the curve, where the velocity is slower, sediment accumulates on the curved point bars. Meanders are unstable; erosion along the outer banks and deposition on the inner bends causes the meandering river channel to migrate downstream as well as laterally.

Meanders do not always migrate evenly. Sometimes an upstream limb will shift more rapidly than the downstream limb, and the space between them will decrease. When the river floods, it may then break through its banks, cutting off the entire loop, thus shortening its course. The abandoned meander bend, blocked on both ends, becomes what is known as an oxbow lake. Such areas then fill with sediment, and soon support a variety of wetland plants.

The spectacular bends of the North Fork of the Shenandoah River do not follow this usual pattern. For instance, they are *incised*, or cut deeply into the bedrock, which prevents their migration. While meanders are generally somewhat symmetrical and linked by wide arcs, here one finds long, straight stretches, joined by short, tight bends. In addition, the amplitudes of these meanders, which are irregular, are unusually large.

Incised meanders have been traditionally interpreted as old stream meanders which deepened their valleys in response to a change such as vertical uplift of the land. The Shenandoah meanders, however, owe their peculiarities to the bedrock over which they flow. This section of river coincides with a belt of Martinsburg shale, a tightly folded belt of thin, alternating layers of fine-grained sandstone, weak siltstone, and shale. While elsewhere in its valley, the river flows across other, more resistant bedrock, generally well covered by gravel and cobbles, here the water flows mostly on exposed bedrock. This happens because the shale breaks down into small particles that are readily removed, and the current is strong enough to remove the larger pieces of rock brought downstream and washed in from tributaries. Prominent, closely-spaced joints, or fractures, that run on northwest-southeast cut through this rock. Although the formation as a whole is not resistant to erosion, the water can carve more easily through the rock by following these planes of weakness. It is this structure which gives rise to these elongated, parallel meanders. Although they are not typical, such meanders are not unique. Similar features are found elsewhere on the Martinsburg shale as well as on other rock formations with similar structural weaknesses.

Remarks: *Woodstock Tower can be a good viewing spot for fall hawk migration flights (see #5 and #78). The Massanutten Mountains are partly built of layers of shale. Where the shale layers are exposed along roads and stream, and face south, they frequently house a unique plant community. Patches of these shale barrens can be seen alongside Route 678. Just look—do not pick any plants or walk on the shale, as these fragile habitats are very easily disturbed. (See #91 for more information on shale barrens.) The Massanutten Mountains lie within the George Washington National Forest, which offers picnicking, hiking, camping, fishing (with license, trout stamp, and National Forest stamp), and hunting (be careful during deer season—see #47). Little Fort Recreation Area, just south of Woodstock Tower on Route 758, and Elizabeth Furnace Recreation Area, on Route 678 northeast of Route 758, have campgrounds and some other facilities. For more information contact George Washington National Forest, Lee Ranger District, Professional Building, Edinburg, Va. 22824, (703) 984-4101.*

95.
Seneca Rocks

Directions: **Pendleton County, W.Va. From Washington, D.C., take I-66 west about 65 miles. Take I-81 southwest 4 miles to Exit 74. Follow Route 55 about 48 miles to its end in West Virginia. Take U.S. 220 and Route 28 south and west 13 miles to Petersburg, then stay on Route 28 west and south about 22 miles to the town of Seneca Rocks, also called Mouth of Seneca. On the left just before the junction with U.S. 33 is a U.S. Forest Service visitors' center. Seneca Rocks is right behind it. Continue a short distance south on Route 28; immediately after crossing the bridge over Seneca Creek, take the first left turn onto Roy Gap Rd. Go 0.2 mile down this small dirt road to the end and park. To the right, a swinging footbridge crosses the creek and a trail leads to Seneca Rocks.**

Seneca Rocks Formation

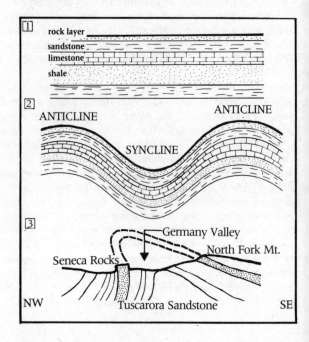

Ownership: **Monongahela National Forest, U.S. Forest Service.**

Seneca Rocks, a vertical wall soaring 960 feet above the valley floor, is one of the most spectacular rock formations in the Appalachians. The rock is Tuscarora sandstone. Composed almost entirely of quartz grains cemented together by quartz, it is one of the most resistant rocks in the Ridge and Valley Province and thus is the major ridge-maker (see **Ridge and Valley**). The Tuscarora sandstone was folded along with the other layers of rock when the Appalachian Mountains were built. At one time, this sandstone continued up and over to the east, connecting Seneca Rocks with North Fork Mountain in a huge arch known as the Wills Mountain Anticline (see **#92**, **#93**, and Nearby Places of Interest). Anticlines are large-scale upward folds, ranging from several hundred feet to several hundred miles across. The oldest rock is found in the center of these arches. In comparison, synclines, or downwarpings, have the youngest rock in the center. In the early stages of folding, the anticlines form ridges and the synclines are valleys. Over time, erosion alters the land surface. The ages of the rocks exposed at the surface may no longer reflect the underlying geological structure, and the resistance of individual rock layers, rather than the geological structure, controls the topography. As the tough Tuscarora sandstone was worn away off the top of the anticline here, the softer, underlying rock was exposed and more easily eroded. All that remains of the sandstone is this bladelike section of the anticline's steeply plunging western limb. The center of this structure is now a broad valley (see diagram).

The short, steep trail climbs up the back side of Seneca Rocks to the 15-foot-wide ledge at the top. After crossing the footbridge, follow the dirt road through the stream-cut gap in the Tuscarora sandstone. On the left, a yellow-blazed trail leads through the underlying red sandstone and shales of the Juniata formation to the top of Seneca Rocks. The view from this precarious, but thrilling, spot is worth the effort of the climb. You can see the Allegheny Front to the west (see **#121**), and look up and down the valley of the North Fork of the South Branch of the Potomac River nearly 1000 feet below.

The sandstone weathers slowly, so only a thin sandy soil has accumulated. A few plants, however, manage to survive. Stunted table mountain pines cling to the narrow ledges. Various grasses, alumroot, bluets, and blueberries also grow on the moss-and-lichen-covered rock. This is the best-known location for silvery whitlowwort. In West Virginia this uncommon plant is found only on outcrops of Tuscarora sandstone.

Remarks: *The hike to the top of Seneca Rocks is short but very steep and strenuous. Wear sturdy shoes and allow at least an hour to make the trip. Be careful on the high, narrow ridge; it is a long, nearly sheer drop to the bottom. The visitors' center offers exhibits and an excellent view of Seneca Rocks and the rock climbers who frequently scale the wall. This is reputed to be one of the best vertical climbs in the east. For climbing information or lessons, contact Gendarme or Seneca Rocks Climbing School, Box 53, Route 1, Seneca Rocks, W.Va. 26884, (304) 567-2600. Seneca Rocks is part of the Spruce Knob–Seneca Rocks National Recreation Area. Nearby there is picnicking, miles of hiking, trails, camping (private campgrounds on Route 28 or a Forest Service campground in Onego), backpacking, fishing (with a license, trout stamp, and National Forest Stamp), and canoeing. Hunting is also permitted, so hiking during deer season can be dangerous. Deer season varies yearly, falling in late November to early December; no hunting on Sundays. For more information, contact Potomac Ranger District, U.S. Forest Service, Route 3, Box 240, Petersburg, W.Va. 26847, (304) 257-4488, or call the Seneca Rocks visitors' center at (304) 567-2827.*

Nearby Place
of Interest

Seneca Caverns is a commercial limestone cavern in Germany Valley. Continue south from Seneca Rocks on Route 28 about 7 miles to Riverton. Turn left onto Route 9 and proceed to the caverns. For a scenic drive, continue on Route 28 about 3 miles beyond Riverton, then east on U.S. 33, which crosses North Fork Mountain. Drive about 3 miles to an excellent viewpoint overlooking the scenic Germany Valley. From here, you can see Seneca Rocks. Remember that the Tuscarora sandstone once arched from Seneca Rocks to the crest of this mountain just to the east. Once the limestone beneath the Juniata formation was exposed, the valley was rapidly widened. Germany Valley, 8 miles long, is a large intermountain *karst,* or limestone, valley whose floor is riddled with caves, sinkholes, and narrow ravines. These features form as surface water dissolves the limestone and is captured by an underground drainage system.

96.
Ramsays Draft

Directions: Augusta County, Va. From Richmond, take I-64 west about 100 miles to Staunton, then take U.S. 250 west about 19 miles. Turn right at the sign for Ramsays Draft and the Mountain House Picnic Area. Follow the road straight ahead 0.4 mile, passing the picnic area on the right, and park by the Game Commission building. The trail follows the road, which is blocked to vehicles, for much of its 5-mile length.

Ownership: George Washington National Forest, U.S. Forest Service.

A clear mountain stream tumbles and glimmers in pools as sunlight pierces through the old forest along Ramsays Draft, one of the few virgin tracts of its size in the east. Over 6000 acres of magnificent forest, inaccessible on the steep and rugged terrain, were never logged.

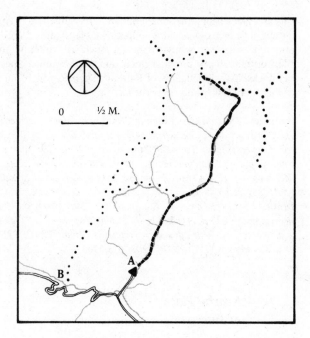

Lofty hemlocks, tuliptrees, white pines, and oaks, conspicuously larger than the typical second-growth trees found elsewhere, line the valley floor. Azaleas and mountain laurels provide bursts of color, and spring wildflowers put on quite a display. The valley steepens and narrows along the upper reaches of Ramsays Draft, where cathedrallike stands of majestic hemlocks create the impression of a primeval forest. Some of these trees are more than 300 years old. The dense, cool shade of the high canopy limits the ground cover to ferns and mosses. In summertime, it is often 15°F cooler than by the picnic area.

Bordered by ridges rising 1000 feet above the stream, this narrow valley shows virtually no signs of disturbance. No one ever settled here—there are no flat places. Fires have burned here in the past, scarring some of the large trees, but only one has occurred since 1935. The ridgetop vegetation of chestnut oaks (along with scarlet, bear, and northern red oaks, and pitch pines) has been more heavily influenced by fire. The road that follows the lower stretch of the stream is no longer maintained; plants are encroaching and the bridges and culverts have been washed out.

Grouse, turkey, and white-tailed deer are numerous. A few bobcats and black bears still remain but are rare sights. You may catch a glimpse of ravens, pileated woodpeckers, black-capped chickadees, and red crossbills. Northern species, such as winter wrens, and Blackburnian, black-throated green, and parula warblers, nest in the hemlocks. Two inhabitants of Ramsays Draft to watch out for are timber rattlesnakes and copperheads.

Remarks: *The trail crosses Ramsays Draft many times; sneakers are advised for times and places when fording is inevitable. This 10-mile round trip is an easy, fairly level walk. Hiking, camping, fishing (with a license, trout stamp, and National Forest stamp), and hunting (be careful during deer season—see* **#47**) *are permitted. This area is being considered for wilderness designation. For more information contact Deerfield Ranger District, 2304 W. Beverley St., Staunton, Va. 24401, (703) 885-8028. The nearby Sexton Cabin, operated by the Potomac Appalachian Trail Club, is available for use with advance reservations. Contact PATC, 1718 N St. NW, Washington, D.C. 20036, (202) 638-5306.*

Nearby Place of Interest

About 1 mile west of Ramsays Draft on U.S. 250 are the Confederate Breastworks; an interpretive trail leads through what remains of some Civil War fortifications. This is also where the Shenandoah Mountain Trail begins (see map).

97.
Goshen Pass

Directions: Rockbridge County, Va. From Richmond, take I-64 west about 100 miles to where it joins I-81. Continue south on the combined highway about 35 miles. Near Lexington, I-64 heads west again; take it about 1 mile west to Exit 13. Take U.S. 11 north 0.3 mile; take Route 39 north and west about 13 miles to Goshen Pass. You can observe the pass as you drive through, or stop at the numerous pulloffs (see Remarks).

Ownership: **Virginia Division of Parks; Virginia Highway Department; and Virginia Commission of Game and Inland Fisheries.**

Goshen Pass features steep, rugged slopes towering some 1000 feet above the surging water of the Maury River. It is an unspoiled and scenic place that attests to the power of rivers. The Maury River has drained this area for millions of years. As the Appalachian Mountains formed, the river continued to flow and cut down into the land. As layer after layer of rock was worn away, the hard, quartz-rich sandstone that now caps Little North Mountain, the first ridge of the Ridge and Valley Province (see **Ridge and Valley**), was exposed. Over time, the erosive forces of the river carved a narrow passageway through the resistant ridge, creating this water gap. Vertical cliffs of quartzite standing 50 feet or higher break the slopes here and there. Some of those exposed along the road display layers that were folded as the Appalachian Mountains were formed. Large angular blocks succumbing to weathering and the forces of gravity have broken off the cliffs and have come to lie on lower slopes. Others, which landed in the river, have been smoothed and rounded and will eventually be worn away.

Various plant communities grow on the adjacent mountains, the tallest of which reaches over 3400 feet. Because the quartzite is slow to break down and the terrain is so steep, only shallow, acidic soil that is low in minerals develops. Acid-loving plants such as rhododendrons, mountain laurels, and huckleberries are abundant throughout the area. Elevation and moisture availability influence which trees grow where. Hemlocks, along with sycamores and yellow poplars, line the river. White oak, red maple, yellow poplar, basswood, and white pine reach up the moist slopes to elevations of 1700 to 1800 feet. Hickories and black locust are prevalent on drier slopes. In contrast, table mountain pine and bear oak dominate the high, dry ridges. Below them, chestnut oaks, blackgum, and Virginia and shortleaf pine cling to the mountainsides. Lush pockets of ferns, mosses, and various wildflowers grow where water seeps to the surface. Most of the surrounding area has been cut over, grazed, or burned in the past. In contrast, on the northeast side of the river is a section (Goshen Pass Natural Area) that is so steep and inaccessible that it has probably never been logged, even though the trees appear to be young because they are so slender.

The thick woods house a variety of animals. Black bear and white-tailed deer share the forest with smaller mammals such as rabbits, gray squirrels, and opposums. Wild turkey and ruffed grouse are numerous. Birds, including summer tanagers and blue grosbeaks, are summer residents in the lower reaches of Goshen Pass. Among the other birds to be found in this area are mountain dwellers such as scarlet tanagers and various warblers—black-throated blue, black-throated green, and Blackburnian. June is the best time to visit, for then the birds are singing their courtship and territorial songs, and the rhododendrons are in bloom.

Remarks: *The road through Goshen Pass has numerous parking areas with picnic grounds, but there are no trails through the pass. The Maury River offers fishing for trout (with a license and trout stamp), small mouth bass, and redeyes, as well as swimming and wading (at your own risk). Hunting and camping are permitted in the Goshen–Little North Mountain Wildlife Management Area. Hiking here during deer season is not advised, as the area is heavily used by hunters (see #47). For more information contact the Virginia Commission of Game and Inland Fisheries, Route 6, Box 484A, Staunton, Va. 24401, (703) 885-9030. Several dirt roads penetrate the wildlife management area to the southwest. One trail, 3 to 4 miles long, follows Laurel Run to the top of the ridge, where it intersects with the road from leading Guys Run to Hogback Tower on the top of Big Butt (elevation 3451 feet).*

98.
Rich Hole

Directions: **Alleghany and Rockbridge counties, Va. From Richmond, take I-64 west about 100 miles to where it joins I-81. Continue south on the combined highway about 35 miles. Near Lexington, I-64 heads west again; take it west about 14 miles to Exit 11 for Goshen. Turn off; after 0.3 mile, turn left onto U.S. 60 and continue west 2.6 miles. Just beyond the crest of the hill, an unmarked parking area can hold about six cars. The white-blazed trail begins as a dirt road at the northeast end of the parking lot (A).**

Ownership: **George Washington National Forest, U.S. Forest Service.**

The entire watershed of Alum Creek lies protected between the long parallel ridges of Brushy Mountain and Mill Mountain. The upper basins of the creek's two tributaries are deep, northeast-facing coves that house notable examples of a "cove hardwood" forest. Although most of the surrounding area has been logged, pockets of trees remain undisturbed by either man or disaster. Off the trail in the coves to the north are a number of outstanding trees. On the rich soil in these protected hollows stand tall oaks, hickories, green ashes, sugar maples, basswoods, and cucumber trees. Some reach up to 125 feet, with straight, unbranched trunks ranging from 30 to 52 inches in diameter. They are widely spaced, with many smaller trees between. With a closed canopy high above an open understory, this forest is reminiscent of the mature woodlands of the past.

Climb steeply up Brushy Mountain. By pausing at a ledge partway up in one of the few places where rock is exposed at the surface on these steep slopes (**B**), you can see across the countryside to the southeast, watch for hawks gliding by, and take a last look at the highway before escaping into the quiet calm of this undeveloped wilderness. Continue about a mile up to the ridge of Brushy Mountain, then along the headwall ridge above the coves. This ridge divides the two adjacent watersheds: Alum Creek flows to the northeast, and the North Branch of Simpson Creek drains to the southwest. Both streams support native trout.

The stands of mature cove hardwoods are off the trail to the right

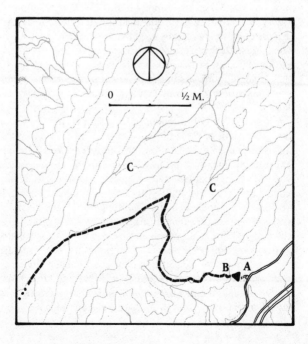

(north) below the ridge (**C**). If you leave the trail to explore the coves, walk carefully so as not to disturb the soil on these steep slopes—as well as for your safety. Because the large trees are not clustered together, they may not be obvious at first. After exploring the coves, return to the trail and either retrace your steps to the trailhead or extend your walk. The Rich Hole Trail continues down the west side of Brushy Mountain to become the North Branch Trail, which parallels the North Branch of Simpson Creek.

In contrast to the cove hardwoods, various other plant communities share the mountainous terrain as a result of environmental conditions and some minor past disturbances. Scrubby thickets of bear oaks, chestnut sprouts (see **#30**), azaleas, and rhododendrons cover the ridgecrest. Some of the well-drained steep slopes along the ridge have mixed communities of pitch pines, chestnut oaks, mountain laurels, and rhododendrons, while hemlocks line gullies and ravines that dissect the mountainsides. Throughout the area, evidence of slight grazing and faint traces of roads long gone have been found, indicating that some usage must have occurred within the past century. Fire scars, from a hot blaze 30 to 70 years ago, remain. Apparently the large trees survived unscathed.

Be on the lookout for the wildlife that thrives in this remote and well-buffered area, a National Natural Landmark. The quick thrumming of a startled grouse taking briefly to wing is a common sound. A deer is likely to notice your intrusion and dash away. Although deer are common here, they are still more numerous in other nearby woodlands. They prefer open areas, where young trees and shrubs provide abundant browse, to mature forests. With less available food, Rich Hole supports a smaller population (see **#59**). A few black bears roam here, but your chances of encountering one are very slim.

Another permanent resident of Rich Hole is the wild turkey. You may catch sight of these birds running along the ground for cover. This is their usual means of escape, but turkeys will also fly, swiftly and strongly, for short distances. Wild turkeys are the largest game birds in North America. Males measure 3 to 4 feet long and stand, when alert, 3 to 4 feet high, with a wingspan of 4 to 5 feet; females are somewhat smaller. If the trail appears to have been swept off with a broom, turkeys were probably there scratching the dirt and leaf litter for food. Seeds, nuts, and acorns are their staples, but grasshoppers and other insects are summertime supplements. Frogs, toads, salamanders, and lizards may also be eaten. In early spring when food is scarce, turkeys feed on new grass and tree buds. When heavy snowfalls blanket the ground, they fast for as long as a week, but when eating is good, a large turkey can consume a pound of food in one meal. Wild turkeys travel in flocks of as many as forty or fifty members. Males and females segregate in winter. With springtime comes breeding season, and the polygamous males, or gobblers, gobble wildly to attract mates. The hens then nest on the ground in depressions, the edges of thickets, or under the branches of a fallen tree, where they lay about a dozen eggs 2 to 2.5 inches long.

Back in colonial days, wild turkeys were very abundant throughout the east. Subsequent expansion of human settlements took its toll through increased hunting and loss of the mature open woods and clearings that provided habitats for the turkeys. Now that habitats have improved and are being protected, turkeys have been successfully reintroduced and their numbers are increasing.

Other inhabitants of the forest are those typical for these mountains: grey squirrels and other small mammals, rattlesnakes, some copperheads, and black snakes. Owls roost in the trees as do downy, hairy, yellow-bellied, and pileated woodpeckers. Also living here are nuthatches, sapsuckers, tufted titmice, chickadees, and thrushes.

Remarks: *The walk takes about 3 hours and is fairly strenuous. Fishing (with a license, trout stamp, and National Forest stamp) and hunting (be careful during deer season—see* **#47***) are allowed. For information contact the James River District, George Washington National Forest, 313 S. Monroe Ave., Covington, Va. 24426, (703) 962-2214.*

99.
Natural Bridge

Directions: **Rockbridge County, Va. From Richmond, go west on I-64 about 100 miles. Turn southwest on I-81 and go about 45 miles to Exit 49. Well-marked signs lead to the Natural Bridge.**

Ownership: **The Tolly Family.**

Natural Bridge, a National Natural Landmark, is a spectacular arch of limestone, 200 feet high, that soars over a narrow wooded gorge. The sight is particularly impressive on winter evenings under a translucent sky with great horned owls calling from the nearby cliffs. In summer, noisy crowds make the scene less inviting.

The bridge is part of the same system of limestones and dolomites found throughout the Shenandoah Valley. Millions of years ago Cedar Creek, which now runs beneath the bridge, was not one but two streams. One was a small tributary of Cascade Creek, which now joins Cedar Creek just south of the bridge. The other ran to the north, where it joined the Poague River. Cascade Creek dropped sharply, and its waters had strong cutting power. Working its way northward it came close to the Poague River tributary and captured it (see **#104**). These waters made their way through an underground passage, which became larger and larger as the slightly acid water ate at the limestone (see **#100**). Natural Bridge is all that remains of that passageway, and Cedar Creek is now the main stream, with Cascade Creek as its tributary.

The steep-sided gorge has a wide variety of trees; seventeen species have been recorded. The shade and moisture in the ravine provide a habitat for such northern species as hemlocks and beeches. Beside the path leading down into the gorge are several very old arborvitae or northern white-cedar, trees commonly associated with limestone outcroppings.

Remarks: *Entry fee of $3 (as of 1983). The well-marked pathway down is short but somewhat steep; a bus runs from the parking lot. Open all year round from 7:30 a.m. to late evening. Early morning is a good time to avoid the crowds. Camping at many private campgrounds in the area and at Shenandoah National Park. For further information contact Natural Bridge Hotel, Natural Bridge, Va. 24578, (703) 291-2121.*

100.
Falls Ridge
Preserve

Directions: **Montgomery County, Va. The preserve is about 16 miles southwest of Roanoke, Va. For permission to see the area and detailed directions, contact Mr. William Bradley, manager, (703) 382-2220.**

Ownership: **The Nature Conservancy.**

At Falls Ridge, steep rocky hills rise and fall along the valley of the North Fork of the Roanoke River. A major geological fault runs across the hills, like an invisible barrier. On one side is ancient cal-cium-bearing rock called dolomite. On the other are younger shales and sandstones. Because of their high quartz content, the latter rocks produce acid soils in which azaleas, mountain laurels, rhododen-drons, and hemlocks flourish. These plants stop abruptly at the fault. The fault runs through the yard of the manager's house, and the different plant communities are visible there. On the dolomite side, you will find columbine, walking fern, and other plants that thrive only in calcium-rich soils (see **#74**).

This dramatic contrast of rock, soils, and associated plant life makes Falls Ridge a unique site. The stage was set 225 to 250 million years ago when, during one phase of the long period of upheavals that lifted the Appalachians, a shelf of dolomite was pushed up over younger shales and sandstones. The dolomite, a rock similar to lime-stone which contains magnesium as well as calcium, was formed on the floor of an ancient ocean from the shells of marine organisms that accumulated there 500 million years ago. The sandstones and shales date from about 400 million years ago.

As you drive up the steep road to the manager's house, you are tracking one side of a syncline, or a U-shaped fold in the rock layers where the rock strata have been contorted (see **#95**). The road cuts through distinct bands of shale and sandstone, the shale being brittle and crumbly, the sandstone more blocklike.

From the house, the manager will direct you down the short, steep road to the travertine cliff, a much younger formation than the surrounding rock. It sits right along the fault zone. Groundwater carries carbonic acid, a result of the interaction of water and plant material. This acid is strong enough to dissolve calcium out of the dolomite. As the calcium-laden stream flows over the fault, there is a pH change as the water strikes the more acid rocks. This causes the water to deposit small amounts of calcium carbonate. The cal-cium carbonate has built a waterfall, which now aerates the water as it tumbles over. This leads to yet another chemical change, whereby more calcium carbonate is brought out of solution. This is then deposited on rocks, twigs, and piles of leaves, eventually forming a cliff such as the one seen here. In the stream itself, you can see new formations of travertine beginning to grow on the debris there. The cliff is wide because the stream has changed course many times, building up the cliff in a new place with each shift. The holes and crevices are largely due to organic material that has rotted away after the rock was formed. The cliffs are used by a nesting pair of northern ravens every year, birds usually found much farther north.

Around and on the travertine, a variety of special plants can be found. In early spring the sharp-leaved hepatica blooms; in late spring and summer come stonecrop, bellwort, walking fern, and columbine. By August the narrow-leaved spleenwort is sprawling in the cracks of the rocks.

There are two other intriguing aspects to the ecology of Falls Ridge. The sudden drop from the mountaintops to the valleys creates enormous differences in the moisture content of the terrain. The ridges are dry, especially where the cracked and brittle shales allow rain water to pass through like a sieve. Here the ground is sparsely covered with moss, lichens, and table mountain pines. Several hundred feet below, in the hollows and along the hillsides, are pockets of swamp and damp woods, where one finds dogwood, redbud, and an assortment of flowers common to moist deciduous woods.

Many northern, southern, and mountain species are near the edge of their range at Falls Ridge, which helps add to the plant and animal diversity found here. Yellow buckeye and table mountain pine are trees of the central Appalachians. The table mountain pine is found only on the dry shale ridgetops. There are chinkapin oaks, commonly associated with limestone outcroppings in the mountains of the central United States. Northern species include eastern hemlock, northern white-cedar, and white pine. Among the southern species are post oak and Virginia pine.

Remarks: *The walk down to the cliffs and waterfall and back takes about 20 minutes. Wear good walking shoes. The manager will direct you to other trails on the preserve. Camping at Roanoke Mountain on the Blue Ridge Parkway just south of Roanoke.*

Nearby Place
of Interest

Just north of Roanoke, along the Blue Ridge Parkway at mile post 95.3, is Harvey's Knob. This is an excellent hawk watch lookout during the fall migrations. The second and third weeks of September are the peak of broad-winged hawk migrations. They are followed by ospreys and sharp-shinned hawks. With the stronger winds of November come large numbers of red-tailed hawks. Northern harriers, American kestrels, Cooper's hawks, and red-shouldered hawks are also seen.

Mountain Lake Wilderness Study Area

Mountain Lake, one of the only two natural lakes in Virginia, sits on private property near the crest of Salt Pond Mountain in Giles County. (The other is in the Great Dismal Swamp in the southeast corner of the state; see Mid-Atlantic coastal volume.) The existence of this sizable lake—two-thirds of a mile long and nearly a fifth of a mile wide—appears to be the result of several factors. The depression in which the lake lies was initially formed as the underlying rocks were dissolved and eroded. The depth of the lake is partially caused by rockslides and talus, which dammed the stream's outlet. Records over the past 200 years show that the water level has fluctuated; falling levels could be accounted for by drought or by increased flow through the rock dam.

Within its 8400 acres adjacent to the lake, the Mountain Lake Wilderness Study Area encompasses a great variety of habitats, such as high, dry ridgetops; low stream valleys; sandstone ledges; and red spruce bogs. Variations in elevation and exposure to the sun increase the diversity. In addition, this area is located in a zone where northern and southern species overlap. A great variety of flowering plant species has been counted just in the vicinity of the University of Virginia Biological Station.

Northern plants such as red spruce, hemlock, and yellow birch grow in the cool climate high on Salt Pond Mountain, typical of the high mountains in Virginia. Red spruces, which are rare in Virginia, are clustered in bogs, from which several creeks emanate. They are also found scattered throughout stands of hemlocks elsewhere on this mountain. Thickets of bear oaks, rhododendrons, azaleas, and blueberries dominate the dry ridges. Other oaks, hickories, and tuliptrees are also found here, while Virginia, table mountain, and pitch pines grow where it is rocky. Pines and oaks, plus red maples, redbuds, black walnuts, and sassafras trees grow along low-lying streams like Johns Creek. Shrubs, ferns, spring wildflowers, and mosses are plentiful beneath the forest canopy. Ferns are particularly abundant and varied; any widespread species of eastern fern might be seen.

The birdlife also reflects a northern element. Many northern birds breed here near the southern limits of their ranges. Found only in high elevations this far south, they are not widely distributed in Virginia. Warblers—Blackburnian, Canada, black-and-white, black-throated blue, and black-throated green—solitary vireos, golden-crowned kinglets, winter wrens, and red-breasted grosbeaks breed here, as do least flycatchers, which are found in only one other location in the state. Also some southern species, such as hooded warblers, venture north to this area. Black-capped chickadees, the species most common in the north, and Carolina chickadees, the common one in the southeast, are both found here. Over a hundred species of birds have been recorded.

The other wildlife is also quite varied. Deer, beaver, muskrat, and gray fox are among the forty-five mammal species recorded here. Although they are scarce, a few bobcats and black bears still roam the woods. Thirty-six reptile and amphibian species, including timber rattlesnakes, northern copperheads, and at least nine species of salamanders (see **#58**) have also been counted. Native brook trout swim in the streams (see **#53**).

Mountain Lake is on private property; the "no trespassing" policy is enforced. The Mountain Lake Wilderness Study Area offers many miles of trails for hiking and cross-country skiing, and stocked streams for fishing (with a license, trout stamp, and National Forest stamp). Camping is permitted anywhere in the National Forest; a Forest Service Campground is located at White Rocks (off Route 613, about 4.5 miles past the War Spur Branch parking area, near Route 635). For more information contact the U.S. Forest Service, Blacksburg Ranger District Office, Route 1, Box 404, Blacksburg, Va. 24060, (703) 552-4641.

101.
Bear Cliff

Directions: **Giles County, Va. From Roanoke, take U.S. 460 west, then southwest (combined with U.S. 11), then northwest past Blacksburg, about 40 miles in all. Continue on U.S. 460 about 6.5 miles beyond the junction with Business U.S. 460, just west of Blacksburg. Turn north (right) onto Route 700 and drive up the mountain. At Mountain Lake, the road merges with Route 613; soon the pavement ends, just past Mountain Lake. At the fork in the road, 8 miles from U.S. 460, bear right to the University of Virginia Biological Station. The road forks again just ahead. Park off the road; be sure you are not blocking traffic. Walk up the left fork, past the gate, to the caretaker's red house on the left to get permission to hike here. The trail begins at an unmarked, gated dirt road on the right where you parked (A).**

Ownership: **Leased by the University of Virginia Biological Station from the Commonwealth of Virginia.**

The easy, yellow-blazed trail to Bear Cliff (**B**) follows along the flat ridge about a mile, passing through thickets of mountain laurel and rhododendron. Follow the dirt road until it comes to a small building. Go around it to the right and a footpath continues to Bear Cliff. The mountainside drops abruptly some 800 feet from the windswept cliff, then continues steeply down to the valley of Johns Creek below. Rows of parallel, narrow ridges separated by equally narrow valleys lie off to the south and east (see **Ridge and Valley**).

The rock exposed at Bear Cliff is the resistant Tuscarora sandstone that caps most of the ridges in the province (see **#95**), including Salt Pond Mountain. The outcrop was broken apart into enormous blocks during the Ice Age, when the climate was much colder than it is today, although the glaciers never extended this far south. As a result of the severe conditions, including large daily temperature fluctuations, the rock split and was wedged apart (see **#118**), forming cavelike passageways between the blocks.

The plants that grow here are often found on rocky ledges at this elevation. Dwarfed yellow birches are interspersed with mountain laurels, rhododendrons, and other members of the heath family.

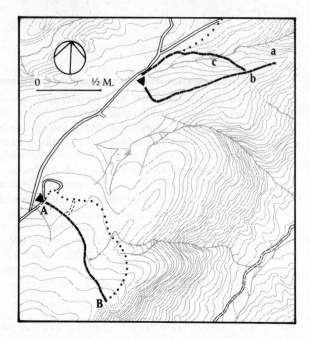

Because the soil here is thin and low in nutrients, the plants remain small, even when mature. The buffeting winds help limit their size.

Northern plants, such as mountain wood fern and starflower, thrive in the cool climate at this high elevation. Mountain wood fern thrives in the shaded, moist, and chilly environment within the passageways through the rock. During the Ice Age, extensive forests of northern species covered the land. Once the glaciers melted and the climate warmed, these northern plants were able to survive only high in the mountains, where we find them today. Growing side by side with them are a number of southern species, including fly poison, common along the trail; galax, near its northern limit; and Michaux's saxifrage, found only on rocky cliffs and in crevices.

In fall, when the winds blow from the south or east, migrating hawks (see **#5** and **#78**) soar past Bear Cliff, which faces east. The dominant winds, however, are out of the west, so hawks generally follow the other (western) side of the ridge (see **#102**). Though the most numerous hawks are broad-winged, others—such as red-tailed, red-shouldered, and sharp-shinned—may also be seen. Northern ravens also ride on the air currents above the ridge.

102.

War Spur Trail

Directions: **Giles County, Va. Follow directions for Bear Cliff (#101). As you follow Route 613 up Salt Pond Mountain, bear left at the first fork in the road and continue on Route 613, instead of bearing right toward the University of Virginia Biological Station. Go 1.8 miles past the fork. The parking area, which has a large wooden trail map, is on the right.**

Ownership: **Jefferson National Forest, U.S. Forest Service.**

Like the trail to Bear Cliffs, the War Spur Trail passes through a forest of oaks, hickories, pitch pines, and rhododendrons. Walk a mile and a quarter out to the War Spur Lookout (**a**). Here, a break in the forest shows where the Tuscarora sandstone comes to the surface, as at Bear Cliffs. From here, the green, thickly wooded valley of the War Spur Branch can be seen below. Salt Pond Mountain is part of the eastern continental divide. War Spur Branch flows east (to the left) through the deep valley below, into Johns Creek and then the James River before reaching the Atlantic Ocean. Little Stony Creek, whose headwaters are just on the other side of the ridge facing you, flows in the opposite direction. It joins the New River, which eventually empties into the Gulf of Mexico.

Retrace your steps to the trail junction (**b**) and turn right. As the trail descends, the oaks, hickories, and pines give way to thickets of rhododendron and tall hemlock trees. Alongside the upper reaches of War Spur Branch (**c**) is an old-growth forest of hemlocks and some hardwoods, principally white oak. It is silent and still in the dark cool shade of these towering, majestic trees. Some of them, with diameters approaching 3 feet, are more than 300 years old. Although the rest of Salt Pond Mountain and the surrounding area were cleared or burned in the 1920s, the trees in this steep and inaccessible ravine escaped cutting.

After crossing the stream and leaving the hemlocks, the trail climbs easily three-quarters of a mile up to the ridge. At the trail junction, turn left. Route 613 lies a quarter-mile ahead.

Remarks: The loop trail to the War Spur Lookout and back through the hemlocks is a fairly easy walk, under 3 miles.

Nearby Places of Interest

Wind Rock: From the parking area for the War Spur Trail, continue 1.9 mile farther north along Route 613 and park on the right. Follow the Appalachian Trail (white blazes) beyond the parking area for about half a mile to Wind Rock. This is a good local hawk-watching spot and offers extensive views toward West Virginia.

Interior Bogs: Continue another 3 miles along Route 613 to Route 635, which is paved, and turn left. About 4.4 miles down this road on the left, just before you reach Interior, are several small boggy areas. Pull off the road to park. These wet patches have filled in to varying degrees. Some places have been taken over by alder thickets; others, fringed with cattails, remain open. Nodding ladies' tresses, sundews, club mosses, and quillworts all grow here. Big Stony Creek flows through this valley and, over the ages, has altered its course. Several thousand years ago it probably flowed where these bogs are now located.

Cascades: Continue west and then south on Route 635 for 12 miles until it intersects with U.S. 460. Turn left onto U.S. 460 and travel 2.6 miles to Route 623 in Pembroke. Turn left and proceed 3.4 miles to the parking area. A 4-mile loop trail leads to the Cascades, where water pours some 60 feet over a sandstone ledge. The lower trail is posted with interpretive signs and follows Little Stony Creek. Return from the falls along the upper road.

The Appalachian Plateau:
A Furrowed Upland

The Appalachian Plateau is a broad, sweeping region about 300 miles across at its widest point, in northern Pennsylvania. Once a level highland, it has been sculpted into many land forms, from the rounded hills of the Poconos, to the deep canyons of the Loyalsock River and Pine Creek, to the steep, cool heights of the Catskills. The Appalachian Plateau stretches across southern New York and northern Pennsylvania, then arches southward along the western edge of the Appalachian Mountains through West Virginia and south to Alabama. This guide, however, covers primarily the strip of the plateau running through southeastern New York and northeastern Pennsylvania, a tract averaging 120 miles wide by 140 miles in length. The western area gently slopes toward the Susquehanna River, while the eastern portion descends toward the Delaware River. Between lie smooth, rolling hills blanketed in hardwood forests and numerous lakes and swamps of glacial origin. Towering some 2000 feet over the surrounding Appalachian Plateau are the Catskills, where mountain summits rise over 3500 feet. Elsewhere on the plateau, too, are marked shifts in elevation, ranging, for example, from 2100 feet in western Wayne County north of Scranton, Pa. to as low as 500 feet along the Delaware River in eastern Pike County, Pa.

This part of the Appalachian Plateau was once a lowland inundated by a shallow ocean. During the Devonian period 405 to 365 million years ago, continental land masses collided, forcing up ancient mountains along the eastern edge of the North American plate. These moun-

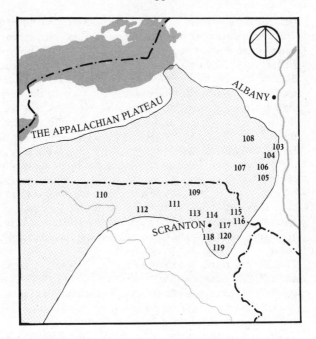

tains separated the Appalachian Plateau from the ocean and created an island sea, bordered by the mountains to the east. Erosion carried millions of tons of earth from the mountains to the west into this inland sea, and layer upon layer of sediment was deposited on the bottom. As millions of years passed, this sediment was compressed and cemented into thick beds of sandstone, shale, limestone, siltstone, and other sedimentary rocks, thousands of feet thick. Subsequent mountain-building continued over several hundred million years climaxing between the Permian and Triassic periods, 250 million years ago.

This portion of the Appalachian Plateau has been above the sea for more than 200 million years. Surprisingly, while the sedimentary rock of the Appalachian Mountains was contorted into folds, the rock strata of the plateau, which are of the same origin, were gently lifted and remain basically horizontal. The Poconos, the Catskills, and other high ridges on the plateau result from the erosion by streams through the horizontal layers of rock.

Much of the topography of this region was sculpted by the four glacial advances that began about 2 million years ago and by the tremendous quantities of meltwater that accompanied their retreat. These great glaciations occurred during the Pleistocene epoch, which ended approximately 10,000 years ago when the Wisconsin Glacier had retreated. Throughout the northern portion of the Appalachian Plateau, the glaciers deposited piles of gravel, sand and other sediments called *glacial till,* much of it swept away by the meltwaters and deposited as dams across streams and rivers. The ice sheets themselves also acted as barriers, changing the courses of rivers and the patterns of drainage. Such sites as Kettle Creek Gorge and the Lehigh River Gorge in Pennsylvania were created this way. Within the ice sheets were huge boulders. Borne along by the massive wall of ice, these boulders scoured out shallow depressions and deep hollows in the bedrock. These low areas have become swamps and bogs, such as the alder swamp at Woodbourne Sanctuary in Pennsylvania. Elsewhere, swirling glacial meltwaters carved large basins in the rock, such as Archbald Pothole and the Tubs, also in Pennsylvania.

Today, the climate of the Appalachian Plateau is generally cool and wet. The average January temperature is 22°F, while July averages 66°F. Mean precipitation ranges from 40 to 48 inches, with the Catskill Mountains consistently one of the wettest areas. The abundant rainfall tends to leach minerals from the soils, and the cool temperatures inhibit bacteria that break down organic matter, an essential process in the development of rich fertile soils. Relatively poor soils called gray-brown podzols cover most of the Appalachian Plateau.

Yet, even so, vast woodlands thrive on the plateau. Oaks and hickories predominate in the south, giving way to beeches, maples, and hemlocks, and ultimately spruce, fir, and birch forests in the north. In the Catskills, shifts between northern and southern plant communities occur according to changes in elevation. The 4000-foot summit of Slide Mountain is almost exclusively fir; beech, maple, and hemlock grow on the slopes and in the valleys below.

Paleo-Indians arrived in the Appalachian Plateau region as the Wisconsin Glacier was retreating northward 15,000 to 10,000 years ago. They were nomadic hunters and gatherers whose life-style centered around the movements of animals such as the mastodon, muskox, elk, moose, and caribou. Around 8000 B.C., the Paleo-Indians evolved into the Archaic Indians. The Archaics remained predominantly transients, though annual cultivation of domesticated plants had begun. When the Europeans arrived, they found the Mohawk, Oneida, Seneca, Iroquois, and Delaware Indians. These peoples were much more sedentary than their ancestors, establishing villages, usually in bottomlands, where they grew squash, corn, beans, and sunflowers along fertile streambeds.

The influence of the European settlers on the Appalachian Plateau region was rapid and substantial. Trapping of native furbearers such as fisher, pine marten, and otter was followed by the logging of Penn's Woods and abrupt changes of natural habitat. The newly cleared land created meadows for animal husbandry—of sheep, then dairy cows. As lines of transportation to eastern population centers improved, annual crops such as potatoes, corn, apples, tomatoes, and melons were shipped to eastern markets. This change in natural habitat resulted in increased numbers of forest-edge and meadow fauna—cottontail, woodchuck, eastern meadowlark, red-winged blackbird, and meadow vole. Creatures of the deep woods such as the eastern elk, cougar, bobcat, and wild turkey decreased or vanished altogether.

Today only the steepest or remotest areas support virgin stands of forest. However, the shift from agriculture to industry has allowed for the regeneration of native forests on old fields. Most of the forested land is at various stages of second or third growth. In addition, county-based conservation districts and the state Bureau of Forestry have provided thousands of trees for selective forest plantings. In the Pocono area, where the number of full-time and weekend residents continues to increase, many people are occupying abandoned farmland and planting ornamental and fruiting trees, often within sections of older forest.

In spite of human impact, much of the plateau seems remarkably remote from civilization. Bobcats, considered a sign of wildness, roam the forests. The large tracts of wooded land, the rugged mountains, and the deeply etched stream valleys are threaded with many miles of trails. Less traveled than the Appalachian Trail of the Ridge and Valley, these tracks offer solitude and adventure.

—Jack L. Ferrell

The Catskill
Mountains

The Catskills, within easy reach of New York City, are surprisingly remote mountains characterized by deep valleys and narrow gorges, rocky ledges and sheer cliffs, waterfalls and dense forests. Thirty-four of the peaks are over 3500 feet high. The mountains are well worth a visit at any season, each boasting its specialty: fall paints the trees with glorious colors; winter brings the stillness and serenity of snow; spring wildflowers are the first plants to burst to life. The Catskills receive the most visitors in summer, when the days are often hot and humid.

In spite of the proximity to New York City, the Catskills were not inhabited until the 1800s. Prior to this, the Indians of the Hudson River Valley ventured to the mountains only to hunt and fish. Likewise, the Dutch settlers of the 1600s stayed in the lowlands. (The influence of these first settlers is reflected in the place names. *Kill*, applied to small streams, comes from a Dutch word meaning "inlet or channel of the sea." *Clove*, or *kloove*, means a cleft, or here, the narrow, steep mountain passes often thought to be the haunts of witches and devils.) With the opening of the Catskill Mountain House in 1823, the eastern Catskills became a major vacation spot, their romantic beauty attracting many artists, writers, and celebrities. Throughout the century, the tourist trade and other industries grew and the population expanded. In 1885, sections of the Catskills were designated as forest preserve in a footnote to the establishment of the Adirondack Forest Preserve. (New York City businessmen feared their harbors would fill with silt if logging activities in the

Adirondacks continued unabated.) Later, Catskills Park, an area of 700,000 acres including both public and private lands, was established with the intent that it become forest preserve and remain forever wild. Today, more than a third of that land is state forest preserve, covered with dense second- or third-growth hardwoods and pockets of virgin timber too stunted or too inaccessible to have been logged.

The Appalachian Plateau, which includes the Catskills, is not like the rest of the Appalachian Mountains, which were folded complexly and twisted by internal earth pressures (see **Appalachian Plateau**). The rocks here are thick, nearly horizontal layers of relatively undeformed red conglomerate, sandstones, shales, and siltstones. Over the ages, deep valleys have been carved by streams into this section of the plateau. The uplands separating the streams now stand out as the topographic highs of the Catskills. The peaks, all on roughly the same level, show where the surface of the plateau once was.

During the Devonian period, which lasted from 405 to 365 million years ago, a shallow arm of the ocean covered the land from what is now New York west to the Mississippi Valley. This was a time of great upheaval—the Acadian Orogeny. As the plates of the earth carrying the North American and European continental land masses moved gradually toward each other, mountains were uplifted along the leading (eastern) edge of the North American plate as the proto-Atlantic Ocean became continually smaller (see **#45**). As the land was raised and eroded, streams carried enormous amounts of sediments westward to the inland sea. Near the mountains, where slopes were steep, streams flowed rapidly and deposited coarse sediments. As they encountered the more level coastal plain en route to the sea, stream velocity decreased and finer-grained materials collected. Thousands of feet of sediments accumulated between the mountains and the sea. An extensive wedge-shaped deposit, typical of a delta, developed. The thickest part, composed of the coarsest material, lies to the east, comprising the Catskill Mountains. Overlying rocks deposited after the Devonian period were eroded away.

Mountain-building episodes continued to occur over the subsequent ages, thrusting up the Appalachian Mountains. The Permian period, which ended some 225 million years ago, signified the final closing of the proto-Atlantic Ocean. The Catskills did not buckle with the rest of the Appalachians, although they may have been uplifted at various times.

The Catskills tower some 2000 feet over the surrounding Appalachian Plateau. The sandstones and conglomerates that resulted from these thick, coarse-grained deposits are more resistant to erosion than the finer-grained rocks to the west. Because they are also more porous, much of the precipitation seeps into the rock. Therefore, streams here are farther apart and stream erosion is less. In addition, the Catskills' steplike terrain hinders soil erosion, since the soil either rests on gentle slopes or is absent altogether from the vertical cliffs.

The glaciers that extended across much of North America during the Pleistocene ice ages (about 2 million to 10,000 years ago) covered the Catskills. Perhaps only the highest peaks jutted above the ice. The mountains guided the glaciers, which, following paths of least resistance, crept down the Hudson Valley and across the Mohawk Valley, although local variations occurred. The moving ice altered preexisting features somewhat, scraping the landscape and, at the same time, depositing other rock debris gathered along the way. Although the degree of glacial scouring was not great, a few lakes and ponds now lie where glaciers carved basins in the bedrock (see **#103**). Most of the glacial features are difficult to discern now that vegetation has covered the landscape.

The polar climate, which crept south as the glaciers advanced, lingered even after the glaciers had retreated, exposing newly barren rock surfaces in its wake. The arctic pioneer plants that first colonized the bare rock were eventually followed by spruce and fir, the only trees able to survive in the cold, wet climate. As conditions gradually became more hospitable, hemlocks and hardwood trees shaded out and replaced the firs and spruces. Today, these spruce and fir remnants of the Ice Age remain as shrinking mountaintop islands.

The Catskills harbor a rich and diverse plant community, largely because of the great changes in elevation within short distances, which directly affect both temperature and precipitation: the higher the elevation, the lower the temperature and the greater the precipitation. Wind, the type and depth of soil, and the degree of disturbance an area has suffered are other factors that determine what species of plants can grow there.

The Catskills can be divided into three vegetational zones. Oaks, hickories, pitch pines, and mountain laurels grow along the Hudson River and inch up the slopes to an elevation of about 1000 feet. Along the exposed east escarpment, however, these trees are found as high as 2500 feet (see **#103**).

A forest of American beeches, yellow birches, and sugar maples growing on the moist soil, and hemlocks, which flourish on the north slopes and in deep, cool ravines, cover more than three-quarters of the Catskills. The seedlings thrive in the shade of the dense canopy under which oaks and hickories cannot survive. Black cherry, white ash, basswood, and hophornbeam are other members of the reproducing forest community. The understory is a tangle of various shrubs, ferns, wildflowers, and mosses.

As one climbs higher, a shift to more northern species occurs. Paper, or white, birch becomes increasingly abundant as the other trees dwindle in number, with yellow birch being the last to disappear. Red spruce and balsam fir dominate on some ridges over 3000 feet, where conditions are harsh. Although the elements constantly test the resiliency of the ridgetop trees, conditions are not severe enough for a treeline to develop. Unlike most hardwoods, spruce and fir are able to grow in dense thickets on shallow soil and where drainage is poor. The trees are short and stunted due to wind, snow, and ice breakage, coupled with the short growing season and shallow soil. The hardwoods that are found in the higher elevations are also stunted and gnarled.

It is because they tolerate similar conditions that spruce and fir are often found in mixed stands. Pure stands of red spruce are not common. Their small and shallow root systems require moist soil and make them vulnerable to windthrow—strong winds, which dry the soils and thus aggravate a drought, may knock over whole stands of trees. Once a blowdown has occurred, constant exposure inhibits repair. The mosses, which cover the needle litter and normally help retain ground moisture, dry out from the lack of shade. In addition, reproduction of spruce is hampered by fir seeds that germinate more vigorously and whose taproots are deeper. Even though red spruce does not reproduce well, it is long-lived and persistent, and therefore dominates locally. Balsam fir, being more drought-resistant and less subject to exposure, is more abundant than spruce and dominates in elevations above 3700 feet.

Today's forest is similar to that of the seventeenth century, when majestic hemlocks, 60 to 100 feet tall and 2 to 4 feet in diameter, graced the slopes. The Catskills were once known as the "Blue Mountains," because the thick canopy of hemlock and other boughs locked in the high humidity and gave rise to a haze which, from a distance, colored the mountains blue. In the 1800s, much of the forest was cleared for agriculture and industry. Tanning was the most prevalent business and had the greatest impact. Abundant hemlocks (for tannin), clean water (to prevent rotting), and numerous waterfalls (for power) attracted a total of fifty-nine tanneries. A cord of hemlock bark was needed to tan ten hides. Between 1820 and 1870, when tanneries flourished, an estimated 70 million trees were destroyed to produce 7 million cords of bark. After the bark was peeled off the logs, the wood—95 percent of the tree—was burned or left to rot. By 1870, the supply was depleted, leaving only those trees that were too inaccessible. The felling of the hemlocks resulted in considerable losses of soil. No longer shaded, the streams were warmed beyond the tolerance of the native trout, which perished (see **#53**). Organic wastes from the tanning process rendered the water undrinkable as well, although the streams recovered soon after the industry died out. By the 1900s, abandoned open areas were reverting to hardwood forest. Now, over 100 years later, hemlocks are again significant members of the forest.

The Catskills are a haven for a variety of wildlife. White-tailed deer, nearly eliminated by 1880 from loss of habitat, made a strong comeback as farmlands were abandoned. Bears and bobcats inhabit the region, but sightings are extremely rare. Raccoons, skunks, squirrels, and other small mammals are prevalent, as are porcupines, which eat the paint off metal trail markers and devour plastic ones. Snowshoe hares, gray foxes, and minks live here; wild turkeys are becoming more numerous as the forest matures.

The dense foliage often turns birding more into a matter of sound than of sight. Woodpeckers, chickadees, sparrows, great horned owls, and ruffed grouse can be found. Red-tailed and broad-winged hawks are often seen circling below high lookout points, along with the more common turkey vultures. Living in the higher altitudes are northern bird species such as gray-cheeked thrushes, which are at their southernmost breeding limit, slate-colored juncos, white-throated sparrows, and winter wrens. Also present at various times of the year are nuthatches, yellow-bellied sapsuckers, flycatchers, and numerous warblers.

To reach the Catskills from New York City, drive north on I-87 to Exit 19, about 100 miles. Directions from here are included in each site description. There are over 200 miles of trails crisscrossing the Catskills. Each is blazed with color-coded markers: generally red designates east–west trails, blue-blazed trails run north–south, and yellow indicates a side trail. A register is located at most trailheads. Please sign it—both in case of an emergency, and so the Department of Environmental Conservation can record usage of each area to justify the funding received for trail work. Wear proper footgear; most trails are rocky and steep. Be sure to carry sufficient drinking water with you, as water is not always available and none is tested. The bugs are prolific in June, but lessen in number by late August.

The state land within the Catskills offers picnicking, camping (off the trails as well as in campgrounds), fishing (with a license), and hunting (be careful during deer season; see **#64**). Private campgrounds are numerous throughout the Catskills. For more information, contact the appropriate regional office of the Department of Environmental Conservation. For Greene County: P.O. Box 430,

Catskill, N.Y. 12414, (518) 943-4030. For Ulster and Sullivan counties: 21 South Putt Corners Rd., New Paltz, N.Y. 12561, (914) 255-5453. For Delaware County: Route 10, Stamford, N.Y. 12167, (607) 652-7364. See the books and maps listed in the **Bibliography** for additional historical background and information on campgrounds, other trails, and backpacking opportunities. In 1983, the New York–New Jersey Trail Conference (Box 2250, New York, N.Y. 10001) and the Appalachian Mountain Club (5 Joy Street, Boston, Mass. 02108) published a hiking-trails-map set for the Catskills. This fine five-map set is available from either organization.

103.
The Escarpment Trail

Directions: **Greene County, N.Y. From Kingston, continue north on I-87 to Exit 20. Take Route 32 north about 8 miles. Turn west (left) on Route 23A and drive for 7 miles. Turn right at the sign for North Lake, bear right again, and continue 3.8 miles to the park entrance. The parking lot for day use is by the beach, 1.6 miles farther along the park road. The trailhead is on the right, just before the parking lot.**

Ownership: **New York State Department of Environmental Conservation.**

The North Lake area is the most spectacular and heavily visited section of the Catskills. This 4.5-mile hike will award you views down to the Hudson River some 9 air-miles away and to the Taconic and Berkshire Mountains beyond. Walking along the rocky ledges of the escarpment and through wooded valleys, you will pass through all three major forest communities as the elevation increases from 2200 to 3000 feet.

Rising from 500 feet to a maximum of 3900 feet within 3 miles, the escarpment, a sheer cliff in many places, extends 20 miles. It is an asymmetrical ridge, or *cuesta,* sloping gently away to the west in contrast with the abrupt dropoff to the east. The western slope parallels that of the sea floor on which the sediments were deposited. The uppermost rock layers are resistant to erosion and maintain the gentle westward slopes. The steep, exposed eastern face is the result

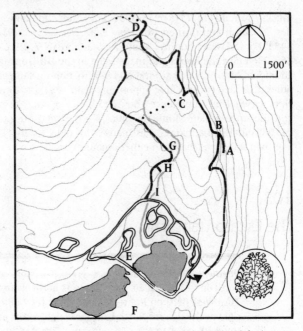

Inset: Pitch pine cone

of erosion. As the softer layers below are exposed and eroded away, the overlying resistant rock is no longer supported and breaks off.

The blue-blazed trail to North Point begins along the edge of the escarpment, where only shallow-rooted pitch pines can cling to the rocky surface. Where there is enough soil, red and chestnut oaks stand watch over mountain laurels and blueberry and huckleberry bushes. Pines and oaks fill the lower elevations of the Hudson Valley, but also grow along the edge of the escarpment where this dry, exposed eastern slope is warmed by winds from the valley. Away from the escarpment's edge, the trees are those typifying the beech–yellow-birch–sugar-maple forest (see **Catskill Mountains**).

Rising above the trail on the right is Sunset Rock (**A**), a massive outcropping of conglomerate covered profusely by lichens (see **#115**). A conglomerate is a sedimentary rock containing a large proportion of pebbles and gravel. This brown sandstone is generously endowed with quartz pebbles up to 3 inches in diameter, giving it the name "puddingstone," an old term that refers to any conglomerate in which the pebbles resemble plums or raisins. Just beyond the outcrop, turn sharply right and take the yellow-blazed side trail to the top of Sunset Rock, where lichens and small plants breaking down the rock to soil disguise the bold texture of the conglomerate. Constant winds blowing from the northwest have sculpted the few persistent trees into "flags" whose branches point away from the wind.

Return to the blue-blazed trail and continue to Newman's Ledge (**B**), where a 100-foot cliff drops to a steep 2000-foot slope that runs down to the Hudson Valley. This conglomerate ledge is one of many such in the Catskills (see **#106**).

As the trail climbs higher, spruce and fir, with a dense undergrowth of huckleberries, outnumber the hemlocks and hardwoods. The trail swings by a swamp (**C**) full of spruce and leatherleaf, vivid purple in early summer with blooming wild irises. Mountain holly, meadowsweet, and mountain laurel also grow here, along with paper birch, red maple, and hemlock. Ridgetop swamps such as this are common in the Catskills, where slight depressions in the nearly horizontal bedrock retain water.

A final steep climb of a quarter-mile brings you to North Point (**D**) and excellent views to the north, east, and south. The land atop the escarpment received the most intensive glacial scouring of the Catskills during the Ice Age, as evidenced by the bare rock ledges and thin soils. North and South lakes (**E**), clearly visible to the south, lie in basins scooped out by the ice. The barrier of land that separated the two lakes was removed by the Department of Environmental Conservation in the early 1970s to enhance the recreational use of the water. The field (**F**) beyond the lakes, which is maintained, is where the Catskill Mountain House was located (see **Catskill Mountains**). A narrow-gauge cable railroad, quite a feat of engineering, carried passengers straight up the escarpment to the Catskill Mountain House in the late 1800s.

On your return, take the red-blazed trail to the right through the thick woods of Mary's Glen (**G**). Where the trail crosses a rocky creek bed, detour carefully left along the creek to the brink of the falls (**H**).

The wet area at the end of the trail (**I**) is an old beaver pond. In 1980, a beaver dammed the stream near the road but, due to the lack of rain, had to move to the lake. The dam has since been removed, but the area remains swampy. Just before reaching the road, notice a large tree on the left. Like many nearby, it was gnawed on by the beaver, who stripped the lower bark. Porcupines completed the job by chewing on and removing the rest of the bark.

The parking lot is three-quarters of a mile to the left along the park road.

Remarks: *Day-use fee is $3. Other activities at North Lake include camping, swimming, boating, fishing (with a license) and naturalist activities. Rowboats and canoes can be rented at the lake, and horses may be rented outside the park. The area is open in winter for cross-country skiing. Be careful along the cliffs. For more information, contact the Department of Environmental Conservation regional office for Greene Co. (see* **Catskill Mountains***).*

104.
Kaaterskill
Falls

Directions: **Greene County, N.Y. From Kingston, continue north on I-87 to Exit 20. Take Route 32 north about 8 miles. Turn left and head west on Route 23A up Kaaterskill Clove 5.8 miles to the big horseshoe bend in the road. The trail to the base of the falls begins on the right; park 0.2 mile beyond on the left (A). If you don't want to make the steep climb to the top of the falls, continue 1.2 miles beyond A on Route 23A to the North Lake turnoff and turn right. After 1.7 miles on this road, turn right onto a rutted dirt road marked by a telephone pole in the middle of the intersection. Drive 0.4 mile to the parking lot. On foot, follow the wide gravel path beyond the yellow gate to the top of the falls (D). The drop is precipitous; be careful.**

Ownership: **New York State Department of Environmental Conservation.**

The blue-blazed Escarpment Trail begins at Bastion Falls **B** a lovely wide waterfall tumbling over fern-laden ledges in Spruce Creek, which drains North and South lakes to Kaaterskill Creek. The splendor of these falls is, however, far surpassed by that of Kaaterskill Falls, reached by a steep half-mile walk.

After skirting the falls, walk across the needle-blanketed floor of the hemlock grove. These original growth trees, many of which reach 3 feet in diameter, are 250 to 300 years old. Follow the Blue Trail along Spruce Creek, then turn left onto a short yellow-blazed side trail that leads to the base of the falls (**C**). At 260 feet, Kaaterskill

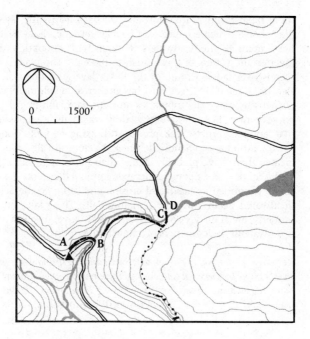

Falls are the highest in the East, falling straight for 180 feet, then cascading another 80 feet over sandstone tiers. Return to the blue-blazed trail. You can continue, and make the steep climb to the top of the falls (**D**), or return to your car, drive to the top, and reach the falls by a very short and easy stroll (see Directions). From this vantage point, one gets a good sense of the narrowness and depth of the valleys of both Spruce Creek and Kaaterskill Creek.

The steep gorges and falls are the result of a process called "stream capture" and stream erosion. Kaaterskill Clove is a classic example of this capture process. Kaaterskill Creek flows sharply down the east escarpment (see **#103**), traveling several miles to the Hudson River. The steep gradient caused by the sudden change in elevation enables the creek to erode away the soft shales and undercut the more resistant sandstones at its headwaters, rapidly carving a gorge into the escarpment. In contrast, Schoharie Creek flows west then north on the elevated upland to join the Mohawk River before reaching the Hudson River. It travels more gently over a greater distance, slowly wearing away the uppermost, resistant sandstone layers. Although a small creek, Kaaterskill Creek, by virtue of its more rapid headward erosion, has cut back across the divide into the Schoharie drainage area. At two different times, Kaaterskill Creek has "captured" the headwaters of a branch of Schoharie Creek and diverted the waters of this branch to the east. The water now descends over falls en route to the lower level of Kaaterskill Creek. Because Kaaterskill Creek now has an increased volume of water, it deepens its gorge. Its tributaries also cut back, forming their own gorges which, likewise, are headed by waterfalls. Kaaterskill Creek first captured Spruce Creek, previously flowing west into Gooseberry Creek, a tributary to Schoharie Creek. Kaaterskill Falls, which were created then, have probably shifted their position farther upstream as the Spruce Creek gorge undergoes continued erosion. Kaaterskill Creek continued its headward erosion and captured the Schoharie headwaters again, this time at Haines Falls. These falls, on private property, are at the very head of Kaaterskill Clove; the present divide is now about three-quarters of a mile farther west.

Remarks: *Kaaterskill Falls are most spectacular in spring when the water level is high. In winter, a cautious walk will reveal frozen castles of ice. For more information, contact the Department of Environmental Conservation regional office for Greene Co. (see* **Catskill Mountains***).*

105.
Slide—Cornell—Wittenberg Mountains Trail

Directions: **Ulster County, N.Y. From Kingston, head west about 25 miles on Route 28, and turn left at the Woodland Valley sign onto Woodland Valley Rd., about 1 mile west of Phoenicia. Crossing the bridge after 0.2 mile, turn right, and continue 4.8 miles to the road's end at Woodland Valley Campground. Park in the first lot, on the right. The red-blazed trail begins across the road between Campsites 70 and 71 (see Remarks).**

Ownership: **New York State Department of Environmental Conservation.**

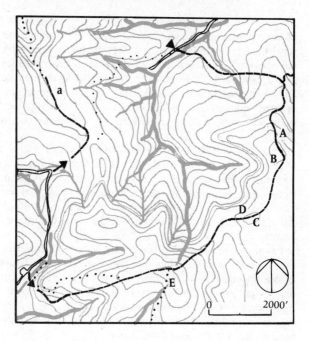

Slide Mountain, at 4180 feet, is the Catskills' highest peak. Together with Wittenberg (3780 feet) and Cornell (3860 feet) mountains, Slide Mountain forms one of the dominating topographic features of the Catskills. From Woodland Valley, the trail leads up Wittenberg Mountain through a mature forest of beech, yellow birch, and sugar maple (see **Catskill Mountains**). Large boulders lie everywhere, giving testimony to the power of the glaciers that once moved through this region, tearing away pieces of rock, transporting them, then dropping them where they rest today. Hemlock groves are frequent along this segment of trail.

About 2 miles and a half up the well-marked, red-blazed trail are high ledges (**A**) that interrupt the steady, gentle slope with a sudden change in elevation, causing abrupt changes in vegetation. Paper birches increase in number and once the top of the ledges are reached, one is suddenly surrounded by spruces and firs, the understory painted green with ferns, mosses, and grasses (see **Catskill Mountains**).

Just beyond the ledges and the 3500-foot marker (posted because camping is not allowed in the fragile environment above this level) is a huge outcrop of sedimentary rock that gives clues to the history of these mountains. A close look at the layers, or *strata*, will reveal some made of grains so small that they are barely discernible to the naked eye while others are composed of much larger particles. Probably deposited in an ancient river, the various layers indicate differing stream currents that prevailed over time. The intersecting layers, or cross-bedding, obvious in the middle of the outcrop, are "fossilized" remnants of dunes once formed by the water currents (see **#3**).

As the summit (**B**) is approached, Slide Mountain can be seen to the west (right). It was named for the 1200-foot rockslide that slashed across its north face in the 1830s. Rockslides often occur on these steep slopes during spring rainy seasons. The broad, flat summit of Wittenberg Mountain offers expansive views to the southeast—the Ashokan Reservoir, the Hudson Valley, and the distant mountains beyond.

The trail drops down off Wittenberg Mountain, traverses a narrow ridge, Bruin's Crossing, and then ascends Cornell Mountain, whose summit (**C**) is about three-quarters of a mile away. Its upper reaches are also forested by spruce and fir. The old-growth spruce trees, weakened by exposure and dry conditions, are not reproducing (see **Catskill Mountains**). The balsam fir saplings growing beneath them will eventually take over.

Leading a quarter-mile down Cornell Mountain, the trail passes through a stand of virgin spruce (**D**). The taller trees, rising above thickets of younger spruce, have lost their upper branches to wind, snow, and ice. The degree of descent, as the trail continues down before climbing to the top of Slide Mountain, about 2 miles away, is marked by the reappearance of paper and yellow birch, then red maple and beech.

The climb up Slide Mountain is difficult and very steep. After scrambling up rocky ledges and some partly eroded sections of trail, you arrive at the summit, (**E**), which is covered by fir trees along with some paper birches. The spruces that probably once grew here are gone; it is thought that they were blown down. A plaque commemorating John Burroughs, a nineteenth-century naturalist who frequented the Catskills, is attached to the face of a conglomerate outcrop full of quartz pebbles. This is the youngest rock found in the Catskills and dates back more than 360 million years to the late Devonian period. Although this type of rock once covered the entire region, it has been eroded away everywhere except from the top of this highest peak (see **Catskill Mountains**). Glaciers inundated the Catskills throughout the ice ages. Striations, or grooves, in the summit rock indicate that these glaciers even covered this high peak at one time. However, whether Slide Mountain was completely engulfed by the ice of the most recent, or Wisconsin, glacier remains a matter of debate.

The gradual descent down Slide Mountain brings with it an equally gradual change in vegetation as the fir trees give way to the beech–yellow-birch–sugar-maple community. The red-blazed trail ends 2 miles below the summit at the Phoenicia–East Branch Trail. The parking lot on Big Indian–Oliverea Rd. is 1 mile to the right of this yellow-blazed trail.

Remarks: *This strenuous hike of roughly 9 miles can be done in a full day by leaving a second car at the finishing point on Big Indian-Oliverea Road: On Rt. 28, continue 7.5 miles west past Woodland Valley Rd. to the village of Big Indian. Make the first left turn onto Big Indian–Oliverea Rd. (Route 47). Follow this road 9 miles, past Winnisook Lake and Lodge, to the Slide Mountain parking lot on the left. The summit of Slide Mountain can be reached by an easier, and more popular, 3-mile hike from this access point. If you wish to hike over Slide, Cornell, and Wittenberg Mountains, however, it is best to begin at Woodland Valley as described here, as it is easier to ascend the steep, slippery passages. Parking at Woodland Valley for the day costs $2.50. The office is on the left 500 yards beyond the parking lot. Alternatively, a 14-mile circuit can be made by continuing on the yellow-blazed Phoenicia–East Branch Trail about 5 miles past the Slide Mountain parking area back to the Woodland Valley Campground. Camping is permitted along the trail, but not less than 100 feet from any trail, parking area, or water source and not above 3500 feet. For more information, contact the Department of Environmental Conservation regional office for Ulster Co. (see* **Catskill Mountains***).*

106.
Giant Ledge

Directions: **Ulster County, N.Y. From Kingston, take Route 28 west about 32 miles to Big Indian. Make the first left turn onto Big Indian–Oliverea Rd. (Ulster Route 47), and continue 7.1 miles. Parking is on the right, just below the hairpin turn; the yellow-blazed trail begins across the road.**

Ownership: **New York State Department of Environmental Conservation.**

This trail, a 3.5-mile round trip, is shorter and easier than the Slide–Cornell—Wittenberg Mountain Trail (see **#105**), but passes through similar changes in vegetation. The rocky trail ascends about three-quarters of a mile to the Giant Ledge shelter through a mature beech, yellow birch, and sugar maple forest, then climbs steeply almost half a mile to the spruce-and-fir-covered top of Giant Ledge (see **Catskill Mountains**). As on Wittenberg Mountain, the rocky ledges that cause sudden changes in topography bring equally abrupt changes in vegetation.

Giant Ledge extends about three-quarters of a mile. Both sides offer views of the surrounding mountains. The east face (**a**) is a vertical 300-foot cliff. Its massive sandstone breaks off in huge blocks as the softer underlying layers are eroded away. This is one of the most dramatic of many such ledges located throughout the Catskills. The views of the surrounding green hills and valleys are excellent, but exercise caution near the cliffs. Below the ledge is a stand of virgin hemlocks and spruces. As old as 300 years, some of the hemlocks reach diameters of 39 inches; the largest spruce trees are 31 inches across. Clearly visible from the ledge, these trees are not accessible by trail.

Remarks: *The trail, an easy walk of a mile and a quarter, continues to the top of Panther Mountain where thickets of stunted balsam firs and scattered paper birches flourish. To return, retrace your steps across Giant Ledge and down to your car. For more information, contact the Department of Environmental Conservation regional office for Ulster Co. (see* **Catskill Mountains***).*

107.
Balsam Lake
Mountain

Directions: **Ulster County, N.Y. From Kingston, take Route 28 west about 35 miles to Highmount. At the post office, turn southwest (left) onto Route 49A, which ends at a T intersection in about 5 miles. Turn south (left) onto Route 49 (Dry Brook Rd.). Make the first right turn, after a mile, onto Millbrook Rd., marked by a small wooden sign on a building. Millbrook Rd. climbs steeply uphill for 2.1 miles**

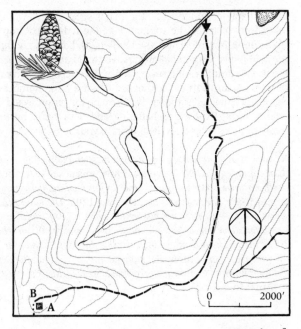

Inset: Balsam fir

**to the trailhead at the second set of trail signs. Pull off the
road on the right to park; the blue-blazed trail begins on
the left.**

Ownership: **New York State Department of Environmental
Conservation.**

The 3-mile hike up Balsam Lake Mountain provides a fairly easy
excursion through the western portion of the Catskill Mountains.
The western Catskills are less visited than the eastern mountains, as
they lack the striking scarps and unobstructed lookouts. However,
glimpses of valleys far below attest to their heights.

Gradual changes in the vegetation occur as one ascends this 3720-
foot mountain. The trail leads first through woods thick with American beech and sugar maples; saplings of both species are crowded
beneath the taller canopy trees. Ferns flourish between the moss-
carpeted rocks that litter the forest floor. Mountain maple and hobblebush are conspicuous in the understory. Black cherry and yellow
birch become more plentiful as the trail climbs higher, but beech and

sugar maple continue to be the major species at elevations up to 3475 feet. To reach the summit, take the red-blazed loop trail. As the summit is approached, the hardwoods, battered and broken by the wind, give way to balsam firs. Scattered at first, firs abound on the broad summit (**A**), growing densely between towering skeletons of trees. A storm in 1950 knocked down a large number of trees. Some firs remained standing, but were no longer protected by other, nearby trees. Exposed to battering and desiccation by the wind, many of these taller trees died. Retrace your steps back to your car.

Remarks: *A 15-acre bog of sphagnum moss and balsam fir is located less than a quarter of a mile from the firetower, and about 40 feet lower, to the north-northwest (**B**). Unusually large for this mountaintop setting, the bog formed where drainage was blocked (see #120). The adventurous bushwhacker can search for the bog by following a faint trail through thick vegetation (look for it between the firetower and small, nearby cabin). While the bog itself is nearly impenetrable due to the balsam fir, its edges can be explored more easily. For more information, contact the Department of Environmental Conservation regional office for Ulster Co. (see* **Catskill Mountains***).*

108.
Gilboa
Fossil Site

Directions: **Schoharie County, N.Y. From Kingston, go north on I-87 to Exit 21. Take Route 23 west about 38 miles to Grand Gorge. Turn north (right) onto Route 30 and drive 2.9 miles. Turn right at the sign for Gilboa. There is a pull-off on the right after 1.1 miles, just before the bridge.**

Ownership: **Power Authority of the State of New York.**

For the avid fossil buff or the curious passerby traveling through the western Catskills, this is a roadside stop that, despite its humble appearance, provides a glimpse into the earth's environment millions of years ago. If you are passing by, stop for a minute to take a look at the seven large fossils—the stumps of trees from one of the oldest known forests in the world—lined up along the fence by the road's edge. Fossils of this kind, called *Eospermatopteris*, were first exposed by a flash flood of the Schoharie Creek in 1869. Further investigations of this area in 1920 uncovered hundreds of fossils, indicating that these trees were a major component of an ancient forest.

These fossils date back more than 365 million years to the Devonian period, when fish were the most highly developed animals. Presumably, the Gilboa trees grew in dense forests near the edge of a shallow sea that once covered much of what is now New York State (see **Catskill Mountains**). Radiating, unbranched, straplike roots held these bulbous-based trees upright in the muddy swamps. In contrast, a modern tree widens at its base and its many-branched roots are continuous with the tree's trunk. The forests apparently underwent several cycles of flooding, burial, and regrowth. The tree trunks were broken off near their bases, their centers decayed and were filled with sand, which now forms the fossils.

Another type of fossil, of a plant unlike any presently found on earth, was discovered in the same rocks. These fossils, known as *Aneurophytons*, were formed from the foliage of ancient trees. What might be called leaves consisted only of veins; and lacked the flat green surfaces of modern leaves. Photosynthesis could take place nevertheless, just as it does in green stems and branches today. Like ferns, these plants reproduced via spores instead of seeds. However, their internal structure closely resembled that found in pines and other conifers today.

To date, no one has been able to prove that the tree stumps and foliage came from the same plant. What the Gilboa trees looked like and the role they played in plant evolution still remain issues of conjecture.

Nearby Place of Interest

Mine Kill State Park is about 3 miles north of the fossil site. Return to Route 30 and turn north (right). After 2.7 miles, turn right into the Mine Kill Falls Overlook parking lot. One trail leads to the overlook and another branches off to the bottom of the falls. The main park entrance is 0.6 mile farther north on the right. Activities include swimming, hiking, picnicking, and both fishing (with a license) and boating on the Blenheim-Gilboa Pumped Storage reservoir. For more information, contact Mine Kill

State Park, Box 921, North Blenheim, N.Y. 12131, (518) 827-6111. The Blenheim-Gilboa project visitors' center is located 1.1 miles north of the park entrance; turn right at the sign for Lansing Manor.

109.
Woodbourne
Sanctuary

Directions: **Susquehanna County, Pa. From Scranton, go north on I-81 about 20 miles to Exit 64. Take Route 106 northwest 5.8 miles to Kingsley. Continue west across U.S. 11 toward Brooklyn and Dimock. Follow the twisting road around three left-hand curves. Turn right at 2.3 miles, going through Brooklyn and on to Dimock. Turn north (right) on Route 29. Woodbourne is 1 mile up the road toward Montrose. Park on the right at the crest of the hill.**

Ownership: **The Nature Conservancy.**

This sanctuary contains a magnificent stand of virgin hemlock and mixed hardwood forest, the largest of its kind remaining in northeastern Pennsylvania. (When the Europeans first settled America, such forests covered all of the northeastern United States and southern Canada.) Some of the hemlocks here are 350 years old. At least twelve different species of ferns grow in the moist woods, along the edges of an alder swamp, and in the succession forest at the edge of the virgin stand.

Underlying the sanctuary are layers of sedimentary rock, running roughly parallel with the ground. This sediment, comprising sandstone and shale, was deposited at the bottom of a shallow sea that covered much of Pennsylvania in the Devonian period, 405 to 365 million years ago. Several glaciers later crept across the plateau; each time they receded, the meltwaters eroded layers of younger rock from the surface of the plateau, revealing the Devonian deposits. Since then the deposits have again been covered by newer layers of soil. One relic of the glacial age, though, is the alder swamp, which sits in an area that was compressed by the thick wedge of ice that passed over it.

The short circular nature trail begins at the parking area and passes through old fields and a young hardwood forest. Within five minutes you will enter the stand of virgin timber. Here hemlock, beech, and red maple predominate; sugar maples, red oak, yellow birch, and black birch are also present. This is a climax forest—the variety of species will remain constant, rather than shifting in favor of different species—until disturbance of some kind begins a new process of succession (see **#41**). Few shrubs are found here, because the canopy of trees is dense, allowing little light to reach the forest floor. Those that do grow are northern species such as hobblebush, mountain maple, and striped maple, which like the sanctuary's cool climate, enhanced by its altitude of 1600 feet. This cooler climate may also explain why hemlocks, which just a short distance to the east and south in the Delaware Valley are confined to shady ravines and north-facing slopes (see **#69**), are found here on top of the plateau. Christmas and wood ferns grow in the moist soil under the trees, as do many wildflowers.

Northern species of birds and animals are also present in the preserve. Along the swamp, northern waterthrush and Canada warblers may be heard. Winter wrens, commonly associated with coniferous forests of the north, sometimes nest in the sanctuary along with hermit thrushes, solitary vireos, and the black-throated green warbler. These species breed in northern woods, and in the south as far as North Carolina and Tennessee in the higher mountains.

Snowshoe hares also winter here. Porcupines, unusual for this area, are sometimes seen, as well as otters, red foxes, long-tailed weasels, and bobcats, whose more northerly habitats have been encroached upon, have taken refuge in the sanctuary.

The trail winds around the edge of the alder swampland. A wide variety of ferns flourishes here: cinnamon, marsh, sensitive, crested, Glinton's, Bott's, royal, and long beech. From here, the path loops back to return to the parking area.

Remarks: *Tours of the areas off the nature trail to bog areas can be arranged by contacting the custodian-naturalists, Joyce and Benjamin Stone, (717) 278-3384. Camping at Lackawanna State Park off I-81, on Route 407.*

110.

Pine Creek

Gorge

Directions: **Tioga County, Pa. From Scranton take U.S. 6 west 117 miles to Wellsboro. Take Route 660 southwest (left) 10 miles over very twisty roads to Leonard Harrison State Park. The road ends at the overlook parking area (A).**

Ownership: **Pennsylvania Bureau of State Parks.**

Standing at the overlook (**A**), you look down 800 feet into a deep gorge, a great rift in the gentle topography of the Appalachian Plateau. This is the Grand Canyon of Pennsylvania, the Pine Creek Gorge, a National Natural Landmark. For 25 miles it gouges a trough into the bedrock. At the southern end of the gorge near Waterville, the walls rise 1450 feet above the river. Standing at the park lookout, you will see the flattened topography, characteristic of sites within the Appalachian Plateau (see **Appalachian Plateau**). Hills shaped and etched by the force of water recede one behind the other into the distance, a heavy green in summer, brilliant with color in autumn.

The canyon below is a product of the recent Ice Ages, which began about 2 million years ago. Before the great sheets of ice advanced across the northern United States, the upper branch of Pine Creek flowed northeast and the lower branch flowed southwest. The two streams were separated by a divide about a mile north of the lookout. (A divide is an area of high ground separating one drainage area from another.) As each mass of ice moved south, it blocked the northern portion of Pine Creek. The waters rose behind the dike of ice and spilled over the divide to join the lower creek, in the process eroding a pathway through the divide. As each of the glaciers continued to advance, it moved up over the divide, gouging and scouring it further. Then, as the ice sheets retreated, the stream was again dammed and tremendous amounts of meltwater were released. Carrying tons of rock, gravel, and other glacial debris, lower Pine Creek now had tremendous cutting power. In the course of each glaciation, the stream dug deeper and deeper into the sandstones and softer sedimentary rocks of the plateau.

The outlook is an excellent place to watch bird migrations in spring and fall. Suddenly the September air comes alive with squeakings, bits of song, rustling movement. A wave of warblers is moving through, perhaps pushing south in front of a storm. Warblers are notoriously hard to distinguish in the fall. The males, having lost their bright breeding plumage, are muted versions of their spring selves. This makes excellent sense. Courting is over; the males no longer need to attract the attention of the female; they will be much safer from predatory hawks if they are less noticeable (see **Wissahickon Valley** on warblers). While not as spectacular as at the Kittatinny Ridge near the Delaware River, hawk flights are worth watching for (see **#78**). Waterfowl also use the gorge as a flyway. Spring landbird flights peak in late April and early May.

Turkey Path, a mile-long trail, descends to Little Four Mile Run and follows the stream to the bottom of the gorge. At the top of the trail where the soils are dry and have been disturbed by construction, white or paper birch, aspen, and red pine cover the hill. Almost immediately as the trail begins to descend, hemlock, black birch, yellow birch, red and white oaks, and American beech take over the

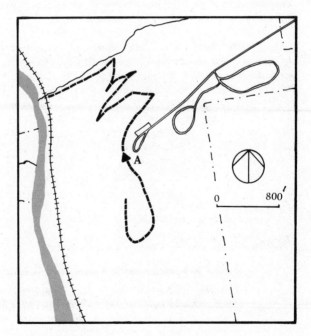

canopy. Striped maple is common in the understory. This is an example of the hemlock–northern-hardwood forest, which covers virtually all of the Appalachian Plateau Province (see **Appalachian Plateau**). These forests have nesting populations of birds whose range extends southward of the plateaus only at higher elevations. They include the hermit thrush, yellow-bellied sapsucker, winter wren, solitary vireo, northern junco, red-breasted nuthatch, golden-crowned kinglet, purple finch, and a variety of warblers, including the magnolia, Blackburnian, black-throated blue, black-throated green, and Canada warblers, and the northern waterthrush.

As you make your way to the bottom of the gorge, you will pass a variety of outcroppings. There are blocks of sandstone containing cracks and fine line fractures. There are red and greenish-gray shales and mudstones, which break easily into flakes and fragments (see **#111**). In some places the sandstone blocks sit on top of beds of shale or mudstone. The softer material has eroded away and the sandstone is left as an overhang. Eventually, when more of its support disappears, the sandstone block will fall under its own weight.

At the bottom of the ravine are a series of waterfalls. Little Four Mile Run flows over sandstones and fossil-bearing shales here. Look for bulblet fern along the falls. Maidenhair fern and marginal wood fern also grow along the lower portion of the trail.

Remarks: *The trail is about 2 miles round trip, and portions of it are steep. From Colton Point on the west bank of the gorge an even steeper trail winds down to the river. To reach the trail go back along Route 660 to Route 362 and turn left toward Ansonia. In Ansonia pick up U.S. 6 west and drive over the gorge. On the far side take the first left to Colton Point. Several hiking trails crisscross the area. For maps of the Tiadaghton and Tioga state forests contact the Bureau of Forestry, P.O. Box 1467, Harrisburg, Pa. 17120. There is excellent trout fishing in Pine Creek and many of its tributaries. A license is required.*

111.

World's End State Park

Directions: Sullivan County, Pa. From Scranton go west on U.S. 6 about 25 miles to Russell Hill. Turn west (left) on Route 87 and go 26 miles to U.S. 220. Turn south (left) and go 11 miles. Turn northwest (right) on Route 154. Go 6.5

miles to the World's End camping area on the left. Just past the campground, turn left onto Mineral Springs Rd. and turn left again after about 500 feet. Drive to the trailer dump station on the left side of the road. Park here and walk south, picking up the blue-blazed Canyon Vista Trail at Mineral Springs Road (A). To reach the High Knob Overlook, continue driving west on Route 154 toward the park office. Make a sharp left onto Double Run Rd. Go 2.7 miles to Dry Run Rd. and turn west (right). Drive 2.3 miles and turn right onto High Knob Rd.; a sign marks the turn. Drive to the end and park. To see a good exposure of fossil lungfish burrows, continue west on Dry Run Rd. for 3.2 miles beyond High Knob Rd. to a pulloff by a large face of red rock. Look for the burrows about 20 feet up the cliff. To reach Route 87 continue west 0.5 mile on Dry Run Rd. Alternatively, from Williamsport go about 6 miles east to Route 87. Turn north (left) and go about 25 miles to Route 154. Turn southeast (right) and go about 3.5 miles to Mineral Springs Rd.

Ownership: Pennsylvania Bureau of Forestry.

This 1-hour walk on the blue-blazed Canyon Vista Trail takes you up through 100 million years of geological history and presents you with the sight of a deep, wild gorge cut into the Appalachian Plateau. Like all the surface rock formations of the plateau, the rock here is sedimentary, a layered stack of sandstone, shale, and conglomerate (see **Appalachian Plateau**).

Where the trail begins (**A**), the rocks are covered with soil and the trees are of the hemlock–northern-hardwood association (see **Catskill Mountains**). Black birch, yellow birch, and sugar maple are abundant. In the moist shade a variety of ferns grow, including broad beech fern, spinulose wood fern, marginal wood fern, and Christmas fern.

Stay on the Blue Trail for about three-quarters of a mile till it strikes the Red X Trail. Turn sharp left and continue about a quarter-mile to the Vista.

Near the top of the climb, the ground is covered with bits of broken red shales belonging to the Mauch Chunk Formation. This formation makes up the rim and upper walls of the gorge throughout the park. From the overlook (**B**) there is wide view of the precipitous gorge and the plateau topography.

Turn and walk straight back from the overlook to a tumble of vast rocks (**C**). Made up of conglomerate and sandstone, these are the

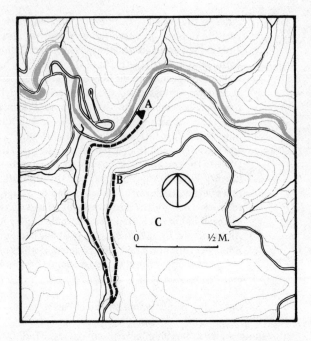

youngest rocks in the gorge (see **Shawangunks**). They are also the hardest. They belong to the Pottsville Group. The repeated freezing and thawing of water has broken the formation apart into huge boulders (see **#118**). The large cracks in the rock run roughly parallel to each other along a horizontal axis. Between the fractures, you can see series of diagonal patterns, known as *cross-bedding*. These patterns were laid down by a stream with changing currents. The Pottsville Formation was deposited by a *braided stream*, a stream carrying so much material that it deposits countless islands of rock, gravel and other sediments. Such streams are commonly associated with the meltwaters of glaciers. As new islands are formed and old ones change shape, the river currents shift, accounting for the cross-bedding you see here.

These sedimentary rocks which make up the Mauch Chunk and Pottsville formations formed as mud, gravel, sand, and clay washed off highlands to the east and deposited in lowlands by streams and rivers. Although 95 percent of the rock in the earth's crust is igneous or metamorphic, most of the rock we encounter is sedimentary. This is because sedimentary rock is made up of the products of erosion, a continuous process that happens at the surface of the earth, while igneous and metamorphic rocks are formed in heat and pressure deep below the earth's surface (see **#16**). Here the sedimentary material came to rest on a vast delta complex that covered this part of Pennsylvania about 330 million years ago. Tons of sediment thousands of feet thick accumulated, compressing the layers below. As each layer was compressed it slowly changed from loose material into stone. About 250 million years ago these layers were lifted up and erosion began to wear away into a pattern of intersecting gorges and flat hills (see **Appalachian Plateau**).

To return to your car, continue on the Canyon Vista Trail northeast from **B** about a third of a mile. Turn left on the red-blazed Loyalsock Trail and descend the slope about half a mile to return to the Canyon Vista Trail. Turn right toward the parking area. Continue the tour, stopping at High Knob Overlook and the fossil lungfish burrows (see Directions). The lungfish burrows are in the oldest rocks at the bottom of the gorge. These rocks are part of the Huntley Mountain Formation and are made up of olive-gray sandstones and reddish shales. Depending on the size of the particles, mineral composition, the cementing materials, and the pressures to which they have been subjected, each type of sedimentary rock has a different hardness. Shale, made up of fine, clay-sized particles, feels smooth to the touch. The clay particles were deposited in thin beds on the bottom of calm water. The particles do not form a tight bond, and so the shale breaks apart easily into small flat flakes. Each flat plane is the surface of a bedding layer. Sandstone is a much harder rock with coarser grains. The grains of sand have been cemented together more firmly, through several processes. Water carries new minerals into the pores between the grains and deposits them. The new minerals bind the sediments together. The simple pressure of tons of material lying above the sediments weld them together, and if the material has been deeply buried, the minerals may start to recrystalize. Cementation also can occur as a result of chemical changes.

The lungfish burrows offer a clue to the environment that existed here about 370 million years ago. Like the lungfish still living today, this ancient freshwater species could breathe oxygen. These were shallow-water creatures, and in periods of long drought, their habitat often dried out. In order to stay moist and survive, the lungfish burrowed their way tail-first into the soft muds. At the top of the burrow they left a small opening, allowing them to breathe. Then the fish went into a kind of suspended animation, during which their metabolic rate dropped dramatically. With the return of wet weather, the fish roused themselves and became aquatic again. The empty burrows sometimes filled with sediments that became harder rock than the original muds. On this rock face the siltstones around the burrows have eroded away more quickly, leaving the shape of the burrows standing out against the siltstone as long narrow columns in bas-relief.

Remarks: *The climb to the canyon vista is about half an hour at moderate speed. Wear hiking shoes. For a longer hike, stay on Canyon Vista Trail as it makes a wide loop before returning to the campground. Camping is available at the park. Other activities include trout fishing with a license in Loyalsock Creek, supervised swimming by the park office, backpacking along the Loyalsock trail and other park trails. For information on the Loyalsock Trail see #112. The creek is a favorite run among experienced whitewater kayakers. Water levels in the creek change rapidly and kayakers should contact the park office for updated information. Nearby is Kettle Creek Gorge, a beautiful natural area maintained by the Wyoming State Forest. For further information contact World's End State Park, Department of Natural Resources, P.O. Box 62, Forksville, Pa. 18616, (717) 924-3287.*

112.
The Allegheny Front

Directions: **Lycoming County, Pa. From Williamsport go about 6 miles east to Route 87. Turn north (left) and drive 10.1 miles to the trailhead of the Loyalsock Trail. There is a parking area on the south (right) side of the road. Alternatively, from Scranton, follow the directions to World's End State Park to the junction of U.S. 220 and Route 87. Continue west on Route 87 approximately 35 miles. The parking area will be on the left.**

Ownership: **Pennsylvania Bureau of Forestry.**

The Allegheny Front marks the edge of the Appalachian Plateau, where the flat-topped hills give way to the rise and fall of the Ridge and Valley Province. The front runs north along the outer edge of the Appalachians up through Virginia, West Virginia, and Maryland and then in central Pennsylvania curves eastward toward the Catskills. Over much of its course it is elusive. Here it stands forth, a great, unmistakable escarpment.

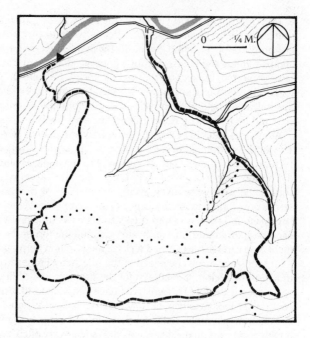

The trail ascends steeply from the parking area through a stand of hemlocks. After about half a mile, it breaks over the top of the slope onto a gently rising flat covered with mountain laurel. In late May and early June, the laurel fills the woods with pink blossoms. The canopy is made up of mixed oaks, primarily white oaks. Like virtually all woodlands on the plateaus, this is a second-growth stand. In among the oaks are some eastern white pines. White pines have long been prized. The long straight trunks became the masts of colonial ships, while pine boards made excellent floorboards and furniture. The great virgin stands that once covered the northeast have long vanished.

At **A** follow the Loyalsock Trail across the old forest road. About half a mile farther, follow the trail as it bears left onto a woods road and then leaves the road, turning sharply east (left) up toward the rim of the front. After 2 miles, you will reach the edge of the escarpment. Here on the very dry soils, chestnut oaks form the canopy, while lowbush blueberries and huckleberries fill the shrub layer.

The trail follows the very edge of the front for about a mile and a half. There are several lookouts along the path. The top of the ridge is 1800 feet, about 1000 feet above the valley below. The long line of the Allegheny Front marks the meeting point for two very different products of the same event. To the south, where the Appalachians wrinkle the landscape, the upheavals that raised the mountains contorted, broke, and tortured the rock layers into undulating folds full of faults and fissures. Weaker layers of rock were worn away, leaving behind deep valleys. Harder formations resisted erosion and became rocky ridges (see **Ridge and Valley**).

Atop the Appalachian Plateau, the upheavals ran a different course. The land was uplifted evenly, so that the horizontal layers of sedimentary rock remained largely in place. Erosion and glacial scouring did remove upper layers of rock; but because the layers were horizontal, the rock wore away evenly. Formations of resistant sandstones now form a protective cap over the softer rocks below. Where streams found their way into cracks and crevices, the landscape has been sculptured into hills and valleys. Along the top of the escarpment, you can see the exposed rocks of the Burgoon Formation. This hard sandstone forms the bench of the Allegheny Front throughout much of the region. It is known for the strong cross-bedding of the rock layers (see **#111**). Geologists have determined that the Burgoon sandstones were deposited by torrential braided streams. Braided streams carry so much sediment that bars and islands of gravel and boulders are continually deposited. Such streams are often associated with cross-bedding.

Remarks: *Allow 4 to 5 hours to climb up and retrace your steps. The best time of year for this hike is when the leaves are off the trees. To make a circle route continue east another 2 miles to the Bear Creek Ranger Station. Follow the road north about a mile out to Route 87 and turn west (left) back to the parking area, about 0.5 mile down the road. The circle route is about 10.5 miles. The Loyalsock Trail runs for over 50 miles east into Wyoming County. Backpacking campsites are scattered along the way. A trail guide is available from the Alpine Club of Williamsport, P.O. Box 501, Williamsport, Pa. 17701. The trail markers are red disks with a yellow LT. Two disks indicate a turn in the trail. Side trails that return to the main trail are marked with a yellow disk and a red X. Other side trails are marked with blue or white disks. Camping is available at World's End State Park, northeast on Route 87. (See **#111**).*

113.
Ricketts Glen
Natural Area

Directions: **Luzerne County, Pa. From Scranton, take I-81 south about 25 miles to the Nanticoke exit. Go west (right) 4 miles on Route 29 to U.S. 11. Turn southwest (left) for 1 mile, then go north, still on Route 29, for 10 miles. Turn west (left) on Route 118 and go 11 miles. Turn north (right) on Route 487; after 3.3 miles turn right. Park headquarters are 0.4 mile up the road on the right. To reach the head of the Glen Trail, turn right by the park office and drive 0.5 mile. Park at the end of the road. The Ganoga Glen Trail leads south from the parking area and is well marked.**

Ownership: **Pennsylvania Bureau of State Parks.**

In the heart of Ricketts Glen, a National Natural Landmark on the banks of Kitchen Creek, are stands of white pine and hemlock that were young when Columbus crossed the Atlantic. They are among the oldest trees in the eastern United States. Farther upstream the tributaries of Kitchen Creek hurtle down the face of the Allegheny Front in waterfall after waterfall. In the forests, bobcats and bears can still be found and northern species of birds such as black-throated blue warblers and hermit thrushes nest on top of the plateau. This is one of the most outstanding natural areas in the eastern United States, set in the midst of 13,050 acres of state park.

As you drive up toward the park headquarters along Route 487, park on the left after 2 miles and walk a half-mile to the overlook at Grand View (**A**). Standing at the lookout, you are on the edge of the escarpment known as the Allegheny Front. It stretches to the east and west, marking the boundary between the harder, younger conglomerates and sandstones of the plateau to the north (see **Appalachian Plateau**) and the softer, older sandstones, siltstones and shales of the Ridge and Valley Province to the south. The rocks of this region began as river-borne materials deposited 340 to 315 million years ago during Pennsylvanian and Mississippian periods. A hundred million years of pressure and compaction transformed the gravels, sands, and mud into rock. Then, about 250 million years ago, upheavals within the earth contorted the surface, erecting the

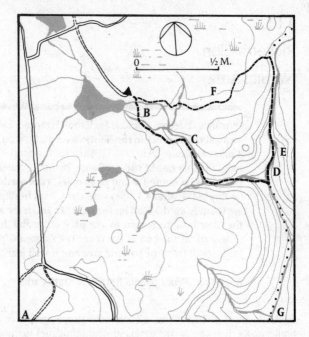

mountains of the Appalachians and shaping the more rolling relief of the Appalachian Plateau. This massive event—which took millions of years—was followed by further periods of uplift, which continued to raise rock strata. Throughout these tens of millions of years, erosion was also at work, wearing down and carving away, removing hundreds of feet of rock and gradually creating the escarpment on which you stand. In more recent times, over the last 1 to 2 million years, at least four glaciers have etched a path across the landscape. At Grand View you can find whitish boulders of Pocono Conglomerate. These are glacial erratics, remnants of one of the earlier glaciers, brought from the north and deposited here when the ice sheet melted. The most recent glacier, the Wisconsin, did not cover Grand View; its path lay just to the east.

From the overlook, drive to the head of the Ganoga Glen Trail. The start of the trail slopes gently down hill. On top of the plateau where the trail begins (**B**), the ground is very rocky and the soil thin. This is because the hard rocks resist erosion. The forest here is made up of northern species: groves of hemlocks mixed with red maples, sugar maples, and American beeches are dominant. The dense shade of the hemlocks allows few shrubs to grow on the forest floor (see #67). Mosses and ferns such as Boots fern, spinulose wood fern, and rock polypody thrive in the moist shade.

Walk about half a mile to Ganoga Glen Falls (C). As you approach the falls, the trail becomes rocky. The great number of waterfalls indicates the youth of Kitchen Creek. Though the creek probably began etching its pathway several hundred million years ago, the main work of cutting the glens was done by the meltwaters of the last glacier. Over thousands of years to come, the creek will erode away the rocks so that the falls run together, becoming higher and fewer. As you stand by the falls, you can see that the erosive force of the water is working away at the top and the lip of the falls. Gradually, the lip of the falls is migrating back toward the base of the falls upstream, Cayuga.

Ganoga, Cayuga, and the other falls in the upper glens run across the hard sandstones of the Huntly Mountain Formation; their characteristic shape is a series of steps. About a quarter-mile down the trail, the two streams come together at Waters Meet. Go left on the Glen Leigh Trail. At Wyandot Falls (D) and R. B. Ricketts Falls (E), the stream spills over in dramatic cascades called "bridal veils." Here the water flows over a gray sandstone that forms a cap over softer red shale. The water eats away the shale more quickly, leaving an overhang of sandstone. These rocks are part of the older Catskill Formation, which lies at the base of the Allegheny Front.

The constant spray from the falls creates a moist environment throughout the ravine, in which certain plants thrive. Look for long beech fern, silvery and maidenhair spleenworts, and liverworts along the banks and in the rocks by the stream. The creek provides a corridor of light in the forest canopy, in which less shade-tolerant species like the yellow birch can grow. Clutching onto the bare rocks, their roots trap soil and provide nurseries for ferns and seedlings.

From Waters Meet walk up hill about 1 mile to the Highland Trail. Turn left. About three-quarters of a mile along the Highland Trail is Midway Crevasse (F), a narrow cleft through a tumble of huge rocks. These chunks of Pocono conglomerate were not transported here directly by glacial movement. Instead, they broke off a ledge 100 feet to the north during the bitter post-glacial period, when frequent freezing and thawing of water within cracks in the rock eventually broke it apart (see #118). Continue about half a mile to Ganoga Glen Trail. Turn right to return to your car.

To reach Ricketts Glen itself, either walk south (left) along Kitchen Creek from Waters Meet about half a mile or, from the parking area, return to the junction of Route 118 and Route 487. Go 1.5 miles to a parking area on the right. Cross the road and walk north along Kitchen Creek for 15 minutes and you will enter a stand of great hemlocks (**G**). Partly because of their inaccessibility and partly because of the foresight of Col. R. B. Ricketts, who owned this land, these trees were not cut when the plateau was logged extensively in the 1890s. There is virtually no undergrowth at all beneath these trees because of the dense shade they cast. This is the forest that the earliest settlers knew. To the south of the parking lot is the Evergreen Nature Trail, where the very oldest white pines and hemlocks are located. Recently some trees blown down in this area were examined and found to be 900 years old.

Remarks: *Allow 2 hours to make the circuit of the upper glens. The walking is rough, slippery, rocky, and very steep in some places. Wear hiking boots with good treads. Activities include boating on Lake Jean (permits available at park office), lake and stream fishing (with a license), and swimming. Camping at the park. For more information contact Ricketts Glen State Park, R.D. 1, Box 251, Benton, Pa. 17814.*

114.
Archbald
Pothole

Directions: **Lackawanna County, Pa. From Scranton, go northeast on Route 6 about 6 miles beyond I-81. Immediately beyond Eynon shopping center, take a sharp right into the parking area.**

Ownership: **Pennsylvania Bureau of State Parks.**

This is reputed to be the largest pothole in the world, 38 feet deep and 41 feet across at the widest point. Although potholes are frequently found below waterfalls or in fierce rapids, there is no evidence of a stream in this area; thus, it is probable that Archbald Pothole was created during the melting of the last glacier, about 15,000 to 10,000 years ago. A stream of glacial runoff probably found its way into a crack in the glacier and plunged hundreds of feet to the bedrock below. It began to eat out a cavity as it swirled pieces of rock and sand and gravel against the stone. The glacial stream carved a hole through layers of sandstone, shale, and coal belonging to the Pennsylvanian period. The sandstone is thinner and weaker than the shale beneath it and breaks apart more easily. The mouth of the hole is, therefore, considerably wider than the bottom. The shale on the north face of the hole has been polished and smoothed by the action of water and grit.

The Archbald Pothole is located off a main highway in a heavily built-up area and bears the scars of heavy use, but it is an intriguing phenomenon.

Remarks: *There is camping at Tobyhanna State Park, about 20 miles southeast of Scranton along I-380.*

115.
Lacawac
Sanctuary

Directions: **Pike County, Pa. From Scranton, take I-380 southeast, then take I-84 east 16 miles to Exit 6. Go north 0.7 mile on Route 507. Turn west (left), following signs to Ledgedale Campground, 1.8 miles. Road ends at T junction; go east (right) 0.5 mile to another T; take sharp right (southeast). Road becomes gravel. Take the second right, at the sign for Lacawac. Follow road to the end and park by the manager's house.**

Ownership: **The Nature Conservancy. Open to the public by appointment. Write or call the Lacawac Sanctuary, R.D. 1, Lake Ariel, Pa. 18463, (717) 689-9494.**

Lacawac Sanctuary, a National Natural Landmark, is a small, diverse preserve of 500 acres perched 250 feet above the Wallenpaupack Valley. It contains two outstanding natural features: the southern-most unpolluted glacial lake in the northeast, and a series of steep rocky ledges which support unusual vegetation. Although the surrounding land has been farmed and logged for centuries, the ledges and the lake have remained undisturbed for about 100 years.

The Catskill sandstone and, beneath it, the red Catskill shale were deposited in the shallow seas of the Devonian period, about 380 million years ago. The layers of rock are horizontal, much as they were laid down, for this area was not as contorted by mountain-building as was the Ridge and Valley Province to the east (see **Ridge and Valley**). The sandstones and shales contain large amounts of silica and no calcium, and the soils which have developed from these rocks tend to be acidic (see **#100**). The abundant hemlocks and rhododendron reflect this. When the last glacier had receded from the region, about 10,000 years ago, it exposed the rock ledges of the Wallenpaupack Valley and gouged out Lake Lacawac.

The lake has remained unpolluted and undisturbed largely because its watershed is contained within the boundaries of the sanctuary. The watershed of any body of water is the surrounding area that supplies water to that body by surface runoff or tributary streams. Any activity in the watershed will affect the condition of the lake or stream. In this region, lime fertilizer is often washed off the fields and into the ponds. If lime were to seep into Lake Lacawac, it would drastically change the character of the lake. Vegetation would dramatically increase and the acidic bog which lies at one end might be destroyed.

The rock cliffs overlooking the Wallenpaupack Valley are highly inaccessible. This has prevented loggers both from disturbing the unique plant life found here and from destroying the shade that these plants require. Giant lichens, or rock tripe, sit on the ledges; measuring 7 inches in diameter, these leathery plants are probably over 100 years old.

Lichens are really two plants masquerading as one. The visible form is a fungus, more specifically the reproductive appendage of the fungus. Attached to it is a species of algae, invisible to the naked eye. Each fungus is associated with only one species of algae. The algae contain chlorophyll, the green pigment that allows a plant to produce its own food through photosynthesis. Using carbon dioxide, water, and the energy of sunlight, green plants manufacture sugars and starches. These are the basic ingredients necessary for growth and reproduction. The fungi do not contain chlorophyll and cannot produce their own food. Instead they absorb it from the algae. In return for this service the algae have an anchor and perhaps some protection against dehydration. Botanists have yet to agree on whether this relationship is truly symbiotic, that is, that each organism derives equal benefits from the arrangement.

Lichens are often the first visible sign of primary succession (see **#63**). Growing on the barren surface of bare rock, they play an important part in breaking down the rock into soil. The ledges are also an excellent place for spring wildflowers and ferns.

Remarks: *To protect the site from too much disturbance, visitors are given guided tours, which must be arranged ahead of time. An extensive walk will take about 2 hours. When possible, the staff will suit the walk to visitors' requests. The terrain is gentle. Ledgedale Campground is located in Greenood on the road to the sanctuary (see Directions).*

116.
Bruce Lake
Natural Area

Directions: **Pike County, Pa. From Scranton, take I-380 southeast, then take I-84 east 22 miles to Exit 7, and head south on Route 390. Go 1.5 miles and pull into the parking area on the left. Walk to Bruce Lake along the dirt-road trail.**

Ownership: **Pennsylvania Bureau of Forestry.**

On a cool morning in May, the woods and wetlands along the way to Bruce Lake are alive with birds. White-tailed deer dash off into the trees. A gray fox trots purposefully across the path. Blueberry bushes flower in the woods; cranberry blossoms by the edge of the lake. Fall is as lovely. The red maples and sugar maples gleam against a background of dark hemlock and balsam fir.

Bruce Lake lies on the Pocono Plateau (see #119). The glaciers marked the topography well, scooping out depressions in the flat bedrock of sandstone and shale; today they are the lakes, bogs, and swamps of the region.

The trail begins in a young second-growth forest. White oaks and northern red oaks and a few hickories make up the canopy. Red maples are prominent in the understory. The oaks have been damaged by gypsy moths in recent years, which may change the look of these woods considerably. For the time being the understory and shrub layers are sparse. There is a scattering of blueberry and mountain laurel. Hayscented fern carpets large areas. If the oaks are killed, the undergrowth will become more dense, taking advantage of the increased light.

Several types of wetland are scattered along this hike. After about 500 feet, Panther Swamp (**A**) stretches to the north. Dead and dying trees fringe its edge, indicating that water levels have risen here. This is the result of beaver activity. Beavers have played an important role in maintaining and rejuvenating bogs and swamps in the northeastern United States. Holes in dead snags such as these are

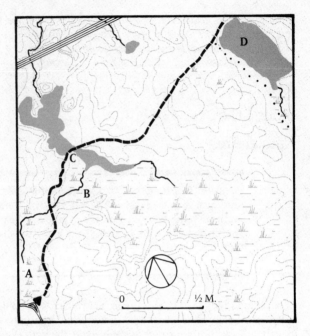

often used as nesting sites by wood ducks. Watch for nesting mallard, too. Earlier in spring, migrating waterfowl settle into the Pocono wetlands to feed and rest as they move north. Hemlocks and balsam firs form a dense tangle around much of the swamp. Balsam fir is typical of mountain bogs as far south as Virginia. The balsam fir is distinctive, neat, compact, and conical—the perfect Christmas tree. Like the hemlock, it is an important food tree in winter. The seeds are eaten by ruffed grouse, the twigs by deer and an occasional snowshoe hare, and the bark is stripped off by porcupines.

Beyond Panther Swamp the land dips slightly and the woods are shadier and cooler. Sugar maple and American beech dominate the canopy here. A few larger trees appear. Soils are moister here thanks to the lower topography. Northern species of warblers and other birds nest in the woodlands of the Poconos. Search for black-throated blue warblers, black-throated green warblers, solitary vireos, hermit thrushes, and others along this walk.

About a mile from the trailhead, Balsam Swamp begins to emerge on the right side of the trail (**B**). This wetland is marshier than Panther Swamp, covered with hummocks of sedges. Through the process of succession common to bogs and swamps, this area is gradually becoming dry land (see **#120**). There is a good view of the swamp as the trail crosses the bridge at Egypt Meadow Lake (**C**). The wetlands of the Poconos are nesting grounds for a variety of warblers and other songbirds. Look and listen for the common yellowthroat and the swamp sparrow.

Once past Balsam Swamp the trail rises onto a small rocky ridge. The vegetation changes abruptly; oaks reappear, with chestnut oaks on the driest part of the ridge. The abundance of oaks in the forests of the Poconos is a reminder that this section of the Appalachian Plateau is at the southern limit of the province. To the south are the oak-hickory forests of the Piedmont (see **#10**). To the north are the northern forests of hemlock and hardwoods (see **Catskill Mountains**).

At Bruce Lake (**D**), about 2.5 miles from the trailhead, the western shore is low and boggy. A mat of peat with cranberry, St. Johnswort, sundews, and other bog species lines the bank (see **#120** and **#65**). Succession is only just beginning to change the face of this lake. Following the probable course of events, this lake, if left to itself, should gradually shrink as the bog species grow out over its surface.

Remarks: *From here you can retrace your steps, for a walk of 5 miles. Allow 2 hours or more. For a long circle hike of almost 8.5 miles, turn south (right) just west of Bruce Lake along the West Branch Bruce Trail with yellow blazes. The intersection is well marked. The trail is somewhat overgrown. After .5 miles turn west (right) onto Rock Oak Ridge Trail, which is well marked. Go another 1.5 miles to a junction of several trails. Go north (right) along the Brown Trail. It is the most traveled path. After about 1.5 miles the trail joins the Bruce Lake Trail just northeast of Panther Swamp. Though long, the trail is not too difficult. In places it is rocky and thick with brush. This is a good trail for snowshoeing or cross-country skiing in winter. A new trail is planned for 1984. Camping is available at Promised Land State Park. Contact the park office for a permit: R.D. 1, Box 96, Greentown, Pa. 18426. Other activities at the park include swimming, fishing (with license), and boating (rentals available).*

117.

Devil's Hole

Directions: **Monroe County, Pa. From Scranton, take I-380 southeast about 25 miles to Exit 7. Go southeast on Route 611 about 5 miles to Mount Pocono. Turn east (left) onto**

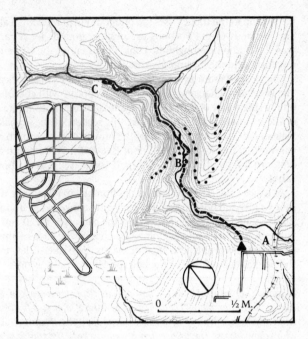

Route 940 and go 0.8 mile. Turn north (left) onto Devil's
Hole Rd. and travel 1 mile. Where the road turns sharply
east (right), drive straight onto the parking area for State
Game Lands #221, directly ahead on the left.

Ownership: Pennsylvania Game Commission.

From the parking area, walk south about a quarter of a mile to the
railroad tracks. Turn east (left) along the tracks a short distance.
Here, 100 feet above Devil's Hole Creek, an overview of the whole
region is at your feet (**A**). To the northwest, the creek has cut a deep
canyon, cool and lined with tall trees, wild and scenic in any season.
In the distance, to the northeast is the high ridge of Seven Pines
Mountain, where a few large white pines tower above the mixed
oaks to mark the edge of the Pocono Plateau (see **#119**). Beginning
in the boggy wetlands on the plateau, the clear, trout-filled stream
drops 500 feet in the nearly 2 miles it travels from the falls to this
vantage point. In winter, the strong winds blowing across the plateau make strange wailing sounds as they flow across the canyon.
Eerie and haunting, these noises may be the source of the name of

the area. You can hear these moanings from various points along the hike if the wind is strong enough.

Return to the parking area and start up the old road running northward beyond the large steel-pipe gate. The dressed stones that pave the road were cut from quarries up on Seven Pines Mountain. Some people hold that the name "Devil's Hole" was given to the ravine by the nineteenth-century stonecutters who labored long and hard in these quarries.

Beyond the parking area the trail drops rapidly into the first stream crossing. Some evidence remains of a number of stream-improvement projects, which were designed to create and improve native brook-trout habitat. Today there is a flourishing population of both brook and brown trout (see **#53**). The vegetation changes from the oak-dominated upland woods to a cool, moist ravine habitat where American beech, sugar and red maples, and black birch are the principal species. Mountain laurel and rhododendron grow abundantly in the shrub layer.

The trail winds along the road for about a mile and a quarter, occasionally fording the rocky stream. Small, scattered evergreen plantations begin to appear on both sides of the stream, marking the beginning of an old estate built at the turn of the century (**B**). The tall stand of trees here is sheltered by the steep canyon wall and nurtured by the rich alluvial soils that have collected in this small hollow. On closer inspection you will find a startling collection of trees imported from all across the country and around the world. Thilenius, the well-to-do food importer who built the estate, planted cypress, firs, spruces, cedars, and numerous unknowns. The cedar trees are distinctive, for the bark is often shredded and claw-scarred. The resident black bears tear up the bark as a way of declaring their territory. Both males and females mark the trees in this way.

You will be lucky to see a bear. They are solitary animals, shy of humans. Although nocturnal, they occasionally scrounge for food in the day as well. They will eat almost anything, including ants, fish, frogs, berries, insects, and garbage. Contrary to popular myth, bears do not really hibernate in the winter; in fact the females give birth in midwinter. The bears lay up a large store of fat in the autumn and retire only when their layer of fat is thick enough. The animals spend the winter in their dens, moving little. One rather startling aid for surviving this foodless period is a fecal plug about 6 inches long. The bear eats a final meal of indigestible material such as pine needles, dry leaves, hair, and mucus. This wads into a tight mass which isn't expelled until spring.

As you leave the site of the old estate, the canyon deepens and narrows. The temperature drops. This natural refrigeration is a blessing in summer, as the hiking becomes more difficult from this point. The trail peters out, and you must make your way up the streambed, going from boulder to boulder. A change to more northerly vegetation occurs. Two species, mountain maple and striped maple, now dominate the understory. Northern shrubs found here include purple-flowering raspberry, red baneberry, and red-berried elder.

After another half-mile of scrambling over the rocks, you will reach a cascading waterfall that plunges down the edge of the plateau in a series of steps culminating in a 20-foot fall (**C**). At its foot is a large dish-shaped basin or pothole. Most of it was eroded by a swirling whirlpool formed during the retreat of the Wisconsin Glacier 15,000 to 10,000 years ago (see **#75** and **#114**). It was also the glacial meltwater that shaped the canyon, gouging it out with tons of rock and gravel. The steep cliff face and the pool below are also known as Devil's Hole, a wonderful place to swim after a hot hike.

In addition to bear, other species found in these quiet woods include white-tailed deer, turkey, grouse, snowshoe hare, and bobcat.

Remarks: *More hiking trails lead up to the top of Seven Pines Mountain. From the estate area, a series of stone steps leads up to the east (right as you walk out to the falls) and strikes an old quarrying road. Turn right to hike up to the ridge. Including the detour to the overlook at* **A**, *allow 4 to 5 hours for this walk. The easiest time to make this expedition is in low water in late summer and autumn. During winter, spring, and early summer wear rubber-soled boots or sneakers and be prepared to get wet. There is access to a network of jeep trails and hiking paths along Route 191 in Mountainhome. To reach them go back to Route 940. Turn east (left) and drive about 3.5 miles to Route 191. Turn north (left) and go about 4 miles. Turn west (left). The road branches almost immediately. The right fork goes to the Rattlesnake Creek area and the left to Mill Creek. There is fishing (with a license) in the creek. Camping at Tobyhanna State Park just a few miles northwest of Mount Pocono along Route 423. For further information contact the Pennsylvania Game Commission, P.O. Box 1567, Harrisburg, Pa. 17105. The area is open for deer hunting in the fall.*

118.

Hickory Run
Boulder Field

Directions: **Carbon County, Pa. From Scranton, go south about 35 miles on the Northeast Extension of the Pennsylvania Turnpike. Turn west on I-86 and go 3 miles to Exit 41; go south on Route 534. After 1.6 miles, make a sharp turn to the west (left); continue 3.3 miles to Hickory Run State Park headquarters. The trailhead is 5.3 miles farther, just beyond the underpass of the turnpike. Park opposite the old farm; cross the road and walk north, up behind the house, to the edge of the field to pick up the well-worn Boulder Field Trail.**

Ownership: **Hickory Run State Park, Pennsylvania Bureau of State Parks.**

The Hickory Run Boulder Field, a National Natural Landmark on the southwest edge of the Pocono Plateau (see **#119**), developed during the severe arctic climate that accompanied the advance and retreat of the Wisconsin Glacier over many thousands of years. It looks now much as it did then. It is a disconcerting place, seemingly barren of plants, mysterious, a relic of the geological past. The 3-mile hike to the field takes the visitor along rolling terrain through a second-growth forest typical of the plateau: eastern hemlock, tuliptree, black birch, gray birch, red, white, and black oaks, white pine, American beech, and maples. Rhododendron and mountain laurel are common shrubs.

Three species of club moss, which grow well in the cool, moist, shade, can be found as you walk along the trail. The forest floor is often pocked with small humps and depressions, the scars of old treefalls. The soils of the plateau are relatively thin, so trees are often blown over, pulling up hunks of earth and leaving a hole. Although the tree eventually rots, the hummock of earth around its roots remains, serving as a nursery for tree seedlings and rhododendron plants.

In spring and summer the woods are full of nesting woodpeckers, flycatchers, vireos, and thrushes. Wild turkeys are also plentiful, having made a comeback in the last few years (see **#98**). Black bears, as well as smaller mammals, are seen on this trail.

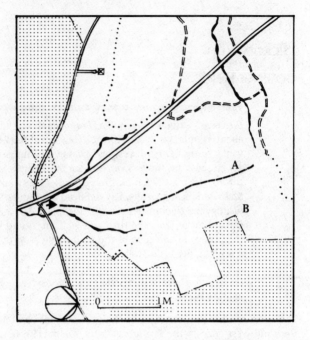

After about 2 miles, the trail passes up over a small rocky ridge covered with mountain laurel and gray birch, a species that is one of the first trees to move into open spaces. The trail then drops down through increasingly stony ground and groves of hemlocks. The trail is occasionally confusing here. Watch for lime-green blazes on the trees.

You will enter the boulder field (**A**) from the south. The field is made up of rounded boulders of red sandstone and red conglomerate of the Catskill Formation, 380 to 385 million years old. Conglomerate is sedimentary rock made up of various sizes and types of material, in this case principally sandstone and quartz, that have been bonded into a solid mass by chemical cementation and pressure (see **Shawangunks**).

When the Wisconsin Glacier drew to a halt about 18,000 years ago—just a mile to the north and east of the boulder field—the great mass of ice radically changed the surrounding environment, creating arctic conditions. During the summer months, rocks at the surface of the earth were subjected to a continual, daily cycle of thawing and freezing, while the ground beneath remained frozen.

On two high ridges to the north and south of the boulder field, meltwater from the glacier seeped into fractures in the red sandstones and conglomerate. Upon freezing, the water expanded, pushing at the rock and wedging each crevice and crack farther apart. After many such cycles, huge angular chunks of stone broke off.

These large pieces of rock were mixed with clay, sand, and ice. As the ice melted in the summer heat, the top layer of material shifted and ground its way down the slope over the frozen earth. In the process, the boulders were smoothed and rounded. Finally, after the passage of thousands of years, the glacier withdrew northward as the climate warmed. The silt and fine debris were washed away by the rush of meltwater from the retreating glacier, leaving only the boulders.

At first glance, the boulder field seems lifeless, but the forest is gradually encroaching. Lichens cover the rocks, slowly working at the surface of the rock, breaking it into tiny pieces. Shrubs and trees are beginning to colonize the perimeter of the boulder field. In the southwest corner of the field, where hemlocks and birches have begun to encroach, are the largest rocks, huge slabs 11 feet long and 4 feet thick (**B**). From their unrounded shape, it is clear that they did not move much from their original position. These rocks were broken up in place by the same cycles of freezing and thawing that affected the others.

To return to your car, retrace your steps. As you drive back toward the park office on Route 534, go 2 miles and stop at a dirt road leading off to the north (right). A 5-minute walk will take you to a firetower. You can climb the tower for a fine view of the Pocono Plateau. From the top level, look northeast. You will see one of the long ridges from which the boulders slid down to the field.

Remarks: *This walk is about 5.5 miles round trip. Allow 3 hours to give yourself time to explore the boulder field. It is a rough, rocky trail on level ground. Wear sneakers or hiking shoes. Take water, as streams are dry in summer. Be careful in the woods to the southwest of the field (**B**); it is easy to get disoriented. If you have two cars, one can be left at the parking area to the northwest of the boulder field. There is camping within the park. For further information, write or call Hickory Run State Park, R.D. 1, Box 81, White Haven, Pa. 18661, (717) 443-9991.*

119.

Camelback Mountain

Directions: **Monroe County, Pa. From Scranton go south-east on I-380, then I-80, about 45 miles to Exit 45. Take Route 715 west 0.4 mile to Sullivan's Trail. Turn north (left) and go 5.3 miles to Wilke Rd. Turn southwest (left) and follow Wilke Rd. for 4.3 miles; it ends at the parking area by the ranger station (A).**

Ownership: **Big Pocono State Park, Pennsylvania Bureau of State Parks.**

Camelback Mountain, at the southeastern corner of the Pocono Plateau, towers 1000 feet above the lowland to the east and the rolling country of the Appalachian Mountains to the south. From its summit, the view spreads out in every direction, revealing the topography of the land like a huge relief map. Camelback is not a true mountain at all; it is part of a plateau region that was lifted up during the building of the Appalachian Mountains but was only gently folded. Then the region was sculpted by erosion, largely during the ice ages. In that process the less resistant rock around Camelback Mountain was stripped away, leaving this ridge behind (see **Appalachian Plateau**). Beneath the thin soils are rugged outcrops and boulders of gray quartz-bearing sandstone. Beds of softer siltstones and shales deposited at approximately the same time, about 380 million years ago, may also be present, but are covered with soil and vegetation.

Stand at the marker by the ranger station and look to the north across the Pocono Plateau. The height of the summit is 2133 feet, only a 100 feet or so above the rest of the plateau. The small "hills" are all approximately the same altitude, which is typical of an eroded plateau. To the east, south, and southwest runs the Kittatinny Ridge, which is here called Blue Mountain (no relation to the Blue Ridge Province to the south; see **#68**). The rocks forming the ridge are older than the rocks on top of Pocono Plateau by about 38 million years. In it, three great passages have been carved. To the east is the Delaware Water Gap and to the southwest is the Lehigh Gap. Through these gorges flow the rivers which made them and for which they are named. Between them is Wind Gap, also cut by a river, but this one has since become part of another stream (see **#94**).

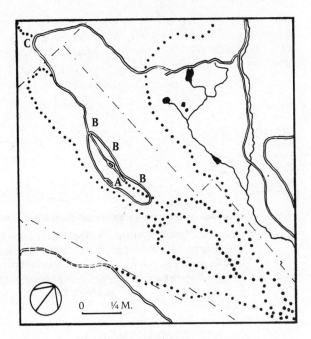

One finger of the last glacier just reached out to touch the top of Camelback Mountain and wrap around it. As the ice receded, it left a huge jumble of sand, gravel, and boulders north and south of the summit (**B**). This sheet of debris is called a *terminal moraine*; it accumulated because even as the southern edge of the ice sheet was melting away new ice continued to form at the cold, arctic heart of the glacier to the north and east and continued to transport material southwestward (see **#66**).

The vegetation at the summit is stunted and adapted to dry, poor soils. Scrub oak, quaking aspen, dwarf sheep laurel, pin cherry, and black chokecherry are among the common species. Ice storms in winter and frequent strong winds create severe conditions at the summit; until recently, it was also swept by frequent fires. Several trails drop off the escarpment to the east. As soon as you leave the exposed ridgetop, taller gray and white birches and chestnut oaks begin to appear. In the shade of these trees, mountain laurel grows abundantly.

Remarks: *The park includes 10 miles of trails. The mountain laurel blooms in the latter part of June. Black bears are sometimes seen at Deep*

Lake; the trail to it starts at (**C**)*. No hunting on Sundays. For further information contact Big Pocono State Park, Box 173, Henryville, Pa. 18332, (717) 894-8336 or 894-8337. Camping is available at Hickory Run and Gouldsboro–Tobyhanna state parks.*

120.
Tannersville
Cranberry Bog
Preserve

Directions: **Monroe County, Pa. The bog is located near Tannersville, Pa. about 11 miles west of the Delaware Water Gap (see #68). Open by appointment only through the Meesing Nature Center, Monroe County Conservation District, R.D. 2, Box 2335A, Stroudsburg, Pa., 18360, (717) 992-7334.**

Ownership: **The Nature Conservancy.**

The Tannersville bog, a National Natural Landmark, is a mat of floating vegetation surrounding a small eye of open water. The bog mat is made up of sphagnum moss and a wide variety of special bog shrubs and plants. Around its edges is a dense swamp of red maple. The bog is very gradually becoming dry land, and various successional stages are visible here. Because the sphagnum moss and associated bog plants are so easily destroyed by human traffic, access to the wetland areas of the preserve is limited.

This is the southernmost low-altitude boreal bog along the eastern seaboard. Boreal forests are those found in the sub-arctic regions of Canada. Black spruce and tamarack, typical of these forests, grow in the bog at Tannersville and are visible from the 350-foot boardwalk that goes into the heart of the preserve. Other northern species found here include bog and sheep laurel, large and small cranberry, dwarf mistletoe, Labrador tea, bog rosemary, and sphagnum moss. The snowshoe hare, seen here in the winter, is at the southernmost limit of its range.

Tannersville bog is also special because it has remained relatively undisturbed for eons. Many other bogs have been destroyed by efforts to mine the peat, which is partially decayed sphagnum moss and which is often used as fuel, a soil conditioner, and a planting medium. Here, although the peat is 50 feet thick in some places, it is a treacherous, quaking mass too soft for men, wagons, and horses to work in safely.

Experts currently believe that the bog was formed as the Wisconsin Glacier retreated about 15,000 to 10,000 years ago, leaving behind it a huge hunk of ice. Embedded within the ice were great quantities of rocks and debris, picked up as it traveled southward. As this ice melted, heavier pieces of rock around the outside of the ice fell out first, creating a rough circular dam. The finer bits of debris and silt were deposited later. The pressure of the water on top crushed the sediments down until they were eventually packed into an impenetrable lining.

The ice mass that moved down from the north brought with it the seeds of northern plants, which flourished in the cool, wet climate created by the melting ice. Today one can see a variety of species whose normal range runs from Manitoba to Labrador and south to Wisconsin and Ohio.

From the end of the boardwalk, you can look across the sphagnum-moss mat. This mat forms the bed for these northern plants. Sphagnum moss contains air sacs which enable it to absorb many times its own weight in water. It acts as a sponge to soak up and retain rainwater, which is the primary source of moisture in the bog. This helps to maintain a very stable level of water in the bog and in the watershed, the area around the bog that drains into it.

The water and soils of bogs are highly acid, due to a combination of factors. Nutrients such as calcium, phosphorus, nitrogen, and potassium are washed away from the soil almost as soon as they accumulate and are replaced by hydrogen, which comes from molecules of water. Beneath the green mat of living sphagnum moss is a layer of dying moss. As it decays, it also releases acids. Below a certain depth, the acidity of the bog becomes strong enough to inhibit bacteria that complete the breakdown of dead plant material into its nutrient parts. This increases the infertility of the bog. It is this partially decayed plant material that forms the peat layer of the bog. At the upper surface of the bog, the living sphagnum moss draws on the scant supply of nutrients in the water, leaving less for other species. Nitrogen is one of the most important nutrients, and one of the scarcest in a bog. Some plants have compensated for the scarcity of nitrogen by becoming insectivorous. The pitcher plant and the round-leaved sundew (see **#65**) are two plants that obtain nitrogen by trapping and digesting bugs. These plants are found only in bogs; in other habitats they cannot compete with plants that thrive in less acid soils.

A resident black-bear population is sustained by the abundant blueberries, raspberries, and serviceberries that grow at the edge of the bog. Beavers (see **#64**), river otters, bobcats, gray foxes, and red foxes, as well as the rare bog turtle, are found in the sanctuary. There is also a variety of birdlife.

Remarks: *It is sometimes possible to arrange a special winter tour to other points of interest in the preserve, when ice protects the sphagnum mat and other plants. Camping nearby at Scotrun Park on Route 611, and at Tobyhanna State Park, 26 miles northwest of Stroudsburg along Route 611.*

121.
Dolly Sods

Directions: **Tucker and Grant counties, W. Va. From Washington, D.C., take I-66 west about 65 miles, then I-81 southwest 4 miles to Exit 74. Follow Route 55 north and west about 48 miles to its end in West Virginia. Take U.S. 220 and Route 28 south and west 13 miles to Petersburg, then stay on Route 28 west about 10 miles more. At Route 4 (Jordan Run Rd.), turn north (right) and go about 1 mile. Turn left onto Route 19, which leads westerly for 9 miles to the top of the Allegheny Front. At the intersection, turn north (right) onto Forest Service Rd. 75, which follows the crest of the Allegheny Front north. Mileages measured from this intersection to specific points are included in the text.**

Ownership: **Monongahela National Forest, U.S. Forest Service.**

Perched on the brink of the Allegheny Front (see **#112**) and extending several miles west across the Appalachian Plateau is a desolate, uninhabited, and fascinating place known as Dolly Sods. Windswept expanses of heath barrens, interrupted by rock ridges and patches of trees, cover thousands of acres. Sphagnum glades, with their northern plants, and unexplained grass balds add to its diversity. Although rugged in appearance, this tundralike area is actually quite fragile.

Dolly Sods' high elevation—over 4000 feet in many places—and its exposure to the elements result in a climate similar to northern Canada. The weather here is frequently terrible. Spring arrives late, fall early. Storms crop up suddenly, and thick, soupy fog can descend at any time of year. On those seemingly rare days of clear skies and sunshine, the view east from the edge of the Allegheny Front is stupendous. The land drops steeply some 2500 feet to the stream valley below, and long parallel ridges and valleys (see **Ridge and Valley**), beginning with the Wills Mountain Anticline (see **#92**), line up in the distance.

Two wonderful stops are the established overlook, just a short distance up Forest Service Rd. 75 on the right, and Bear Rocks, 7.7 miles up this road. Leave your car at the pulloff and walk to the edge of the Front, to your right. Then drive up the road, park on the left just before the hairpin turn, and walk out to Bear Rocks. The ridge of the Allegheny Front is made of the highly resistant Pottsville conglomerate (see **#122**), blocks of which lie broken and scattered from thousands of years of frost-wedging (see **#118**). Below the escarpment are a series of smaller hills, the Fore Knobs, where the Pocono group, older but similarly resistant rocks, are exposed. The layers of softer limestones and shales that lay above these hills have long since been removed by erosion.

Under certain conditions in fall, flights of migrating hawks pass by Bear Rocks, sometimes several hundred in a single day. Winds from the east strike the Allegheny Front and rise, providing updrafts on which the hawks ride. When there are no winds, they may ride on thermals, rising currents of warm air (see **#5** and **#78**). The winds at Dolly Sods are generally out of the west, however, often bringing flights of southbound warblers by Bear Rocks. Since these winds cross the plateau without creating updrafts, the hawks continue their migrations along other ridges. During the fall, many people are involved in netting and banding migrating birds here, in a widespread effort to track and understand their migration patterns.

Heath barrens—open, windy flats of huckleberries, blueberries, and cranberries, along with laurels, azaleas, chokeberries, speckled alder, bleeding hearts, and many other plants—cover most of the plateau near Bear Rocks. These are easily explored by walking west, away from the front, only a short distance from Bear Rocks. Also called huckleberry plains or roaring plains, this habitat is commonly found in these mountains above 3800 feet. Although the thin soil, severe winds, and cold temperatures inhibit plant growth, destructive activities of man are, ironically, responsible for the formation of this alluring place. Dense forests of hemlocks and spruce trees, reportedly up to 9 feet in diameter, growing on peaty soil 8 to 15 feet thick once covered this land. By the mid-1920s, logging activities and uncontrollable fires totally destroyed this forest and the peat, leaving only ashes and mineral soil, or bare rock. Rainwater carried away all the nutrients, and flash floods swept through stream valleys. Recovery is progressing slowly, as more soil accumulates. In spite of the many stages of succession present (see **#41**), Dolly Sods is far removed from its earlier state. Today, no evidence of the original forest remains.

Scattered red spruces are reestablishing themselves throughout the heath barrens, while in other parts of Dolly Sods, forests of these trees shade dense thickets of rhododendrons. The stream valleys harbor other northern species—yellow birch, beech, maple, and hemlock. Most of the birds typical of northern red-spruce forests breed here in summer, including hermit and Swainson's thrushes, veeries, Nashville warblers, purple finches, and winter wrens.

A northern element of plant life also appears in the sphagnum glades that dot the plateau. These sphagnum bogs, while similar to northern bogs (see **#120**), have different origins. Northern bogs lie in depressions gouged into the rock by glaciers. The bogs here are found in low spots where the hard, underlying rocks merely slow or block the drainage of a stream. Beaver ponds are generally associated with these bogs, in which cranberries, bog rosemary, yellow-fringed orchis, and sundews grow. One small sphagnum glade can be seen along the Northland Loop Interpretive Trail, located 4.6 miles up Forest Service Rd. 75. Another accessible one is Dobbin Slashing, a large bog west of Bear Rocks, on Western Maryland Railroad Co. property, reached on foot by a dirt road that veers left just before the hairpin turn by Bear Rocks on Forest Service Rd. 75.

Several natural grass balds occur at Dolly Sods, though they are more common farther south in the Appalachians. These meadows are treeless, although they occur within a heavily forested region. In them grow mountain oat grass (known locally as Allegheny flyback) and other grasses, bracken fern, goldenrods, violets, and a number of other flowers. Mosses lie directly on the ground between individual plants. At their perimeters, the balds grade into the surrounding heath barrens. The causes for the grass balds are unclear, but possible influences include climate (storms or changes wrought by the presence of glaciers to the north during the last Ice Age), biotic factors (grazing by wildlife has at least maintained the meadows), topography, fire, and early human influences. That grass balds have been here for at least two centuries is evident in the name Dolly Sods. Settlers in the nearby valleys who used the meadows as grazing lands for their animals referred to them as sods. A family named Dahle was one of the early owners, back in the late 1700s.

Remarks: *Hiking, camping, fishing (with a license, trout stamp, and National Forest Stamp), hunting (be careful during deer season—#95) and cross-country skiing are common activities. The only facility is a primitive campground located 5 miles up Forest Service Rd. 75. The weather is often severe year round; be prepared for sudden storms. It is easy to get lost on the open plains in the frequent fogs. Winter explorers should be well prepared. Cold, wind, and abundant snow make Dolly Sods a dangerous place; the road is not plowed in winter.*

For more information contact the Potomac Ranger District, Monongahela National Forest, Route 3, Box 240, Petersburg, W.Va. 26847, (304) 257-4488.

Nearby Places of Interest

Smokehole Caverns, which are commercial and open to the public, are located 6 miles west of Petersburg on Route 28. Also off Route 28 is the road leading through the Smokehole area, a scenic canyon of geologic interest through which the South Branch of the Potomac River flows. There is camping at the Smokehole Recreation Area. Shale barrens line the roadsides in the vicinity of Petersburg (see #91). On the Appalachian Plateau near Davis are Canaan Valley State Park and Blackwater Falls State Park, both worth a visit.

122.
Spruce Knob

Directions: **Pendleton County, W.Va. Follow directions for Dolly Sods (#121) as far as Petersburg. Continue southwest on Route 28 about 30 miles (9 miles past Seneca Rocks—see #95). Following signs, turn right onto Briery**

Gap Rd. and drive 11.5 miles to the parking lot at the top
of Spruce Knob.

Ownership: **Monongahela National Forest, U.S. Forest Service.**

At 4861 feet of elevation, Spruce Knob is West Virginia's highest
point. It is not really a knob, but a ridge about a mile long that stands
only slightly higher than the rest of Spruce Mountain's summit ridge,
which extends 12 miles to the north. The mountainside drops off
gradually to the south and west, but falls steeply to the east. This
escarpment is part of the Allegheny Front, the physiographic feature
separating the Ridge and Valley Province to the east from the Appalachian Plateau (see **Ridge and Valley, Appalachian Plateau,** and **#112**). Spruce Knob and the nearly level ridgeline of the
Allegheny Front are capped by the resistant Pottsville conglomerate,
composed of various-sized quartz grains cemented together mainly
by quartz.

Various layers of the Pottsville Group cap most of the ridges in
this central region of the Appalachian Plateau, just as the similar
Tuscarora sandstone is the major ridge-former in the Ridge and
Valley Province. These hard, resistant rocks withstand the forces of
erosion well, and by protecting the softer rocks beneath them, they
form highlands. In places where they have been worn down and
the softer rock has been exposed, the land has been eroded into deep
valleys (see **#95**). The Pottsville conglomerate, formed more than
300 million years ago, seems ancient, but it is over 100 million years
younger than the Tuscarora sandstone, which lies deeply buried
beneath the surface of the Appalachian Plateau.

The rock exposed at the summit of Spruce Knob is covered with
lichens, mosses, and club mosses. Flowers and ferns cling to what
little soil accumulates in crevices. The cold and windy summit of
Spruce Knob supports a sparse cover of red spruce and yellow birch
trees. These trees, typical of northern boreal forests, range this far
south only in the mountains, generally at elevations higher than
3500 feet. Apparently, they are remnants of a more extensive forest
that thrived during the last glacial period. The climate then was cold
and wet, although the advancing ice sheets did not travel this far
south. Harsh winds and violent storms frequently batter the trees so
that the red spruce trees stand only 10–15 feet tall although they are
more than 50 years old. Where they are most exposed to the wind,
the trees have been pruned into "flags" with branches growing only
on their leeward sides (the side toward which the wind is blowing).
On more protected spots, the trees are less deformed, although still

dwarfed by the harsh conditions. Mountain ash, red maple, mountain holly, and serviceberry also manage to survive in these wooded patches.

According to local history, this spruce and yellow birch forest was once more dense and widely spread before fires and logging destroyed it. Much of this knob and the surrounding ridges are now covered by heath barrens (see **#121**). Black huckleberry, south mountain cranberry, and minniebush are among the low shrubs that compose these barrens. Gooseberry, teaberry, bracken fern, club mosses, sedges, and skunk currant are some of the many other plants found here. Painted trillium and clintonia bloom in spring, followed by northern bush honeysuckle, then pearly everlasting and fireweed. The heath barrens are being invaded by trees in those spots protected from the wind, which otherwise keeps the shrubs well pruned. Why heath barrens form and how permanent they are remain an unsolved mystery.

Remarks: *A very short level trail leads from the parking lot to the lookout tower and connects with a nature trail. From the tower is an excellent 360° view of the Appalachian Plateau and the Ridge and Valley Province. Spruce Knob is within the Spruce Knob–Seneca Rocks National Recreational Area. See #95 for more information.*

Nearby is an 86-acre tract of old-growth hemlocks, the Fanny Bennet Tract, which will give you an idea of how this area once looked. Go south on Route 28 about 9 miles past Briery Gap Rd. Turn north (right) onto Saw Mill Rd. and go 2 miles. The Fanny Bennet Tract, marked by a sign, is on the left by the first intersection.

Spruce Knob Lake and campground are also nearby. Go back down the mountain 1.8 miles and turn right onto Route 112. After nearly 6 miles, bear right at the road junction and continue 1 mile to the man-made lake and campground.

Recent Changes
in Common Bird Names

The following species have recently been given new common names by the American Ornithologists' Union. As most guidebooks still have the old names, we provide the new designations here rather than in the text.

Old	New
Louisiana heron	tricolored heron
common pintail	northern pintail
common scoter	black scoter
common bobwhite	northern bobwhite
common gallinule	common moorhen
northern phalarope	red-necked phalarope
barn owl	common barn-owl
common screech owl	eastern screech owl
saw-whet owl	northern saw-whet owl
common flicker	northern flicker
eastern pewee	eastern wood-pewee
rough-winged swallow	northern rough-winged swallow
northern raven	common raven
short-billed marsh wren	sedge wren
long-billed marsh wren	marsh wren
American golden plover	lesser golden-plover

Glossary

acidic: Containing an abundance of hydrogen.

alga: Any of a large group of aquatic plants ranging from tiny one-celled to large multicelled organisms.

bog: A wet, soggy area with little or no drainage.

bottomland: Low-lying ground that may be flooded from time to time.

brackish: A term used to describe water that is somewhat salty but not as salty as seawater.

calcite: A mineral made up of calcium, carbon, and oxygen; also known as calcium carbonate.

canopy: An umbrella of trees formed by the tallest trees in a stand.

climax forest: A forest in which the mix of species is relatively stable over time.

competition: Rivalry of plants or animals for the same resources or habitat.

coniferous: Evergreen and cone-bearing.

deciduous: Shedding leaves annually.

disjunct: Set apart from the main distribution of the species.

ecosystem: The interaction of plants, animals, and their environment.

erosion: The process by which the earth's surface is worn away by water, wind, or waves.

fault: A fracture in a body of rock along which displacement has occurred.

glacial erratic: A chunk of rock transported from its original location and deposited elsewhere by a glacier.

glacier: A mass of ice formed from recrystallized snow flowing over the land.

habitat: The natural environment of an animal or plant.

Ice Age: A period from about 10,000 to 2 million years ago during which a large portion of the earth was covered by glaciers; also called the glacial epoch.

igneous rock: Rock formed from cooling magma either beneath the earth's surface or through volcanic eruptions.

impoundment: An artificial pond or lake.

interglacial periods: Warm periods that occurred between the glacial advances when the ice sheets withdrew toward the poles.

joint: A fracture in a rock mass where displacement has not occurred.

larva: The immature, wingless stage of certain insects.

litter: The layer of slightly decomposed plant material on the surface of the forest floor.

magma: Molten material beneath the earth's surface.

marsh: Low, wet land covered by grassy vegetation.

meander: The curve of a river.

metamorphic rock: Rock that is formed from preexisting igneous or sedimentary rock through heat or pressure or both.

mica: One of a large family of minerals containing silica. Mica splits easily into thin, pliable flakes and is commonly found in igneous and metamorphic rocks.

migration: The rhythmic seasonal movement of certain birds and other animals.

old field: A stage in the succession of cleared land to forest characterized by grasses, flowering plants, and shrubs.

orogeny: The process of mountain building.

peat: Partially decomposed plant material common to wet areas.

photosynthesis: The process by which plants convert water and carbon dioxide into carbohydrates.

pioneer: One of a number of plants that appears early in the process of succession.

Pleistocene epoch: The Ice Age or glacial epoch.

raptor: One of a group of birds that includes hawks, owls, and eagles.

runoff: Rainwater or melting snow that drains away across the surface of the ground.

secondary growth: The forest that appears after land has been cleared.

sedimentary rock: Rock formed from sediments deposited on or near the earth's surface.

shorebirds: Species that frequent coastal areas and inland beaches, such as sandpipers and plovers.

species: A group of related plants or animals that interbreed to produce fertile offspring.

strata: Distinct layers of sedimentary or igneous rock.

succession: The process by which the vegetation of an ecosystem changes over time.

swamp: Low, wet forest that is regularly flooded.

tannin: Any one of a variety of large, complex molecules contained in most woody plants.

understory: The trees found growing beneath the canopy species and above the shrub layer.

waterfowl: Aquatic birds, including geese, ducks, and swans.

Bibliography

General Reference

Angel, H., and Pat Wolseley. 1982. *The Water Naturalist*. New York: Facts on File.

Argow, Keith. 1976. Rev. ed. *Appalachian Natural Areas Directory*. Washington, D.C.: Society of American Foresters.

Barbour, Michael G., Jack H. Bork, and Wanna D. Pitts. 1980. *Terrestrial Plant Ecology*. Menlo Park, Calif.: Benjamin/Cummings Publishing Co.

Braun, E. Lucy. 1950. *Deciduous Forests of North America*. Philadelphia: Blakiston Co.

Brooks, Maurice. 1965. *The Appalachians*. Boston: Houghton Mifflin Co.

Brown, Lauren. 1979. *Grasses: An Identification Guide*. Boston: Houghton Mifflin Co.

Crain, Jim, and Terry Milne. 1975. *Camping Around the Appalachian Mountains: Including the Blue Ridge and the Great Smokies*. New York: Random House/Bookworks.

Dickerson, Mary C. 1969. *The Frog Book*. New York: Dover Books.

Eyre, F. H., ed. 1980. *Forest Cover Types of the United States and Canada*. Washington, D.C.: Society of American Foresters.

Fernald, Merrit Lyndon. 1950. *Gray's Manual of Botany*. New York: D. Van Nostrand Co.

Godfrey, Michael A. 1980. *A Sierra Club Naturalist's Guide: The Piedmont*. San Francisco: Sierra Club Books.

Harding, John J., and Justin J. Harding. 1980. *Birding the Delaware Valley Region*. Philadelphia: Temple University Press.

377

Hatch, F. H., A. K. Wells, and M. K. Wells. 1972. *Petrology of the Igneous Rocks*. London: George Allen & Unwin/Thomas Murby & Co.

Hunt, Cynthia, and Robert M. Garrells. 1972. *Water: The Web of Life*. New York: W. W. Norton & Co.

Hurlbut, Cornelius S., Jr., and Cornelis Klein. 1977. 19th ed. *Manual of Minerology*. New York: John Wiley & Sons.

Keeton, William T. 1972. 2nd ed. *Biological Science*. New York: W. W. Norton & Co.

Korling, Torkel, and Robert O. Petty. 1978. *Wild Plants in Flower: Eastern Deciduous Forest*. Chicago: Chicago Review.

Mason, Roger. 1978. *Petrology of the Metamorphic Rocks*. London: George Allen & Unwin/Thomas Murby & Co.

McPhee, John. 1983. *In Suspect Terrain*. New York: Farrar, Straus & Giroux.

Orr, Robert T. 1970. *Animals in Migration*. New York: Macmillan Co.

Palmer, E. Laurence, and H. Seymour Fowler. 1975. *Fieldbook of Natural History*. New York: McGraw-Hill Book Co.

Perry, John and Jane G. 1980. *The Random House Guide to Natural Areas of the Eastern United States*. New York: Random House.

Press, Frank, and Raymond Siever. 1974. *Earth*. San Francisco: W. H. Freeman & Co.

Odum, Eugene P. 1971. 3rd ed. *Fundamentals of Ecology*. Philadelphia: W. B. Saunders Co.

Ray, Peter Martin. 1972. 2nd ed. *The Living Plant*. New York: Holt, Rinehart & Winston.

Reid, George K. 1961. *Ecology of Inland Waters and Estuaries*. New York: Reinhold Publishing Corp.

Reifsnyder, William E. 1980. *Weathering the Wilderness*. San Francisco: Sierra Club Books.

Ricklets, Robert. 1976. *The Economy of Nature: A Textbook in Basic Ecology*. Portland, Ore.: Chiron Press.

Riley, Laura and William. 1979. *Guide to the National Wildlife Refuges*. Garden City, N.Y.: Doubleday & Co., Anchor Press.

Shelford, Victor E., ed. 1926. *The Naturalist's Guide to the Americas*. Baltimore: Williams & Wilkins Co.

Stearn, Colin W., Thomas H. Clark, and Robert L. Carroll. 1979. *Geological Evolution of North America*. New York: John Wiley & Sons.

Terres, John K. 1980. *The Audubon Encyclopedia of North American Birds*. New York: Alfred A. Knopf.

Thomas, Bill. 1976. *The Swamp*. New York: W. W. Norton & Co.

Usinger, Robert L. 1967. *The Life of Rivers and Streams*. New York: McGraw-Hill Book Co.

Vankat, John L. 1979. *Natural Vegetation of North America*. New York: John Wiley & Sons.

Von Frisch, Karl. 1974. *Animal Architecture*. New York: Harcourt Brace Jovanovich.

Welty, Joel Carl. 1962. *The Life of Birds*. Philadelphia: W. B. Saunders Co.

Delaware

Delaware Geological Survey. 1980. *Delaware: Its Rocks and Minerals*.

Fleming, Lorraine M. 1978. *Delaware's Outstanding Natural Areas and Their Preservation*. Hockessin, Del.: Delaware Nature Education Society.

D.C. Area

Shosteck, Robert. 1976. *Potomac Trail and Cycling Guide*. Oakton, Va.: Appalachian Books.

Thomas, Bill and Phyllis. 1980. *Natural Washington*. New York: Holt, Rinehart & Winston.

Wilds, Claudia. 1983. *Finding Birds in the National Capital Area*. Washington, D.C.: Smithsonian Institution Press.

Maryland

Hahn, Thomas F. 1978. 2nd ed. *Towpath Guide to the C & O Canal: Section 4*. Shepardstown, W. Va.: American Canal and Transportation Center.

Hahn, Thomas F. 1981. 3rd ed. *Towpath Guide to the C & O Canal: Section 3*. Shepardstown, W. Va.: American Canal and Transportation Center.

Mittenthal, Susan Meyer. 1983. Rev. ed. *The Baltimore Trail Book*. Baltimore: Johns Hopkins University Press.

Robbins, Chandler S., and Danny Bystrak. 1977, 2nd ed. *Field List of the Birds of Maryland*. Maryland Avifauna no. 2. Baltimore: Maryland Ornithological Society.

New Jersey

Boyle, William J., Jr. 1979. *New Jersey Field Trip Guide.* Summit, N.J.: Summit Nature Club.

Robichaud, Beryl, and Murray F. Buell. 1973. *Vegetation of New Jersey.* New Brunswick, N.J.: Rutgers University Press.

Walking News, Inc. The Hikers Region Map series covers trails in New Jersey and New York. A free key map is available from Walking News, Inc., P.O. Box 352, New York, N.Y. 10013.

Wolfe, Peter E. 1977. *The Geology and Landscapes of New Jersey.* New York: Crane Russak.

New York

Adams, Arthur G., et al. 1975. *Guide to the Catskills.* New York: Walking News, Inc.

Bennett, John, and Seth Masia. 1974. *Walks in the Catskills.* New York: East Woods Press.

Boyle, Robert H. 1969. *The Hudson River.* New York: W. W. Norton & Co.

Evers, Alf. 1972. *The Catskills: From Wilderness to Woodstock.* Garden City, N.Y.: Doubleday & Co.

Kudish, Michael. 1979. *Catskills Soils and Forest History.* Arkville, N.Y.: Catskill Center for Conservation and Development.

Kudish, Michael. 1971. *Vegetational History of the Catskill High Peaks.* Available from University Microfilms International, 300 North Zeeb Rd., Ann Arbor, Mich. 48106.

McIntosh, Robert P. 1977. *The Forests of the Catskill Mountains, N.Y.* Cornwallville, N.Y.: Hope Farm Press.

New York–New Jersey Trail Conference and American Geographical Society. *New York Walk Book.* 1971. 4th ed. Garden City, N.Y.: Doubleday & Co./Natural History Press.

Rich, John Lyon. 1934. *Glacial Geology of the Catskills.* New York State Museum, Bulletin no. 299. Albany, N.Y.

Scheller, William G. 1980. *Country Walks Near New York.* Boston: Appalachian Mountain Club.

Schuberth, Christopher J. 1968. *The Geology of New York and Environs.* New York: Natural History Press.

Thomas, Bill and Phyllis. 1983. *Natural New York.* New York: Holt, Rinehart & Winston.

Pennsylvania

Geyer, Alan R. 1969. *Hickory Run State Park Boulder Field.* Bureau of Topographic and Geologic Survey, Park Guide no. 2. Harrisburg, Pa.

Geyer, Alan R., and William H. Bolles. 1979. *Outstanding Scenic Geological Features of Pennsylvania.* Harrisburg, Pa.: Bureau of Topographic and Geologic Survey.

Goodwin, Bruce K. 1964. *Guidebook to the Geology of the Philadelphia Area.* Bureau of Topographic and Geologic Survey, Bulletin G41. Harrisburg, Pa.

Hoffman, Carolyn. 1982. *Fifty Hikes in Eastern Pennsylvania.* Woodstock, Vt.: Backcountry Publications.

Inners, Jon D. *Ricketts Glen State Park.* Bureau of Topographic and Geologic Survey, Park Guide no. 13. Harrisburg, Pa.

McGlade, W. G. 1969. *Archbald Pothole State Park: Archbald Pothole.* Bureau of Topographic and Geologic Survey, Park Guide no. 3. Harrisburg, Pa.

McGlade, W. G. 1970. *Leonard Harrison and Colton Point State Parks: The Grand Canyon of Pennsylvania.* Bureau of Topographic and Geologic Survey, Park Guide no. 5. Harrisburg, Pa.

Thwaites, Tom. 1979. *Fifty Hikes in Central Pennsylvania.* Somersworth, N.H.: New Hampshire Publishing Co.

Virginia

Beck, Ruth and Richard Peake, eds. "Site Guide to Birds of Virginia." Unpublished. Available through the Virginia Society of Ornithologists, 520 Rainbow Forest Dr., Lynchburg, Va. 24502.

Gathright, Thomas M. II. 1976. *Geology of the Shenandoah National Park.* Virginia Division of Mineral Resources, Bulletin no. 86. Charlottesville, Va.

Heatwole, Henry. 1978 and 1981. *The Guide to Skyline Drive and Shenandoah National Park.* Shenandoah Natural History Association, Bulletin no. 9. Luray, Va.

Reed, John C., Jr., Robert S. Sigafoos, and George W. Fisher. 1980. *The River and the Rocks: The Geologic Story of Great Falls and the Potomac River Gorge.* U.S. Geological Survey, Bulletin no. 1471. Washington, D.C.: Government Printing Office.

Shelton, Napier. 1975. *The Nature of Shenandoah.* Washington, D.C.: National Park Service.

White, Mel. *A Guide to Virginia's Wildlife Management Areas.* Richmond: Virginia Commission of Game and Inland Fisheries.

Wuertz-Schaefer, Karin. 1977, 1980. Rev. ed. *Hiking Virginia's National Forest.* Charlotte, N.C.: East Woods Press.

West Virginia

Clarkson, Roy B. "The Vascular Flora of the Monongahela National Forest, West Virginia." *Castanea* 31, no. 1 (March 1966).

Core, Earl L. 1966. *Vegetation of West Virginia.* Parsons, W. Va.: McClain Printing Co.

Field Guides

Audubon Society Field Guide Series. New York: Alfred A. Knopf. The series includes guides to birds, reptiles and amphibians, insects, shells, butterflies, mushrooms, mammals, trees, and wildflowers.

Brockman, George A. 1958. *A Field Guide to Trees and Shrubs.* New York: Golden Press.

Elias, Thomas S. 1980. *The Complete Trees of North America.* New York: Van Nostrand Reinhold Co.

Farrand, John, Jr., ed. 1983. *The Audubon Society Master Guide to Birding.* 3 vols. New York: Alfred A. Knopf.

Klimas, John E., and James A. Cunningham. 1981. *Wildflowers of Eastern America.* New York: Galahad Books.

Newcomb, Lawrence. 1977. *Newcomb's Wildflower Guide.* Boston: Little, Brown & Co. This guide contains an easy-to-follow key for flower identification.

Peterson Field Guide Series. Boston: Houghton Mifflin Co. The series includes guides to birds and bird songs, reptiles and amphibians, ferns, butterflies, animal tracks, the Atlantic seashore, wildflowers, trees, and shrubs.

Pettingill, O. S., Jr. 1977. *A Guide To Bird Finding East of the Mississippi.* Boston: Houghton Mifflin Co.

Robbins, Chandler S., Bertel Broun, and Herbert Zim. 1966. *Birds of North America.* New York: Golden Press.

Watts, M. T. 1963. *Master Tree Finder.* Berkeley, Calif.: Nature Study Guild. An excellent guide for beginners.

Index

Except for bird species, of which every citation is included, the index lists only those plant and animal species that are significantly mentioned or described in detail. *Italic* figures refer to major discussions; **boldface** figures refer to site numbers.

A Note
About the Authors

Susannah Lawrence is a graduate of the University of Wisconsin. From 1972 to 1975 she worked as a researcher, writer, and lobbyist on environmental and consumer issues for Consumer Action Now, a public interest group based in New York City. From 1975 to 1980 she was a lobbyist in Washington, first as executive director of Consumer Action Now and subsequently as a staff member of Solar Lobby. She now lives in Manhattan.

Barbara Gross received a B.A. in earth and environmental science from Wesleyan University and has spent several summers working as a naturalist for the National Park Service.

NOTES

NOTES

NOTES